14TH EDITION

The
Melaleuca
Wellness Guide

Recommended uses for Melaleuca products
based on research and the clinical experiences
of health care professionals and veterinarians
and
Proven household solutions recommended by
people who use Melaleuca products every day

For more Melaleuca information,
visit our website, **www.RMBarry.com**

DISCLAIMERS:

RM Barry Publications is an independent publishing company and is not affiliated with or related to Melaleuca, Inc. We specialize in providing educational information to Melaleuca Marketing Executives about and related to Melaleuca, Inc. and its products. However the claims and information contained in the publications distributed or authored by RM Barry Publications are not endorsed, approved or sponsored by Melaleuca, Inc.

Every effort has been made to ensure that the information contained in this book is complete and accurate. However, neither the publisher nor the author is engaged in rendering professional advice or services to the individual reader. The ideas, procedures and suggestions contained in this book are not intended as a substitute for consulting with your physician. All matters regarding health require medical supervision. Each person's health needs are unique. To obtain recommendations appropriate to your particular situation, please consult a qualified health care provider. RM Barry Publications, its authors, and Melaleuca, Inc. shall have neither liability nor responsibility to any person or entity with respect to any loss, damage, or injury caused or alleged to be caused by any information or suggestion in this book.

This book is intended to supply educational information to users of products manufactured by Melaleuca, Inc. It should not be used as sales literature or for business promotion.

All product names in this book (in italics) are registered trademarks of Melaleuca, Inc. of Idaho Falls, Idaho.

Portions of this book were compiled or written by D.S. Church, Ph.D.

Published by:
RM BARRY PUBLICATIONS
P.O. BOX 3528
LITTLETON, CO 80161-3528

Toll-Free **1 (888) 209-0510**
Local (303) 224-0277
Fax (303) 568-0224

Web Site: **WWW.RMBARRY.COM**
E-mail: **INFO@RMBARRY.COM**

ISBN 978-0-9801117-4-3
Printed in the United States of America

Table of Contents

Introduction

How to Use this Book

We hope you enjoy this newly updated version of the popular *Melaleuca Wellness Guide* book. Since 1995, the *Melaleuca Guide* has been the most authoritative and comprehensive resource for users of Melaleuca, Inc. products. Actually, earlier versions of the *Melaleuca Guide* go back as far as 1986, shortly after Melaleuca, Inc. was founded, and approximately one million copies of different versions have been sold. In recent years, Melaleuca, Inc. has unveiled some remarkable products that warranted several new editions of this book. Here is a quick review of the major version changes from recent years:

9th Edition: Added "Products Index" as a supplement to "Problems Index." Changed cover art to current. Three new chapters: "Heart Disease Risk Factors," "Digestive Health," "Urinary Tract Infections." Added *Phytomega*, *Florify*, and *Cranbarrier* as suggestions in appropriate "Healthy Body" entries. Updated prices in "Product Price Comparison."

10th Edition: Added *Sol-U-Guard Botanical* and *CounterAct Cough Drops* in the appropriate "Healthy Body" entries.

11th Edition: Added chapter tabs. Added *ProStolic*, *Tough & Tender Wipes*, *Clear Defense Wipes*, and *Prenatal Omega-3* in appropriate "Healthy Body" and "Healthy Home" entries. Expanded on "Heart Disease Risk Factors" chapter. Added "Nutritional Supplements" chapter. Revised vision chapter. Improved the "Problems Index." Updated prices in "Product Price Comparison" chart.

12th Edition: Enlarged chapter tabs. Added *Unforgettables* in the appropriate entries. New entries: Alzheimer's disease, bedbugs. Changed recommendations for tick removal. Several product name changes.

14th Edition: Skipped 13th edition to match version numbers with the *Melaleuca Quick Reference* booklet. Several product name changes. Revised "Heart Disease" chapter. "Healthy Home" recipies now formulated for 16 oz spray bottle.

We highly recommend that you **turn to the Problems Index first** if you are looking up a certain condition. It may be listed under a different term than you originally thought.

We're confident you will find this newly updated and expanded *Melaleuca Wellness Guide* to be the most complete resource for Melaleuca customers ever.

CHAPTER ONE

The Melaleuca Story

by Richard M. Barry

Portions of this chapter have been taken from "Built On Solid Principles: the Melaleuca Story" by R.M. Barry. The book is a fascinating, in-depth portrayal of Frank VanderSloot, his mission, and how this former Idaho farm boy, once rated as lacking in leadership qualities, led Melaleuca, Inc. to phenomenal success in just a few short years. Informative, captivating, and truly inspirational, this fascinating portrait of a business founded on principles and integrity is a "must read" for anyone who wants to understand the company and the people who are drawn to it.

The story of Melaleuca, Inc. as we know it today actually began back in the mid-eighties when a gifted American businessman had the insight to recognize the vast potential possessed by the unique substance we now call *Melaleuca oil*, and the foresight to evolve a business strategy based on its therapeutic properties. That man is, of course, Frank VanderSloot, co-founder of Melaleuca, Inc.

The early days of the original company, Oil of Melaleuca, Inc. were beset with difficulty. At the time, Frank VanderSloot seemed an unlikely candidate for such a venture. He was already a successful man. His personal abilities had enabled him to rise above his simple origins in rural Idaho to become Regional Vice President of Cox Communications, Inc.

Initially, he was called into Oil of Melaleuca, Inc. by the Ball brothers who wanted a man of his prestige and prowess at the helm. They finally managed to convince Frank of the vast, untapped potential of this wonderful substance from Australia. After some investigation, Frank was sold on the product, and decided to join the Balls in the business, which had already been operating for several months. He intended to help out the Ball brothers for eighteen months and pick up his bonus check to pay off his new house ... end of story.

It didn't quite work out that way.

On his first day at work, VanderSloot heard the tape of a radio interview given by one of the Ball brothers. This tape was being sold as a marketing tool, and when he listened to it VanderSloot was astounded to hear, among other claims, that *Melaleuca oil* was being touted as a cure for herpes and gonorrhea. VanderSloot immediately ordered the tape to be withdrawn, but it was too late. The very next day he was informed that a representative of the FDA was waiting to see him in the reception area.

In his speech at the Melaleuca Caribbean Cruise of 1999, Frank describes the incident very wittily. At first Frank was not worried. He went into the reception area, leaned across the oak desk and offered his hand to the FDA officer. Frank says, "Have you ever extended your hand to someone to shake it and they didn't shake it? It's not a good feeling. And that's what happened. I reached my hand out and instead of extending his, he reached into his back pocket and pulled out a wallet. A big, black wallet, and did what I know he'd done a hundred times before. He did a little flip with it. He flipped it open and it went 'thud!' right on that oak countertop and I was staring at the ugliest badge I have ever seen in my life. It said 'FDA'—and some other things on it—United States Government. He said, 'I'm Ed Edmunsen and I'm here to close your doors if you don't cease this illegal and unethical advertising.'"

With a gulp, Frank ushered the man into his office to be told in no uncertain terms he would not be allowed to operate while making such claims.

"I said, 'Hey, well, you'll be happy to know, sir, today's my second day on the job and yesterday, my first day, I took that tape off the market. We're not selling it anymore. And besides, the guy that you're after is in Australia.'"

Frank later consulted an FDA expert to find that none of the literature could be used to promote Melaleuca. Whether the claims were true or not, in strict FDA terms, legally they could not be advertised.

Everything that could go wrong in a business did, though it was through no fault of Frank or the Ball brothers. Not only did the FDA totally clamp down on any advertising claims for the product, but the company's business plan floundered mainly because it was saddled with weaknesses inherited from an MLM-type structure.

The death knell was sounded with some more bad news. Frank had initially been attracted away from his secure job by the exciting potential of the oil itself. A partner in the business, an Australian plantation owner, had promised a world monopoly on the supply of high-grade oil. Given the enthusiasm that Frank had for the product after researching its benefits, the promise of a world monopoly had been a major clincher. It seemed too good to be true. And, in fact, it was. The Australian plantation owner's promises turned out to be false, and their world monopoly melted away.

Plagued with problems and unforeseen legal complications, VanderSloot and the Ball brothers made the inevitable decision to close the company.

Rather than see this as a failure, VanderSloot seized upon the demise of the original company as a starting point for an entirely new company. In doing so, he used the new company as the platform to launch an ideal so basically American that it seems innovative only because so many modern businesses have lost sight of it. Namely, that the Free Enterprise system does not have to be exploitative to succeed. To initiate his strategy, one of the first things VanderSloot did was to formulate a

Mission Statement—*"Enhancing the Lives of Those We Touch by Helping People Reach Their Goals."*

From the beginning, Frank VanderSloot was adamant that the 'new' Melaleuca should help people to reach their goals in such a way that no one should get hurt, either in the business or by the business. This credo, coupled with his insistence on diligent legal and scientific research, led to the impeccable Melaleuca product line—"quality products made from natural substances supported by intensive research."

Perhaps the key to the heart of Melaleuca lies in VanderSloot's determination to "build a business to last a lifetime." Frank was a shrewd businessman and experience had taught him that continued growth needs two essential resources—product and personnel. In the case of Melaleuca, where the Marketing Executives are drawn from people with homes and families—and full-time jobs—the only factor which will attract people and keep them is belief. It is impossible to foster this in people unless the products are the best and the morals of the company are beyond reproach.

Wary of the pitfalls of inventory loading and the multitude of traps in the MLM structure, VanderSloot evolved his now-famous system of Consumer Direct Marketing. Quite simply, it meant that any average person could gradually work towards financial independence, risk-free, without quitting his or her day job, spending vast amounts on products, or working countless hours processing customer orders on a monthly basis.

Listening to Frank VanderSloot's Melaleuca speeches over the years, it is possible to see how much his own personality has grown along with the company—a classic case of a man growing to fulfill the role he's defined for himself by sharing his heart-felt values. Though a fuller analysis of the man and his novel business methods are beyond the scope of this chapter, they are, in fact, covered in depth in a fascinating book, *Built On Solid Principles: The Melaleuca Story.*

Frank's accomplishments are many. Not only does he serve on the Board of Directors of the prestigious United States Chamber of Commerce, but Idaho State University named him Business Leader of the Year, to mention but a few. Typically, VanderSloot shrugs off the glory of such successes, saying, "There were many people besides myself who contributed to Melaleuca's success."

Nevertheless, inadvertently, Frank tapped into something that is the model for new millennium business success as touted by America's top economic experts.

Charles Handy, "the philosopher for the world of business and management," foresaw in his book, *The Age of Unreason*, the collapse of the 45-year job and the paternalistic company which is taking place around us now. His blueprint for success in the next century provides a radical break with the 'take-no-prisoners' attitudes of 1990s business practice. Handy says, "The old-fashioned models of corporate control and contracts of employment are meaningless. Organizations have to be based on trust."

Similarly, Peter Drucker, one of the most perceptive observers of the American business scene stated, "The kind of organization [that will succeed] will be built around family and regional ties that, unlike American business, are personal rather than impersonal."

The fact is Frank VanderSloot must have gotten something right—the growth of Melaleuca has been staggering. In comparison with other product-based companies, there are no unseen pitfalls, no 'trickle-downs' from upper Executives making a fortune at the expense of those lower down the scale. The system works for everybody. Melaleuca's Marketing Executives have become a market force to reckon with and, as their scope and power have grown in keeping with the demands of the market, so has Melaleuca.

Despite these changes, the basic principles of Melaleuca have remained untouched. Time itself has shown that it is these very principles that have enabled Melaleuca to flourish at an amazing rate when traditional companies are going under. That these principles are touted by experts as "cutting-edge" may give rise to a chuckle. Melaleuca's principles were not formulated in an oak-paneled room in Princeton or Harvard. They are simply the down-home values Frank acquired from his hard-working Idaho father. It is these simple truths that empowered Melaleuca to rise above the shaky start of Oil of Melaleuca, Inc. and chart a path through the shark-infested waters of the 90s business world into the bright future of the next century.

It also attests to something that Frank VanderSloot believes we all possess—the ability to affect the lives of others in a positive way. He says, "We don't have to do great, newsworthy things to have a great influence on this world. We only need to live a life others can follow. It is impossible to measure the impact that one life can have on thousands of others."

VanderSloot calls this principle...

THE POWER OF ONE

The success of Melaleuca is living proof of this principle for, in VanderSloot's case, his main influence—an influence that is prevalent everywhere in the "Melaleuca philosophy"—came from his father.

Peter Francis VanderSloot is typical of the millions of "quiet Americans" who formed the backbone of America in the 1950s and, in many ways, enabled it to rise to its status as the leader of the economic world. They did this simply by being who they are—simple, working folk who work. And how they work. With only a third-grade education, Peter VanderSloot labored up to sixty hours a week on the railways, sometimes away from home a week at a time. He spent his whole life just feeding his kids and providing a home and values that would serve them in the future.

There is in such people a quiet wisdom which is the way of those who tend animals, till the soil and wake each morning without complaint, ready for a day of toil. Frank imbibed this wisdom from his father wholesale—and is eternally grateful for it. He says, "If I had not had the influence of my father in my life...it's doubtful that Melaleuca would exist as it does today."

Life on a small farm is not easy. Rural Idaho in those days was very poor. Work was hard to come by and it was mostly just logging. Such environments breed common sense, and Mr. VanderSloot, Sr., instilled his values in Frank not by preaching sermons but by practical example. For example, when he wanted Frank to have the education he had missed himself, he gave Frank a milk cow! Frank would milk that cow morning and night. He'd churn up the milk with a hand paddle and, making sure to keep his brother away from the final product, Frank would sell the cream for a few dollars at the market. Amazingly, Frank used this money to finance his college education. And, in keeping with the hard lesson learned, he actually paid for his own college expenses by living in and watching over a Laundromat.

It was quite an eye-opener for Frank seeing people at college with new clothes when all his were bought at the Salvation Army thrift store, but he was never jealous. In fact, it reinforced his first lessons—keep out of debt, work hard and, as he never heard his father tell a lie, always be honest.

For those approaching the Melaleuca organization for the first time or even those within it, it is important to understand VanderSloot's assertion that he is "not especially gifted." In his early years, he actually hated standing up in front of people and failed a leadership-attitude test because of his shyness. But through the example of his father and other key figures in his life, he came to realize the importance of self-esteem and the impact that the right kind of influence can have on the future of a so-called "average" person.

After the demise of Oil of Melaleuca, Inc., VanderSloot had to work late into the night to salvage a viable business from its shipwreck. He was not simply struggling with facts and figures. Rather, he was determined to develop a business that was built on the solid foundation of his home values. Also, it had to be a business that was readily available to not just a gifted few but to anyone with the desire and determination to succeed.

In picturing Frank at this stage, it should be remembered that when he began with Oil of Melaleuca, Inc., he was already a very successful businessman. As Regional Vice President of Cox Communications, Inc., a Fortune 500 company, he'd served his time in the 'war trenches' of modern business and had come out tops. The fact is, once the initial shock of the Oil of Melaleuca, Inc. failure had settled, he realized that he now had the chance to start something new, something that had been hovering at the back of his mind for years.

He embarked on a quest for knowledge. He consulted marketing gurus, direct-sales experts and FDA attorneys. From them he took what he thought was the best and incorporated it into his own methodology. What he came up with was a risk-free plan with a low monthly production requirement well within the scope of any American household.

The plan was elegant in its structure, economically sound—and innovative. VanderSloot was no longer in pursuit of a dream but possessed of a viable strategy to facilitate it. It was to become no less than the 'Melaleuca Way.'

THE MELALEUCA WAY

"Give a man a fish; it feeds him for a day. Teach him how to fish and he can feed himself for a lifetime." VanderSloot's idea was not to give away opportunity but to empower people to make their own. And from the well of this simple philosophy have sprung many statements and slogans which are at the heart of the Melaleuca experience:

- "No one must get hurt from what we do."
- "The magic is in helping others reach their goals and not in trying to reach our own goals."
- "No amount of wealth will bring true happiness if it is gained unethically."
- "We are not a multi-level company...Multi-level marketing has been used to con [people] into money-making schemes. We have never done that."
- "We don't have a right to be here unless we are marketing the best products for the best prices at the best value of anybody in this nation."
- "Don't quit your job."
- "We're telling about Melaleuca, not selling it."
- "The marketing and delivery of exceptional products at reasonable prices has been the key to our success."

Hundreds of thousands of people are now taking advantage of the opportunity to compete against the huge conglomerates. Marketing Executives are pulling customers away from these giants in tens of thousands by using Melaleuca's unique Marketing Plan.

However, when VanderSloot hears his Executives enthusing about his "wonderful Marketing Plan," he gives them a few home-truths. "I feel that sometimes there's a tendency for people to perceive that it's the Marketing Plan that brings us our success. It is not so." His conviction is deep on this matter. "Without having the best products that money can buy, we don't really have an excuse to be here."

THE BEST OF SCIENCE AND NATURE

It is for this reason that he was determined that, in the future, Melaleuca would use only those products that were the very best in nature, as supported and guided by scientific research. VanderSloot sought tirelessly to form relationships with pharmacists, nutritional experts, allopathic and homeopathic doctors, herbal experts, and scientists from all fields. His aim was to sort out the product wheat from product chaff.

As an illustration of how VanderSloot spent his time during this

period, here's an example of one of his contacts. Frank located a doctor
who was something of an expert on tea tree oil. For more than ten years,
this man had been using the oil in his practice to treat a wide variety
of complaints. Frank spent the entire day with the doctor, extracting
every scrap of information he could about the uses of tea tree oil and
the various mixtures used to treat different complaints. They must have
been mutually impressed with each other because when Frank established Melaleuca, Inc., the man became a loyal customer. So much so that
in 1986 the doctor published his first book about Melaleuca products.
Then, in 1995, the doctor greatly expanded his book and called it the
Melaleuca Guide. It is said that the test of time is the true judge of all
things. If so, his books have passed with flying colors, since approximately
one million copies have been sold. In fact, a historical footnote is that this
worthy doctor has since moved on to other things. However, the book
in your hand at the moment, *The Melaleuca Wellness Guide*, is a new
and radically-revised book, but is still based on all the tried and tested
product knowledge from the original *Melaleuca Guide*.

THE PIONEER PRODUCT: MELALEUCA OIL

To create the exceptional product line he needed for the new
company, VanderSloot had to have a dependable supply of high-
grade *Melaleuca oil*. He went to great lengths to secure a crop which
could propagate a superior tree line. No two strains of the *Melaleuca
alternifolia* tree provided the same quality of oil. His investigations
took him to Australia. The best stands of *Melaleuca alternifolia* trees
are in an area called the Bungawalbyn Reserve.™ The Bungawalbyn
varieties produce genetically-superior trees that give the highest quality
oil. The properties of the tree were so highly thought of by the local
Aborigines that the very word *Bungawalbyn* means 'healing ground.'
Thus, VanderSloot was able to secure exclusive rights to oil harvested
from natural stands; these Bungawalbyn trees had never been treated
with herbicides or pesticides.

Under Melaleuca's incentive, the growers sought out more robust and
higher-yield trees, took seedlings from them, and from this superior line
began establishing plantations of trees. The enthusiastic participation of
the Australian growers was ensured by Melaleuca who supported them
through years of poor yields, and the growers responded with a greater
diligence in producing the highest-quality yield possible.

As research on *Melaleuca oil* progressed, it became obvious that its
medicinal properties were directly proportional to its quality of oil. Higher
grades of the oil have greater levels of the therapeutic agent Terpinen 4-ol
and less of Cineole, which can be irritating to sensitive skin.

Other companies were selling substandard grades of the oil as "pure
oil of *Melaleuca alternifolia*." Some of these oils have very little, if any,
medicinal value. VanderSloot wanted to make sure that Melaleuca sold
only the highest-quality oil available, and that customers could clearly see
what grade they were getting. He decided to place the grade designation

right on the label, and hence the name "*T36-C7*" for the standard high-grade oil, and "*T40-C5*" for the ultra-rare grade oil. These pure oils have been shown to be superlative treatments for stings, burns, skin rashes and a host of topical applications. Because the higher grade of the oil comes from trees with rare genetics and the supply is limited, it is more expensive.

Melaleuca recently raised the standards for both grades of their oil to "*T36-C5*" and "*T40-C3*," which demonstrates a commitment to making the very best oil available as growing and harvesting techniques continue to improve. The standard high-grade oil is used in a wide range of Melaleuca products, most notably in skin care, hair care, dental care, and medicine chest products.

Even though reputable organizations the world over have validated *Melaleuca oil's* effectiveness and safety, VanderSloot is always cautious about its claims. By 1996, over six million bottles of the oil had been sold. Nevertheless, when describing its uses, Frank insisted on erring on the conservative side, saying, "It's clear that *Melaleuca oil* has some very unique and unusual properties. Many people have experimented and reported very favorable results on conditions such as cold sores, canker sores, candida, chicken pox, herpes, thrush, etc. Several studies have been done on some of these conditions that appear quite promising. But more research needs to be done to verify its efficacy before being able to make legitimate claims in regard to these conditions."

The book is not yet closed on *Melaleuca oil.* In some ways, it is still a mystery and, as of yet, not all of its properties are fully understood. New research is expanding its possibilities every day. One thing is certain—as new uses are discovered for this wonderful substance, Melaleuca will ensure that any potential benefit is passed on to customers.

BEYOND MELALEUCA OIL

Nearly 30% of Melaleuca's revenues go into product quality. Compared to this, traditional manufacturers only spend about 10% for the same purpose. By pouring revenue back into product development, Melaleuca has been able to provide an ever-widening range of new products, many of which are not based on *Melaleuca oil* at all.

Melaleuca's research and development team continually searches for natural ingredients with known restorative or curative powers. Having found such an ingredient, Melaleuca will either closely examine any former research on it, or they will initiate fresh research. As a result of such investigations, Melaleuca now distributes a line of products which use ingredients that go far beyond the original flagship product, *Melaleuca oil*. Nowadays, many of the products are not based on the oil at all but on other natural botanicals—plants and herbs whose health-promoting properties have been known for years and whose viability has been established by further testing. These include household products that are safe to both the health of the user and that of the environment, and a wide range of personal care and cosmetic products.

Americans are slowly becoming aware that protecting our health and the environment is not just the province of the fanatical few. The gap between the violation of nature's delicate balance and its rebound effect on humanity is growing narrower every year. Melaleuca's household and personal care products offer a solution where the giant corporations have simply turned a blind eye. This has created a competitive edge for the company as it attracts more and more people who realize they can now exercise personal and environmental responsibility without sacrificing effectiveness.

UNLOCKING NATURE'S SECRETS WITH SCIENCE

As Melaleuca expands, there seems to be a peculiar sense of appropriateness in the direction taken. Following its establishment of safe household and personal care products, Melaleuca's move into the area of nutrition and personal health aids seemed a natural step. "We have found that mother nature has provided a natural solution for almost every health problem that confronts us. Our task is to use science as the key to unlock the secrets that nature has to offer," states VanderSloot.

As Melaleuca R&D uncovers fresh developments in natural health, the flexibility of their infrastructure facilitates their ability to investigate and incorporate such developments into an enhanced product line. This is accomplished on a time scale which would be impossible for the gigantic corporations. Not only does this put Melaleuca on the cutting edge, but the speed at which it takes place does not compromise safety or quality.

FRUCTOSE COMPOUNDING

Given some of the negative factors of modern life—stress, pollution, over-processed foods—it is even more essential that our body receive an adequate supply of vitamins and especially minerals. A healthy diet which includes the recommended intake of fruits and vegetables does not always provide the necessary nutrition. If the minerals are not in the soil, they won't be reproduced in the food. Thus, the degeneration of soil quality and the practice of over-processing food has given rise to a peculiar phenomenon—people who overeat and are still malnourished.

Furthermore, nutritional research has also shown that even when there is an adequate mineral supply within certain foods, it doesn't necessarily mean that the body will receive the full benefit. This anomaly came to the attention of nutritionists in Egypt, Libya, and Iran in the 1970s, where children were suffering from horrible symptoms of zinc deficiency—severe growth retardation and dwarfism—even though the local foods contained an adequate supply of zinc.

The explanation is that the zinc attaches itself to certain acids in the food and is passed right through the body as "waste," without even getting to the cells. This happens, though to a lesser degree, with the minerals in our diets as well. The problem is solved by using an innovative process which binds a mineral to fructose, a substance found in fruit which is very readily absorbed by the cells. By using this "fruit sugar" messenger to carry the minerals piggy-back style, the mineral is passed through to the tissues and its full benefits can be utilized by the body.

This patented process called "fructose compounding" is exclusive to Melaleuca. No one else has this cutting-edge technology, which is one of the features of Melaleuca's *Vitality Pack*.

THE CASE OF BOBBI MCCAUGHEY

Melaleuca's emphasis on using only those quality products which have been validated and well researched has had some interesting repercussions in the community at large. Not the least of these is the case of Bobbi McCaughey, the Iowa woman whose claim to fame is the delivery of seven living children at one birth.

To fully appreciate the magnitude of this feat, it has to be remembered that formerly in cases of multiple births, all or some of the children died. In fact in two previous cases of septuplet births, all the babies died.

When Bobbi had recovered from the news that she was pregnant seven times over (if, indeed, she ever will recover!), the primary concern was her physical robustness. Could she withstand the severe assault of this incredible event?

Her pastor's wife, Ginny Brown, is a Melaleuca Marketing Executive. Ginny suggested that Bobbi use the *Vitality Pack*. Of course, Bobbi had to have her doctors look over the specifications of the *Vitality Pack*. They examined the ingredients closely before approving them. Bobbi embarked upon a regimen of taking the *Vitality Pack* three times a day and three *ProVex-Plus* capsules a day. The most distinctive advantage of the *Vitality Pack* is the high absorption of minerals due to Melaleuca's patented fructose-compounding process.

Bobbi says, "We thought it would be a great help during the pregnancy and that it would be much more usable—as far as being absorbed by my body—than a regular prenatal vitamin would be."

A pregnant woman has very special nutritional needs. For instance, Bobbi was supposed to eat 4,000 calories a day, but she could not eat that much. "I needed to eat something every forty minutes and I just couldn't."

Zinc and calcium are especially needed, even during a normal pregnancy. In this case, the situation was even more extreme—Bobbi was carrying seven babies. So it was absolutely essential that she had the right nutrition. But, for the first five months of the pregnancy, she was so sick she could hardly eat at all. Once she got to the hospital she was able to eat a little bit more, but she says, "But then I had hospital food, so I didn't want to eat any more! So it was good to have something that was really able to boost the vitamins and minerals I didn't get from the food."

The circumstances of a pregnancy seven times over needed very special precautions. Bobbi was told by her doctors to stay in bed for the last five months of the pregnancy. This immediately introduced other possible problems—blood clotting in the legs, reduced muscle tone, and loss of bone mass. Also, a common aspect of multiple pregnancies is that blood pressure can rapidly escalate to abnormal proportions. The doctors who had examined the ingredients of the *Vitality Pack* told Bobbi to take the *Vitality Pack* three times every day, and she never had any problems with blood pressure.

Ginny, knowing that it might be difficult for the McCaughey's to pay for the vitamins in such quantities, called Tish Poling at Melaleuca, and Tish discreetly arranged that the McCaughey's would get everything they needed from Melaleuca without any intrusive publicity.

When Bobbi was asked how she felt during this period, she replied, "I felt really good. It wasn't until probably the last week and a half that I really felt terrible. By that time, the contractions had started and I was on other medications to stop them."

Of course, Frank VanderSloot was proud that Melaleuca's vitamins and minerals had been used in such a medically-sensitive situation. He said, "We're really pleased that the McCaugheys decided to use our vitamins, and that the result has been so great. Our hopes and prayers are with them as they prepare for the wonderful experiences ahead."

Well, the results have become worldwide news. Bobbi did deliver her seven bouncing bundles of joy—the first woman in known history to do so. Of course, Bobbi's major feat attracted worldwide attention. One day, when Bobbi was back in the hospital post-delivery, the phone rang. Ken McCaughey picked up the phone. A voice said, "Mr. McCaughey, you have a phone call from the President of the United States."

The McCaugheys were astonished. The President had phoned to offer his personal congratulations. Bobbi's marathon feat had even caught the imagination of the President of the United States!

Naturally, the credit should go to Bobbi and her team of doctors. Still, there is no doubt that Melaleuca's policy of credible testing and high-quality product meant that the *Vitality Pack* was well up to their standards.

A comic side-light to the Bobbi McCaughey case took place during one of Frank VanderSloot's talks. While addressing a roomful of people, Frank mentioned that Bobbi had been taking the *Vitality Pack*.

"All of a sudden," Frank said, "from the back of the room, a woman screamed, 'OH MY GOSH!!' It seems she was a new customer and she'd just started taking the *Vitality Pack* herself. She was concerned that somehow that was what caused the seven babies!"

Partly because of Bobbi McCaughey's experience with the *Vitality Pack*, Melaleuca has now introduced the *Vitality Pack Prenatal*. This new formulation is specifically designed for the nutritional needs of a woman during her pregnancy.

THE ACCESS PERFORMANCE BAR

As we move into the first century of the new millennium, the greatest change in health care is the trend towards prevention rather than cure. In particular, lifestyle has been designated as a major causal factor in disease.

Exercise is a key element in a healthy lifestyle. Obesity is a major concern, and lack of exercise is a main contributor to strokes and heart attacks. The *Access Performance Bar* was developed specially to ensure that the maximum possible benefits were obtained from exercise.

Through Melaleuca's practice of networking with cutting-edge doctors, they became aware of Dr. Lawrence Wang's studies into fat metabolism. Dr. Wang, Ph.D., is the Professor of Animal and Human Physiology at the University of Alberta, Edmonton, Canada, and a member of the prestigious Royal Society of Canada.

His research into fat metabolism led him to a substance called adenosine which exerts a blocking effect on the burning of stored fat during exercise. Adenosine, a by-product of activity, leads to the familiar sensation in fatigued muscles, expressed in the old exercise slogan as "feel the burn." It is adenosine which is indirectly responsible for that burning sensation and muscle soreness after exercise. Normally, exercise burns off glucose, not fat, but by utilizing a natural substance which inhibits the effect of the adenosine, Wang was able to increase the direct burning of fat, not glucose, during exercise.

This led to the *Access Performance Bar,* a product made from natural substances which has become a mainstay for both athletes and casual exercisers alike. Taken approximately fifteen minutes before exercise, the bar ensures that the body will burn less glucose and more fat. Fatigue and soreness are minimized and exercise can continue for longer periods. This simple, safe exercise bar ensures that maximum benefits can be attained during any exercise routine.

THE EVOLUTION OF PROVEXCV®

Melaleuca's interest in formidable health issues did not stop with obesity. In 1995, Melaleuca announced that they were committed to becoming a world leader in research and development into a group of substances known as flavonoids. This was in direct response to the enormous medical problem of heart disease and the related medical and lifestyle factors associated with it.

The results have been quite amazing. VanderSloot remarked, "We never dreamed that when we said we would become a world leader, we would actually become the world leader in the development of products to reduce the risk of heart disease."

Melaleuca's interest in flavonoids had been aroused by a peculiar phenomenon known as the French Paradox which came to the attention of the public in 1990. The way in which the story develops is a prime example of Melaleuca's product development methodology.

Apparently, the French consume 2.8 times the amount of lard as

Americans and 3.8 times as much butter. The French are also a nation of very heavy smokers. Yet, despite the fact that they have higher blood cholesterol levels and higher blood pressure readings than Americans, the French have only one-third the rate of heart attacks.

Subsequent research led scientists to attribute this odd paradox to the French's habitual consumption of red wine with meals. This led to further studies into the constituents of red wine, aimed at pinpointing the connection between the wine and their lowered incidence of heart attacks. Over the years, many such experiments gradually eliminated different factors until, finally, something concrete was established. It seems the lowered incidence of heart attacks in the French was due to a substance in grape skins and seeds known as flavonoids. Flavonoids are present in red wine and purple grape juice.

The basic causes of heart attacks had already been well established by earlier researchers. It stems from two factors—the buildup of "oxidized" cholesterol on artery walls, which causes the artery to become restricted, and the "stickiness" of blood platelets which may cause a blockage in the restricted artery.

The buildup of "bad" cholesterol has been shown to be minimized by antioxidants such as Vitamin E. Also, as early as 1974 it was demonstrated that aspirin can reduce artery blockage by inhibiting platelet clotting.

This simplified explanation indicates that any attempt to reduce heart attacks has to be a two-fold attack—one, to produce an antioxidant that reduces the oxidation of "bad" cholesterol, and two, to reduce blood platelet "stickiness" in a similar manner to the action of aspirin.

Aspirin has one major drawback. Most heart attacks are induced through stress, and it was found that aspirin's effect is minimized in the presence of adrenaline, which is released during stress—the "Catch 22" of using aspirin for this purpose.

Melaleuca, in responding to the challenge of this new area, formed an alliance with Dr. John Folts, the man who had conducted the original research into the beneficial effects of aspirin. Folts had already spent several years researching the effects of flavonoids on platelet stickiness. He believed that flavonoids were the key to the 'French paradox.' Folts says, "Focusing on flavonoid supplements was the next logical step. Everyone has been asking when they'll be able to get the same benefits [of red wine] from a pill."

Melaleuca's goal was to develop a flavonoid-based dietary supplement that would be effective at preventing heart disease. Initial research revealed that flavonoids extracted from plants are not absorbed completely by the body. At first this was very disappointing news.

Other manufacturers of flavonoid supplements were touting them as being effective against heart disease based on tests which were done in test tubes only. Melaleuca's research had been done in living subjects and clearly showed that the claims made by the other manufacturers were greatly exaggerated.

The researchers set out to solve the problem of absorption so the benefits of the flavonoids could be utilized by the body. After almost two years they discovered that a particular mixture of flavonoid extracts combined with a special blend of enzymes greatly increased the absorption of the flavonoids. This was the breakthrough they had been looking for. This led to the development of the first flavonoid-based supplement which has been proven (in living subjects) to be effective in curbing the two primary causes of heart disease.

"WHEN THE TRUTH IS ALMOST TOO GOOD TO BE TRUE"

This was the title of Frank VanderSloot's September 1997 President's Message, which was a direct response to the results of Dr. Folts' research. These results, to put it mildly, were overwhelming. A ripple of excitement fluttered through the Melaleuca world as the breakthrough product, known as *ProvexCV,* was made available to Melaleuca Marketing Executives at the 1997 Convention.

Frank VanderSloot, in accordance with long-established Melaleuca principles, asked for restraint. He urged his Marketing Executives to refrain from any publicity until Dr. Folts and his researchers could publish their findings in appropriate medical journals.

Melaleuca's success with *ProvexCV* is not a lucky accident. Melaleuca is ever sifting through the enormous number of natural remedies to all kinds of illnesses. The larger corporations simply will not take time to investigate natural remedies. One reason for this is they cannot be patented. And smaller companies simply don't have the funds to pursue the kind of research that led to *ProvexCV.* So Melaleuca has carved out a huge niche for itself in the marketplace as the leading manufacturer of beneficial natural products.

In his February 1997 address, Frank VanderSloot illustrated the importance of R&D. "If any company, large or small, comes out with a great product, rather than competing with it, we'll incorporate it into our own product line-and we will challenge our own scientists to improve on it. We did exactly that with *ProVex*—instead of becoming a competitor or follower in that industry, we found a better way, and we became the leader."

Melaleuca, Inc.'s astute methods of uncompromising testing have borne fruit in more ways than one. In the words of Frank VanderSloot, "As our ongoing research continues to uncover more of nature's secrets, we promise to keep you informed. We believe this is a never-ending story, but the first chapter is now complete. Stay tuned for more information."

Well, more information did come and this time it raised a ripple of excitement not just amongst Melaleuca Executives but the world.

The Press has always been intrigued by the idea of the French Paradox—the idea that drinking alcohol could actually promote health is something of a teaser. Unfortunately, this was always its weak point medically.

Then, in November 1998, Dr. Folts delivered a presentation to the American Dietetic Association. In the context of numerous other presentations, this was the one that attracted the attention of the Press.

Folts had experimented with a supplement consisting of carefully researched amounts of grape seed, grape skin, Gingko biloba, bilberries and a specific flavonoid called quercetin. Folts found that his test subjects showed a "significant and encouraging" reduction in the contributing factors responsible for heart disease.

This was the news that sent the Press racing for the door. The news was circulated very rapidly via Associated Press, Reuters, and numerous other agencies. Over 100 articles were generated in different newspapers around the nation and on numerous television news programs. Here was absolute verification that a non-alcoholic substance in pill form could be effective against heart disease.

Folts' talk was a major breakthrough. But for Melaleuca, it was, in some sense, old hat. For, of course, the supplement Folts tested was none other than *ProvexCV.*

Earlier that year, VanderSloot had said, "We have also learned some exciting things about the most effective way to extract the nutrients from grape seeds and grape skins...We have learned exactly how to do it and we are not telling anyone else. And much of what we know is now protected by patent."

A patent? Yes. Melaleuca, Inc. had the foresight to contract with the only manufacturer who knew the special process needed to obtain the maximum result from the grapes. Melaleuca even arranged with the manufacturer to have a special factory built. Melaleuca's contract ensures that they, and only they, are eligible to receive this special extract for the next twenty years.

It is ironic that originally Frank VanderSloot had taken over the reins of a new company based on the promise of another monopoly—the world monopoly of *Melaleuca oil*. Sadly, it turned out to be too good to be true. Now Melaleuca, Inc. stands on the threshold of an incredible medical coup. And this time, the monopoly is signed, sealed, and water-tight.

As the new millennium begins and Melaleuca trembles on the brink of a solution to America's *number one* health problem, the future is looking brighter than Frank VanderSloot could ever have dreamed. With an air of barely-concealed excitement, he states ...

"I do not know of any company, regardless of size, let alone a Direct Marketing company, that has had the opportunity to take a product of this magnitude to market. A product that is so far advanced beyond anything else in the marketplace...! It's wonderful to be in a position where the truth is almost too good to be true. Thank goodness it is true. I cannot imagine a better situation for us to be in."

Indeed.

The complete 128 page book, "Built on Solid Principles: the Melaleuca Story," is available from RM Barry Publications. Call 1 (888) 209-0510 or visit us on the internet at www.RMBarry.com.

CHAPTER TWO

That Amazing Tea Tree Oil!

ABOUT THE AUTHOR

Karen MacKenzie began her investigation into Tea Tree oil in 1989 while working as a researcher for an essential oil company. During this time, she began to develop a strong interest in alternative medicine and nutrition. When, in 1991, she developed an allergy to chemicals in many personal care products and make-up, she was forced to search for chemical-free alternatives. Unfortunately, there were very few alternatives available back then. Her quest led her to begin using Tea Tree oil in a variety of ways with spectacular results, and her allergy eventually subsided.

She began writing about Tea Tree oil to share her experiences with others. In 1996, she founded the Tea Tree Oil Information Service in Great Britain to help spread the word and to assist medical professionals as well as the general public in using this valuable natural gift.

INTRODUCTION

When I initially heard about Tea Tree oil, I could not believe it. It was too good to be true. Why had we not heard about it before? The truth is we had, but then we had chosen to ignore it!

I have traced Tea Tree oil back to its roots in Aboriginal Australia, through its popularity during the Second World War, right up to the present day world-wide acclaim. I have read the research papers, used it for first aid applications, treated my pets, and even cleaned many household accessories and furnishings with it.

I am constantly amazed by its versatility and effectiveness. I would never have believed that an essential oil from one plant could lend itself so successfully to so many different applications. No one but God, through nature, could have created such a valuable broad-spectrum substance, and that is the beauty of Tea Tree oil—it is totally natural.

I wrote this in an effort to bring Tea Tree oil to your attention, so you, like I, could read about its history, study the research work, utilize its many properties, and make up your own mind about nature's potent gift. After all, Tea Tree oil was created for each and every one of us.

PREFACE

Every week we see the same headlines in the newspapers "Head Lice Shampoo Cancer Scare"…"The Age of the Superbug is Here"… "Household Chemicals and Pollution Linked to Cancer"…"Acne Treatment Damages Skin Cells"… and so on.

We are now just beginning to wake up to the fact that the synthetic chemical cocktails we encounter during the course of a lifetime—hairsprays, cosmetics, deodorants, polishes, detergents, toothpastes, perfumes, aftershaves, first aid treatments, medicines, air fresheners, etc. —are systematically weakening our bodies. It is undeniable that our health is beginning to suffer. Where will it all end?

Germs, bacteria, and other parasites are evolving to beat their chemical killers. The "superbugs," including MRSA (Golden staph), thrive. Mystery illnesses are on the increase. Do we then try to make stronger chemicals? You bet we do!

Are we not forgetting one simple, fundamental fact? Bacteria is a basic, one-celled form of life, and these chemicals are harmful to all life—including our own!! When we use harsh chemicals against bacteria we can also unbalance and even destroy our own body cells, too.

I am not denying that synthetic medicine was, and is, a great gift. But it is its indiscriminate use, in addition to all other synthetics and chemicals, that is causing the problem. Over fifty years ago society started to turn its back on nature, and the chemical industry took center stage. We seemed to forget that we were part of nature and that to turn against it, we would be turning against ourselves. It is only now that we are beginning to pay the price.

Now, wouldn't it be marvelous if we could find a safe, non-toxic, non-irritating substance that would play a role in replacing many of the strong chemicals in our cupboards? Well, we have!

Here is a product that is made by nature, for nature. It is a completely natural, topical, clinically proven anti-bacterial and anti-fungal substance. It has anti-inflammatory, immune system strengthening, pain killing, and wound healing qualities. It also exhibits anti-viral, expectorant, and balsamic characteristics.

All this, and it can be used as a powerful antiseptic, parasiticide and insecticide. AND it's also kind to our skin cells. The pure Tea Tree oil of the *Melaleuca alternifolia*, works with the body, not against it. Research shows it has rapid results against the new "20th Century Superbugs" including MRSA.

I still find it ironic that if man had made such a synthetic substance and had spent millions of dollars on the development program, it would have been hailed as the wonder of the century. Everyone would have known about it, and everyone would be utilizing its many properties. But because Tea Tree oil is found in nature, it is viewed with suspicion.

The sooner we all once again wholeheartedly embrace a more natural approach in both medicine and in industry, the sooner we will begin to stem the tide of the so called "superbugs" and "mystery illnesses."

THE TEA TREE OIL STORY

To trace the history of the "healing Tea Trees" we have to start on the North Eastern coastal region of New South Wales, Australia—the only place in the world where the *Melaleuca alternifolia* tree yields the "real" Tea Tree oil.

We then have to travel back centuries, long before Australia was "discovered," and long before scientific evidence began, to a time when Australia belonged to its native inhabitants, the Aborigines. In particular, the Bundjalong Aborigines inhabited the wetlands around the Bungawalbyn Creek and, according to legend, were well aware of the medicinal qualities of their many "healing trees." Although not documented, it is widely understood that they treated various wounds and skin infections with an early form of poultice made from crushed leaves and warm mud from along the banks of the creek. The poultice was excellent for drawing out infection and healing the skin.

These Aborigines also used the healing waters of the pools in the area which were surrounded by the trees. Falling leaves and twigs leached their "magical" healing liquid into the water, turning it a deep yellowish color. The Aborigines bathed and washed in this natural healing "spa" to treat any number of conditions from sore muscles to serious diseases. Maybe this is why they named the area "Bungawalbyn" in the first place. The name means "healing ground."

The "healing trees" did not become commonly known as "Tea Trees" until around 1770 when Captain Cook, along with a botanist named Joseph Banks and the crew of The Endeavour, used the leaves with their distinctive aroma to brew a spicy and refreshing "tea." It is most unfortunate that they did not "discover" and publish the unique healing qualities of the "Tea Trees." But according to the account of that time, they drank the essence in varying concoctions, even alcoholic beverages such as a "Tea Tree beer."

Thus the name "Tea Tree" became popular, especially with the first "white" settlers who colonized the low-lying areas around the Clarence and Richmond Rivers. From the 1790s on, they watched and learned from the Aborigines how to use the leaves and waters in various inhalations, poultices, and rubbing mediums. Because these first settlers rarely had medical or botanical backgrounds, there was no real "scientific" evidence recording the healing qualities of the Tea Trees. The European community was very skeptical of these "anecdotal stories." It could not have helped that the Aborigines were often thought of as primitives from an uncivilized world. In the words of the settlers, "They didn't want to work or better themselves… they were always disobedient and lazy." Thus the healing remedies, along with the Aboriginal way of life, were treated with contempt.

As new settlers arrived, they struggled to clear the harsh native vegetation to make way for settlements and dairy farms. They cursed every Tea Tree for its hardy and persistent hold on its own natural habitat. The Tea Trees tenaciously survived drought, fire, flood, and even frost, and resisted any attempt to destroy them. Fortunately for the rest of the world, the only way they could have been eradicated was by the physical removal of every part of the tree, including the extensive root system.

It is ironic that while the settlers battled to destroy the Tea Trees, they were only too willing to use the healing leaves for poultices and inhalations to stem infection and disease.

It is to our loss that the Tea Tree, although used as an effective "bush remedy" by subsequent generations of farmers, did not reach our attention until the early 1930's. It was not even mentioned in the British Pharmaceutical Codex until 1949, where it was listed as "Oleum Melaleuca." [1]

In Australia it was not until the early 1920's that Arthur de Ramon Penfold, FCS, Chief Chemist at the Museum of Applied Technology, Arts and Sciences in Sydney, extracted the oil of the Melaleuca alternifolia and announced that "yes indeed!" it did have antiseptic and anti-bacterial properties.[2] The accepted anti-bacterial agent at that time was carbolic acid (known as phenol). Imagine the stir it must have caused when it was determined that "an old Aboriginal remedy" was up to 13 times stronger! and was non-toxic and non-irritating—unlike carbolic acid! [3]

When the results were finally published in 1925, there was great enthusiasm among doctors of the time and "Penfold's discovery" was immediately put to the test.

In 1930 the *Medical Journal of Australia* published an article, "A New Australian Germicide," by Dr. E.M. Humphrey.[4] It stated "that what he found most encouraging was the way that the oil from the crushed leaves of the *Melaleuca alternifolia* dissolved pus and left wounds and surrounding areas clean." He tested and enthused about this great substance, highlighting Tea Tree oil as never before.

He noticed "that the germicidal action became more effective in the presence of living tissue and organic matter, without any apparent damage to healthy cells."...

He suggested "that it would be particularly good for applying to dirty wounds caused in street accidents."...

He also found "most encouraging the results on nail infections. Particularly those infections that had resisted various treatments for months which now were cured in less than a week!"...

"The pus solvent properties of Tea Tree oil made it an excellent application for the fungal nail disease paronychia, which if left untreated could result in the deformity and even eventual loss of the nail."...

1 "Oleum Melaleuca," *British Pharmaceutical Codex,* 597-598, 1949.
2 Penfold, A.R. and Grant, R. "The Germicidal Values of Some Australian Essential Oils and Their Pure Constituents," *Journal Proceedings of the Royal Society of NSW,* 59:3, 346-50, 1925.
3 This was determined by the Rideal-Walker co-efficient, a method used at that time to determine the germicidal properties of compounds.
4 Humphrey, E.M. "A New Australian Germicide," *Medical Journal of Australia,* I, 417-418, 1930.

He urged the dental industry to "take seriously the antiseptic properties for infections of the gum and mouth.".…

He noted that "just two drops of Tea Tree oil in a tumbler of warm water made it a soothing and therapeutic gargle for sore throats in the early stages.".…

He wrote that "it would probably be effective for most of the infections of the naso-pharynx.".…

That it "was an immediate deodorizing medium on foul-smelling wounds and pus-filled abscesses.".…

And, "if it was added to hand soap it would make the soap up to sixty times more effective against Typhoid bacilli than the so-called 'disinfectant soaps' of the day.".…

He felt "that if an ointment could be made from the oil it would help to eradicate several parasitic skin diseases.".…

He concluded "that it was a rare occurrence because most effective germicides actually destroyed healthy living tissue along with the bacteria.".…

The Scientific and Medical worlds were intrigued. More research was funded and articles began appearing in additional publications such as the *Australian Journal of Pharmacy*[5] and the *Australian Journal of Dentistry*.[6] World-wide appetites were whetted. Articles were presented and published in the *Journal of the National Medical Association* (USA)[7] and the *British Medical Journal*.[8]

As the reputation of Tea Tree oil spread, there was a great deal of anecdotal evidence about its effectiveness in a wide range of topical applications, both medical and veterinary. From diabetic gangrene in man[9] to diseases of poultry and fish, it was recognized as a safe, effective, non-toxic, non-irritating, antiseptic disinfectant.[10]

If Penfold was the "Founding Father," Humphrey was certainly the "Metaphorical Mother." His enthusiastic writings opened up a multitude of medical and practical uses for Tea Tree oil. Others have tried, tested, and approved of its healing properties, but thanks to Penfold and Humphrey the world would no longer be denied the miraculous healing powers of the Aborigine "healing tree," the Tea Tree— *Melaleuca alternifolia.*

5 Anon, "Tea Tree Oil," *Australian Journal of Pharmacy,* p274, 30th March 1930.
6 MacDonald, V. "The Rationale of Treatment," *Australian Journal of Dentistry,* 34, 281-285, 1930.
7 Anon, Journal of the *National Medical Association* (USA), 1930.
8 Anon, "Ti-trol Oil," *British Medical Journal,* 927, 1933.
8 Anon, "An Australian Antiseptic Oil," *British Medical Journal,* 966, 1933.
9 Halford, A.C.F. "Diabetic Gangrene," *Medical Journal of Australia,* 2, 121-122, 1936.
10 Penfold, A.R. and Morrison, F.R. "Some Notes on the Essential Oil of *Melaleuca alternifolia,*" *Australian Journal of Pharmacy,* 18, 274-5, 1937.

A Growth Industry

By the start of the Second World War, Tea Tree oil from the *Melaleuca alternifolia* had earned its reputation as a miracle healer. It was medically recognized world-wide for the successful treatment of a whole range of conditions including:

- Ear, nose and throat infections: tonsillitis, gingivitis, pyorrhea, etc.
- Gynecological infections: candida, thrush, etc.
- Nail infections: paronychia, tinea, etc.
- Skin infections: impetigo, pediculosis, ringworm, etc.
- And a wide range of other contagious and non-contagious fungal, bacterial and parasitic infections (It was considered especially effective for pus filled and dirty infections.)
- Dental nerve capping
- Hemorrhages, wounds, first aid, etc.
- Not to mention all of the many and varied veterinary applications.[11]

A bottle of Tea Tree oil was a standard Government Issue in Australian Army and Navy first aid kits, especially for those soldiers serving in tropical countries. It was initially used in munitions factories to inhibit the high air-borne bacteria count. Then it was found that, by adding it to the machine cutting oils, it substantially reduced infections, especially those from abrasions caused by the off-shoot of metal filings. The production of Tea Tree oil was considered of such great importance that bush cutters were exempt from doing national service.

Surgeons, doctors, dentists, vets, and even housewives were utilizing its many healing properties. The Australian division of Colgate-Palmolive manufactured a Tea Tree oil "germicidal" soap that was very popular for a number of years.

During this meteoric rise in popularity, the actual Tea Tree industry was very modest indeed, with just over twenty steam distillation units (stills) in the Bungawalbyn area, and those were mostly small family run businesses. The cutting and harvesting was completed totally by hand, mainly from trees growing wild in the swampy bush lands. Successful harvesting depended wholly upon manpower against the harsh elements of the Australian climate and the many hazards of working alongside the carnivorous and poisonous wildlife. Inevitably demand became far greater than supply. Throughout the war years all available stocks of good quality Tea Tree oil were taken under government control. There was little or none left for the developing marketplace. Scientists concocted cheaper synthetic alternatives. Although not as effective as Tea Tree oil, for their germicidal qualities, they were much more readily available. In the post war era the pure oil of the Melaleuca alternifolia was almost impossible to buy.

---

11 Penfold, A.R. and Morrison, F.R. "Some Notes on the Essential Oil of *Melaleuca alternifolia,*" *Australian Journal of Pharmacy,* 18, 274-5, 1937.

Right up until the middle of the 1940s the pure Tea Tree oil was still highly regarded and sought after. It had been the heyday of the Tea Tree oil industry.

During the earlier years, as the popularity of Tea Tree oil was growing, so too was medical technology. In 1928, Scottish biologist Alexander Fleming first observed the effect of penicillin on bacteria, and the antibiotic was "born." By 1941, the drug was developed and on its way to becoming established. By the 1950s it was heralded as the new "wonder drug." It was the age of synthetic and semi-synthetic medicine. Infections that were usually fatal were now virtually wiped out—tuberculosis, pneumonia, and venereal disease to name but a few. There was now hope where there had been despair. The new drugs went from strength to strength. Everyone wanted them, and everyone got them. Antibiotics were the theme of the day, and man rejoiced in the fact that he had finally triumphed over nature. The Tea Tree industry went into steep decline as natural remedies were classed as quack cures. Modern medicine was being built on synthetic chemicals and, for more than a decade, they reigned supreme.

Unfortunately the developing drug manufacturers were not interested in natural or preventive medicine, or indeed actually curing non-pathogenic diseases. The "BIG" money was in controlling symptoms so that the sufferers would be using a drug for the rest of their lives. Yes, there were side effects, but there were more drugs to control the side effects. Big money spawned big power. The press was courted, and the diminishing herbal medicine sector was held firmly down. Fortunately, as the saying goes, "You can fool some of the people some of the time, but you can never fool all of the people all of the time."

In the 1960s the "hippie" revolution started. Suddenly there was a growing awareness and unease concerning the whole scenario. Chemical pollution, animal testing, cover-ups, the addictions to synthetic drugs, and the hazardous side effects all added to the rumblings of disquiet. Then came a bombshell—an emergence of the "superbugs." Virulent strains of pathogens had evolved and were becoming immune to the antibiotics. It was clear that within the next few years these new strains could infect the population as before. With the dubious environmental and social implications all this held, once more, people were beginning to look for alternatives. "Natural" remedies were gaining in popularity, and before long the "Herbal Renaissance" had begun.

Like the tenacious hold those newly discovered Aboriginal "healing trees" had had on their natural habitat, so too the Tea Tree oil of the *Melaleuca alternifolia* was waiting in the background, forgotten but not gone. New research work was funded and the popularity of the Tea Tree was once again starting to flourish.

The first signs of the Tea Tree revival appeared when Dr. Henry Feinblatt published his work in the *Journal of the National Medical Association* (USA) in January of 1960. It was a favorable study about the action of a "Cajeput-type oil for the treatment of Furunculosis"(boils).[12] Two years later, Dr. Eduardo F. Peña (USA) completed a successful study of 130 women entitled *"Melaleuca alternifolia* Oil—Its use for Trichomonal Vaginitis and Other Vaginal Infections."[13] In April 1972, Dr. Morton Walker published the results of a study entitled "Clinical Investigation of Australian *Melaleuca alternifolia* for a Variety of Common Foot Problems" (Tinea pedis, Bromidrosis, corns, bunions, etc.) in the *Journal of Current Podiatry*.[14]

As word spread from journals to newspapers, a slowly increasing demand for both information, and indeed for the oil itself, started to grow. Articles appeared in such publications as the *Perfumer & Flavorist*[15] the *Planta Medica*,[16] the *Manufacturing Chemist*,[17] etc. The perfume and cosmetic industries and the botanical and medical faculties were just beginning to take a renewed, albeit cautious, interest.

The ups and downs of what was little more than a bush industry meant that during the 1970s the Tea Trees were still being harvested by hand from the snake and spider infested wet-lands around the Bungawalbyn Creek.

The cutters used machete-like knives to hack off the leaves and the terminal branches, which were then transported out of the swamp to the stills. Many of the wide-tired trucks could not even attempt to make a track through the dense undergrowth, so the cutters themselves manually carried their yield out of the swamps to the awaiting transport. On a good day, one skilled worker could cut and load a truck with up to one ton of leaves and twigs.

Arriving at their destination the cuttings would then be emptied into a container over one of the large distilling vats. Using a simple wood fired steam-distillation method, these vats were fired up and allowed to reach boiling point. The resulting steam would pass through the leaves and twigs, bursting the oil bearing sacs and vaporizing the oil. The vapors then were condensed, mixed with the distillation water in the collection tank, and the pure oil was siphoned off into drums. Each standard vat could quite easily be filled by one skilled cutter and yield around 7–10 liters of pure oil. Depending on the quality of the cuttings, the process could be repeated several times until the last drop of oil had been fully extracted.

TEA TREE OIL

---

12 Feinblatt, H.M. "Cajeput Type Oil (Tea Tree oil) for the Treatment of Furunculosis" (boils), *Journal of the National Medical Association* USA, 52: 32-4, 1960.

13 Peña, E.F. *"Melaleuca alternifolia*: Its Use for *Trichomonal vaginitis* and Other Vaginal Infections," *Obstetrics and Gynecology*, 19:6, 793-795, 1962.

14 Walker, M. "Clinical Investigation of Australian *Melaleuca alternifolia* oil for a Variety of Common Foot Problems," *Current Podiatry*, April 7th to 15th, 1972.

15 Beylier, M.F. "Bacteriostatic Activity of Some Australian Essential Oils," *Perfumer and Flavorist International*, V4, 23-5, 1979.

16 Low, D., Rowal, B.D. and Griffin W.J. "Antibacterial Action of the Essential Oils of Some of Australian Myrtaceae," *Planta Medica*, 26, 184-189, 1974.

17 Pickering, G.B. "Cedarwood Oil Compounds, Silica Gel Separation and Tea Tree Oil as Nutmeg Substitute," *Manufacturing Chemist*, 27, 105-6, 1956.

As demand was once again on the increase, so too, the Tea Tree industry itself started to rapidly expand, and inevitably the natural stands of Tea Trees were being systematically destroyed along with the associated eco-systems. It was obvious that something had to be done. So by the start of the 1980s farms were set up. Tea Trees were now being cultivated on the fertile farmlands and the oil was produced on a semi-commercial scale. From the late 1980s sustainable plantations were established and mechanical cutting was introduced. Tea Tree oil production was substantially increased to meet the ever-growing demand for high quality oil.

During this time new research work was being funded, and in 1985, Dr. Paul Belaiche completed three studies at the University of Paris, France on the use of *Melaleuca alternifolia* for the treatments of (1) Candida albicans, (2) Cystitis (urinary tract infections), and (3) Paronychia (Pus infections of the skin and nail bed). All three trials proved a success for the continued use of Tea Tree oil, and his results were supported by a number of doctors.[18, 19, 20]

More and more positive studies started to appear, like one on oral pathogens in periodontal disease by Walsh and Longstaff, published in *Periodontology* in 1987.[21] And another in 1988 by Williams and Home, "The Composition and Bacteriocidal Activity of the Oil of Melaleuca alternifolia."[22] And two others by P.M. Altman; "Australian Tea Tree oil," in 1988[23] and "Australian Tea Tree Oil—a Natural Antiseptic," in 1989.[24] Over the next few years there began a whole plethora of Tea Tree studies, some pilot, some in-vitro, and others clinical. Applications were being tested and tried all over the globe.

In October 1990, Bassett, Pannowitz, and Barnetson published a clinical, double-blind comparison of the efficacy of 5% Tea Tree oil to 5% benzoyl peroxide in the *Medical Journal of Australia*. The results prompted the comments, "Both had a significant effect in ameliorating (improving) the patients' acne...encouragingly fewer side effects were experienced by the patients treated with Tea Tree oil."[25]

In 1994, a study by Buck, Nidorf, and Addino, "Comparison of Two Topical Preparations for the Treatment of Onychomycosis: *Melaleuca*

18 Belaiche, P. "Treatment of Vaginal Infections of Candida albicans with the Essential Oil of Melaleuca alternifolia- Cheel," *Phytotherapy,* 15, 13-14, 1985.

19 Belaiche, P. "Treatment of Chronic Urinary Tract Infections with the Essential Oil of *Melaleuca alternifolia* - Cheel," *Phytotherapy,* 15, 9-12, 1985.

20 Belaiche, P. "Treatment of Skin and Nail Infections with the Essential Oil of *Melaleuca alternifolia* - Cheel," *Phytotherapy,* 15, 15-18, 1985.

21 Walsh, L.J. and Longstaff, J. "The Antimicrobial Effects of an Essential Oil on Selected Oral Pathogens," *Periodontology,* V8, 11-15, 1987.

22 Williams, L.R., Home, V.N., Zhang, X. and Stevenson, I. "The Composition and Bacteriocidal Activity of Oil of *Melaleuca alternifolia,*" *International Journal of Aromatherapy,* 1:3, 15-17, 1988.

23 Altman, P.M. "Australian Tea Tree Oil," *Australian Journal of Pharmacy,* 69, 276-78, 1988.

24 Altman, P.M. "Australian Tea Tree Oil - A Natural Antiseptic," *Australian Journal of Biotechnology,* 3:4, 247-8, 1989.

25 Bassett, I.B., Pannowitz, D.L. and Barnetson, R.St.C. "A Comparative Study of Tea Tree Oil Versus Benzoyl Peroxide in the Treatment of Acne," *Medical Journal of Australia,* 153:8, 455-458, 1990.

alternifolia (Tea Tree oil) and Clotrimazole" was completed. It concluded that Tea Tree oil was as effective, if not more so, as the Clotrimazole treatment for nail bed fungus.[26] Medical practitioners were beginning to notice the "good effects" on a variety of ailments including abrasions, abscesses, acne, athletes foot, canker sores, chicken pox, dandruff, eczema, hemorrhoids, head lice, infections (ear, nose, and throat), psoriasis, stings and bites, shingles, wounds, etc.

Since the beginning of the 1990s a scientific research team, led by associate Professor Tom V. Riley (including C.F. Carson and K.A. Hammer) at the Microbiology Department of the University of Western Australia, has published many papers and letters, and is continuing to study the anti-microbial properties of *Melaleuca alternifolia*. Their most notable laboratory based studies and subsequent papers include the following:

In 1993, a review into the history and unique anti-microbial properties of this ancient aboriginal oil.[27]

In 1994, two studies were published. The first was a study into the unique anti-bacterial properties of Tea Tree oil.[28] The second was a positive study into the effect of Tea Tree oil on the bacteria that can cause acne and related problems.[29]

During 1995 four studies were published. The first, and most important to mankind, was an in-vitro study into how Tea Tree oil can inhibit and destroy the bacteria that has become immune to methicillin, an antibiotic normally used to combat the *Staphylococcus aureus* species of gram-positive bacteria. Hospitals all over the world are finding more and more isolates of *Staphylococci* that are becoming immune to the once effective drugs. This study successfully showed that all sixty-six isolates were susceptible to the oil of *Melaleuca alternifolia* even at a quite low dilution.[30]

The next study that year detailed a broth micro-dilution method that could effectively be used to detect the susceptibilities of *E. Coli* and *Staphylococcus aureus*.[31]

The third in 1995 was a study into eight of the major components that make up the unique composition of Tea Tree oil, including Terpinen 4-ol

26 Buck, D.S., Nidorf, D.M. and Addino, J.G. "Comparison of Two Topical Preparations for the Treatment of Onychomycosis: *Melaleuca alternifolia* (Tea Tree Oil) and Clotrimazole," *Journal of Family Practice,* 38, 601-5, 1994.

27 Carson, C.F. and Riley, T.V. "Antimicrobial Activity of the Essential Oil of *Melaleuca alternifolia* (A Review)," *Letters in Applied Microbiology,* 16, 49-55, 1993.

28 Carson, C.F. and Riley, T.V. "The Antimicrobial Activity of Tea Tree Oil," *Medical Journal of Australia,* 160, 236, 1994.

29 Carson, C.F. and Riley, T.V. "Susceptibility of *Propionibacterium acnes* to the Essential Oil of *Melaleuca alternifolia*," *Letters in Applied Microbiology,* 19, 24-25, 1994.

30 Carson, C.F., Cookson, B.D., Farrelly, H.D. and Riley, T.V. "Susceptibility of Methicillin-resistant *Staphylococcus aureus* to the Essential Oil *Melaleuca alternifolia*," *Journal of Antimicrobial Chemotherapy,* 35:3, 421-4, 1995.

31 Carson, C.F., Hammer, K.A. and Riley T.V. "Broth Micro-dilution Method for Determining the Susceptibility of *Escherichia coli* (*E coli*) and *Staphylococcus aureus* to the Essential Oil of *Melaleuca alternifolia*," *Microbios,* 82, 181-185, 1995.

and Cineole, etc. This is extremely useful for all sectors of the Tea Tree industry, helping to determine the best possible composition of an oil for medicinal effectiveness, etc.[32]

The final study that year took a critical look at the toxicity of Tea Tree oil, opening the way to discovering which components cause a reaction in those who are susceptible.[33]

In 1996, an in-vitro study showed that Tea Tree oil could inhibit the pathogenic bacteria that inhabits the skin's surface but could, in turn, still maintain the essential skin flora. This had good implications for using a low dilution in personal care products and skin creams.[34]

Also in 1996 an important study into the effectiveness of Tea Tree oil against the various gram-positive *Streptococcus spp. Streptococci* bacteria is implicated in many lesser (group B) and major, sometimes fatal, (group A) infections including Strep Throat and the flesh eating *Necrotizing fasciitis* (Type II).[35]

In 1997, their in-vitro study found that Tea Tree oil could inhibit the fungi *Malassezia furfur* (formally known as *Pityrosporum ovale*) which can contribute to dandruff and other various skin conditions.[36]

Their work in 1998 found that commercial Tea Tree products were as effective an anti-fungal agent as a Tea Tree dilution for inhibiting superficial *Candida albicans* type infections.[37]

And in the last year of this century, one of their in-vitro studies suggested that Tea Tree oil may also have a place in combating bacterial vaginosis.[38]

Two projects due to be completed soon are research into the anti-inflammatory properties and the anti-viral activity of Tea Tree oil. Various trials, projects, and medical collaborations are also in the pipeline. At last, mainly due to their invaluable in-vitro studies, things are really starting to move and are actually gathering momentum. Hopefully this will give Tea Tree oil the much needed credibility with those who choose not to see the healing of generations of people as proof of efficacy.

32   Carson, C.F. and Riley, T.V. "Antimicrobial Activity of the Major Components of the Essential Oil of *Melaleuca alternifolia," Journal of Applied Bacteriology,* 78:3, 264-9, 1995.

33   Carson, C.F. and Riley, T.V. "Toxicity of the Essential Oil of *Melaleuca alternifolia* (or Tea Tree Oil)," (Letter) *Journal of Toxicology-Clinical Toxicology,* 33:2, 193-4, 1995.

34   Hammer, K.A., Carson, C.F. and Riley, T.V. "Susceptibility of Transient and Commensal Skin Flora to the Essential Oil of *Melaleuca alternifolia* (Tea Tree Oil)," *American Journal of Infection Control,* 24:3, 186-9, 1996.

35   Carson, C.F., Hammer, K.A. and Riley, T.V. "In-vitro Activity of the Essential Oil of *Melaleuca alternifolia* Against *Streptococcus Spp.," Journal of Antimicrobial Chemotherapy,* 37:6, 1177-8, 1996.

36   Hammer, K.A., Carson, C.F. and Riley, T.V. "In-vitro Susceptibility of Malassezia furfur to the Essential Oil of *Melaleuca alternifolia," Journal of Medical and Veterinary Mycology,* 35:5, 375-7, 1997.

37   Hammer, K.A., Carson, C.F. and Riley, T.V. "In-vitro Activity of Essential Oils, in Particular *Melaleuca alternifolia* (Tea Tree Oil and Tea Tree Oil Products) Against *Candida spp.," Journal of Antimicrobial Chemotherapy,* 42:5, 591-5, 1998.

38   Hammer, K.A., Carson, C.F. and Riley, T.V. "In-vitro Susceptibilities of Lactobacilli and Organisms Associated with Bacterial Vaginosis to *Melaleuca alternifolia* (Tea Tree oil)," (Letter) *Antimicrobial Agents and Chemotherapy,* Jan 1999.

TEA TREE OIL APPLICATIONS—AN AMAZING ANTISEPTIC AND MUCH MUCH MORE!

In the early days of Tea Tree oil, back in the 1930s and 1940s, when the scientific evidence was in its infancy, it became clear that Tea Tree oil was a very valuable commodity. Humphrey's paper, "A New Australian Germicide," published in the *Medical Journal of Australia*, was really the catalyst that started the commercial ball rolling. Ever since the very first evidence, new testing methods, superior emulsifiers and more advanced surfactants have all helped us to understand and use Tea Tree oil in a vast array of products.[39, 40]

ANTIBACTERIAL SOAPS

The first commercially blended Tea Tree oil product was an antiseptic soap, which was manufactured by the Australian division of Colgate-Palmolive. The soap all but disappeared after the war years with the rise in synthetic disinfectants. In the early 1980s antiseptic soaps, creams and lotions started to emerge on a wider scale. A positive trial conducted by The Associated Foodstuff Laboratories of Australia in 1983 showed that the bacterial count on hands was substantially reduced by washing with Tea Tree products. Dr. Humphrey had long advocated the use of its superior germicidal action, and many other clinical trials have later confirmed this.[41, 42, 43]

ACNE CREAMS AND LOTIONS

Many people suffer from acne and facial boils at some time in their lives. There have been quite a few positive trials using Tea Tree oil in various products for these conditions. The unique penetrating action of the Tea Tree oil helps to rid the dermal layers of the invading bacteria. A soon to be friend of mine who had four boils on her chin and was at her wits end contacted us to ask our advice. She had been on antibiotics for over three months, but the boils were still thriving. We suggested she use a Tea Tree problem skin lotion, so she went back to her doctor who agreed to take her off the antibiotics. Within two weeks, two of the boils had disappeared and the third was shrinking fast. Within one month she had just a faint mark where the last boil had finally admitted defeat. She was amazed with the results. We had seen it all before![44,45,46]

39 Williams, L.R., Home, V.N. and Asre, S. "Antimicrobial Activity of Oil of *Melaleuca alternifolia*. Its Potential Use in Cosmetics and Toiletries," Cosmetics, Aerosols & Toiletries in Australia, 4:4, 1990.

40 Altman, P.M. "Australian Tea Tree Oil," *Australian Journal of Pharmacy*, 69, 276-78, 1988.

41 Hammer, K.A., Carson, C.F. and Riley, T.V. "Susceptibility of Transient and Commensal Skin Flora to the Essential Oil of *Melaleuca alternifolia* (Tea Tree Oil)," *American Journal of Infection Control*, 24:3, 186-9, 1996.

42 Beylier, M.F. "Bacteriostatic Activity of Some Australian Essential Oils," *Perfumer and Flavorist International*, V4:23-5, 1979.

43 Williams, L.R., Home, V.N. and Asre, S. "Antimicrobial Activity of Oil of *Melaleuca alternifolia*. Its Potential Use in Cosmetics and Toiletries," *Cosmetics, Aerosols & Toiletries in Australia*, 4:4, 1990.

44 Bassett, I.B., Pannowitz, D.L. and Barnetson, R.St.C. "A Comparative Study of Tea Tree Oil Versus Benzoyl Peroxide in the Treatment of Acne," *Medical Journal of Australia*, 153:8, 455-458, 1990.

MOISTURIZING CREAMS AND LOTIONS

Although very few clinical studies have been completed in this area, there is much anecdotal evidence detailing the good effects of Tea Tree oil, applied in creams and lotions, to help alleviate skin conditions such as psoriasis and eczema, etc. A large Australian Tea Tree company has done its own investigations into inflammatory skin conditions with some quite positive results. A couple of the studies, "A Clinical Investigation of a Tea Tree Oil Preparation for the Re-hydration of the Skin in Lower Limb" by Jill Fogharty, and "A Pilot Study into Australian Tea Tree Oil" by M. Abdulla, have been successfully completed. Where local inflammation is present due to skin complaints, stings, bites, etc., Tea Tree oil in dilution was effective in soothing local irritation and pain. The best thing about Tea Tree moisturizing creams and lotions is that, even with a quite low dilution of Tea Tree oil, they can inhibit harmful bacteria while maintaining the resident skin flora.[47, 48]

ORAL/DENTAL PRODUCTS

An article in one of Australia's popular health magazines (*Prevention* January 1992), and written by Dr. William Mayo, stated that Tea Tree oil was effectively used in many oral preparations (toothpastes, mouthwashes, lip salves, sore throat sprays, lozenges, cold sore ointments, etc). There have been many clinical studies on oral pathogens. Tea tree oil is second to none for helping to keep teeth healthy and white, or to guard against mouth infections.

Dr. Andrew Weil, the well-known medical author and physician, frequently recommends Tea Tree oil toothpastes and mouthwashes for a number of oral problems. Some of these include halitosis (bad breath), gum disease, and canker sores.[49, 50, 51, 52]

HAIR CARE PRODUCTS

Tea Tree oil is a very effective ingredient in shampoos and conditioners. It helps to keep the hair and scalp in tiptop condition. It was reported as early as 1939 that Tea Tree oil was an excellent

45   Carson, C.F. and Riley, T.V. "Susceptibility of Propionibacterium acnes to the Essential Oil of *Melaleuca alternifolia*," *Letters in Applied Microbiology*, 19, 24-25, 1994.

46   Feinblatt, H.M. "Cajeput Type Oil (Tea Tree oil) for the Treatment of Furunculosis" (boils), *Journal of the National Medical Association* (USA), 52, 32-4, 1960.

47   Hammer, K.A., Carson, C.F. and Riley, T.V. "Susceptibility of Transient and Commensal Skin Flora to the Essential Oil of *Melaleuca alternifolia* (Tea Tree Oil)," *American Journal of Infection Control*, 24:3, 186-9, 1996.

48   Shemesh, A. and Mayo, W.L. "A Natural Antiseptic and Fungicide," *International Journal of Alternative and Complementary Medicine*, Dec. 1991.

49   Shemesh, A. and Mayo, W.L. "A Natural Antiseptic and Fungicide," *International Journal of Alternative and Complementary Medicine*, Dec. 1991.

50   Walsh, L.J. and Longstaff, J. "The Antimicrobial Effects of an Essential Oil on Selected Oral Pathogens," *Periodontology*, V8, 11-15, 1987.

51   Shapiro, S., Meier, A. and Guggenheim, B. "The Anti-microbial Activity of Essential Oils and Essential Oil Components Towards Oral Bacteria," *Oral Microbiolog. Immunology* (Denmark), 9:4, 202-8, 1994.

52   Weil, A. *Ask Dr. Weil*, http://www.drweil.com

ingredient in soaps and shampoos. An Australian chemist advertised the use of a 3% Tea Tree shampoo for the treatment of dandruff. Today *Melaleuca alternifolia* has finally been clinically sanctioned as a possible anti-dandruff shampoo ingredient, and shown that, even at a quite low dilution, it can inhibit the yeast that causes the problem.[53, 54]

PARASITICIDE AND INSECT REPELLENT

There are many anecdotal cases of Tea Tree oil soothing pain and itching after a sting or an insect bite. The analgesic qualities together with its powerful solvent action (dissipating the venom) is probably what makes it so effective. It is also thought that the solvent properties help to dissolve the hard outer case of the insect and so making it an effective insecticide/parasiticide, while the Terpenes present in the oil act as an insect repellent.

Tea Tree has been used for a number of years by doctors for the safe removal of parasites. With the growing concern over the safety of prescription lotions, it was refreshing to actually hear a qualified doctor give his approval. The well-known physician and medical author, Dr. Andrew Weil, recommends the use of Tea Tree oil and other oils for the treatment of head lice.[55, 56, 57, 58]

ANTIFUNGAL CREAMS AND FOOT CARE PRODUCTS

Tea Tree oil is very effective on all sorts of foot problems and infections. Many successful trials have been carried out in this area, from athletes foot (Tinea pedis) and ringworm, to warts, even on rough and cracked skin. It is used by podiatrists all over the world.

On his Web site, *Ask Dr. Weil,* the highly respected medical author writes, "Tea Tree oil is the best treatment I know for fungal infections of the skin (athlete's foot, ringworm, jock itch). It will also clear up fungal infections of the toenails or fingernails, a condition notoriously resistant to treatment, even by strong systemic antibiotics."[59]

We have a lovely letter from a parent whose son's feet were so badly infected with Plantar warts that his doctor had said that surgery was the only option. We put her in touch with a podiatrist who we knew used Tea Tree oil on his patients. After a few weeks of treatment,

53 Goldsborough, R.E. "Ti-Tree Oil," *The Manufacturing Chemist,* 57-58-60, Feb 1939.
54 Hammer, K.A., Carson, C.F. and Riley, T.V. "In-vitro Susceptibility of Malassezia furfur to the Essential Oil of *Melaleuca alternifolia,*" *Journal of Medical and Veterinary Mycology,* 35:5, 375-7, 1997.
55 Veal, L. "The Potential Effectiveness of Essential Oils as a Treatment for Head Lice, *Pediculus Humanus Capitis,*" *Complementary Ther. Nurs. Midwifery,* 2:4, 97-101, 1996.
56 McDonald, L.G. and Tovey, E. "The Effectiveness of Benzyl Benzoate and Some Essential Oils as Laundry Additives for Killing House Dustmites," *Journal Allergy and Clinical Immunology,* 1993.
57 Williams, L.R., Home, V.N. and Asre S. "Antimicrobial Activity of Oil of *Melaleuca alternifolia.* Its Potential Use in Cosmetics and Toiletries," *Cosmetics, Aerosols & Toiletries in Australia,* 4:4, 1990.
58 Weil, A. *Ask Dr. Weil,* http://www.drweil.com
59 Weil, A. *Ask Dr. Weil,* http://www.drweil.com

the son was well on his way to a complete recovery, and without the intervention of surgery.[60, 61, 62]

PERSONAL CARE PRODUCTS

Tea Tree oil products for personal care are gathering momentum. Dr. Humphrey in his writings of 1930 stated that it was a good deodorant, killing the bacteria that produced the odor. Hammer et al found that, at low dilution, it could be used on the skin and still maintain resident skin flora. Today we have a far wider choice of personal care items, as word of the effectiveness of this wonderful oil spreads far and wide. From deodorant to body lotion, cosmetics, sunscreen, hand cream, to aftershave lotion, after-sun cream and bubble bath, its non-sting healing properties are being utilized as never before.[63, 64]

VAGINAL DOUCHES AND GENITAL CREAMS

Unfortunately for us humans, we have many sites that can harbor the pathogenic yeasts and bacteria that cause infection. Central heating, synthetic underwear, tight-fitting clothes, etc., all add to the problem. Fortunately there are many Tea Tree personal hygiene products on the market with plenty of clinical trials to back up the claims that Tea Tree oil can effectively reduce harmful parasites that thrive in dark, warm places on the body. Dr. Andrew Weil claims that, for vaginal yeast infections, Tea Tree oil "is at least as effective as the usual prescription remedy." [65, 66, 67, 68]

INFLAMMATION

Again this is another area where Tea Tree oil has been used for decades by alternative practitioners in the treatment of inflammation and pain. From insect bite salves to rheumatic rubs and sports care products, there is much anecdotal evidence to support its use in this area. The first clinical evidence that Tea Tree oil may be able to reduce inflammation and associated pain has been found in a study by the

60 Tong M.M., Altman, P.M. and Barnetson R.St.C. "Tea Tree Oil in the Treatment of Tinea pedis," *Australian Journal of Dermatology*, 33:3, 145-9, 1992.
61 Walker, M. "Clinical Investigation of Australian *Melaleuca alternifolia* oil for a Variety of Common Foot Problems," *Current Podiatry,* April 7th to 15th, 1972.
62 Nenoff, P., et al. "Antifungal Activity of the Essential Oil of *Melaleuca alternifolia* (Tea Tree oil) Against Pathogenic Fungi In-vitro," *Skin Pharmacology*, 9:6, 388-394, 1996.
63 Altman, P.M. "Australian Tea Tree Oil - An Update," *Cosmetics, Aerosols & Toiletries in Australia*, 5:4, 27-9, 1991.
64 Priest, D. "Tea Tree Oil in Cosmetics- The Promise and the Proof," (Technical paper) *Cosmetics, Aerosols & Toiletries in Australia*, 9:4, 1995.
65 Weil, A. *Ask Dr. Weil*, http://www.drweil.com
66 Peña, E.F. "*Melaleuca alternifolia*: Its Use for Trichomonal vaginitis and Other Vaginal Infections," *Obstetrics and Gynecology*, 19:6, 793-795, 1962.
67 Hammer, K.A., Carson, C.F. and Riley, T.V. "In-vitro Activity of Essential Oils, in Particular *Melaleuca alternifolia* (Tea Tree Oil and Tea Tree Oil Products) against *Candida spp.*," *Journal of Antimicrobial Chemotherapy*, 42:5, 591-5, 1998.
68 Hammer, K.A., Carson, C.F. and Riley, T.V. "In-vitro Susceptibilities of Lactobacilli and Organisms Associated with Bacterial Vaginosis to *Melaleuca alternifolia* (Tea Tree oil)," (Letter) *Antimicrobial Agents and Chemotherapy*, Jan 1999.

College of Dentistry at the University of Tennessee Memphis.[69] The Rural Industries Research and Development Corporation (RIRDC) in Australia has funded further research into this and the results should be published soon.

BURN GELS

There is a great deal of anecdotal (but not very much scientific) evidence that Tea Tree gel helps to alleviate pain and infection when applied to burns. Many leading Tea Tree companies are using the oil of *Melaleuca alternifolia* in a whole range of new and innovative burn gels and impregnated dressings. The water soluble gel helps to quickly cool down the burn while the Melaleuca oil, held in suspension, reduces the pain and inflammation. Healing is accelerated with much less likelihood of infection and scarring—great news for casualty units, fire departments, industry, schools, families, and in fact, anyone who is likely to treat burns and scalds.

Did you know? It was reported that Australian actor Mel Gibson insisted on using Tea Tree impregnated fire blankets on the set during the filming of the amazing fire scenes for the film *Braveheart*, just in case any of the actors or film crew were accidentally burned! Nice one Mel!

HAND AND NAIL CARE

Dr. E.M. Humphrey in the 1930s found that "The pus solvent properties of Tea Tree oil made it an excellent application for the fungal nail disease paronychia, which if left untreated could result in the deformity and eventual loss of the nail." Dr. Andrew Weil claims that Tea Tree oil works better, and is much cheaper, than prescription antifungals for fungal infections of the toenails or fingernails.[70, 71, 72, 73]

COUGHS, COLDS AND FLU

Alternative practitioners have successfully used Tea Tree oil in sprays (for strep throat), inhalations and decongestant chest rubs. There is some evidence available in peer-reviewed journals that can collaborate these facts, but more research needs to be done in this area.[74, 75, 76]

69 Dabbous, K.H., Pippin, M.A., Pabst, K.M., and Pabst, M.J. "Superoxide Release by Neutrophils is Inhibited by Tea Tree Oil," (Supported by NIDR DEO5494) College of Dentistry, UT Memphis, 1993.
70 Penfold, A.R. and Morrison, F.R. "Some Notes on the Essential Oil of *Melaleuca alternifolia*," *Australian Journal of Pharmacy*, 18, 274-5, 1937.
71 Humphrey, E.M. "A New Australian Germicide," *Medical Journal of Australia*, I, 417-418, 1930.
72 Buck, D.S, Nidorf, D.M. and Addino, J.G. "Comparison of Two Topical Preparations for the Treatment of Onychomycosis: *Melaleuca alternifolia* (Tea Tree Oil) and Clotrimazole," *Journal of Family Practice*, 38, 601-5, 1994.
73 Weil, A. *Ask Dr. Weil*, http://www.drweil.com
74 Carson, C.F., Hammer, K.A. and Riley, T.V. "In-vitro Activity of Essential Oil of *Melaleuca alternifolia* against *Streptococcus Spp.*," *Journal of Antimicrobial Chemotherapy*, 37:6, 1177-8, 1996.
75 Coutts, M. "The Bronchoscopic Treatment of Bronchiectasis," *Medical Journal Australia*, July 1937.
76 Shemesh, A. and Mayo, W.L. "A Natural Antiseptic and Fungicide," *International Journal of Alternative and Complementary Medicine*, Dec. 1991.

TEA TREE OIL

THE FIRST ANTI-VIRAL EVIDENCE

Most alternative practitioners have known that Tea Tree oil of *Melaleuca alternifolia* has shown signs of anti-viral activity, especially with the Herpes virus (cold sores, chicken pox and shingles blisters, warts, etc.). Now that the first research report completed by Chris Bishop at John Moores University, Liverpool, UK, has been published, others supported by the Rural Industries Research and Development Corporation (RIRDC) are set to follow.[77]

AT WAR WITH THE SUPERBUGS

Methicillin-resistant *Staphylococcus aureus* (MRSA, Golden-staph, Super-staph) is believed to be at epidemic proportions. The last of the synthesized antibiotics are becoming increasingly less effective against it. Tea Tree oil, at a low dilution of less than 2%, is proving to be the one last hope. Unfortunately, because Tea Tree oil cannot be patented or held exclusive, large pharmaceutical companies do not see the need to help with research. Could this mean that they are more interested in profits than in people's health? [78, 79, 80, 81]

CHILD CARE

There are many safe, dermatologically tested Tea Tree products available that are designed for children. It is comforting to know that Tea Tree is still a very effective pathogenic bacteria inhibitor even at a low dilution of 0.25% in some cases.[82]

PET CARE

The beneficial effects of Tea Tree oil apply to animals as well. Skin problems, wounds, insect bites and stings, and ringworm can all be treated very successfully with the oil or products made with the oil. One property of Tea Tree oil in particular is very beneficial to pets—it is a very effective insect repellent. It's a useful treatment and deterrent for fleas, ticks, and mites.[83, 84]

77   Bishop, C.D. "Anti-viral Activity of the Essential Oil of *Melaleuca alternifolia* (Maiden & Betche) Cheel (Tea Tree) Against Tobacco Mosaic Virus," (Research Report) *Journal of Essential Oil Research,* 7, 641-644, 1995.

78   Carson, C.F., Cookson, B.D., Farrelly, H.D. and Riley, T.V. "Susceptibility of Methicillin-resistant Staphylococcus aureus to the Essential Oil *Melaleuca alternifolia," Journal of Antimicrobial Chemotherapy,* 35:3, 421-4, 1995.

79   Carson, C.F., Hammer, K.A. and Riley, T.V. "Broth Micro-dilution Method for Determining the Susceptibility of *Escherichia coli* (*E coli*) and *Staphylococcus aureus* to the Essential Oil of *Melaleuca alternifolia," Microbios,* 82:332, 181-185, 1995.

80   Carson, C.F., Riley, T.V. and Cookson, B.D. "Efficacy and Safety of Tea Tree Oil as a Topical Anti-microbial Agent," (editorial) *Journal of Hospital Infection,* 40:3, 175-8, 1998.

81   Elsom, G. "Susceptibility of Methicillin-resistant *Staphylococcus aureus* to Tea Tree Oil and Mupirocin," *Journal of Antimicrobial Chemotherapy,* V43, 427-428, 1999.

82   Hammer, K.A., Carson, C.F. and Riley, T.V. "Susceptibility of Transient and Commensal Skin Flora to the Essential Oil of *Melaleuca alternifolia," American Journal of Infection Control,* 24:3, 186-9, 1996.

83   Carson, C.F. and Riley, T.V. "Toxicity of the Essential Oil of *Melaleuca alternifolia* (or Tea Tree Oil)," (Letter) *Journal of Toxicology-Clinical Toxicology,* 33:2, 193-4, 1995.

84   Southwell, I., Markham, J. and Mann, C. "Why Cineole is Not Detrimental to Tea Tree Oil," *Rural Industries Research and Development Corporation,* Research Paper Series 97/54, 1997.

AGRICULTURAL APPLICATIONS

Although there have not been a great deal of clinical studies on the use of Tea Tree oil in agriculture, its anti-fungal, parasiticidal, and indeed, anti-viral properties can be utilized for use in the greenhouse and garden (see the first anti-viral evidence above). Australian farmers and organic growers have been using Tea Tree products for a number of years.[85, 86]

HOUSEHOLD CLEANING AND LAUNDRY

The solvent properties of Tea Tree oil, which are so useful at dissolving pus and debris in wounds, are also brilliant in household cleaning products and in the laundry. Today, companies all around the globe are utilizing its unique solvent and anti-microbial qualities. There are soaps, stain removers, fabric softeners, laundry detergents and whiteners, copper and brass cleaners, dish detergents, window cleaners, all-purpose cleaners, bathroom cleaners, furniture polish, air fresheners, odor eliminators, floor cleaners, hospital grade disinfectants, etc. Tea Tree oil can also be used very effectively as an anti-microbial surface cleaner. It is many times more "active" than a comparable strength disinfectant.[87, 88]

The household of the 21st Century has a unique opportunity to say "No!" to those harsh synthetic chemicals that are slowly poisoning our planet. While we still have natural, biodegradable commodities like the oil of the *Melaleuca alternifolia* we have a choice—a greener choice that can not only assist in healing our bodies, but can also safely cleanse all around our homes too, quite literally from basement to attic.

A LESSON IN QUALITY

With the spreading world-wide popularity of Tea Tree oil, there was inevitably a growing demand for high quality oil with consistent healing properties. Unfortunately, less scrupulous companies could easily sell an inferior oil, trading solely on the good reputation earned by the pure oil of *Melaleuca alternifolia*. With no quality standards in place, these companies could quite legally mix the pure oil with a cheaper oil, having little or no healing qualities, and market the blend as "Tea Tree oil" or "Melaleuca oil."

Even if the oil is wholly derived from the *Melaleuca alternifolia* tree, this does not guarantee its therapeutic value. Tree genetics, growing conditions, distillation methods, and storage can all affect oil quality to a degree. This is why, in 1967, in order to protect both

85 Small, B.E.J. "Tea Tree Oil," *Australian Journal of Experimental Agriculture and Animal Husbandry*, V21, 1981.

86 Olsen, M.W. "Control of *Sphaerotheca fuliginea* on Cucurbits with a 1.5% Dilution of an Oil Extracted from the Australian Tea Tree," *Phytopathology*, 78:12, 1595, 1988.

87 Altman, P.M. "Australian Tea Tree Oil," *Australian Journal of Pharmacy*, 69, 276-78, 1988.

88 Altman, P.M. "Australian Tea Tree Oil - A Natural Antiseptic," *Australian Journal of Biotechnology*, 3:4 247-8, 1989.

the consumer and the Tea Tree industry, the Australian Standards Association established a standard for the oil.

This new standard was based on two of the oil's key components—Terpinen 4-ol and Cineole. As far back as 1925, it was known that Terpinen 4-ol was the main anti-microbial component. Obviously, higher levels of Terpinen 4-ol are desirable. Cineole is the component that gives Tea Tree oil its unique penetrating ability. But high levels of Cineole can be irritating to sensitive skin, so lower levels of Cineole are preferable. Consequently, the Australian Standards Association set the 1967 standard so that Melaleuca oil should have a minimum content of 35% Terpinen 4-ol and a maximum of 10% Cineole.

Unfortunately these new requirements led to an over-production of unmarketable oil that failed to reach the required standard. To save the ailing and discontented Tea Tree industry, the standard was relaxed in 1985 to a minimum content of 30% Terpinen 4-ol and a maximum of 15% Cineole. Fortunately for us, there are a number of reputable suppliers who still sell high-quality oil which falls well within the original (higher) standard.

Please be aware that there are many oils that technically can be called "Tea Tree oil" or "Melaleuca oil." There are over 150 species of Melaleuca trees, some with nearly identical main components, but there is only one Melaleuca alternifolia. To be sure that you have the authentic Australian Tea Tree oil, it must state on the label that it is the oil of the *"Melaleuca alternifolia."* It should also contain more than 35% Terpinen 4-ol and less than 10% Cineole. It is very important to know your supplier and to make sure that the oil you purchase is of a high therapeutic grade. If in any doubt, go back to your supplier and ask to see a detailed specification. A reputable supplier would be happy to oblige. There are reputable companies today that have never lowered their standards and have always sold the pure oil of *Melaleuca alternifolia* that is well within the set guidelines.

This all reminds me of a very apt slogan I once saw:

"Nothing added, nothing removed,
  Nature's best cannot be improved."

Tea Tree oil of the *Melaleuca alternifolia* is a uniquely complex substance that continues to delight and surprise us the more we learn about it. It is truly one of "nature's best," and one of nature's most potent, remarkable, and useful gifts.

CHAPTER THREE

Is Your Home a Healthy Home?

How common household chemicals may gradually be making you and your family sick.

by John K. Beaulieu

IS YOUR HOME A HEALTHY HOME?

It's alarming but true—scientists and doctors have discovered that there is a connection between our health and the use of common everyday household chemicals. If yours is the typical home, you probably use dozens of cleaning and personal care products, purchased at the local grocery store, which contain chemical ingredients that could be harmful to your health and the health of your loved ones.

Since World War II, there has been a dramatic rise in the number of man-made chemicals we use in our homes. The typical home now contains over sixty-three hazardous products that together contain hundreds of different chemicals.[1] At the same time there has been an equally dramatic rise in the incidence of certain chronic health problems. Research indicates that it is more than coincidence that the dramatic rise in these various diseases has coincided with the increased use of hazardous, man-made chemicals in the home.

HAVE WE ALWAYS BEEN THIS SICK?

At the beginning of the 20th century the cancer incidence rate was about one in fifty. Today in the US, one in three women and one in two men will suffer with cancer some time in their lives. Cancer is the number two killer of adults and the leading cause of death from disease in children.[2]

The incidence of central nervous system disorders like Alzheimer's and Multiple Sclerosis increases annually.

Birth defects are on the rise as well. Over 150,000 babies are born with defects each year for reasons unknown. Another 500,000 babies

---

1 World Resources Institute, *The 1994 Information Please Environmental Almanac* (Houghton-Mifflin, 1994).
2 American Cancer Society, *Cancer Facts & Figures 2004.*

are miscarried early in pregnancy each year with an additional 24,000 miscarried late in pregnancy or stillborn.[3] Infertility is increasing and widespread with over 2 million couples who want children and are unable to conceive.[4]

Asthma was also once a very rare disease. Now the condition is extremely common. The asthma rate has tripled in the last twenty years with over 30 million Americans currently afflicted.[5]

Attention Deficit Disorder in adults and children is rising. In 1993, two million children took the drug Ritalin so they could sit still long enough to learn. In 1995, that figure doubled to approximately 4 million.[6] In 2000, 17 million prescriptions were written in the US for Ritlin and other drugs to treat ADD, according to NBC's "Dateline."

You or someone you know has probably been touched in some way by one of these illnesses. What could be causing these, and other health problems, to rise and afflict so many otherwise healthy people? Although other factors are involved, more and more scientists are linking these ailments to long-term chemical exposure. And, for most of us, our greatest exposure to chemicals is right in our own homes! We breathe chemical vapors from household products in the air; we absorb chemicals into our skin while using household products to clean our homes or make our bodies clean and smell good; and we swallow small amounts of chemicals when we gargle, or when we eat food from dishes that have been cleaned with chemicals and still contain a thin residue. The home is also where over 1.5 million young children are poisoned each year, and most of the time they are poisoned by a cleaning or personal care product![7]

WHY I WROTE THIS ARTICLE

I realize that you are probably not aware of the potential health hazards present in many household cleaners and personal care products. Unfortunately, most people are not. It is for you that I have written this article. I am not a chemist or a doctor, and I am not trying to promote myself as an expert on household chemicals. However, I have done considerable research on this subject because I want to provide the safest, healthiest home I possibly can for my own wife and children. What I learned is so convincing that I feel I must share it with you and others as best I can.

In this article, you will find quite a bit of information on the connection between household chemicals and your health. I have tried to provide information from the most credible and objective sources possible. You may find the information shocking and very disturbing, as I did. But I want you to know that I do not mean to frighten you. I simply

3 H. Needleman & P. Landrigan, *Raising Children Toxic Free* (Farrar, Straus, & Giroux, 1994).
4 Doris Rapp, *Is This Your Child's World?* (Bantam Books, 1996).
5 American Lung Association, Trends in *Asthma Morbidity and Mortality* (April 2004).
6 Doris Rapp, *Is This Your Child's World?*
7 The National Safe Kids Campaign, *Poisoning* (1996).

want you to be informed so that you can make a simple, rational decision concerning your health and the health of your loved ones.

THIS ARTICLE HAS A HAPPY ENDING

Happily, there is a simple solution to the problem presented in this article. Some conscientious companies now offer household products that are safer and more natural. Most of these people-friendly and environmentally sensitive products work just as well or better than grocery store brands, and in many cases, actually cost less. So, there's really no reason to risk your health, or the health of your loved ones any longer.

Is your home a healthy home? Right now, it's probably not as healthy as it could be. Read on to learn more.

THEY WOULDN'T SELL IT IF IT WASN'T SAFE ...WOULD THEY?

When we pick up a product at the local grocery store, most of us like to think we are getting something that has been tested and proven to be safe. After all, we have laws to protect our health and safety, don't we? Actually, the government has very limited power to regulate manufacturers, or require testing of their products. Here are some disturbing facts:

- A product that kills 50% of lab animals through ingestion or inhalation can still receive the federal regulatory designation "non-toxic."[8]
- Of the 17,000 chemicals that appear in common household products, only 30% have been adequately tested for their negative effects on our health; less than 10% have been tested for their effect on the nervous system; and nothing is known about the combined effects of these chemicals when mixed within our bodies.[9]
- No law requires manufacturers to list the exact ingredients on the package label.[10]

"Personal care product" refers to just about anything we use to clean our bodies or make ourselves look or smell good. The closest thing to a regulatory agency for the personal care industry is the Food and Drug Administration (FDA), and their power is extremely limited. Here are more unsettling facts regarding personal care products:

- The FDA cannot regulate a personal care product until after it is released into the marketplace.
- Neither personal care products nor their ingredients are reviewed or approved before they are sold to the public.
- The FDA cannot require companies to do safety testing on their personal care products before they are sold to the public.

---

8 Doris Rapp, *Is This Your Child's World?*
9 World Resources Institute, *The 1994 Information Please Environmental Almanac.*
10 Debra Lynn Dadd, *Home Safe Home* (Tarcher-Putnam, 1997).

- The FDA cannot require recalls of harmful personal care products from the marketplace.[11]
- The National Institute of Occupational Safety and Health (NIOSH) analyzed 2,983 chemicals used in personal care products. The results were as follows:

> 884 of the chemicals were toxic
> 314 caused biological mutation
> 218 caused reproductive complications
> 778 caused acute toxicity
> 148 caused tumors
> 376 caused skin and eye irritations.[12]

WARNING:
YOU CAN'T TRUST WARNING LABELS!

You may think you know what is in a product and its potential harms by reading ingredient and warning labels. Think again. Manufacturers are not required to list the exact ingredients on the label. Also, chemical names are often disguised by using innocuous "trade names." So even if the chemical is listed on the label, you may not recognize it for what it is.

Even if the harsh and dangerous active ingredients are listed on a package, oftentimes the remainder of ingredients are lumped into a category known as "inert" (not active) ingredients. This term may lead you to believe that these chemicals are not toxic or hazardous. In fact, many of the 1,000 different chemicals used as inert ingredients are more harmful than the active ingredients. The Environmental Protection Agency (EPA) does not require manufacturers to identify most inert chemicals, or disclose their potential harmful effects. Even suspected carcinogens (cancer-causing agents) are used as inert ingredients in household products.[13]

Regarding warning labels, one New York study found that 85% of products they examined had incorrect warning labels. Some were labeled poisonous, but weren't; others were poisonous, but not labeled as such; others gave incorrect first aid information.[14] And there are absolutely no warnings on products about possible negative effects of long-term exposure. This is unfortunate because most diseases linked to chemical exposure are the result of long-term exposure.

If we don't know what's in it, and we don't know if it can hurt us, how are we supposed to make an intelligent decision about whether or not to bring this product into our home?

11   United States Food and Drug Administration, *FDA Authority Over Cosmetics* (Office of Cosmetics Fact Sheet, 1995).
12   Judith Berns, "The Cosmetic Cover-up," *Human Ecologist* 43 (Fall 1989).
13   John Harte, *Toxics A to Z* (University of California Press, 1991).
14   Debra Lynn Dadd, *Home Safe Home.*

WHY AREN'T MANUFACTURERS REQUIRED TO TEST THESE CHEMICALS?

As we've already discussed, the government has very limited power to regulate manufacturers or require testing of their products. The reason has to do with economics and politics. It takes dozens of years and hundreds of thousands of dollars to fully test one chemical. If the government were to require every manufacturer to test every product and prove that it is safe, many manufacturers would be forced to go out of business, and our products would cost about twice as much as they currently do. Besides, who do you think they would test these chemicals on anyway? That's right—animals.

All this would cause a lose-lose situation for politicians. Manufacturers would be angry at them for imposing the expensive testing. And the public would be angry at them for requiring manufacturers to torture and kill all those animals, and for driving the prices of household products through the roof!

Even if a chemical has been tested and found to be harmful, you still may not get the truth from a manufacturer. Just look how long it took the tobacco industry to finally admit cigarettes are addictive and cause cancer. Do not wait for any company to spend hundreds of thousands of dollars to confirm that their product definitely causes cancer. Let's exercise our rights as informed consumers and choose manufacturers who make products with safer, more natural ingredients.

WHICH PRODUCTS? WHICH CHEMICALS?

Chemicals that can cause death, cancer, central nervous system (CNS) disorders, learning disorders, birth defects, respiratory illness, and many other health problems appear in most of the cleaning and personal care products in your home. It may be difficult, however, to tell which health risks a particular product poses. Since manufacturers do not list long-term health effects on the packages and are not required to list the ingredients, it's impossible to learn all the health risks by reading the label.

That's why I have provided a short list of product types and general comments about possible health risks below. Of course, every product is different. Even the same product's ingredients can vary from batch to batch depending on the cost and availability of certain chemicals. The following lists of cleaning supplies and personal care products are by no means exhaustive. The possible health effects do not apply to every single brand. However, based on examination of many grocery store brands, chemicals in the following products cause the listed health problems:

CLEANING PRODUCTS

- Air freshener – toxic; may cause cancer; irritates nose, throat, and lungs.
- Disinfectant – very toxic; causes skin, throat, and lung burns; coma.
- Drain cleaner – toxic; causes skin burns; liver and kidney damage.
- Oven cleaner – toxic; causes skin, throat, and lung burns.
- Window cleaner – toxic; causes CNS disorders; causes liver and kidney disorders.
- Floor/Furniture Polish – toxic; causes CNS disorders; may cause lung cancer.
- Spot remover – toxic; may cause cancer; causes liver damage.
- All-purpose cleaner – causes eye damage; irritates nose, throat, and lungs.
- Toilet bowl cleaner – very toxic; causes skin, nose, throat, and lung burns.
- Chlorinated scouring powder – toxic; highly irritating to nose, throat, and lungs.
- Dishwasher detergent – toxic; causes eye injuries, damage to mucous membranes, and throat.
- Dishwashing liquid – harmful if swallowed; irritates the skin.
- Carpet shampoo – toxic; may cause cancer; causes CNS and liver damage.
- Laundry detergent – toxic; irritates the skin and lungs.
- Bleach – toxic by swallowing; vapors are harmful; causes CNS disorders.
- Stain remover – toxic; may cause cancer; vapors can be fatal.
- Fabric softener – toxic; may cause cancer; causes CNS disorders; causes liver damage.

PERSONAL CARE PRODUCTS

- Shampoo – may cause cancer; irritates eyes, skin, and lungs.
- Dandruff shampoo – may cause cancer; causes organ degeneration; causes CNS disorders.
- Deodorant soap – may cause cancer; causes asthma; irritates lungs.
- Bubble bath – causes bladder and kidney infections; irritates skin and nose.
- Mousse and hair spray – may cause cancer; causes lung disease; irritates eyes and skin.
- Mouthwash – toxic to children; may cause cancer.
- Breath Spray – may cause cancer.
- Perfume/Cologne – toxic; may cause cancer; irritates skin and lungs.
- Cosmetics – may cause cancer; causes CNS damage; irritates skin and lungs. [15, 16, 17]

15 Debra Lynn Dadd, *Home Safe Home.*
16 John Harte, *Toxics A to Z.*
17 Ruth Winter, *A Consumer's Dictionary of Household, Yard and Office Chemicals* (Crown, 1992).

ONE COMMON INGREDIENT

Although it would take a second book to cover all the ingredients commonly used in the products above, I want to let you know about one, formaldehyde, as an example. Formaldehyde is used frequently in both cleaning and personal care products because it is a cheap preservative.

The following information is taken from a Material Safety Data Sheet (MSDS) which, by law, must be supplied to anyone who uses any chemical product in the workplace. The MSDS for formaldehyde warns: "Suspected carcinogen; May be fatal if inhaled, swallowed, or absorbed through skin; causes burns; inhalation can cause spasms, edema (fluid buildup) of the larynx and bronchi, and chemical pneumonitis; extremely destructive to tissue of the mucous membrane."[18]

All these symptoms and more are caused by formaldehyde. Yet manufacturers can put formaldehyde in shampoo and not list it as an ingredient![19] You will be shocked to learn that formaldehyde is a common ingredient in baby shampoo, bubble bath, deodorants, perfume, cologne, hair dye, mouthwash, toothpaste, hair spray, and many other personal care items.

Before I go any further, I want to state that the amount of formaldehyde in many of these products is slight. Brushing your teeth every day probably will not give you cancer, but the risk is still there. After all, formaldehyde is still a suspected carcinogen, and if all cancers start from the abnormal growth of one cell, then why allow any amount into or onto your body?

BEWARE OF AEROSOLS

Both cleaning and personal care products come in aerosol cans. I want to warn you of the dangers of aerosols in your home. First, they send a fine mist of toxic chemicals into the air that is easily inhaled and absorbed. Second, this fine mist settles, leaving a coating of toxins on surfaces where children crawl and play and adults eat and sleep. Finally, many of the propellants used in aerosol cans are toxic themselves. Vinyl chloride, one of the most common, can cause dizziness, lack of coordination, headaches, blurred vision, nausea, and death.[20]

I read of a young man named Stuart who became dizzy and collapsed while spray painting bookshelves in his basement. When his wife found him a few hours later, he was dead.

These chemical propellants are also highly flammable. A woman named Laurie received disfiguring burns when the hair spray she was using was ignited by her cigarette. Each year 5,000 people receive emergency room treatment for aerosol-related injuries.[21]

Jimmy, 8, used a hammer and nail to puncture an old aerosol can.

18 Material Safety Data Sheet - *Formaldehyde.*
19 Debra Lynn Dadd, *Home Safe Home.*
20 John Harte, *Toxics A to Z.*
21 Dr. Ted Ferry, *Home Safety Desk Reference* (Career Press, 1994).

The can exploded, hurling pieces of metal into his face and upper chest, cutting him severely.[22]

When you weigh the short-term and long-term harms of aerosol products, I think the smart conclusion is simply to get rid of them.

TOXIC CHEMICALS AND THE HUMAN BODY

Your body is a very complex, very fragile system of chemical reactions and electrical impulses. When you consider a single cell breathes, uses energy, and releases waste much like your whole body does, you can begin to understand how even small amounts of harmful chemicals can affect the performance of the body's processes. Chemicals enter the human body in three ways: ingestion, inhalation, and absorption.

INGESTION

Ingestion brings to mind the image of a young child opening the cabinet under the sink and drinking something deadly. Well, each year nearly 1.5 million accidental ingestions of poisons are reported to U.S. Poison Control Centers. The majority of the victims are under the age of twelve and have swallowed a cleaning or personal care product.[23] It amazes me how many deadly chemicals are stored under sinks or on bathroom counters and bathtubs within easy reach of young children.

INHALATION

It may surprise you to learn that poisoning by inhalation is more common, and can be much more harmful, than ingestion. When something harmful is swallowed, the stomach actually begins breaking down and neutralizing the poison before it is absorbed into the bloodstream. However, when you inhale toxic fumes, the poisons go directly into the bloodstream and quickly travel to organs like the brain, heart, liver, and kidneys.

Many products give off toxic vapors which can irritate your eyes, nose, throat and lungs, and give you headaches, muscle aches, and sinus infections. This process of releasing vapors into the air is called *outgassing*. Outgassing occurs even when a chemical is tightly sealed in its container. If you doubt this, simply walk down the cleaning aisle at your local grocery store and notice how strongly it smells of toxic vapors even though all the containers are sealed tight.

ABSORPTION

Finally, you need to realize the potential threat absorption poses. One square centimeter of your skin, an area less than the size of a dime, contains 3 million cells, four yards of nerves, one yard of blood vessels, and one hundred sweat glands.[24] We've all heard the ads for nicotine patches and analgesic creams. These medicines work by being absorbed into the bloodstream through the skin. Even some heart medicines are administered through transdermal (through the skin) patches.

Any chemical that touches the skin can be absorbed and spread throughout the body. This can even happen when you come in contact with a surface that was treated with a chemical days, or even weeks earlier. I had no idea that my children could be harmed by crawling across the kitchen floor my wife had just cleaned. I thought we were being conscientious, not reckless. Since we no longer have products which contain harmful chemicals in our home, I no longer worry when I see my baby daughter crawling across the floor or putting her fingers in her mouth. I know she is not absorbing or ingesting toxic residues.

HOME IS WHERE THE CHEMICALS ARE

Home is where you are most likely to be exposed to toxic chemicals. After all, you spend 80 to 90% of your time indoors, most of that at home.[25] This fact is important when you understand that in one five-year study, the EPA found that airborne chemical levels in homes were as much as seventy times higher inside than outside.

When toxic household chemicals release vapors into the air, they have nowhere to go. During the oil shortages of the 1970s, builders began making houses as energy efficient as possible. The result has been homes that keep toxic indoor air tightly sealed inside.

Exposure to toxic indoor air may have a devastating effect on your health. One fifteen-year study found that women who worked at home had a 54% higher death rate from cancer than women who had jobs outside the home.[26] The study concluded that the increased death rate was due to daily exposure to the hazardous chemicals found in ordinary products. Some experts argue that 30% of all cancers stem from exposure to toxic chemicals.[27]

Not all of the health effects are fatal, however. According to a special legislative committee of the Commonwealth of Massachusetts, 50% of all health problems are caused, in part, by deteriorated indoor air quality.[28] A hangover is the side-effect of non-lethal ethanol poisoning (getting drunk). How many days do you wake feeling "hung over," with aches and pains or nausea? Perhaps the air in your home is poisoning you. How many bottles of pain-killers have you purchased to rid yourself of headaches, possibly brought on by your fabric softener?

The good news is that by switching to safer, more natural products, you can rid yourself of these symptoms altogether. You can make your home a healthy home.

24 Nancy Sokol Green, *Poisoning Our Children* (The Noble Press, 1991).
25 World Resources Institute, *The 1994 Information Please Environmental Almanac.*
26 Nancy Sokol Green, *Poisoning Our Children.*
27 John Harte, *Toxics A to Z.*
28 Doris Rapp, *Is This Your Child's World?*

IMMEDIATE EFFECTS OF CHEMICAL EXPOSURE

Could this happen in your home? When Peter Schwabb of Seattle, Washington, was a year old, he crawled over to the dishwasher to watch his mother unloading it. Suddenly, he put a finger into the detergent dispensing cup and ate a fingerful of wet but undissolved Electrasol. In minutes his face was red and blistered, and the inside of his mouth and his tongue were burned white. Because of a series of lucky circumstances, Peter was in the hospital within minutes and he recovered in a few days.

While Peter was in the hospital, there was a little girl across the hall who (according to Peter's mother) ate some dishwashing detergent and required seven operations to reopen her scarred esophagus.[29]

Another 18-month-old boy had to eat through tubes for five months and at last count has had thirty operations. Detergent is what destroyed his throat, too.[30]

Three-year-old Jason Whitely, of Tulsa, Oklahoma, died a lingering and horrible death two weeks after swallowing three ounces of a hair rinse containing ammonia.

Seven-month-old Adrian Gonzalez, Jr., of Belen, New Mexico, crawled through a puddle of spilled bleach, which gave him third-degree burns on 50% of his tiny body and burned his lungs from the fumes as well. It took him four days to die.[31]

The real tragedy here is that all of these accidents could have been prevented. A simple decision to use safer products could have meant that these children would not have had to suffer and die. Unfortunately, most parents don't realize that they have a choice.

MORE DANGEROUS THAN GUNS

It may shock you to learn that according to the National Safety Council, more children under the age of four die of accidental poisonings at home than are accidentally killed with guns at home.[32] Among children age five and under, the most common poison is a cleaner or personal care product.[33]

Ninety percent of all poisonings occur at home between the hours of 4 and 10 PM, when children are home from school and playing in the house.[34] Young children are especially vulnerable. They learn by putting things in their mouths. This is even more frightening when you consider the number of products that look like something else. Window cleaner looks like blueberry drink. Ammonia looks like apple juice. Many poisons come in bright, colorful containers with small, obscure warning labels that young children can't read. Remember the

29 Shirley Camper Soman, *Let's Stop Destroying Our Children* (Hawthorn Books, 1974).
30 Shirley Camper Soman, *Let's Stop Destroying Our Children*.
31 Shirley Camper Soman, *Let's Stop Destroying Our Children*.
32 *Accident Facts* (National Safety Council, 1993).
33 The National Safe Kids Campaign, *Poisoning*.
34 The National Safe Kids Campaign, *Poisoning*.

IS YOUR HOME HEALTHY?

skull and crossbones symbol? It's a symbol that children can identify easily, but manufacturers are no longer required to display it on most household products.

Lennon Miller, 18 months, of Memphis, Tennessee, drank lemon-scented furniture polish, enticed no doubt by the attractive smell. He lived during a day of suffering, and died in John Gaston Hospital of chemically-induced pneumonia.[35]

ACCIDENTS HAPPEN TO ADULTS, TOO

Young children are not the only ones at risk for chemical injury. Poisoning is the number one accidental killer in the home, accounting for over 3,000 deaths in 1985 and over 4,000 deaths in 1990. These chemicals are also responsible for thousands of injuries each year.[36]

A 34-year-old man received burns on his arm after using a caustic drain-cleaner in his bathroom sink. Fifteen minutes after applying the chemical, he ran water into the sink, but the remaining residue splashed on his arm.[37]

A woman poured boiling water into a can of oven cleaner, according to the directions on the can. As she carried the can from the table to the oven, it spilled, burning her hand and producing large quantities of ammonia gas, which gave her a choking cough.[38]

But most of the health problems related to chemicals in the home are not because of accidents like these. Most chemical-related health problems are the result of exposure to toxics day after day, year after year.

LONG-TERM EFFECTS OF CHEMICAL EXPOSURE

Before I begin discussing the long-term effects of exposure to toxic chemicals in cleaning and personal care products, I want to make two points that I think are very important. First, the different diseases and conditions linked to chemical exposure are usually the result of long-term exposure. Just as one cigarette is not likely to give you cancer, one non-acute exposure to chemicals in cleaners probably won't harm you either. But we're talking about cumulative exposure to many different products: your mouthwash, conditioner, cologne or perfume, laundry detergent, window cleaner, and so on. When you consider all the products and all the chemicals you come across each day, you can begin to understand the potential for long-term harm.

Remember, the long-term effects of exposure to most chemicals in household products are not known. And nothing is known about what happens when they mix within our bodies. Drinking alcohol while using certain drugs can be a deadly combination. Could other chemicals mix in our bodies in a similarly fatal way?

35 Shirley Camper Soman, *Let's Stop Destroying Our Children.*
36 Home Safety, *USA Today* (February 13, 1997).
37 Dr. Ted Ferry, *Home Safety Desk Reference.*
38 Dr. Ted Ferry, *Home Safety Desk Reference.*

My second point concerns your body. What most doctors and scientists who investigate and treat chemical-related illness contend is that the *amount* of chemical a person is exposed to is not as important as *how sensitive* a person might be.[39] Some people can drink three beers and not be intoxicated. Others can feel groggy after drinking less than one beer. It all depends on a person's size and weight and the strength of their detox system. The same concept applies to chemical exposure.

YOUR DETOX SYSTEM

Your body has a system that destroys and eliminates toxins. After all, many things that appear naturally in the environment are toxic, and we need to have a strong defense system against them. Organs like the kidneys and liver filter out and remove toxins. Our blood contains T-cells that attack foreign agents. However, many people have overloaded or very weak detox systems. High levels of toxins and a poor nutritional state leave many people more susceptible to the effects of chronic chemical exposure.

Even healthy people can be affected. When exposed to a certain toxin, the body will respond by producing more of the enzymes needed to destroy the poison. In a sense, the body has "masked" the poisoning.[40] It has prevented the effects of the poisoning from being felt, even if the effects would have been mild. But, this has stressed the immune system, possibly leaving a person vulnerable to infection.

By switching to cleaners and personal care products that are not full of toxins, you can reduce the stress on your detox system, possibly leading to a healthier life. I have not missed a day of work due to illness in over two years. I have not seen a doctor for illness in three years. My children have been to the doctor for illness only twice in three years. I believe this is, in part, the result of my wife and me deciding to switch to safer and more natural products. I encourage you to do the same. It's one decision your family can live with.

BIRTH DEFECTS

Birth defects are the leading cause of death among children ages one to four. According to the March of Dimes, one in twelve children is born with a congenital defect. Environmental factors, including exposure to toxic chemicals, cause 7% to 11% of these defects. Sixty percent of birth defects have unknown causes. Toxic chemicals are suspected in these cases as well.[41]

In fact, the Council on Environmental Quality's report on chemical hazards to human reproduction concluded that, "the relationship between exposure to chemicals and human reproductive impairment may be an important area of public health concern that deserves more

39 Dr. Doris Rapp, *Is This Your Child's World?*
40 Nancy Sokol Green, *Poisoning Our Children.*
41 Paula DiPerna, *Environmental Hazards to Children.*

scientific investigation."[42]

Birth defects have been found in a number of animal species where high levels of toxic chemicals are present. A 1996 University of Minnesota study found higher rates of birth defects in children who lived in areas of the state where agricultural chemicals were used the most.[43]

Dr. Marion Moses of the Environmental Sciences Laboratory at Mount Sinai Medical Center in New York strongly recommends that, as far as toxins and carcinogens are concerned, the unborn child should have NO exposure; and where there is doubt about any chemical, err on the side of the child and prevent as much exposure as possible. "If we wait until we have absolute proof for all agents, it may be too late for the child," Dr. Moses stresses.[44]

Thalidomide is a tragic example of a substance that was touted as safe by its manufacturer but was later proven to cause horrible birth defects. Children whose mothers took the drug were born with deformed limbs or no limbs at all. This tragedy destroyed the belief that the placenta was a complete barrier between the baby and the environment. It also served as a wake-up call to how chemicals within the body can disrupt normal fetal development.

The NIOSH study I mentioned earlier stated 314 chemicals that appear in personal care products can cause biological mutations.[45] Many of these chemicals, including known carcinogens, can reach the unborn child.

Chemicals can also cause defects by damaging the egg cells in women. All the eggs a woman will ever have are produced while she is still a baby in the womb. By the fifth month of fetal life, the 3 to 4 million eggs a woman is born with have localized in her ovaries. Chemical exposure at any point can destroy or damage these cells, leaving her infertile or prone to birth defects or miscarriage.[46] Once damage has occurred, repair is almost impossible.

In men, exposure to chemicals can affect sperm development profoundly. A study of male Vietnam veterans found they were 70% more likely to have a child with a birth defect due to chemical exposure.[47] Many of the same chemicals are now found in products used every day around the home.

The presence of solvents in drinking water has been linked to leukemia and birth defects in California, Massachusetts, and New Jersey.[48] You may be exposed to a number of potentially harmful solvents every day, including ethanol, styrene, trichloroethylene, vinyl chloride, diethylene glycol, and toluene. All of these appear in common household products.

42 Paula DiPerna, *Environmental Hazards to Children*.
43 *Dioxins* (National Wildlife Federation Office of Conservation Programs, 1997).
44 Paula DiPerna, *Environmental Hazards to Children*.
45 Judith Burns, "The Cosmetic Cover-up".
46 H. Needleman & P. Landrigan, *Raising Children Toxic Free*.
47 Dr. Doris Rapp, *Is This Your Child's World?*
48 Ruth Winter, *A Consumer's Dictionary of Household, Yard and Office Chemicals*.

INFERTILITY AND MISCARRIAGE

More than 2 million American couples who want to have children are unable to do so. Perhaps you or someone close to you is living with this heartache. It may surprise you to learn that between 1938 and 1991 the sperm count of males in industrialized countries has decreased 50% in quantity and quality. A cross-sectional study of college men found that 25% were sterile. Projected figures place the male sterility rate at over 50% early in the next century.[49]

Women's fertility has also been negatively affected by the increased use of chemicals. In 1934, only twenty-one cases of endometriosis existed in the entire world. Now there are over 5 million women with this condition, which causes infertility, in the United States alone.[50] High levels of toxins have been found in German women with endometriosis. Female monkeys exposed to dioxins had an increased rate of this condition also.[51] Combine the decreased sperm count with the prevalence of endometriosis and you can see just how the infertility rate could grow so large and affect so many.

Even women who can conceive are experiencing extremely high rates of miscarriage. In 1988, more than 600,000 women experienced a miscarriage, and in most cases the cause was unclear.[52] In many cases a woman's body will reject an unborn baby if it detects a profound defect of some kind. We may begin wondering if we are living in a time when more babies have defects. Or perhaps the chemicals that enter the body somehow send mixed or wrong messages.

Many chemicals, including alkylphenol, found in many industrial and household detergents, are known hormone disrupters. This means they act like hormones and can actually change behavior, mood, development and any other bodily functions regulated by hormones. It concerns me that the delicate balance of chemicals our bodies naturally produce and need to function properly can be skewed by synthetic, toxic chemicals.

CANCER

No word strikes more fear into people's hearts than "cancer." Although the death rate from cancer has declined, the incidence rate has not. Cancer rates continue to grow in almost every segment of the American public. Breast cancer and prostate cancers have doubled in the past fifty years. Testicular cancer has tripled during the same period. One in five persons in the United States will die of cancer.[53]

The majority of cancer cases are due to environmental factors.[54] Most experts agree that as many as 80 to 90% of all cancers can

---

49 Dr. Doris Rapp, *Is This Your Child's World?*
50 Dr. Doris Rapp, *Is This Your Child's World?*
51 Dr. Doris Rapp, *Is This Your Child's World?*
52 H. Needleman & P. Landrigan, *Raising Children Toxic Free.*
53 National Cancer Institute, *Cancer Facts and the War on Cancer,* 2004.

be avoided by making certain lifestyle changes. Please understand that "environmental factors" include everything in the environment, including diet, sleep patterns, etc. Some experts argue that 30% of all cancers are caused by exposure to toxic chemicals.[55]

The National Cancer Institute has a list of twenty known carcinogens and over 2,200 chemicals that are probable carcinogens.[56] Many of these chemicals are in the cleaners and personal care products you buy at your local grocery store. The National Toxicology Program is urging that fifteen more chemicals be added to the list of known carcinogens, including an organic solvent used in grease-cutting cleaners.[57]

Cancer tumors start from the mutated growth of one cell. Even minimal exposure over a long period of time can put you at risk of developing cancer. The risk may not be that great, but for me there is no acceptable level of risk when it comes to cancer. I know I can't completely eliminate all potential hazards from my life, but I no longer put myself at risk for cancer by exposing myself to the unregulated, dangerous chemicals that appear in products like laundry detergent, bathroom cleaner, hair conditioner, and cologne.

CANCER IN CHILDREN

I know my children are safer, too. Each year 6,500 children in the United States are diagnosed with cancer. Cancer remains the leading cause of death from disease for children over the age of five, accounting for over 2,100 deaths a year.[58]

The tragedy is that only 20% of cases of childhood cancer are due to genetic factors. Remember, we now know that carcinogens can cross the placental barrier. Exposure to carcinogens in the womb may cause childhood cancer by causing tumor development or by altering the baby's genes, leaving them with a predisposition to cancer. Dr. Robert Miller of the National Cancer Institute states that many carcinogens have a short enough latent period that exposure in the womb could lead to the diagnosis of tumors in the pediatric age period.[59]

Finally, I think it is important to remember that current cancer rates reflect past toxic exposure. Only time will tell what the legacy of our increased use of household products full of toxic chemicals will be.

ASTHMA

The American Lung Association now estimates that 4 million American children and 20.3 million adults presently have asthma. That is three times more victims than just twenty years ago.[60] Once again, environmental factors are under strong suspicion. I have already

54 John Harte, *Toxics A to Z.*
55 John Harte, *Toxics A to Z.*
56 World Resources Institute, *The 1994 Information Please Environmental Almanac.*
57 *Press Release* (National Institute of Health, May 2, 1997).
58 H. Needleman & P. Landrigan, *Raising Children Toxic Free.*
59 Paula DiPerna, *Environmental Hazards to Children.*

told you that most Americans spend 80 to 90% of their time in air-tight buildings, most with less than adequate ventilation. One study concluded that the majority of the 400,000 annual emergency room visits for severe asthma attacks are brought on by poor indoor air quality. Each year, asthma claims the lives of over 4,000 people and costs Americans over 6 billion dollars in medical costs and lost time from work and school.[61]

Doctors know that irritation of the lungs by chemicals can trigger asthma attacks. Long-term exposure to chemicals can contribute to the development of asthma. This is especially true with children. A child's immune system is not fully developed until she is twelve years old. A one-year-old has practically no detox system at all.[62]

Out of germ-phobia, some parents constantly spray disinfectant into the air and on all surfaces in their baby's nursery. What they may not realize is they are exposing their children to formaldehyde, cresol, phenol, ammonia, ethanol, and chlorine. It takes much less of these chemicals to harm a baby than an adult. Babies' bodies are much smaller and they breathe at ten times the rate of adults. The average child visits the doctor twenty-three times in the first four years of life, with the most common complaint being respiratory ailment.[63] When babies get sick, the last thing they need is to have irritating chemicals filling their lungs.

CNS DISORDERS

Central Nervous System (CNS) disorders can range from headaches and dizziness to Multiple Sclerosis, Parkinson's Disease, and Alzheimer's Disease. We know that many chemicals that appear in our household products are neurotoxins. Some act as depressants, some as stimulants, and some cause mood swings. Others act similar to alcohol, leaving a person lethargic, unable to concentrate, and with a loss of balance.

It's important, once again, to remind you that only 10% of the chemicals that appear in household products have been tested for negative effects on the nervous system.[64] And we know nothing about the long-term effects of exposure to these chemicals.

We do know that young people are destroying their brains by abusing aerosol products and inhaling their deadly fumes. In fact, aerosols are the drug of choice for many of these people. This is very frightening.

Doctors have also identified a condition known as toxic encephalopathy, brought on by repeated exposure to solvents over

---

60 American Lung Association, *www.lungusa.org*
61 Mary Ellen Fise, *Indoor Air Quality.*
62 Paula DiPerna, *Environmental Hazards to Children.*
63 National Center For Health Statistics, 1997.
64 Dr. Doris Rapp, *Is This Your Child's World?*

several years. Symptoms include memory loss, behavioral changes, emotional instability, confusion, inability to concentrate, neurological and personality changes, and problems with manual dexterity.[65] Chemicals that cause this condition are in household products. They include chlorinated hydrocarbons, aromatic hydrocarbons and aliphatic hydrocarbons. You need to remember that the amount of chemicals a person is exposed to is not as important as the strength of a person's detox system. Extremely small amounts of chemicals can have severe effects on certain individuals.

Alzheimer's Disease receives so much attention because it is so prevalent and yet remains such a mystery. Around 4.5 million people currently suffer with Alzheimer's.[66] Although we have known about this disease for some time, recently the number of cases has grown dramatically. Approximately 7.7 million people will have the disease by the year 2030, and it may surpass cancer and stroke numbers as a cause of death.[67]

Although there seems to be a genetic link to the cause of Alzheimer's, scientists admit it is too weak to explain the prevalence of the disease. Most research points to environmental factors. Aluminum, a known neurotoxin, is the number one suspect. However, researchers are looking at other toxins and their possible link to this horrible disease. Hopefully, science will find the answers.

Not every CNS problem is as dramatic as Alzheimer's, but some can be almost as debilitating. Betty J., of Albuquerque, New Mexico, suffered from severe migraine headaches for years with major attacks occurring every six to eight weeks. Unfortunately, the medication she was taking was as disabling as the headaches. She would spend a week to ten days in bed until the migraines finally passed and the medication wore off. As you can imagine, this caused great hardship for her, especially with regard to her work.

After doing a little investigation, Betty decided to rid her home of toxic chemicals. She threw out everything she had purchased at the grocery store and used only natural, environmentally sensitive products. Her life changed dramatically. She no longer needed to take painkillers to get out of bed and the recurring migraine attacks stopped.

Disbelieving her own success, Betty purchased a bottle of bleach to see if chemicals were indeed the cause of her problem. Within minutes of opening the bottle, she had another migraine headache. Betty became a true believer in the need to rid your home of toxic, chemical-laden cleaners.

65 N. Ashford & C. Miller, *Chemical Exposures, Low Levels and High Stakes* (Van Nostrand Reinhold, 1991).

66 Alzheimer's Association, "Coalition of Hope," www.alz.org, March 23, 2004

67 Alzheimer's Association, "Coalition of Hope," www.alz.org, March 23, 2004

ATTENTION DEFICIT DISORDER AND OTHER LEARNING DISORDERS

In the year 2000, 17 million children in America were taking Ritalin so they could sit still long enough to learn to read and write.[68] Ritalin is a "Class-2" narcotic. What could be wrong? Why do we need such a powerful drug to help control our children's behavior? Most veteran teachers will tell you that the increased use of Ritalin is not the result of an increased awareness in ADD, as some would argue, but an increase in the actual number of cases. Think back to when you were in school. Was half of your class out of control? Were most of your friends taking medication for hyperactivity? Again, we must find out just what is wrong!

The problem is that many young people are being misdiagnosed. According to Doris Rapp, M.D., an expert on the treatment of environmental illness, as many as two-thirds of the millions of children on Ritalin are actually suffering from acute allergic reactions to environmental agents. Removal of certain chemicals or a profound change in diet could solve the problem.[69] These children do not need powerful drugs.

Young people are exposed to so many chemicals that many of them develop sensitivities. This happens because their detox system burns out even before it fully develops. Then they become susceptible to the effects of even traces of chemicals. I want to state one more time that when it comes to toxins, the amount of exposure is not as important as how sensitive a person is. Children need much less exposure than adults do to develop negative symptoms.

CHEMICAL VAPORS IN SCHOOLS

Take the case of Ryan. When he was four, he began going to school. He would leave feeling fine, but come home feeling weak and tired, clinging tightly to his mother. While in the gym at his school, he became so weak that he had to be carried out. Ryan's mother noticed that they sprayed the table tops and rest area of his classroom with a popular aerosol disinfectant.

Ryan's doctor, an environmental specialist, tested Ryan. She sprayed a four inch area of a paper towel with the same disinfectant and placed it a few feet away from Ryan. Within thirty minutes, Ryan was obviously different. He could no longer hold his pencil and his writing skills completely collapsed. Several tests confirmed his reaction.[70] William, another eight-year-old boy, had a similar reaction when exposed to chlorine fumes.[71]

68 *NBC Dateline*, Episode aired January 15, 2001
69 Dr. Doris Rapp, *Is This Your Child's World?*
70 Dr. Doris Rapp, *Is This Your Child's World?*
71 Dr. Doris Rapp, *Is This Your Child's World?*

Ryan's reaction might be considered severe, but it represents a growing number of young people who are reacting to chemicals in the air in their homes and school. I wonder how many children experience learning problems because of chemicals in the environment. Even if the number is only slight, it is unacceptable. We should try to remove any possible impediment from our children's future, and that begins with providing the healthiest home possible.

Eight-year-old Peter's first class in the morning was taught by a teacher who smoked heavily and smelled strongly of perfume. In this class, arithmetic, Peter typically had difficulty remembering, thinking, and completing his work. His teacher noticed on some days he could not even add two and two.

Peter improved over the course of the morning when he had another teacher who did not smell of either tobacco or perfume. However, the smell of perfume from lunchroom aides and the odor of cleaners from the dish room caused his ability to learn and concentrate to deteriorate again.

Peter's doctor confirmed his sensitivities to many chemicals. Perfumes, colognes, and fragrances can contain harmful chemicals such as formaldehyde, toluene, ethanol, acetone, methyl chloride and benzene derivatives. All can damage the nervous system. Peter now goes to school with an oxygen tank in case he has a severe reaction.[72]

Eleven-year-old Warren always did well in school. His grades were in the 90th percentile. Exposure to phenol caused him to develop multiple ear infections and led to a progressive decline in his grades. After several tests, Warren's doctor confirmed his sensitivity to phenol. Warren eventually transferred schools to escape exposure during the day. Fortunately, his grades returned to normal.[73]

According to Sherry Rogers, M.D., also an environmental specialist, the symptoms produced by chemical sensitivity are as varied as the people affected.[74] While children like Peter and Warren might react with a breakdown of learning ability, children like Chuck become hyperactive. When Chuck was six years old, he would make very loud noises, become uncontrollably bouncy, and hit other children when exposed to certain chemicals. Fumes from furniture polish affected him so strongly that he told his mother he wanted to jump off the roof![75]

These stories hardly reflect the array of reactions that children who are chemically sensitive exhibit. Reaction is unpredictable and can change in time. The bottom line is, you can protect your children. You can limit, if not eliminate, their exposure to neurotoxins. By switching to brands that do not use chemicals like phenol and formaldehyde, you can help them reach their full potential.

72 Dr. Doris Rapp, *Is This Your Child's World?*
73 Dr. Doris Rapp, *Is This Your Child's World?*
74 Sherry Rogers, *Chemical Sensitivity* (Keats Publishing, Inc., 1995).
75 Dr. Doris Rapp, *Is This Your Child's World?*

MULTIPLE CHEMICAL SENSITIVITY

Multiple Chemical Sensitivity (MCS), or Environmental Illness (EI), are the names for an assortment of problems that can affect any part of the human body. Chemicals found in cleaners, personal care products, food, plastics, and even water, can cause this condition. Persons suffering with MCS lack the ability to adequately detoxify their bodies. Symptoms include: headaches, severe fatigue, hyperactivity, muscle pain, joint pain, stomach and bowel problems, constant congestion, muscle twitches, and asthma-type symptoms. Other symptoms include emotional and behavioral problems, depression, loss of memory, and inability to learn or concentrate. More and more people are coming forth, reporting these symptoms, and having their sensitivities confirmed.[76, 77]

I have read the accounts of many victims, and personally spoken with dozens more. Most were very sensitive to chemicals in cleaning and personal care products. They had debilitating body aches, headaches, depression and other nervous disorders. Thankfully, the majority I have talked to received nearly complete relief by switching to people-friendly household products.

Dr. William Rea, a world-known environmental doctor in Dallas, Texas, reports that of all the patients he has seen with MCS, only 13% report developing the condition after a one-time acute poisoning. Sixty percent report developing the condition as the result of long-term slow poisonings involving minimal amounts of toxins. Only 28% of the cases he has documented are work-related. A staggering 72% of the cases are people who have been exposed to chemicals at home or at other places.[78]

Dr. Rea sites the following factors as influencing the onset of MCS:

- Total Toxic Body Burden – This is the sum of all toxins in the body. When the accumulation overloads a person's detox system, MCS can occur.
- Nutritional State – The more nutrient-depleted a person's body is, the more likely they are to develop MCS.
- Synergisms – This means the combination of the different chemicals in the body will have a stronger effect than individual toxins.
- Bioaccumulation of Toxins – This refers to how less dense tissues, like fat cells, can actually absorb and accumulate chemicals. Without the time and nutrition for the body to cleanse itself, the accumulation level can be dangerous.[79]

According to Doris Rapp, M.D., Multiple Chemical Sensitivity is common. Most physicians who practice environmental medicine,

---

76 William J. Rea, *Chemical Sensitivities* (1997).
77 Sherry Rogers, *Chemical Sensitivity.*
78 William J. Rea, *Chemical Sensitivities.*
79 William J. Rea, *Chemical Sensitivities*
80 Dr. Doris Rapp, *Is This Your Child's World?*

including herself, estimate that 25% to 50% of today's population is sensitive to one degree or another.[80]

Nancy, a young, vibrant, well-trained teacher, developed MCS over a period of eight years. She became fatigued, experienced muscle aches, constant ear ringing, difficulty concentrating, blackouts, and severe depression. She became so sensitive that even the nuance of chemical odor made her ill. Scents in her body lotions, make-up and hair spray made her so confused that she could not tell time or recall the names of her students. A whiff of perfume caused her to laugh uncontrollably and twitch.

During a leave of absence, she was too tired to get out of bed, take a shower, or prepare a snack. Her condition was traced to, among many things, phenol in the disinfectants used in the bathroom near her classroom. After two years of therapy, she began to feel better, but she still carries a charcoal filter mask everywhere she goes and fears a total relapse.[81]

Sister Martha, a dedicated teacher, was assigned by her school to tutor students who needed extra help. Unfortunately, the only available room was a converted custodial closet located between two bathrooms. The vapors from cleaners, disinfectants and deodorizers from the bathrooms constantly filtered into this room through vents in the walls.

After tutoring for a while in this room, Sister Martha developed a persistent, nagging cough, joint stiffness and swelling, facial spasms, excessive mucus, and vision problems. She was able to find a doctor who began to treat her sensitivities. Even after extensive treatment, she still lives with many limitations. Although she has eliminated toxins in her home, she cannot remain in a public place like a mall for more than a few minutes. She still needs to take an anti-allergy extract and can drink only purified water.[82]

Both of these stories represent extreme cases of MCS. Most people who suffer with MCS do not have such profound symptoms, but rather experience symptoms like recurring headaches, muscle aches, depression, and chronic fatigue.

Hopefully, more will be learned about MCS and treatments will improve. However, I think the focus should be on prevention. By reducing the amount of toxins in your home, you can help to reduce the risk for MCS in a loved one.

SOME FINAL THOUGHTS

As I am finishing this article, I have just learned that the FDA has proposed a ban on phenolphthalein, a phenol derivative found in laxatives that has been linked to cancer in laboratory animals.[83]

81 Dr. Doris Rapp, *Is This Your Child's World?*
82 Dr. Doris Rapp, *Is This Your Child's World?*
83 HHS News (U.S. Department of Health and Human Services, August 29, 1997).

I believe that many more chemicals will be banned as we learn about the long-term effects of exposure. Other phenol derivatives still appear in many personal care and cleaning products. I strongly urge you not to expose yourself to any chemical that could possibly cause cancer.

At the same time, another company is pulling their tire cleaning product off the shelves because even a tiny amount of the product can kill a child. This product was marketed in a spray bottle! I don't have to tell you parents how children love those spray bottles.

I understand that life is full of risk. When you drive on the highway, there is risk. Going outside in a thunderstorm is risky. It is important to distinguish between what are avoidable risks and what are unavoidable risks. Many Americans have quit smoking, changed their diet, and started exercising because they want to reduce their risk for heart disease, cancer, and a host of other possible conditions. They avoid placing themselves at risk.

In the same way, I encourage you to make your home a healthy home by eliminating toxic chemicals. By removing the dangerous cleaners and personal care products, you remove the potential harms they cause. You eliminate the unnecessary risk for cancer, ADD, nervous disorders, asthma, birth defects, MCS, infertility, and a host of other problems.

I said at the beginning of this article that there is a happy ending—a solution to this problem. Conscientious manufacturers offer people-friendly products at great prices that are just as, if not more effective than hazardous store brands. Talk to the person who cared enough to share this article with you. I am sure they will know where you can get these products.

I am glad you took the time to read this article. I pray that it has opened your eyes to a menace you may not have been aware of before. I hope you now are able to make an informed choice about what you bring into your home.

And may your home be a healthy home.

This chapter is the full text from the booklet entitled "Is Your Home a Healthy Home?" Sharing this booklet is an inexpensive way for you to help your loved ones understand the health risks associated with toxic chemicals in household products. It is available from RM Barry Publications. Call 1 (888) 209-0510 or visit us at our web site www.RMBarry.com.

CHAPTER FOUR

Nutritional Supplements
Are They Doctor Recommended?

It's easy to get discouraged when we visit our doctor, faced with a health challenge, and ask about a promising nutritional therapy we've heard or read about. Unfortunately most doctors are hesitant to recommend anything but pharmaceutical treatments. To understand why doctors are generally slow to recommend nutritional therapies, and sometimes seem to be opposed to dietary supplements, we need to first take a look at their medical school training. During the 1970s and early 1980s, no medical school in the U.S. required students to take a nutrition class. And as of 1985 only two medical schools taught 25 hours or more of courses in nutrition. Even today, too few doctors are offered enough nutritional science training in medical school to understand the fundamental role that vitamins, minerals, and herbs play in the prevention of disease and maintaining good health, and most lack the time to keep up with the latest research in nutrition.[1]

Why didn't medical schools offer nutritional science training in the past?

Good question! Actually, they did at one time. During the early 1900s, researchers discovered evidence for the importance of specific components of foods in maintaining health and in curing or preventing many recently identified deficiency diseases. For two decades, the pioneering work on vitamins and discovery of essential nutrients and their relationship to the prevention of deficiency diseases led to a rapidly growing interest in experimental and clinical nutrition.

During the 1920s and 1930s, the biochemical and clinical aspects of nutrition were being widely taught in medical schools. New organizations were formed to foster nutrition education, and to encourage application of nutrition principles in medical practice. However around 1949, concern for deficiency diseases diminished since they ceased to be a major problem in the U.S., and nutritional problems no longer offered the same challenge for scientists. With new advances in food technology and fortified foods, biochemists once deeply concerned with nutritional problems shifted their focus to other areas. As research in nutrition declined, there was a parallel decline of interest in nutrition education.[2] During the 1950s and 1960s, nutrition became a low priority, and was no longer an important part of the medical curriculum.

More recently, advances have been made toward educating physicians in nutrition and the prevention of disease, although most physicians are still inadequately trained in nutritional science.[2] Today, more and more medical schools are requiring standard nutrition courses, but most still don't deal with disease prevention and management.

The good news is that more and more conventional physicians are now registering for postgraduate courses to learn more about using diet to manage patients' health problems. Numerous studies supporting the value of supplemental nutrients for prevention of disease and promoting good health appear in scientific publications each month, and the number of medical schools requiring nutritional science is increasing, but changing the textbooks and curriculum to include this important research takes time. When more medical schools do this, and put nutrition education into the clinical setting, more doctors will see its value. Doctors of the future are likely to look at nutritional supplements as part of the important range of tools they have available to prevent and treat disease.[1]

However, many doctors still believe there's not enough supportive research to justify telling patients about supplements because the role of nutritional supplements in disease prevention and health improvement is often difficult to measure. They may feel comfortable using nutritional supplements themselves, but don't want to be criticized for practicing "unscientific medicine."[1] As medical school curriculum changes, policies will change, but today physicians have little to no support from policy makers and enforcers, and are discouraged from practicing any form of medicine perceived by medical boards as being unconventional.

But what about all the studies published monthly in scientific publications? Isn't that supportive research?

Yes, it is great supportive research, but while there is an abundance of clinical research for all types of dietary supplements, most of this research involves small phase II studies.[3] What concerns many doctors is an insufficient number of long-term safety studies.

While more long-term safety studies would be ideal, it is in fact one of the biggest research gaps in natural medicine. It costs millions of dollars to do these types of studies, and in order to recoup the cost, it would need to be tacked onto the cost of the end product. But since natural nutrients, botanical substances, and even hormones cannot be patented, it's not feasible for companies to conduct research to this extent. Competitors, without the burden of the cost of research, could develop the same product and undercut the cost, leaving the company conducting the research with little chance of a return on investment. Because of this, pharmaceutical companies choose to focus on chemical drugs that *can* be patented.

Finally, another concern doctors have is that patients will use nutritional supplements as a substitute for a healthy diet and regular medical care. These concerns are very real. Nutritional supplements cannot replace a healthy diet and exercise, but are intended to enhance a healthy lifestyle and provide nutrients that may help in the prevention of disease.

So why do I need to include natural supplements in my diet?

Historically, the accepted modality of treatment by conventional physicians has been to diagnose and treat disease, with emphasis on drug therapies. Prevention of disease, on the other hand, was typically considered more of a public health concern, with published recommendations to eat more fresh fruit and vegetables, reduce salt intake, increase dietary fiber, and to lower blood cholesterol and body fat. We, as a society, tend to overlook the importance of good nutrition and prevention until we begin having symptoms of disease.

Only in the past two decades have we come to recognize that many of the diseases common in older people can be tied to nutritional deficiencies. Medical professionals now accept that nutrition is a factor in the onset and the progression of hypertension, strokes, heart attacks, obesity-related disorders, type 2 diabetes, some forms of cancer, and many other chronic conditions. Chronic diseases are the leading causes of death and disability in the United States accounting for 7 of every 10 deaths, and affect the quality of life of 90 million Americans. Chronic diseases are among the most prevalent and most costly, yet they are the most preventable.[4]

Because nutrition affects our immune system, organ function, hormonal balance and cellular metabolism, many of these chronic conditions and diseases can be traced to a nutrition deficiency. When the deficiency is not corrected, symptoms begin to appear and eventually lead to disease and premature aging. While medical science has made astonishing advances in treating and keeping the symptoms of these degenerative diseases in control with conventional pharmaceutical drugs, the key to optimal health is *prevention*.

Natural medicine treats the underlying cause of chronic diseases brought on by nutritional deficiencies. Many times, drug treatments can effectively be replaced with natural supplements, amino acids, prebiotics and probiotics, fresh foods and functional foods, but should be done only under the care of a health care provider. These same nutrients, along with a good diet, exercise and lifestyle changes, can help in the prevention of disease.

Are supplements really safe? Are they regulated by the government?

Natural medicine is not new. It was practiced for thousands of years before pharmaceutical companies began manufacturing the first synthetic drugs. Properly used, and with the blessings of your healthcare provider, quality supplements are not only safe, but can help promote optimal health.

There is a misconception by some that nutritional supplements are not regulated. Before 1994, dietary supplements fell under the same regulations as food. With passage of the Dietary Supplements Health and Education Act (DSHEA) in 1994, the Food and Drug Administration (FDA) was granted authority to ban products proven to be unsafe.[5]

What should I look for in a good multivitamin or herbal supplement?

A common practice is to pick single nutrients, but taking balanced multivitamin and herbal supplements is recommended because nutrients work together to maintain healthy function in your cells, and it's important to maintain a proper balance. Because herbs with similar properties enhance the properties of each, choosing a product containing a combination of different herbs is usually more effective than individual selections.

Minerals should also be in a form that can be readily absorbed by the body. Dr. Carrie Carter, M.D., author of the book, *Woman's Guide To Good Health*, notes that the *Vitality Pack* by **Melaleuca: The Wellness Company** is a high quality supplement that addresses this need. A patent-pending formulation called "oligofructose complex" is used to attach the minerals to organic compounds (oligofructose and amino acids), which helps the minerals to be absorbed inside the body more efficiently than traditional vitamins and minerals.

ConsumerLabs.com tested many different supplements and listed those that met their criteria, but tested only those that met the Daily Recommended Intake (DRI). Dr. Carter explains that supplements exceeding the DRI level in amounts that may decrease the development of diseases were not tested, which explains why these higher quality/ higher priced supplements did not appear on their list. She noted that Melaleuca's *Vitality Pack* is one of two supplements she has personally had positive experience with.[6]

Although we need to be cautious about overloading our bodies with nutrients, most supplements are not harmful in amounts that far exceed the DRI, and many studies show that many nutrients at higher than DRI levels may decrease the development of degenerative diseases.[6]

In conclusion, when choosing nutritional supplements, we need to be sure the company uses 100% pure standardized extracts of the highest quality that are formulated to be bioactive so that our bodies can effectively recognize, absorb, and utilize the nutrients. And finally, ingredients in the supplement should be formulated in proper proportions to work synergistically with other ingredients.

References

1. *Health Care's Nutritional Deficiency.* Jeffrey S. Bland, Ph.D. Nutrition Science News. March 1997. "http://www.vitamintrader.com/articles/1997_03_Nutrition.html"
2. *Nutrition Education in U.S. Medical Schools Commission on Life Sciences.* National Academy of Science. 1985. "http://www.nap.edu/execsumm.pdf/597.pdf" (164 KB)
3. *Biologically Based Practices:An Overview.* National Center for Complementary and Alternative Medicine. "http://nccam.nih.gov/health/backgrounds/biobasedprac.pdf" (371 KB)
4. *Chronic Disease Prevention.* National Center for Chronic Disease Prevention and Health Promotion. Centers For Disease Control And Prevention. "http://www.cdc.gov/nccdphp/"
5. *Overview of Dietary Supplements.* U. S. Food and Drug Administration. Center for Food Safety and Applied Nutrition. "http://www.cfsan.fda.gov/%7Edms/ds-oview.html"
6. *What You Need to Know About Supplements.* CBN.com. A Woman's Guide to Good Health. Dr. Carrie Carter, M.D. "http://www.cbn.com/health/nutrition/womansguide_vitamins.aspx"

CHAPTER FIVE

Grape Seed Extract

"The most potent preventive medicine you can take!"

ABOUT THE AUTHOR, DR. CLARK HANSEN

Clark Hansen, N.M.D., is a Doctor of Naturopathic Medicine with a very busy private practice in Scottsdale, Arizona. He graduated from the John Bastyr College of Naturopathic Medicine in Seattle, Washington, in 1986. Since 1988, Dr. Hansen has served as the President and Medical Director of The Arizona Institute of Natural Medicine, a medical clinic that attracts patients from all over the U.S.

Dr. Hansen is one of the founders of the Southwest College of Naturopathic Medicine and Health Sciences in Scottsdale, Arizona, where he serves as a member of the Board of Advisors and as an Associate Professor of Clinical Medicine. Dr. Hansen is a member of the American Association of Naturopathic Physicians, the Arizona Naturopathic Medical Association, the American Holistic Medical Association, and the Physicians Committee for Responsible Medicine.

THE DISCOVERY OF A LIFETIME

Proanthocyanidin (PCO) is a natural plant bioflavonoid extracted from the seeds of grapes. Also known as Pycnogenol, this potent bioflavonoid is so essential to our existence that it should be considered a vitamin, because our bodies cannot make it and we cannot survive without it. Its healing and preventive benefits are simply phenomenal. It has been used in France for more than 40 years but has only recently been discovered by Americans. PCO has been found to be the most potent antioxidant ever discovered. It is 20 times more potent than Vitamin C and 50 times more potent than Vitamin E. It is also anti-inflammatory, anti-allergic, and anti-mutagenic. PCO bioflavonoids are found in the peels, skins, and seeds of fruits and vegetables, and the barks of certain trees, including the lemon tree, the French maritime pine tree, and the leaves of the hazelnut tree. Grape Seed Extract yields a 95% concentration of PCO, the highest of any source. Pine bark is second, with an 85% concentration.

DISCOVERY OF PCO

In 1948, Jacques Masquelier, a young Ph.D. candidate from the University of Bordeaux, France, isolated PCO from peanuts. In his doctoral thesis, Masquelier demonstrated the ability of PCO to double the strength of blood vessels within a few hours after administration to laboratory animals. In 1951, Professor Masquelier patented a PCO extract from pine bark. Nineteen years later, in 1970, he patented a second PCO extract from grape seeds which he found to yield a 10% higher concentration. In 1986, Dr. Masquelier discovered that PCO from grape seeds has an intense free radical scavenging effect. These discoveries were laid down in his U.S. Patent #4,698,360 of October 6, 1987. After years of continued research he said, "The test showed that in this respect PCO from grape seeds has an advantage over PCO from pine bark. PCO from grape seeds contains the gallic esters of PCOs. These PCO-esters have been recently described as the most active substances in the battle against free radicals."

NATURE'S MOST POTENT ANTIOXIDANT

PCO bioflavonoids have a specific affinity for the connective tissue (collagen and elastin) of the body, providing stabilization and protection from premature breakdown. When you eat them they become incorporated into the connective tissues of your skin, blood vessels, joints, and cell membranes. They protect your body from free radical damage. Free radicals are produced from oxygen metabolism within the body and from exposure to certain chemicals, environmental pollutants, sunlight, radiation burns, cigarette smoke, drugs, alcohol, viruses, bacteria, parasites, dietary fats, and more.

Free radicals destroy cell membranes, damage collagen and other connective tissues, disrupt important physiologic processes, and create mutations in the DNA of cells. They are implicated in more than 60 diseases, including heart disease, hardening of the arteries, arthritis, Alzheimer's disease, cataracts, and cancer. Free radicals are oxygen molecules with a missing or unpaired electron which spin erratically throughout the body, damaging every tissue they bounce into until they are finally quenched by an antioxidant such as vitamin C or E, beta-carotene, bioflavonoids, or certain enzymes produced by the body. As we grow older, the body's inherent production of free radical deactivating enzymes decreases. As this happens, the skin becomes leathery and wrinkled, arteries lose their elasticity, joints and cartilage stiffen, vision becomes cloudy, the spine becomes stooped, and every part of the body gradually deteriorates. PCO prevents the cross-linking of body tissues that is associated with aging. It blocks connective tissue-destroying enzymes that otherwise would have a cumulative thinning and weakening effect on the body's connective tissue over time.

THE SECRET TO YOUTHFULNESS

PCO helps protect the skin from ultraviolet radiation damage that leads to wrinkles and skin cancer. Because it stabilizes collagen and elastin, PCO can help to improve the elasticity and youthfulness of the skin. Its potent antioxidant effect in the skin has even been found to reverse the process of pigment lipofuscin, causing unsightly age spots to fade and disappear. Many individuals taking PCO have seen it reduce the appearance of surgical scars and stretch marks.

The ability of PCO to stabilize and protect collagen and elastin within joints has demonstrated remarkable effects in the relief of pain and inflammation associated with arthritis. In clinical and experimental studies, PCO has been shown to inhibit inflammatory swelling including postoperative swelling. Many arthritis sufferers say that PCO completely eliminates stiffness and restores their mobility. It also inhibits excessive production of histamine that causes allergic disorders and the inflammatory swelling related to allergies. In fact many cases of arthritis are due to allergies.

PCO has been shown to: improve blood vessel elasticity; increase red blood cell pliability; inhibit platelet stickiness and clumping; normalize blood flow; improve oxygenation of ischemic areas; decrease bruising, bleeding and edema; prevent blood clots; and reduce elevated blood pressure. People taking Grape Seed Extract have found that it can lower their cholesterol levels remarkably, and researchers have found that PCO reduces the size of cholesterol plaque in the blood vessel walls of animals.

Patients with Multiple Sclerosis (MS), a syndrome of progressive destruction of the myelin sheath that surrounds the nerves, have reported significant improvement while taking PCO. Many studies have demonstrated that patients with MS have reduced activity of the antioxidant enzyme Glutathione peroxidase. The ability of PCO to reduce the progressive symptoms of MS may be the result of the fact that it is one of the few antioxidants that can cross the blood-brain barrier.

PCO has also been shown to protect cell membranes and thereby prevent mutations caused by damage to DNA. This may help prevent the onset of cancer. One study has shown that the risk of developing cancer is 11.4 times higher in those with low levels of the antioxidants vitamin E and Selenium. Since PCO is 50 times more potent than Vitamin E as an antioxidant, it is expected to have an even greater individual cancer-preventing effect. Additionally, PCO may work with Vitamin E to enhance the body's ability to fight and prevent cancer by protecting the cancer-fighting cells known as *natural killer cells*. PCO is also known to work synergistically with Vitamin C to increase the longevity of natural killer cells.

Due to its protective effects on connective tissue within the eye, PCO is effective in stopping the progression of cataracts and reversing glaucoma and age-related macular degeneration, the leading cause of blindness.

Grape Seed Extract is the most potent preventive nutrient you can buy. It can prevent the cross-linking of your connective tissue, promote new collagen and elastin production, and slow down or reverse the biological process of aging to help prevent heart disease,

ARTICLES

cancer, strokes, diabetes, cataracts, glaucoma, arthritis, allergies, wrinkles, cellulite, and more.

Bioavailability: PCO is water soluble, readily absorbed within 60 minutes, and actively circulates in the body for three days. Unlike most antioxidants, PCO can even cross the blood-brain barrier.

Safety: PCO is nontoxic, noncarcinogenic, non-teratogenic. It has been thoroughly tested in France for more than 40 years and used by more than 10 million people. Because grape seeds are so bitter, occasional nausea or stomach upset has been reported.

Dosage: Take 50 mg to 300 mg per day depending on intensity of condition. As a general guideline a recent European Symposium on PCO recommended a starting dose of 25 mg for every 25 pounds of body weight for the first 3 days, enough to saturate the body tissues, then the amount can be reduced to ½ that amount.

CASE HISTORIES

Beverly J., Dallas, Texas

I have been taking Grape Seed Extract for 2 months now. The brown spots on my skin are clearing up, the arthritic lumps on my fingers have gone down, and my gums are more firm. The dentist was concerned about the pockets around my back teeth and was amazed when this condition had disappeared. I feel wonderful. I'll never stop taking it.

Tim B., Scottsdale, Arizona

Grape Seed Extract is awesome! I suffer from seasonal allergies and in the past have tried over-the-counter antihistamines which caused me to feel mentally dull and drowsy all the time. After taking the Grape Seed Extract for three days, my allergies cleared up completely without causing any drowsiness. Now I have a clear head and a clear mind. Thanks!

Christine P., Los Angeles, California

I used to be embarrassed to wear a two-piece bathing suit because of a surgical scar on my abdomen. But since I have been taking Grape Seed Extract over the last two months, the scar has shrunk and now is only faintly visible. Thanks! This means more to me than you can imagine.

Bill G., Franklin, Texas

Grape Seed Extract basically gave my life back to me a few months ago when I was very ill with extremely high cholesterol over 400 and triglycerides over 700. I started taking 300 mg Grape Seed Extract per day and continued limiting my fat and sugar intake. Within two months my cholesterol was down to 202 and my triglycerides to 78.

Dr. Hansen has also created an excellent 60 minute audio presentation on Grape Seed Extract. It is available in cassette and CD formats from RM Barry Publications. Call 1 (888) 209-0510 or visit us at our web site www.RMBarry.com.

CHAPTER SIX

Reducing Risk Factors for Heart Disease

OVERVIEW

Cardiovascular disease has been the number one killer of Americans since 1919. The chances are very good that you know someone struggling with heart disease. In 2005, one in 2.8 deaths was attributed to cardiovascular disease. The World Heart Federation reports that heart disease is also the number one killer worldwide. According to the American Heart Association, nearly 80 million Americans, or one in three, live with one or more types of cardiovascular disease, including high blood pressure, coronary heart disease, heart failure, stroke, and congenital heart defects (birth defects).

VARIOUS FORMS OF HEART DISEASE

High blood pressure is also known as hypertension and is measured by the force of blood pumped from the heart against the walls of your arteries. It is often called a "silent" killer because it usually has no signs or symptoms. The heart rhythmically pumps and rests. During a pump, your blood pressure is at its highest and that measurement is called *systolic pressure*, the top number of a blood pressure reading. While at rest, between beats, your blood pressure falls and that measurement is called *diastolic pressure*, the bottom number of a blood pressure reading. A healthy blood pressure is at or below 120/80. High blood pressure is considered a reading of 140/90 or higher. High blood pressure can cause heart failure, and can also lead to stroke, kidney failure, and other health problems.

Coronary heart disease, the most common form of heart disease, is the narrowing of the blood vessels (or coronary arteries) that supply blood and oxygen to the heart. A build-up of fatty material and plaque in the blood vessels leads to coronary heart disease, which then causes angina (chest pain) and heart attacks.

Heart failure means the heart is not able to pump blood through the body as well as it should. It does NOT mean the heart literally stops. Heart failure develops slowly over time and can have a big impact on a person's life and ability to perform daily routines, such as dressing, bathing, and walking.

Stroke is a "brain attack" and is precipitated by lack of blood flow to the brain from a blood clot, or bleeding in the brain from a broken blood vessel. Without a good blood supply, brain cells cannot get enough oxygen and begin to die. High blood pressure, smoking, and diabetes all increase your risk for stroke.

CONTROLLING THE RISK FACTORS

The most important thing you can do to control your risk of heart disease is to make sure your blood pressure and cholesterol levels are in an acceptable range. Get thirty minutes of moderate physical exercise a day. Stop smoking if you're a smoker. Eat a balanced diet including five servings of fruits and vegetables daily. Limit your alcohol consumption. And lose weight if you are overweight.

OBESITY

Obesity increases the risk factor of every major chronic disease, cardiovascular disease included. Most of the time obesity is caused by taking in more calories than are used up in physical activity. The World Health Organization reports that in 2005 there were 1.6 billion overweight adults in the world, with at least 400 million of them obese. Overweight is defined as a body mass index (BMI) of 25 or greater, and obesity is a BMI of 30 or greater, which is approximately 30 pounds or more overweight for the average adult.

Obesity is on the rise worldwide, and is even considered an epidemic. The World Heart Federation noticed that in England the prevalence of obesity *doubled* between 1980 and 1990. Obesity puts a person at higher risk for heart disease by raising blood cholesterol and triglyceride levels. It actually lowers HDL "good" cholesterol, raises blood pressure levels, and can induce diabetes.[1] Please see the obesity section in the "Healthy Body" chapter of this book.

CHOLESTEROL

Your body makes all the cholesterol it needs, but most people get even more cholesterol from the foods they eat, which increases the chances that the waxy substance will line the artery walls and clog up the blood vessels. A cholesterol-screening blood test gives you some numbers measured in milligrams of cholesterol per deciliter of blood. So what do all those numbers mean? Total cholesterol level should be at or below 200 mg/dL. A range of 200–239 mg/dL is borderline high, and 240 mg/dL and above is very high. Doctors will also take readings from LDL and HDL cholesterols. For LDL, the "bad" cholesterol, a level of 160 mg/dL or above is high. For HDL "good" cholesterol, a level of 60 mg/dL or more is good and helps to lower your risk for heart disease. Remember that HDL cholesterol protects against heart disease, so for HDL, higher numbers are better. A level less than 40 mg/dL is low and increases your risk for developing heart disease.[2]

USING STATIN DRUGS TO LOWER CHOLESTEROL

Statins are a family of drugs used to treat high cholesterol and are effective at lowering cholesterol. Generally they are tolerated well by most people, but they have been shown to have some negative side effects. Nausea, diarrhea, gas, constipation, rashes, sleep problems, headaches, and aching muscles are some of the common side effects of statin drugs. However, there are more serious side effects which occasionally occur. (Never stop using a statin drug on your own. Discuss this with your doctor.)[3]

FOODS THAT LOWER CHOLESTEROL

Nature has provided cholesterol-lowering foods as a first defense against heart disease. Two foods, in particular, have proven cholesterol-lowering benefits.

Phytosterols, also known as plant sterols, have a similar chemical structure to cholesterol, but the way the body metabolizes them is completely different. Phytosterols can actually block the absorption of cholesterol and help it to be eliminated naturally through the system, thereby reducing the amount of cholesterol circulating in the bloodstream. Phytosterols are naturally found in vegetable oil, seeds, nuts, and coniferous trees. They need to be absorbed along with fat to be effective, and have traditionally been added to margarines or milk. Research confirms that supplementing with at least 1500 mg of phytosterols daily can result in a 10-15% reduction in LDL levels.[4]

Omega-3 fatty acids, especially from fish oil, are essential to good health. They are called "essential fatty acids" because the human body does not produce them, and we must obtain them from our foods. Oily-fleshed, cold water fish like salmon and sardines are the best sources of EPA and DHA, the two types of omega-3 fatty acids that have been proven to reduce the incidence of heart disease. Omega-3 fatty acids prove beneficial not only with heart health by keeping cholesterol levels low and reducing blood pressure and triglyceride levels, but they also help in the prevention and/or treatment of depression, diabetes, cancer, and rheumatoid arthritis. They have been shown to have good effects on an irregular heartbeat, and appear to reduce instances of sudden death.

In a 25 year survey (1950–1974) of chronic diseases in Northwest Greenland, one of the last whaling communities of 1800 inhabitants were studied. The Greenlanders showed a lower frequency of acute myocardial infarction (heart attacks), diabetes mellitus, hyperthyroidism, asthma, multiple sclerosis, and psoriasis than West European populations. This was attributed to the Greenlanders' diet of cold water fatty fish, high in concentrations of omega-3 fatty acids.[5]

Recent studies also confirm a higher concentration of combined DHA and EPA, both found in cold water fatty fish, is associated with a lower risk of fatal ischemic heart disease, whether the subject is middle aged or an older adult. Also note that higher dietary intake of alpha linolenic acid, found in flax seeds, walnuts, soybean oil, pumpkin seeds, and canola oil has a tendency to lower risk of fatal ischemic heart disease.[6]

PHYTOMEGA® FROM MELALEUCA, INC.

Phytomega, a supplement from Melaleuca, combines these two heart healthy ingredients—phytosterols and omega-3 fatty acids—in a new and effective way. Instead of using the unhealthy saturated fat from margarine as a phytosterol carrier, Melaleuca's scientists use the more heart-healthy omega-3 fatty acid in their supplement *Phytomega*. Research confirms that the combination of phytosterols with omega-3 fatty acids has advantages for health. Evidence shows that this combination is effective in reducing the levels of several cardiovascular risk factors including rapid heart rate and triglyceride concentrations.[7]

Phytomega also has smaller amounts of other heart-healthy ingredients: bromelain, CoQ-10, and alpha-lipoic acid.

Bromelain is an enzyme that is extracted from the stems of pineapples. It has many health giving properties, especially for maintaining a healthy cardiovascular system. Results of several clinical trials indicate that bromelain acts as a blood thinner and can help relieve the symptoms of chest pain and inflammation of a vein caused by a blood clot. Bromelain therapy leads to formation of platelets with increased resistance to aggregation.[8]

CoQ-10 is an antioxidant enzyme made in the body and is also present in small amounts in most foods. Levels of CoQ-10 decline as we age, and some doctors suggest patients older than forty should supplement with CoQ-10. Supplementation is advisable because of the compound's energy-generating properties, and some experts suggest that CoQ-10 might ease congestive heart failure by increasing the amount of cellular fuel available to the heart, enabling it to pump more effectively.

Alpha lipoic acid is an essential fatty acid that converts glucose into energy and is found in all cells of the body. It is an antioxidant that recycles other antioxidants like vitamin C after they are used up. It can neutralize harmful free radicals, the damage from which is thought to contribute to aging and chronic illness.

Phytosterols and omega-3 fatty acids work together to lower cholesterol and maintain healthy triglyceride levels, and without the potential negative side effects of the statin drugs. *Phytomega* is a wonderful supplement to take if you are in any of the high risk categories mentioned. If you are already on a statin drug, continue its use and consult with a doctor about starting *Phytomega*. There is no other supplement on the market that combines plant-based phytosterols with omega-3 fatty acids to help reduce your risk for cardiovascular disease.

CARDIOVASCULAR HEALTH FACTORS

Maintaining a healthy heart involves managing more than just your cholesterol levels. One needs to also take into consideration the following factors which determine the overall functioning of the heart: cholesterol, triglyceride levels, LDL oxidation, endothelial function, platelet activity, and blood pressure.

Melaleuca offers supplements that address each of the factors to cardiovascular health. In addition to *Phytomega*, there are also *ProvexCV* and *FiberWise*. *ProvexCV*, formulated with grape seed extract *(see also Chapter 4, "Grape Seed Extract")*, will help to reduce platelet aggregation, help lower LDL cholesterol, maintain healthy blood pressure, and help prevent free radical damage while strengthening all blood vessels. Only *ProvexCV* has the patented blend of grape seed and grape skin extracts. New ingredients in 2009 are resveratrol and green tea extract. Additionally it has a proprietary enzyme blend of ginkgo biloba, bilberry, and quercetin that ensures absorption.

Resveratrol has been added to *ProvexCV* because it can neutralize free radicals and also inhibit LDL oxidation. Low doses produce cellular protection and reduce damage to cells.

Green tea extract in *ProvexCV* provides better blood vessel function. Specifically, green tea improves the function of endothelial cells. Endothelial cell dysfunction plays a key role in the development of clogged arteries, a process called atherosclerosis.

FiberWise (see Chapter 6, "Digestive Health") lowers cholesterol because of the soluble fiber in psyllium husk. Fiber works to bind LDL cholesterol to the bulk of the stool, and thus pass the bad cholesterol out of the body. Fiber also can help to reduce the production of cholesterol in the liver. The next time you think of fiber, think heart health along with digestive health.

MAINTAIN HEALTHY BLOOD PRESSURE WITH PROVEXCV FROM MELALEUCA, INC.

Introduced in January of 2007, *ProStolic* joined the suite of heart supplements from Melaleuca to compliment cardiovascular health from every angle. *ProStolic* included a proprietary blend of tripeptides, pomegranate juice powder, and potassium to relax blood vessels and allow a healthy blood flow. It proved to be a fantastic product, helping many maintain healthy blood pressure readings naturally. In 2009 Melaleuca improved the formula for *ProvexCV* by adding resveratrol and green tea extract. When the formula was tested, they found the new *ProvexCV* maintained blood pressure as well as the original *ProStolic* formula! Instead of taking two supplements, customers could now take one supplement to both protect the heart and maintain healthy blood pressure.

ARTICLES

DEFENSE AGAINST THE SILENT KILLER BEGINS WITH YOU

Although blood pressure and cholesterol medications as well as natural therapies are helpful in reducing your risk factors for heart disease, your body's best defense against high blood pressure and high cholesterol is your lifestyle. The foods you choose to eat and your exercise habits play the biggest part in your cardiovascular health. As fast-paced as today's world is, making healthy food choices can be difficult. Fortunately, most fast-food restaurants offer alternatives to the normally greasy and deep-fried fare. Now we can choose salads over french fries, fruit over ice cream, and bottled water over soda. The National Institutes of Health Heart Lung and Blood Institute has provided guidelines to help direct you in making lifestyle changes to your diet with hypertension in mind. It's called the DASH (Dietary Approaches to Stop Hypertension) diet. See reference 9 below to download your copy.

Adding exercise to a healthy diet slims not only your body, but your risks for developing cardiovascular disease, too. Melaleuca has developed an online tool to encourage, inform, and challenge you to meet your exercise and diet goals. *VFL.com* is a place for you to log all your food and exercise and see if there are areas you need to improve upon. There are step-by-step exercise and meal recommendations, as well as the community support of your peers in the online forums. It is an excellent place to start or continue on your journey to total wellness.[10]

ARTICLES

References

1   "Obesity and Overweight" American Heart Association, http://www.americanheart.org, 2005

2   "Heart and Cardiovascular Disease" The National Women's Health Information Center, http://www.4woman.gov, Nov 2002

3   Pasternak RC, et al., ACC/AHA/NHLBI "Clinical Advisory on the Use and Safety of Statins." Journal of the American College of Cardiology, vol. 40, No 3, 2002.

4   Normen L.; et al., "Combination of Phytosterols and Omega-3 Fatty Acids: A Potential Strategy to Promote Cardiovascular Health," Current Medicinal Chemistry - Cardiovascular & Hematological Agents, January 2004, vol. 2, no. 1, pp. 1-12(12)

5   Kromann N, Green A. "Epidemiological studies in the Upernavik district, Greenland. Incidence of some chronic diseases 1950-1974." Ata Med Scand 1980;208:401-406

6   Emaitre RN, et al., "n-3 polyunsaturated fatty acids, fatal ischemic heart disease, and non fatal myocardial infarction"

7   Normen L.; et al., "Combination of Phytosterols and Omega-3 Fatty Acids: A Potential Strategy to Promote Cardiovascular health," Current Medicinal Chemistry-Cardiovascular & Hematological Agents, January 2004, vol. 2, no. 1, pp. 1-12(12)

8   Felton GE. "Fibrinolytic and antithrombotic action of bromelain may eliminate thrombosis in heart patients." med hypotheses 1980;6:1123-1133

9   National Heart Lung and Blood Institute http://www.nhlbi.nih.gov then search on "DASH Guide PDF"

10 Vitality For Life – physical wellness system, http://www.vfl.com

CHAPTER SEVEN

Digestive Health

The Benefits of Adding Fiber and Digestive Flora to Your Diet

OVERVIEW

While the subject isn't a popular one in many circles, digestive health is an important topic when discussing optimal wellness and nutrition. In the past, many folks would shy away from talking about digestive health concerns because it was just too personal and seemed a bit off color. Recent press and public attention has helped to lift the taboo around digestive and intestinal health discussions. When we read that 60 to 70 million in the U.S. alone are affected by digestive diseases, or that 146,000 people will be diagnosed with colorectal cancer this year in the U.S., it is difficult not to wake up and want take notice.

Any discussion on digestive health should focus on two key elements of digestion—fiber and gut flora (bacteria). Collectively, fiber and good flora deliver the one-two punch when it comes to excellent digestion. If your system is deficient in either of these, you may experience health problems ranging from benign, such as indigestion and constipation, to serious, such as irritable bowel syndrome and colon cancer.

FIBER

The National Cancer Institute, U.S. Surgeon General, and the American Heart Association recommend between 25-35 grams of dietary fiber a day, but the average person in the U.S. only consumes around 10 grams a day. Typically our modern diets can't deliver enough fiber to meet the minimum recommendations because our foods are overly processed, which is why supplementation is so critical to proper digestion and intestinal health.

There are two types of dietary fiber—soluble and insoluble. Soluble fiber is characterized by its ability to dissolve in water. Soluble fiber is found in oat bran, apples, pears, citrus, legumes, and psyllium. Insoluble fiber can be found in whole grains, whole grain cereals, wheat bran, seeds, celery, cucumbers and a host of other vegetables.

While it is common knowledge that fiber is part of a healthy diet, it is less well known that diets rich in fiber may help to reduce the risk of heart disease, diabetes, diverticulitis, and deep vein thrombosis. Two research studies confirmed these findings. The first study of 40,000 male health professionals found that high fiber intake was linked to a 40%

lower risk of coronary heart disease. The second study, again of male health professionals and female nurses, found that a diet high in cereal fiber was linked to a lower risk of type 2 diabetes.

One of the best ways to supplement your fiber intake is to add fiber from psyllium into your diet. Again, research shows that psyllium has numerous benefits besides regularity. The Food and Drug Administration suggests diets low in saturated fat and cholesterol that include 7 grams of soluble fiber per day from psyllium husk may reduce the risk of heart disease. Studies show another side benefit to psyllium consumption is that individuals who consume psyllium 15 minutes prior to eating report they are less hungry hours after eating than those who don't consume psyllium.

Doctors at the Robert Wood Johnson Medical School in New Brunswick, N.J. found that supplements with psyllium are as effective at lowering LDL cholesterol levels (bad cholesterol) as doubling the dose of the drug simvastatin (brand name Zocor). Dr. Abel Moreyra and his colleagues state, "We found out that adding psyllium to 10 milligrams of simvastatin was equal to doubling the dose of simvastatin," Moreyra says. "We think this is an alternative to escalating the dose of a statin." Doctors like Moreyra are concerned about the negative side-effects of statin drugs.

As mentioned earlier, supplementing the diet with both soluble and insoluble fiber will help promote the elimination of toxins and other wastes. Insoluble fiber, which is available in foods like wheat bran and whole rice bran, is a great bulking agent that effectively pulls toxins from your system and assists with the elimination of waste materials. Whenever your daily intake of fiber is increased, it is crucial to increase your water intake as well, because fiber absorbs water. Fiber works indirectly to detoxify your system and additional water helps to eliminate toxins.

FLORA

Proper intestinal health has numerous benefits besides regularity. Too often we associate poor intestinal tract health with simply being constipated or having an upset stomach. In reality an imbalance of the bacterial flora in the system can lead to many other conditions or symptoms such as diarrhea, reduced immunity to pathogenic bacteria, irritable bowel syndrome (IBS), inflammatory bowel disease (IBD), diverticulitis, and a host of other less common conditions.

The bacterial flora in your large intestine can weigh around 7 ounces (200 gm) and function almost like an organ. This biomass is roughly as large as your spleen or kidney and contains more than 400 species of bacteria. There are literally billions of flora in your "gut" system and they work symbiotically to assist with digestion, nutrient absorption and elimination of waste matter. Good bacteria are also referred to as "probiotic" and work to counteract bad or harmful bacteria. Lactobacilli and bifidobacterium are two strains that help to maintain a healthy balance of intestinal flora. They produce organic compounds like lactic acid, hydrogen peroxide and acetic acid which increase acidity in the intestine and ward off many harmful bacteria.

Re-colonization of good flora is critical to good health because our modern lives negatively impact bacteria populations. Antibiotics, age, alcohol, chlorinated water, diet, disease, and stress are contributing factors that reduce microflora colonies in our gastrointestinal (GI) tract. Antibiotic treatments kill off harmful bacteria that may be causing adverse conditions and disease, but also kill off "friendly" bacteria in our digestive system. This is why it is so important to start a regiment of probiotics anytime you take an antibiotic. Oddly enough, probiotic bacteria produce natural antibiotics which inhibit the growth of harmful pathogenic bacteria throughout the GI tract.

It has become increasingly easy to supplement our diets with probiotics. Years ago the only practical way to supplement was to increase the intake of cultured dairy products like yogurt. Even then it was difficult to get an adequate dose of probiotics because the concentration of healthy bacteria in dairy products may not have been high enough to do any good. Today there are many probiotic (flora) supplements on the market. When looking for a supplement, look for a product that contains no less than 1 billion colonies of flora and preferably between 3 to 5 billion colonies.

Something else to look for in a probiotic supplement is prebiotic ingredients like fructo-oligosaccharides (FOS). Prebiotics (like FOS) boost the growth of beneficial probiotics in the GI tract. FOS are naturally occurring carbohydrates that cannot be digested or absorbed. Essentially they are sugars that ferment in the large intestine and serve as fuel or food for probiotics. FOS also help fight diarrhea, yeast infections, bad cholesterol, and constipation. In Japan more than 500 foods have been fortified with FOS. Similarly, you can find fortified foods in Denmark, Luxembourg, and Portugal.

Research suggests that FOS enhance magnesium absorption in humans and have been shown, in animal models, to reduce colon tumor development by enhancing both colon butyrate concentrations and local immune system effectors.

Increasingly, probiotics and prebiotics are being prescribed to treat the following conditions:

* irritable bowel syndrome (IBS)
* traveler's diarrhea
* diarrhea due to antibiotic use
* prevention of vaginal yeast infections and urinary tract infections
* immune system support
* canker sores
* Crohn's disease
* prevention of colon cancer
* decreasing symptoms of milk sensitivities
* candida, candidiasis

If you are looking to improve your digestive and intestinal health, Melaleuca, Inc. has two outstanding products that you may want to consider using. The *FiberWise* line of products are smart ways to supplement your daily fiber intake with 5 grams of fiber or 20% of the daily recommended intake. In addition to adding both soluble and insoluble fiber to your diet, *FiberWise* also provides 12 additional vitamins and botanicals to assist with digestion. As if this wasn't enough, Melaleuca also includes powerful pre- and probiotics which are essential to the digestive process.

It is difficult to compare *FiberWise* to any other fiber product on the market such as "Metamucil" because Metamucil and other products deliver 30% less psyllium fiber and none of the vitamins, botanicals, pre- and probiotics. With Metamucil you gain only 3 grams of fiber or 12% of the daily recommended allowance, and none of the additional therapeutic ingredients that you get with *FiberWise*.

The second product that Melaleuca offers to help improve intestinal health is *Florify*, with two strains of flora to enhance digestion, absorption, and elimination. Each dose delivers over 5 billion colonies of flora, which research suggests is optimal for good health. Other commercially sold flora products typically provide only 1 billion colonies. Additionally, *Florify* contains FOS (fructo-oligosaccharides), calcium phosphate, and green tea extract to promote the growth of healthy probiotics.

References

Klaper, Dr. Michael., "Is Your Acidophilus Alive and Well? How To Tell", Institute of Nutritional Education and Research, Manhattan Beach, CA

Pereira, M., et al., Archives of Internal Medicine, Vol. 164 No. 4, February 23, 2004

Van Horn L., "Fiber and lipids and coronary heart disease. A statement for healthcare professionals from the Nutritional Committee", American Heart Assoc. Circulation 1997; 95: 2701-4.

Harvard School of Public Health, web site

Agatston, Dr. Arthur., "The South Beach Diet", Rodale Press, New York, 2003

Bornet, F., et al., Digestive and Liver Diseases, Vol. 34, Suppl 2, 2002

CHAPTER EIGHT

You Can Activate Your Immune System

As the world gets smaller, contact from person to person becomes more frequent and germs grow more prevalent, what are we to do to protect our health? The answer is often much closer than we may think, for operating inside each one of us is a very powerful and effective defense called the "immune system."

Much like any other biological system, the immune system is a reflection of our overall health. Eat too much fat, smoke cigarettes, get little sleep, and experience a lot of stress, and your immune system will become weak and less able to protect you. Some studies have found that even negative emotions can detrimentally affect a strong immune system.

For over 4,000 years, the Chinese have used herbs to prevent common diseases. They knew nothing of bacteria or viruses, yet some of these herbs were said to "strengthen the exterior," or the "shield." Modern scientific research is confirming that they were right. We are coming to realize that it is possible to boost the immune system, which can then fight naturally against infectious agents, without the drawbacks of antibiotic therapy.

One of the known immune stimulants is the purple coneflower, Echinacea, which has appeared in over 300 scientific journals with relation to its immune boosting effects. Clinical studies have shown that astragalus, a Chinese plant, has the ability to stimulate the immune system, and pure arabinogalactan (a specific compound found in Western larch trees) has also been found to have a significantly positive effect on the body's natural defenses.

Echinacea (pronounced ek-in-NAY-sha) is one of America's most popular herbal products, used to prevent and treat the common cold, influenza, and infections. If you feel a cold or the flu coming on, you may want to take Echinacea every day for about two weeks or until symptoms disappear. It may also help fight off other viral and bacterial infections such as strep throat, staph infections, recurring vaginal yeast infections, urinary tract infections, herpes, bronchitis, and ear infections. Thirty million Americans take it each year. It is the best known and one of the most researched of immunostimulants.

Astragalus stimulates virtually every phase of immune system activity and has been used as an immunity booster in China for nearly

4,000 years. It is suggested for people who have chronic recurrent infections, especially respiratory infections. It is also recommended for many cancer patients, both those undergoing conventional treatment and those who have completed treatment. It doesn't interfere with chemotherapy or radiation and can be used concurrently.

Though all vitamins and minerals are necessary to maintain a strong immune system, certain nutrients have demonstrated a unique power effect. The first of these is vitamin C, which enhances white blood cell response and function. A common partner with vitamin C, vitamin E has also shown strong immune-enhancing properties, and supplementation with vitamin E has been found to positively affect the immune system.

In addition, studies have found that folic acid, a B vitamin, is necessary for proper immune function. Minerals like zinc and selenium, as well, are crucial to the development of white blood cells.

Echinacea, astragalus, and a good vitamin program are an excellent start for a good immune stimulant program. When you add arabinogalactan, you find a combination that is hard to beat.

Arabinogalactan is a pure, renewable resource that has been discovered to help strengthen the immune system. In fact, it has demonstrated many talents, one of the most prominent being its effect on the body's defense.

Whether at the office, around the kids, at school, or traveling on the airplane, there are many microscopic organisms lurking in our everyday world. To stay healthy enough to enjoy our lives to the fullest, we need a strong immune system. It's important to start with a healthy lifestyle. Trying to get 7–8 hours of sleep every night, eat a healthy diet, exercise regularly, manage your stress and thinking positively can only improve your chances for good health. Taking advantage of dietary supplements such as those offered by Melaleuca can boost those chances. *Activate Immune Complex* contains Echinacea, astragalus, arabinogalactan, vitamin C, vitamin E, folic acid, selenium, and zinc. It is formulated specifically to help strengthen the immune system and is effective and safe for both adults and children.

As Melaleuca says, "When you are feeling like you need a little boost, take *Activate Immune Complex*, and activate your body's natural defenses."

References

"Astragalus Asserts Immunity" *Nutrition Science News* (October, 2000)"

Carper, Jean, "Unique Infection Fighter (Echinacea)," *Miracle Cures,* HarperCollins Publishers, Inc. New York, (1998): 108-119

Leigh, Evelyn, Editorial Director, HRF Greenpapers, Boulder, Co., (2001) *"Echinacea"*

Kelleher, J., "Vitamin E and the Immune Response," *Proceedings Nutr. Soc.* 50 (1991): 245-9

CHAPTER NINE

Depression

The Natural Way to Emotional Health

Every day it seems our lives are moving faster, giving us less time to adjust to, cope with, and enjoy the world around us. We have the same difficult events to deal with, like deaths in the family, divorces, lost jobs, financial difficulties, health problems, and just the trying task of keeping up with things. Though the world would like us to just "deal with it" and move on, our emotions don't work this way. At times we feel overwhelmed, tired out, unmotivated, and unable to handle everything life throws our way.

Depression is a common illness that strikes perhaps 1 in 15 Americans each year. A person's mood, thoughts, physical health, and behavior all may be affected. Symptoms can include a persistent sad, anxious, or "empty" feeling, loss of energy, appetite, or sexual drive, and lack of interest in socializing, work or hobbies.

Researchers have found that certain chemical messengers in the brain affect our mood and our ability to cope with the stresses of life. Fortunately, they have also found nutritional compounds that help maintain the health and levels of these brain messengers, thus supporting our efforts to deal with our fast-paced lives and with the many events that can throw us off balance.

Can chemicals really affect the way we feel? Though some may be skeptical that brain chemicals can actually affect mood, when one considers the effects of alcohol, nicotine, caffeine, prescription drugs, and other compounds on disposition and emotional outlook, it is easy to see that many of our emotional reactions are affected by factors other than our thoughts. The good thing is that, similar to the way we can support the body's physical health through good diet and exercise; we can do the same for our emotional health. In addition, researchers have discovered natural plant extracts and specific vitamins that can help support a strong sense of well being.

The fastest rising star in herbal medicine in Germany and now the United States is the St. John's Wort extract. Why? The simple answer is that St. John's Wort produces equal or better results than prescription drugs in relieving depression, but has far fewer side effects.

Three trials examining treatment of depression compared St. John's Wort with prescription antidepressants. Two studies compared extracts of St. John's Wort with the selective serotonin reuptake inhibitors Prozac and Zoloft. In all three studies, St. John's Wort matched the effectiveness of the prescription antidepressants. Patients taking St. John's Wort experienced fewer and milder side effects than patients receiving prescription antidepressants. St. John's Wort also costs far less than prescription antidepressant medication.

Another herbal extract that researchers have found that may possess abilities to maintain healthy neurotransmitters in the brain is 5 HTP, which is extracted from the seed of a plant that grows in Africa—called Griffonia simplicifolia. It is an amino acid that is the intermediate step between L-tryptophan and the important brain chemical serotonin. There is a massive amount of evidence that suggests that low serotonin levels are a common consequence of modern living. As a result, many people are overweight, crave sugar and other carbohydrates, experience bouts of depression, get frequent headaches, and have vague muscle aches and pain. All of these maladies are correctable by raising brain serotonin levels.

Studies of patients with major depressive disorder have also found that the lower the level of folic acid, the longer and more severe the episode. Another study found that individuals with low folic acid levels were not only more likely to experience depression, they were less likely to respond to antidepressant treatment with a pharmaceutical drug.

In addition, deficiencies of various B complex vitamins have been strongly implicated in depression. Researchers have found a connection between levels of B-12 and the age at which depression symptoms may begin to appear. B-12 deficiencies are linked with poorer cognitive performance in individuals with depression.

Luminex is a dietary supplement specifically formulated to help maintain good emotional health. A unique combination of St. John's Wort, Griffonia seed, folic acid and vitamin B-12, *Luminex* works with the brain's own natural systems to help sustain a strong sense of well-being.

But remember, lifestyle changes can provide a pathway for getting beyond prolonged therapy. Maintaining a well balanced diet, with good nutritional supplements, getting regular exercise and cutting back on sugar and caffeine are a good start. Other things that could help would be to spend more time with positive people, become better at a sport or a craft, or start a new project with a goal. Be good to yourself. Treat yourself to something you enjoy and always make plans for the future.

References

Birdsall, Timothy C., N.D., "5-Hydroxytryptophan: A Clinically-Effective Serotonin Precursor"

Levitt, A. J., Joffe, R. T., "Folate, B12, and life courses of depressive illness", *Biol Psychiatr* 1989 25(7):867-872

"St John's Wort", *National Institutes of Health,* Gaithersburg, MD (July 25, 2001)

CHAPTER TEN

Glucosamine

The Arthritis Nutrient

INTRODUCTION

Jason had been the athletic type, but no longer. That was before a string of sports injuries had damaged the cartilage in his joints and left him with two bum knees and a bad elbow. The diagnosis: osteoarthritis—a crippling, painful, usually permanent condition. When several surgeries failed to fix the problem, Jason almost gave up hope that he would ever be active again. "I was doing everything that medicine said I should, and it wasn't enough," he says. After a year of taking high doses of anti-inflammatory pain medications, he decided that he had to find another solution.

In his search to learn everything he could about osteoarthritis (OA), Jason discovered that a promising treatment for OA had been used in parts of Europe and Asia for decades. The treatment involves supplementing the diet with an inexpensive nutrient called glucosamine. Glucosamine is a substance which occurs naturally in the body and is necessary for building the cartilage which cushions the joints. Anxious to become active again, Jason dug up research dating back to 1959. The largest of these studies had 1,208 participants who took glucosamine daily. Ninety-five percent of them reported that pain was reduced and mobility increased, with no significant side-effects, and with a continuing benefit 6 to 12 weeks after they stopped the supplement.[1] In another study, microscopic examination of the cartilage before and after treatment showed it had been at least partly repaired.[2] And, in yet another experiment, glucosamine was compared with a commonly prescribed anti-inflammatory pain medicine. By the end of the study, those receiving glucosamine experienced significantly greater mobility and freedom from pain than those receiving the pain medicine.[3] The results of these studies have been duplicated in other significant

1 Tapadinhas, M.J., Rivera, I.C., and Bignamini, A.A. "Oral Glucosamine Sulphate in the Management of Arthrosis: Report on a Multi-Centre Open Investigation in Portugal." *Pharmatherapeutica* 3(3): 157-168, 1982.

2 Dovanti, A., Bignamini, A.A., and Rovati, A.L. "Therapeutic Activity of Oral Glucosamine Sulphate in Osteoarthrosis: A Placebo-Controlled Double-Blind Investigation." *Clinical Therapeutics* 3(4):266-272, 1980.

3 Vaz, A.L. "Double-Blind Clinical Evaluation of the Relative Efficacy of Ibuprofen and Glucosamine Sulphate in the Management of Osteoarthrosis of the Knee in Out-Patients." *Current Medical Research and Opinion* 8(3):145-149, 1982.

research over the last two decades.[4, 5, 6, 7, 8]

Jason found the research compelling, as was the fact that European physicians use glucosamine to treat OA, so he began taking the supplement himself. Within two weeks of starting on glucosamine, Jason felt significantly better. Later clinical examination showed that his damaged cartilage was actually repairing itself. Now he says, "I'm back to being a real jock."

But that's not the end of the story. You see, the patient in this story is also a doctor—Jason Theodosakis, M.D. In fact, he's a respected and well-known physician and lecturer in preventive medicine who has trained extensively in exercise physiology and sports medicine. Dr. Theo, as he likes to be called, is also the director of the Preventive Medicine Training Program at the University of Arizona College of Medicine in Tucson.

After his personal success with this "new" OA treatment, Dr. Theo began giving glucosamine to his patients. "The results have been impressive," he says. "I've helped hundreds of people either eliminate the need for surgery or greatly reduce the effects of osteoarthritis." He calls the treatment "the most overlooked medical miracle in America today." His message to OA victims is "There's no reason to suffer any more."

Other respected physicians are beginning to use glucosamine as a part of their OA treatments as well. Andrew Weil, M.D., the best-selling medical author, says "Happily, this seems to be one case where a health fad may actually merit all the attention it's receiving."

Dr. Amal Das, an orthopedic surgeon, has been recommending glucosamine to his patients for three years. "If more people start taking these supplements, it's going to cut down on my business," he says. "I'm having to do less surgery."

Dr. Joseph Houpt, a rheumatologist at the University of Toronto, learned that some of his patients were taking glucosamine on their own. "Enough of them have come back feeling better that I feel it's worth doing a study," he says. He is currently conducting research on 100 patients in his practice.

The mainstream media is beginning to report on glucosamine as well. For example, Newsweek says "...unlike many arthritis fads, this one has some science behind it," and "...if half the people now lining up for the stuff respond to it, arthritis treatment will never be the same."[9]

4 Muller-Fasbender, H., et al. "Glucosamine Sulfate Compared to Ibuprofen in Osteoarthritis of the Knee." *Osteoarthritis and Cartilage* 2:61-69, 1994.

5 Noack, W., et al. "Glucosamine Sulfate in Osteoarthritis of the Knee." *Osteoarthritis and Cartilage* 2:51-59, 1994.

6 Pujalte, J.M., Llavore, E.P., and Ylescupidez, F.R. "Double-Blind Clinical Evaluation of Oral Glucosamine Sulphate in the Basic Treatment of Osteoarthrosis." *Current Medical Research and Opinion* 7(2):110-114, 1980.

7 Vajaradul, Y. "Double-Blind Clinical Evaluation of Intra-Articular Glucosamine in Outpatients with Gonarthrosis." *Clinical Therapeutics* 3(5):260, 1980.

8 Crolle, G., and D'Este, E. "Glucosamine Sulphate for the Management of Arthrosis: A Controlled Clinical Investigation." *Current Medical Research and Opinion* 7(2):104-109, 1980.

9 "The Arthritis Cure?" *Newsweek*, Feb. 17, 1997: 54.

OSTEOARTHRITIS FACTS

Approximately 16 million people in the U.S. have osteoarthritis, a painful condition also known as degenerative joint disease. It is the most common form of arthritis, mostly affecting middle-aged and older people. Osteoarthritis is characterized by pain and loss of movement in the hands and weight-bearing joints, such as the knees, hips, feet, and back. What's alarming about OA is the fact that most people over sixty show to have it on X-ray, but may not have actual symptoms yet, according to the Arthritis Foundation.[10]

Currently, the standard treatment for OA involves the use of anti-inflammatory pain medications which only mask the symptoms and do nothing to correct the underlying cause. In fact, regular use of pain killers may actually accelerate the degeneration of cartilage, making the problem worse.[11] When taken regularly, common pain medications have significant side effects like gastrointestinal bleeding and kidney or liver damage.

By contrast, glucosamine has no significant known side effects. It does not mask the pain, it works to help repair damaged cartilage—the root of the problem. In other words, glucosamine relieves pain by helping to restore and normalize joint function. Most people begin to notice a difference in about two to six weeks after beginning to take glucosamine. Then they are able to wean themselves off the pain medicines.

DOCTOR RECOMMENDED?

Is glucosamine the universally recommended treatment for OA here in America? Not yet, but this is quickly changing. There is an extensive body of clinical research proving that glucosamine is an effective OA treatment in both humans and animals. But most of the research has been done in other countries, and doctors here are slow to accept medical advances from abroad.

Why haven't there been American studies? It all boils down to money. Since glucosamine is a nutritional supplement, it cannot be given patent protection as with new drugs. Consequently, there is very little incentive for drug companies to fund research or promote glucosamine by flooding doctors offices with free samples.

However, some American studies are currently in progress. Results from several studies are being analyzed at the Harrington Arthritis Research Center in Phoenix, according to Dr. Louis Lippielo, the center's senior scientist and biochemist. "I think it's pretty promising," he says. "I'd call it the most promising thing in the last twenty years." But for now, you may have to search to find a doctor who is familiar

10 The Arthritis Foundation. *Osteoarthritis Fact Sheet,* 1997.
11 Hodgkinson, R., and Woolf, D. "A Five-Year Clinical Trial of Indomethacin in Osteoarthritis of the Hip Joint." *ACTA Orthop. Scand.* 50:169, 1979.

with glucosamine and has read the research. Or you may want to give your doctor a copy of this book and ask him to read the research articles which are listed here.

WHICH GLUCOSAMINE IS BEST?

There are several different types of glucosamine. The two most common are glucosamine HCL and glucosamine sulfate. After they are metabolized, both supply the body with the same active ingredient—glucosamine. However, glucosamine HCL is purer, more stabile, and delivers more of the beneficial glucosamine than the sulfate version. And glucosamine HCL has the added benefit of being less expensive, especially when you account for concentration.

Quality is a big issue as well. A University of Maryland analysis found that some brands contained significantly less glucosamine than was stated on the label. So, for best results, buy from a source you know and trust.

This chapter is the full text from the pamphlet entitled "Glucosamine—the Arthritis Nutrient." Sharing this pamphlet is an inexpensive way for you to introduce glucosamine to your loved ones. It is available from RM Barry Publications. Call 1(888)209-0510 or visit us at our web site www.RMBarry.com.

ARTICLES

CHAPTER ELEVEN

Prostate Health

"A Natural Alternative"

If you are a man over age fifty, the chances are 50/50 that you have an enlarged prostate, medically known as benign prostatic hyperplasia (BPH), and the odds escalate as you grow older. It is no picnic—a swollen prostate gland typically two to three times normal size can squeeze your urethra, interfering with normal urination. Symptoms range from having to get up frequently at night to urinate, to pain from obstruction of urinary flow and trouble with erections. It is a non-malignant condition.

You can treat it several ways. You can have surgery, which is very effective but carries the risk of incontinence or impotency. You can take prescription drugs that may or may not work, but can also depress your libido and make you impotent. You can try various therapies, such as laser or microwave, to zap or vaporize unwanted prostate tissue. You can just "watch and wait," as some physicians advise, to avoid drugs and surgery as long as possible. You may also get rid of the symptoms by taking a berry extract, a successful treatment widely used in Europe that costs about one-third as much as conventional drugs and has virtually no risk of side effects. It has worked for millions of men.

A number of conventional drugs are used in the treatment of BPH, most notably finasteride (Proscar®). Several clinical studies have shown that it produces a moderate improvement over placebo. In Europe, up to 90 percent of BPH patients are treated with phytopharmaceuticals or herbal-derived products.

There are about 30 different plant-based compounds currently available in Europe for the treatment of BPH. The most popular (and most effective) is the extract of saw palmetto berry.

It is not clear exactly how saw palmetto works. The most common theory is that saw palmetto reduces levels of a very active form of the male hormone testosterone known as dihydrotestosterone or DHT, thought to be the primary spur to enlargement of the prostate. It is a weird situation. An enzyme switches on the DHT, fooling the cells into thinking they are in puberty again and need to get going. The DHT causes an overproduction of prostate cells, causing the gland to grow bigger. Men with an enlarged prostate have exceptionally high levels of DHT; so do men with prostate cancer. In other words, saw palmetto works as a hormone suppressor.

A major clinical study, which was published in the journal *The Prostate,* involved dozens of researchers in France, Scotland, England, Italy, Portugal, the Czech Republic, Greece, Switzerland, Slovakia and the United States. It compared the use of a commercial saw palmetto extract product available in Europe with the convention drug finasteride (Proscar®) in the treatment of 1,098 patients diagnosed with BPH.

The researchers conclude that both treatments do relieve symptoms of BPH in about two-thirds of patients. This study confirms that the saw palmetto product is equally effective as the conventional drug in relieving symptoms of BPH while producing fewer side effects.

While the drug finasteride (Proscar®) typically takes up to a year to produce significant benefit, saw palmetto extract produces better results in a much shorter period. Most patients achieve some relief of symptoms within the first 30 days of treatment.

The first American randomized clinical trial of saw palmetto shows that the plant reduces swelling in enlarged prostate tissue. The study was published in the March 1999, issue of the peer-reviewed journal *Urology,* followed by a presentation at the Annual Meeting of the American Urological Association in Dallas, Texas, from May 1–6, 1999.

Clearly, saw palmetto offers superior symptomatic relief in prostate disease, as defined by the most common clinical tests. In addition, it improves quality of life and has a "practically negligible side effect risk." This review makes a compelling case for the use of saw palmetto as treatment of choice among physicians and patients concerned with meaningful improvement and greater safety compared with conventional synthetic drugs. (While cost was not a consideration in this review, saw palmetto extract is also significantly less expensive than conventional prescription drugs.)

Like saw palmetto berry extract, pumpkin seed extract helps to ensure normal urinary and prostate function. Initially used in Germany to promote normal urination as well as a healthy urinary tract, recent European tests have shown that pumpkin seed can have a positive effect on the function of the prostate as well.

Pumpkin seed extract is also known to have marked anti-inflammatory action. In other words, like saw palmetto berry, it may help reduce the swelling of the prostate, which is helpful in relieving both BPH and certain types of prostatitis. In addition, pumpkin seed extract has been shown to reduce the symptoms of the disorder, including both the frequent urge to urinate and the amount of residual urine. An added benefit, no unwanted side effects.

Zinc, like saw palmetto berry extract and pumpkin seed extract, has been associated with enhancing prostate health. In one study, more than two-thirds of patients who took zinc supplements daily experienced a positive effect on prostate function. Though it is true that zinc is used internally for bone formation, for the digestion of protein, and for the conversion of nutrients to energy, it is also very crucial to prostate health. Indeed, the prostate gland normally contains 10 times more zinc than any other male body organ.

Unfortunately, older Americans consume less than two-thirds of their Recommended Daily Allowance for zinc. In addition, they don't absorb it as well as they did when they were younger. Consequently, just when a man really needs this nutrient to help the prostate through the changes that occur as he gets older, his diet and his body let him down. Therefore, a supplement rich in zinc can help meet his changing needs.

When considering the overall health of the prostate, it would be negligent not to mention lycopene. Responsible for making tomatoes red, lycopene is a carotenoid (a class of yellow to deep-red pigments occurring in many vegetable oils). It is also considered much more potent antioxidant than beta-carotene.

According to Harvard University researchers, led by Dr. Edward Giovannucci of the Harvard School of Public Health, foods containing tomatoes, which are rich in lycopene, are believed to provide high levels of protection against prostate cancer. In Dr. Giovannucci's detailed studies of 52,000 men over a six-year period, results showed that men with the highest intake of lycopene had a 21 percent lower risk of prostate cancer than men with the lowest intake. Only lycopene had this significant relationship to reducing prostate cancer risk.

If an individual is experiencing some of the symptoms of BPH, it is important that he sees his doctor and not automatically assumes that the problem is, indeed, BPH. After all, there are other possibilities that can cause some of these same symptoms. Examples include a normal bladder that is simply aging, an infection of the bladder, cancer, prostatitis, bladder stones, diabetes, multiple sclerosis, and Parkinson's disease.

Lifestyle changes can also make a difference in lowering the risk of prostate disorders. Consider the following:

1. Cut down on coffee, tea, and cola drinks.
2. Reduce or eliminate beer or other alcohol from your diet.
3. Eat dinner earlier.
4. Eat a diet rich in natural whole foods.
5. Go easy on salt and spices.
6. Increase water intake to stimulate urine flow and prevent urinary retention and kidney infection.
7. Reduce fluids taken after 7 P.M.
8. Stay regular.
9. Keep blood cholesterol below 220 mg per deciliter.
10. Avoid antihistamines and decongestants.
11. Limit exposure to pesticides and other environmental contaminants.
12. Use a well-designed nutritional supplement, which supplies the nutrients important to prostate health.

ARTICLES

Working together, saw palmetto berry extract, pumpkin seed extract, zinc, and lycopene extract assist the body in maintaining proper urinary function and in sustaining a normal, healthy prostate. With the help of a nutritious diet that includes these ingredients, an individual may find himself aging while still maintaining a high level of prostate health.

Melaleuca's answer to a healthy prostate is **ProstAvan**. A natural alternative, **ProstAvan** is made of the highest quality botanical extracts, including saw palmetto berry, pumpkin seed, and lycopene, as well as the nutrient, zinc. European studies have shown that these ingredients maintain normal urinary and prostate function.

For additional information, see the section on *Benign Prostatic Hyperplasia (BPH)* in the *Healthy Body* chapter of this book.

References

Balch, J., M.D., and the Urology Research Center, "Maintaining and Regaining Prostate Health," *Prostate Health*. (Alternative Medicine Updates, Publishers), 1994

Carper, Jean, "Prostate 'Remedy of Choice'", *Miracle Cures,* HarperCollins Publishers, Inc. New York, (1998) 151-158

Foster, Steven, "Men's Health and What you Need to Know about Saw Palmetto" Steven Foster Group

Giovannucci, E., et. al., "Intake of Carotenoids and Retinol in Relation to Risk of Prostate Cancer," *Journal of the National Cancer Institute,* December 6, 1995

Murray, Dr. Michael T., "Saw Palmetto Extract: Nature's Answer to Prostate Enlargement", *Dr. Murray Online*

"Phytomedicines outperform synthetics in treating enlarged prostate," Herb Research Foundation, Boulder, Co.

CHAPTER TWELVE

Menopause

The Natural Way

Hot flashes, night sweats, mood changes, loss of libido and vaginal dryness are some of the most common symptoms of menopause. A single event, menopause is a woman's last period of menstruation. This usually occurs between the ages of 40 and 55 and even though the term "menopause" refers to that single event, the time of change can last for several years. This time is marked by a drastic loss in estrogen, or what is commonly referred to as the "female hormone" and can affect at least 300 of the body's systems. That is why it is beneficial to maintain a normal level of hormones.

But does it have to be done chemically? No. There are natural alternatives. Doctors have turned to hormone replacement therapy (HRT) to combat the symptoms associated with falling estrogen levels. HRT is the administration of the female hormones estrogen and progesterone. Estrogen replacement therapy (ERT) refers to administration of estrogen alone.

ERT is thought to help prevent the devastating effects of heart disease and osteoporosis. However, hormone treatment for menopause is quite controversial. The long-term safety and efficacy remain matters of great concern. There is simply not enough existing data for physicians to suggest that HRT is the right choice for all women.

A study published in the March 21, 2001, issue of the *Journal of the American Medical Association* found that women who used ERT for more than 10 years had twice the risk of dying of ovarian cancer as those who did not use such therapy.

According to an article in the *Journal of the American Medical Association*, the bottom line of a seven-year study of 2,763 women (Heart and Estrogen/Progestin Replacement Study—HERS) is "in these women…the net effect is harm."

An article in the Washington Post on July 3, 2002, stated that other synthetic hormone studies have shown "an increased risk of serious blood clots in the legs and lungs, as well as in increased risk of gall bladder disease…some studies have also noted an increased risk of breast cancer in women who took hormones for longer than about five years."

Is there an alternative? Yes. Herbal medicines have long been used in traditional healing systems to treat conditions of particular interest to women, such as premenstrual syndrome (PMS) and menopausal symptoms. For relief of menopausal symptoms, black cohosh root extract, dong quai, and soy have all proved to provide beneficial effects during menopause.

Dong quai is used for almost every gynecological complaint from regulating the menstrual cycle to treating menopausal symptoms caused by hormonal changes. Dong quai contains vitamins A, E, and B12 and research has shown that it produces a balancing effect on estrogen activity.

Black cohosh has a history of usage for women's gynecological problems dating back to the Algonquian natives living in the Ohio Valley. The eclectic doctors of the 1800s often recommended black cohosh for what they called "hysterical" disease, i.e. female reproductive disease. Today, black cohosh is still used for gynecological problems from menstruation to menopause, with multiple studies over the past 40 years backing this up.

Several studies have shown soy's natural health benefits for menopausal women. In 1998 a study published in the *American Journal of Clinical Nutrition*, found that postmenopausal women who ate 40 grams of soy protein per day significantly increased the bone density in their spines.

If an alternative to HRT is of interest to you, Melaleuca's *EstrAval* is excellent at helping bodies maintain a normal, healthy function both before and after the actual menopause occurs. It is composed of soy extract, black cohosh extract, and dong quai extract. And, best of all, these natural extracts have a minimum potential for side effects. Their natural origins help them to work easily with the body's own system. After all, as Melaleuca says, "*EstrAval*: because you have a lot of living to do."

For more information, see the section on *Menopause* in the *Healthy Body* chapter of this book.

References

Crawford, Sharon, "Black cohosh," *Gale Encyclopedia of Alternative Medicine.*

Hardy, M. L., "Herbs of special interest to women," *J Am Pharm Assoc* (Wash) 2000 Mar-Apr, 40 (2) 234-42: quiz 327-9.

Headline Watch, Mayo Clinic.com, October 27, 2001.

"Managing Menopause," MDchoice.com, October 27, 2001.

"Soy intake related to menopausal symptoms, serum lipids, and bone mineral density in postmenopausal Japanese women," *Obstet Gynecol* 2001 (January, 1997) 109-15.

CHAPTER THIRTEEN

Protect Your Vision

Nutrition for Your Eyes

What handicap do people fear the most? If you guessed blindness, you are right, according to the National Eye Health Education Program of the National Institutes of Health. Our eyes bring in more than 90% of the information that enters our brain. And yet, according to the Louis Harris survey, only 41% of all Americans have an annual eye exam and only 46% have a regular eye doctor.

Vision loss is a catastrophic issue and one particularly facing the aging population. However, proper nutrition can help prevent, and possibly reverse, the most common visual disorders, namely cataracts and macular degeneration. "The traditional thinking is that as age increases, visual sensitivity decreases," says D. Max Snodderly, Ph.D., head of the laboratory at The Schepens Eye Research Institute. "But what we are saying is, maybe that's not inevitable. Improved nutrition could help to retard the loss of visual sensitivity with age."

Cataracts are the leading cause of impaired vision and blindness overall, and age related macular degeneration (AMD) is the leading cause of blindness in people over age 65. Cataracts are opacities or white cloudy spots on the normally transparent lens of the eye. Vision for cataract sufferers is somewhat like trying to see through eyeglasses smeared with salad oil. Macular degeneration is a deterioration or breakdown of the macula. For macular degeneration sufferers, vision is like having a penny taped to the center of your glasses—poor central vision but better peripheral vision.

The consensus is that AMD is a nutritional deficiency disease. The carotenoids lutein and zeaxanthin are most strongly associated with a reduced risk for AMD. "Increasing the consumption of foods rich in certain carotenoids, in particular dark green, leafy vegetables may decrease the risk of developing macular degeneration." Reported Johanna M. Seddon, M.D., of the Department of Ophthalmology, Harvard Medical School.

Although current research does not provide strong conclusive evidence to support the potential role of antioxidants in preventing macular degeneration, many physicians and ophthalmologists do recommend supplementing with these nutrients if it is not contraindicated by other health conditions. In addition, the elimination of the most common risk factors should be carefully considered. Smoking and cardiovascular disease (atherosclerosis, arteriosclerosis, hypertension) are high among the list of risks for AMD, as is a low dietary intake of pigmented antioxidants found in green, orange, and red vegetables and fruits.

Blueberries are recommended for good eye health because they contain high levels of antioxidants, compounds that neutralize free radicals. Free radicals can attack the lens membrane, causing it to harden and relay a fuzzy image. That is why many people who turn 40 joke that "their arms aren't long enough to read." To get the antioxidants that researchers recommend for eye health, you would have to eat a half-cup of blueberries every day. This isn't practical for most people, so Melaleuca combined 100 milligrams of blueberry, and 20 milligrams of bilberry extracts in each *NutraView* capsule.

"Lutein in the lens acts as nature's own sunglasses," says Steven Pratt, M. D., senior staff member at Scripps Memorial Hospital in La Jolla, Ca. Due to the ongoing research of lutein's benefits to eye health, Centrum recently added ¼ milligram to each dose, even though the research on lutein suggests that you must consume six milligrams per day to get the eye care benefits of this nutrient. In other words, to get the research-based recommended dose of lutein by taking **Centrum**, you would need to take 24 tablets per day. In contrast, one capsule of *NutraView* provides 10 milligrams of lutein. That's almost twice the minimum amount recommended by research, all for about 48¢ a day.

Paul Harvey advertises a popular product called "Ocular Nutrition" which also contains 10 milligrams of lutein per daily dose. The price for this product is $40.93 for a 25 day supply, or $1.64 per day. That's more than three times the cost of *NutraView* for the same concentration of lutein!

With Melaleuca's *NutraView*, in one capsule, you receive 10 milligrams of lutein (which protects the eye, especially the macula, from free radical damage), 20 milligrams of bilberry (which helps maintain normal circulation to the eye and helps support night vision), plus 100 milligrams of blueberry powder (a super-powerful antioxidant called the "vision fruit" in Japan), and 150 milligrams of vitamin C (which has been proven to maintain the health of the lens). All of this for only $14.38 for a one month supply. It is exciting to know that certain nutrients may help us to enjoy the miracle of vision far longer than ever before.

References

Aesoph, Lauri M., N.D., "Eat Right for Sharp Eyesight."

Macular Degeneration International 6700 N. Oracle Road, Tucson, AZ 85704.

Quillin, Patrick, Ph.D., R. D., C.N.S., Director of nutrition at the Cancer Treatment Centers of America, Inc., Tulsa, OK, "Sight For Sore Eyes."

CHAPTER FOURTEEN

Urinary Tract Infections

Cranberries—An Old Wives' Tale?

OVERVIEW

Urinary tract infections (UTI) are the second most common type of infection, next to respiratory infections. Women get them more often than men, but when men do get them, they can be more serious and more difficult to treat. Nearly one in five women will get a urinary tract infection during their lives, and of those, 20% will have reoccurrences.[1] Urinary tract infections can be especially dangerous for seniors and pregnant women, as well as for those with diabetes. Symptoms of a UTI include a frequent urge to urinate and pain or burning during urination. The urine may look milky or cloudy, and sometimes only a small amount can be passed. Also there may be abdominal and/or back pain.

Most commonly, UTIs are caused by the bacteria that normally live in the colon, *Escherichia coli*. The *E. coli* usually invade from the lower end of the urinary tract, where bacteria will start multiplying in the urethra, then the infection could spread to the bladder and, if left untreated, bacteria may then infect the kidneys. Signs that the infection has reached the kidneys include fever, pain in the back below the ribs, nausea or vomiting, or blood in the urine. Always see your health care provider immediately if any of these symptoms occur.

There are a few lifestyle changes you can implement to help prevent future UTIs if you are prone to getting them. First, drink six to eight glasses of water a day to flush the bacteria from your system. Avoid alcohol, coffee, and soda because alcohol and caffeine can aggravate the urinary tract. Also, don't hold your urine—go when you feel the urge. Bacteria can grow when urine stays in the bladder too long. Wear cotton underwear and avoid tight-fitting pants. Make sure to use a mild detergent when washing underwear. And finally, use good bathroom hygiene. Keep the genital and anal areas clean. Women should always wipe front to back after a bowel movement. Urinate shortly after intercourse to cleanse the urethra of bacteria.

CRANBERRIES TO PREVENT AND TREAT UTIS

The standard course of treatment for urinary tract infections over the past forty years has been a dose of antibiotics, but hundreds of years of "old wives' tales" have recommended drinking cranberry juice to ward off recurring urinary tract infections. Antibiotics may induce unpleasant side effects and can also upset the normal bacterial flora present in your intestines, which can lead to yeast overgrowth, yeast infections, and diarrhea.

Recommending cranberry juice for UTIs no longer has to be regarded as an "old wives' tale," because numerous studies have confirmed that the phytonutrients in cranberries actually help to block infectious bacteria from clinging to the lining of the urinary tract and bladder. So, instead of clinging and multiplying, the bacteria get washed out of the body when you urinate.

One well conducted double-blind study, published in 1994 in the *Journal of the American Medical Association* found that drinking cranberry juice definitely reduced elderly women's risk of urinary tract infection. A cranberry manufacturer made a placebo drink that had the same taste and vitamin C content as cranberry juice but with no cranberry content. The subjects were 153 elderly women who had a greater than 30% chance of developing a UTI. To prevent the possibility that subjects in the institution who were to be drinking the placebo might inadvertently drink standard cranberry juice somewhere else in the institution, all cranberry drinks were converted to placebo throughout the institution for the duration of the study. Urine samples were collected each month for six months and studied for the presence of bacteria. Bacteria was noted in almost twice as many subjects in the placebo group as in the cranberry group. The difference was noticed between months one and two of the study and remained stable until the end.[2]

Like the cranberry, blueberries contain phytochemicals that inhibit the ability of *E. coli* to adhere to the walls of the bladder. Another nutrient helpful for UTIs is Bearberry (uva ursi), an extract that contains arbutin, a natural diuretic and antibiotic.

Because the cranberry is so bitter, popular drinks are often diluted with water, sugar, and other juices, adding many unwanted calories. A serving of Melaleuca's *CranBarrier* gives you 1,000 mg of cranberry in two chewable tablets, with only 10 calories. And, unlike other cranberry supplements, *CranBarrier* also includes a proprietary blend of blueberry and bearberry, which have been proven to work synergistically with cranberry in the fight against urinary tract infections.

References

1 "Urinary tract infections in adults", National Kidney and Urologic Diseases Information Clearinghouse

2 J Avorn, M Monane, et al., "Reduction of bacteriuria and Pyuria After Ingestion of Cranberry Juice." Journal of the American Medical Association 1994 271: 751-4.

CHAPTER FIFTEEN

Head Lice

Don't Poison Your Child
With Pesticide Treatments!

Few things can strike such fear in the hearts of parents as head lice! While the bloodsuckers rarely, if ever, cause direct harm or transmit disease, they cause parents to engage in everything from blaming to explaining. They wonder where their child got the lice, worry that it reflects on their parenting abilities, and even offer explanations about their housekeeping and cleanliness.

Head lice, according to Harvard researcher Richard J. Pollack, "do not respect socio-economic distinctions. They don't care who you are, and have nothing to do with your level of hygiene. We're just as likely to find them on children who live in million dollar estates as in children who live in far lesser conditions," he adds. "Virtually anyone at some level is at risk."

Every year, an estimated 6 million to 12 million people—mostly children—and their families get head lice and they are becoming resistant to the leading chemical treatment used to combat them.

The treatments can often be worse than the lice. Parents turn to prescription medications with high concentrations of permethrin when over-the-counter versions fail. Some parents resort to everything from kerosene to chemicals intended to put on dogs to kill fleas.

Recommended alternatives to permethrin include pediculicides or anti-louse medications containing lindane and malathion, both available by prescription. But neither is without risk. Dr. Paul Auwaerter, assistant professor of medicine at Johns Hopkins University says that lindane can have unpleasant side effects like stinging sensations. However, others feel much stronger about the negative effects of lindane and pediculicides.

Lindane has been banned in 52 countries and severely restricted in 33 others. It has not been produced in the U.S. since 1977, but it is still imported here. You may still find lindane as the active poison ingredient in flea collars, moth, and other household sprays. As a scabicide poison (against lice) on children it may be present in lotions, creams, and shampoos.

Lindane (gamma-HCH) is one of the few organochlorine pesticides left on the market. It is the active ingredient in products best known by the brand name KWELL, now available only in generic form.

Lindane is frequently used on young children, pregnant women, nursing mothers, and the elderly. These groups are most at risk from lindane's adverse effects."

Chemical treatments for head lice contain potent pesticides and insecticides known as pediculicides. These pediculicides have been known to cause immune suppression, seizures, vomiting, diarrhea, convulsions, circulatory collapse, behavioral change, neuromuscular damage, chronic skin eruptions, liver damage, asthma, respiratory failure, stillbirths, birth defects, cancer and even death.

Also, consider these facts:

- The FDA issued an alert as far back as June 1975 in its bulletin to the medical community regarding the potential harmful effects of lindane.

- The National Pediculosis Association (NPA) testified before the FDA in 1983, 1984, 1985, and 1992 documenting the misinformation, misuse, and abuse of products containing lindane, and the NPA President testified in legal suits on behalf of children permanently disabled after use of lindane in 1990 and 1993.

- On September 5, 2000, California Governor Gray Davis signed Bill AB 2318, banning the sale and use of lindane to treat people for lice and scabies. In 2002, Californial banned pharmaceutical use of lindane due to concerns abut water quality.

Is there an alternative? Many people think so. Check out this notice posted on one school bulletin board:

"Dear Parents, did you know that the leading lice shampoo contains a potent pesticide called LINDANE, which has been known to cause vomiting, diarrhea, convulsions, liver damage and many other health issues with our kids. LINDANE has been banned in 52 countries and severely restricted in 33 others. Why are we using it on our kids' heads? The health of our kids is at stake, don't let them be exposed to this sometimes deadly treatment when there is a natural, safe, non-toxic, chemical free, and effective way to prevent and treat lice infestations. Let's get rid of these pests once and for all in our community! LET'S DO IT FOR OUR KIDS!! For more information call…(Insert your name and number)."

What is the safe alternative? Melaleuca products. How do you use them? See the section on *Head Lice* in the "Healthy Body" chapter of this book.

References:

http://www.lindane.org
http://www.panna.org/lindane
http://www.kidsource.com
http://www.safe2use.com

CHAPTER SIXTEEN

Healthy Body

Every effort has been made to ensure that the information contained in this book is complete and accurate. However, neither the publisher nor the author is engaged in rendering professional advice or services to the individual reader. The ideas, procedures, and suggestions contained in this book are not intended as a substitute for consulting with your physician. All matters regarding health require medical supervision. Each person's health needs are unique. To obtain recommendations appropriate to your particular situation, please consult a qualified health care provider. Always read and follow product packaging directions and warnings. Neither the author nor the publisher shall be liable for any loss, injury, or damage allegedly arising from any information or suggestion in this book.

The five most essential elements of good health are nutrition, exercise, water, rest, and a positive attitude. Fifty years ago we ate fruits and vegetables from our nutritious gardens, and got our exercise from weeding, pushing a lawn mower, and walking to school. In modern society we have almost none of that available. Our gardens and farms are no longer the nutrition providers they once were because of the nutritional depletion of the soil.

It is essential to good health to supplement our diets. The Melaleuca **Vitality 6** pack, which includes the **Vitality Pack** with **Oligofructose Complex**, **CellWise**, **Phytomega**, **ProvexCV**, and **Florify**, is an excellent place to start. This combination of nutritional products is designed to give you basic nutrition, powerful antioxidant protection, healthy intestinal flora, and superior cardiovascular maintenance at a special low price. Packaged in AM and PM packets, and designed for the different nutritional needs of men, women, prenatal, or 50+ years of age, the **Vitality 6** pack is the most convenient way to take the daily supplements essential to good health.

A good night of rest, plenty of water, a few minutes of daily exercise and a good laugh or two and your day is off to a wonderful start! If you are dealing with any of the conditions listed in this chapter and these support products are not mentioned, it should be assumed that they are a part of your overall wellness program.

Here's to good health and happy living!

---

*The information presented in this book is in no way intended as a substitute for medical counseling. Always consult your physician before starting any course of supplementation or treatment, particularly if you are pregnant or currently under medical care. Always read and follow product packaging directions and warnings.

ABDOMINAL DISTRESS

The area between the pelvis and the rib cage contains more organs and more sites for discomfort than any other area of the body. Colic or upset stomach in infants, indigestion, reactions to foods and constipation are common problems that can occur. The bowel, liver, pancreas, kidneys, spleen, stomach and gallbladder are all possible sites of distress.

Of all abdominal distress, gas and indigestion account for 80% of complaints. Abdominal distress is often caused by unhealthy eating habits. While we should all drink at least eight glasses of pure water a day, this water should be consumed between meals rather than at mealtime. When we drink too many liquids with our meal, digestive enzymes are diluted. This, in turn, can be manifested as indigestion or abdominal pain caused by bloating and gas.

Upon feeling discomfort in the abdomen, try to remember if food was ingested which was of questionable freshness. The so-called "summer flu" is actually due to bacterial toxicity from improperly handled food.

Overeating in the evening hours, or eating in a hurry, packs food in the stomach before nerve and hormone stimulation can properly begin the digestive process. Eating rich, fatty meals stresses the stomach, gallbladder, and pancreas, which slows down digestion and allows bacterium to begin fermentation and putrefaction in the bowel.

Constipation is at epidemic levels in our country. Eating high roughage food helps hold moisture in the bowel, giving the muscles of the bowel physical material to propel along its approximately 26 feet in length. The roughage rapidly carries ingested toxins, proliferating bacteria and metabolic by-products out of the body. Experts agree that 20 to 30 grams of fiber per day is advisable for adults. The average American eats approximately 7.3 grams of fiber each day.

*Celebrate eating. Give thanks. Eat as many meals as possible with soft music and candlelight, in the presence of people you love. Drink adequate amounts of liquid each day including 2 or 3 cups of *Melaleuca Herbal Tea* between meals. Slow Down! Use *FiberWise* drink or bars to supplement your daily intake of fiber. Each serving supplies 5 grams of the much-needed fiber. Take *Florify* to help maintain the proper balance of flora in the digestive system. Get 20 to 40 minutes of moderate daily exercise to promote circulation within the abdomen and stimulate bowel peristalsis. Multiple small meals are generally preferable to one or two large meals each day. Take the *Vitality Pack* with *Oligofructose Complex* and *CellWise* daily to encourage proper metabolism and waste excretion from cells. If indigestion occurs, use *Calmicid* as directed. *Calmicid* provides fast relief of acid indigestion, heartburn and gas. It aids digestion with ginger root and helps relieve cramping with chamomile and fennel seed.

To correct colic in infants, give several teaspoons of warm *Melaleuca Herbal Tea* during the day and before bedtime.

See the section on *Indigestion* in this book.

HEALTHY BODY

ABRASIONS

These injuries occur when your skin slides across coarse materials, such as concrete, gravel, or asphalt. The top layers of skin are damaged, causing nerves, blood vessels, and lymph vessels to be exposed to the air. This causes immediate pain and creates an opportunity for germs to enter the body. After the bleeding and oozing stops, a dry protective scab will usually form within a few hours and is nature's protection against infection.

* Washing the area gently, yet thoroughly, with *Antibacterial Liquid Soap* and cool water quickly reduces the pain. (Warm or hot water increases nerve stimulation and pain in most people.) Allow the stream of water to wash off all visible particulates. Pick out any embedded material. Apply *Triple Antibiotic Ointment* or *MelaGel* and allow to remain open to the air if possible. Otherwise, use a loose bandage saturated with *Triple Antibiotic Ointment* or *MelaGel* to prevent sticking. Repeat administration of *Triple Antibiotic Ointment* or *MelaGel* as frequently as needed for several days until the wound is adequately covered with a scab.

ABSCESSES

These painful, pus-filled sacks of infection can occur in or on any surface of the body. Abscesses may start from a cut, scratch, pimple, ingrown hair, ingrown fingernail or ingrown toenail, hemorrhoid, or any piercing of the body. Improper treatment of an infection can produce a characteristic swollen, red, painful lump. The typical bacterium which causes abscesses is Staph epidermis, which is found on healthy skin. While antibiotics are often necessary, the overuse of antibiotics, both by prescription and in the meat we eat, has led to the development of many antibiotic-resistant strains of bacteria.

* Begin drinking *Melaleuca Herbal Tea* in place of other liquids 3 to 4 times each day. Apply *T36-C5* to the abscess. This can help to lessen the pain of the abscess, due to the penetrating effects of the oil.

To encourage drainage and drive the *T36-C5* into the wound, apply hot moist packs over the area. If the abscess can be lanced and drained, soak afterwards in a solution of 1 oz of *Sol-U-Mel* and 2 tbsp of Epsom salts mixed with 1 qt of warm water. Saturate a hand towel in the solution, wring it out, then apply to the affected area for 10 minutes. Repeat every hour to speed the draining. Apply *Triple Antibiotic Ointment* or *MelaGel*. If needed, cover with gauze to absorb any seeping fluid and keep the area clean.

ACHES AND PAINS

A strained muscle does not necessarily cause aches and pains. It may simply be the fatigue of a muscle or set of muscles because of prolonged inactivity, such as sitting in a car or concentrating on a particular task.

HEALTHY BODY

Psychological stress may also be the perpetrator. Generally the aches and pains occur in the lower back or neck and shoulder area, although any muscle could be involved, including the feet.

* When involved in a prolonged activity, be sure that you get up and move around at least once every hour, preferably every half hour. This can prevent a lot of unnecessary aches and pains. When they do occur, **Pain-A-Trate** can give dramatic relief. When time allows, a long soak in a hot bath with **Renew Bath Oil** is very relaxing. If your feet are feeling a little numb from sitting too long, try the **Body Satin Foot Lotion**. It is very soothing.

ACNE

The products of overactive oil glands in the skin can dry and harden, forming blackheads. This may produce a local bacterial infection and pimples. This condition primarily affects adolescents and can occur on almost any part of the body. Outbreaks generally appear on the face, chest and upper back.

Acne is common to those working in hostile chemical environments, people suffering from hormonal imbalances, or those under physical or emotional stress. Additional factors can include the use of oil-based cosmetics, the use of some prescription drugs, heredity (the condition seems to "run" in some families), and changes in the human body at the onset of puberty. Skin blemishes in individuals of all ages arise from improper nutrition, toxicity, and rapidly changing needs for hormonal regulation. Blemishes frequently occur in women during pregnancy. While proper hygiene, including at least twice daily washing of areas most prone to becoming affected, will not in itself prevent acne, it may help to reduce or limit the spreading nature inherent in most acne outbreaks.

* Be aware of food allergies and experiment with elimination diets or get tested by your health care provider. Minimize your sugar intake. Drink 3-4 cups of **Melaleuca Herbal Tea**, hot or iced, each day, in addition to the eight glasses of pure water you should normally drink. Reduce fats to less than 20% of total calories. Perspire for twenty minutes each day, preferably from exercise, but sauna or steam baths work also.

Shower with **Antibacterial Liquid Soap** or **The Gold Bar**. For those who prefer bathing, always put 1 oz of **Sol-U-Mel** in the tub. Avoid eating cooked oils such as are in margarine and potato chips. Get 20 grams of fiber daily including **FiberWise** drink or bar. Take the **Vitality Pack** with **Oligofructose Complex** and **CellWise** daily for the added nutritional benefits of vitamin A, zinc, the B vitamins, and vitamin C. It is also been suggested that **ProVex-Plus** be taken at the rate of 1 capsule for every 25 lbs of body weight each day.

The **Zap-It! Acne Treatment System** was specifically developed for the prevention of acne. Consistent use of this system usually delivers clear skin. Clean skin with the **Zap-It! Facial Wash**; apply **Zap-It! Astringent**, and then **Zap-It! Pore Clarifying Cream**. Carry **Zap-It! Quick Stick** for a convenient treatment away from home.

In addition, you can apply **T36-C5** to any developing pustule. Use the **T36-C5** to clear the plugged oil ducts. The **Renew Intensive Skin Therapy** should be used afterward to keep moisture in the skin and resist oil accumulation. Avoid dry brush or friction rubs with alcohol as this naturally stimulates oil production. Get enough rest.

ADD AND ADHD

Attention Deficit Disorder and Attention Deficit Hyperactive Disorder are found in children and adults who have a reduced attention span and a variable pattern of behavioral challenges. Clinical studies indicate that there is a link to dietary and environmental factors. Simple sugar cravings and intolerance to sugar appear to be indicated. Several studies show a link to essential fatty acid deficiencies within the brain.

* Identify any and all food, food additives, household cleaners, and synthetic substances shown to be reactive, and remove them from the environment. Convert your home to the environmentally friendly Melaleuca cleaning and personal care products. Reduce fried foods, cooked and rancid oils (potato chips, french fries, etc.), sugar (including artificial sweeteners), and food colorings. Have a metabolic and nutritional physical exam by a certified clinician.

The following supplements, along with appropriate dietary changes, may be useful to help improve symptoms. The **Vitality Pack** with **Oligofructose Complex** should be used to help maintain proper nutrition. (Children should be taking the **Vita-Bears**.) **Luminex** will help to maximize cerebral circulation. **ProVex** will reduce free-radical activity and help to reduce sensitivities to allergens. **Phytomega** contains omega-3 fatty acids, which are extremely important for proper brain function. Researchers have discovered a link between mood disorders and low concentrations of omega-3 fatty acids in the body. **CellWise** is used to help maintain cell structure in the brain, and **Sustain Sport** will help maintain proper blood sugar balance and reduce sugar cravings.

When people with ADD took grape seed extract (**ProVex**) for other purposes, such as allergies, they began to notice an improvement in concentration and mental focus. These are classic symptoms of attention deficit. It has been observed that those who took grape seed extract (**ProVex**) on a regular basis showed just as much improvement as those who took stimulant drugs. Generally children fared better on a lower dose (25 milligrams of grape seed extract (**ProVex**) per 25 pounds of body weight daily), and adults did better with a higher dose of 50 milligrams per 25 pounds of body weight daily. Other positive effects such as decreased heartbeat, disappearance of tennis elbow, relief of acne and improvement in sleep and moods were also noted.

Valerian Root found in **RestEZ** has been useful for this disorder with exceptional results and no side effects. The capsule can be opened and mixed with applesauce or juice. One capsule (or ½ capsule if under 80 pounds) two or three times a day can work wonders.

Avoid carbonated drinks. The phosphate additives may be the cause of hyperkinesias (exaggerated muscle activity). The phosphorus found in soft drinks may also leech calcium and magnesium from the body creating a deficiency, which creates further potential for increased hyperactivity and even seizures. Meat and fat are also high in phosphorus. The calcium and magnesium found in the *Vitality Pack* and *Vita-Bears* will provide a calming effect, as well as replenish the body.

AGE SPOTS

Sunspots, liver spots and age spots are all names for skin imperfections. They usually appear when people reach their mid-50s. People who become sun worshippers may find that they have them much earlier.

While most age spots result from an overexposure to the sun, it is important to remember that if the size or color of any spot changes, immediately consult your health care provider. This could be an early warning sign of skin cancer!

* *T36-C5* has been known to fade sunspots in some cases. It certainly won't hurt the skin. Also, *ProVex* and/or *ProVex-Plus* may help to reduce age spots over time. However, to prevent the imperfections as much as possible, use the *Nicole Miller Skin Care* program. The *Day Cover Perfecting Foundation* has an SPF of 10 and the *Day Cover Creme to Powder Foundation* has an SPF of 15. Other exposed parts of the body should always be covered with *Sun Shades Sunscreen* when out of doors. These products will protect you against UVA, UVB and infrared rays.

AIR PURIFICATION

The quality of air you breathe in your home may be robbing you of good health. Modern energy-efficient homes, by virtue of their airtight design, often trap chemical vapors from furniture, carpets, and building adhesives. Condensation from air ducts, houseplant soil, and sink areas can produce harmful mold, fungus, yeast and bacteria. Many respiratory, eye, ear, nose and throat complaints appear in doctors' waiting rooms because of overexposure to foul household air. Changes of seasons often shift populations of these microbial species as growing conditions fluctuate.

* Convert your home to Melaleuca products, replacing toxic cleaning and personal care products with safer Melaleuca products. The outgassing of toxic vapors from both personal care and home hygiene products significantly increases air quality challenges.

Remove browning leaves from houseplants immediately. Provide good drainage for houseplants, and do not overwater.

Change air return filters monthly during extreme weather usage. Frequently spray all filters and vents with diluted *Sol-U-Mel*. To do a Melaleuca oil purge of your house two to twelve times a year, attach an inverted open bottle of *T36-C5* on the furnace intake filter. The high air volume will diffuse the entire contents of the bottle throughout your air ducts and house over the next 12 to 36 hours (depending upon temperature and relative humidity). This treated air flows throughout all the rooms and helps to stop the growth of bacteria, molds, fungus, and viruses.

When using a room humidifier, add a capful or two of *Sol-U-Mel* each time you refill the water tank to help prevent the growth of mold, bacteria, fungus, and viruses in the humidifier and in the room air.

Take *ProVex* and/or *ProVex-Plus* when exposed to toxic substances to help minimize oxidation within the body.

ALLERGIC REACTIONS

Skin rashes, itching skin, sore throat, runny nose, sinus congestion, eye irritation, headaches and fatigue are common symptoms of allergy sufferers. While individuals vary in their degree of sensitivity to allergic substances, it is important to minimize discomfort and prevent complications such as infections. Many of the aromatic oils from Melaleuca alternifolia have local-acting, anti-inflammatory and desensitization effects.

*Always try to avoid the allergen when possible. Your health care provider can help you determine the substances you are reacting to and begin a program to gain permanent desensitization. Applying *T36-C5* directly to exposed skin reaction sites (hands, arms, legs, feet, scalp, neck and abdomen) usually neutralizes the local histamine reaction and reduces symptoms. A word of caution—do not apply any Melaleuca products near or in the eyes. Avoid rubbing the affected skin to prevent further irritation. *Renew Intensive Skin Therapy* or *MelaGel* can be applied afterwards to give long-lasting protection. Soaking in a bath containing 1 oz of *Renew Bath Oil* (and 1 oz of *Sol-U-Mel* if infections are present) offers an added soothing effect.

Remember, allergies are the result of an unhealthy immune system so maximizing your nutrition is essential. Besides eating wholesome food, the *Vitality Pack* with *Oligofructose Complex*, *CellWise*, *ProVex* and/or *ProVex-Plus*, give extra protection against allergies by providing antioxidants in the form of beta-carotene, vitamin C, vitamin E, citrus bioflavonoids, and proanthocyanidins. Antioxidants reduce histamine levels, which cause the itching, rashes, and burning. The calcium in *Vitality Calcium Complete* often gives immediate relief from sneezing and general body aches during a reaction.

For both chronic and acute allergies/hay fever, many people find relief from *ProVex* and/or *ProVex-Plus*. These may need to be taken at the rate of 1 capsule for every 25 pounds of body weight in order to provide the most relief and prevention of allergies.

When your nose and throat are affected by hay fever, dust, pollen or food reactions, try this: breathe hot steam from either a vaporizer or bowl of steaming water with 10 drops of *T36-C5* and 2 capfuls of *Sol-U-Mel* for a minimum of 15 to 20 minutes twice a day (all night is even better). This gives welcome relief.

ALZHEIMER'S DISEASE

Alzheimer's disease is the most common form of dementia experienced by people aged 60 and over. The disease may start with simple forgetfulness (most people with mild forgetfulness do not have Alzheimer's, however), but then may progress to more severe symptoms such as an inability to perform everyday tasks or to recognize faces of loved ones. Researchers have been unable to determine a cause or cure for the disease, but have found that patients who change their diet to lower their risk factors for cardiovascular disease might also lower their risk for Alzheimer's disease.

* Be sure to include plenty of fresh fruits, vegetables, nuts and seeds in your daily diet. Supplement your diet with as many antioxidants as possible, such as in the *Vitality 6 50+* pack, and *Unforgettables* for cognitive health.

AMPUTATION

This is a surgical removal of a portion or all of a limb. The word amputation may also be used to describe the removal of fingers and toes. It is estimated that 70% of all of the non-traumatic amputations are performed annually on diabetics. Diabetes inhibits the free flow of blood to areas farthest from the heart. This means that fingers and particularly toes are susceptible to the development of gangrene.

* Once an extremity has reached the point of gangrene, it must be taken care of by your health care provider. In order to prevent that condition, diabetics in particular need to be very aware of circulation in their extremities. Several things might be tried. Soak the feet or hands in a mixture of *Sol-U-Mel*, mixed with Epsom salts and hot water for up to a half hour at a time. After drying the area, apply either *T36-C5* or *T40-C3*. *Pain-A-Trate* is also good for stimulating the flow of blood and enhancing circulation. See also *Diabetic Gangrene*.

ANAL FISSURES

The anus is a muscle at the end of the digestive path. Many conditions can cause pain in this area, such as hemorrhoids and fissures. If blood is detected in your stool, check with your health care provider immediately. Don't play games with your health. This can be an indication of problems much too serious for self-diagnosis.

* Be aware of whether or not your diet contains enough fiber. Two servings of **FiberWise** can supply nearly half the fiber an average adult needs on a daily basis. In addition to the eight glasses of water that each person should consume daily, drinking multiple cups of **Melaleuca Herbal Tea** would be very helpful. It can be drunk either cold or hot and is quite tasty.

In a warm (not hot) bath, add ½ oz each of **Nature's Cleanse** and **Sol-U-Mel**. After enjoying a healing bath, apply **MelaGel** to the sore anal area.

Be very aware of your nutritional supplements. The **Vitality 6** pack will provide essential supplements that are needed for a healthy lifestyle.

Remember to wear loose-fitting clothing during your healing process. There is no point in further aggravating your condition. Also, consistently use white toilet paper in your bathroom. Many colored or printed toilet papers contain formaldehyde since this chemical tends to hold both the color and the pattern. Formaldehyde is a poison and should be avoided at all costs.

ANEMIA

Insufficient red blood cells and/or hemoglobin cause fatigue and lack of motivation. *Blood loss* due to hemorrhage somewhere within the body or *decreased production* of red blood cells are the two causes. There are several conditions that result in anemia. Iron deficiency due to poor nutrition is most common in teenage girls and the elderly. Those with anorexia, starvation or bulimia-style eating disorders also suffer from anemia since they fail to get the irons and vitamins into their system that can begin to assure some semblance of good health. Heavy menstrual flow is often associated with anemia. Drugs such as aspirin thin the blood and can cause micro-hemorrhage in the gastrointestinal tract. This could cause anemia, especially in women who use this medication for menstrual pain and cramps. Copper, zinc, protein and B vitamins are essential for a healthy supply of red blood cells. Deficiencies of any of these can lead to various types of anemia, which are often difficult to diagnose. A sudden drop in red blood cells (hemolytic anemia) or hemoglobin (hypochromic anemia) is one of the early warning signs of cancer. Infestation of bowel parasites from outdoor pets can also lead to anemia and malnutrition. Often, anemia can only be clearly identified by a complete blood chemistry and blood cell study.

* Avoid over-the-counter drugs. Ask your doctor about the side effects of any prescription medications. Eat an adequate amount of raw fruit and vegetables, whole grains, and fish. Take the **Vitality Pack** with **Oligofructose Complex**, **CellWise**, **ProVex** and/or **ProVex-Plus** regularly to supplement the iron and essential nutrients that are needed to ensure adequate red blood cell building blocks. Drink two cups of *Melaleuca Herbal Tea* each day to maximize kidney detoxification. Get 20 minutes of moderate exercise five times each week to adequately oxygenate the body.

ANTISEPTIC

An ounce of prevention is worth a pound of cure when it comes to germs that cause infection. Any break in the skin is a potential site for infection. Use protective gear, clothing, boots, hats, or goggles when needed.

* Bathe or shower with *Antibacterial Liquid Soap* or *The Gold Bar*, which leaves a fine layer of Melaleuca oil on the skin. For jobs where your hands will become dirty, use *Clear Defense Hand Gel*, *Antibacterial Liquid Soap*, or *Sol-U-Mel* as a preventive hand glove. If an injury occurs, there is a barrier between you and the awaiting germs. You can simply rinse the pre-treated area with warm water and lift the germs off with the soap. Apply *Renew Intensive Skin Therapy* afterwards. This is especially good for mechanics to prevent grease and grime (often loaded with germs) from forcing their way into the skin. It is also especially effective around farm machinery and animals. Carry *Clear Defense Hand Gel* or *Wipes* with you at all times when in public places so it can be used before meals and after the use of a public rest room. Even shaking hands can spread dangerous and contagious germs, so become more aware of where you are and what and whom you touch.

To help prevent the spread of germs in the home or office, spray surfaces with *Sol-U-Guard Botanical*, a broad-spectrum disinfectant that is 99.99% effective against common kitchen and bathroom germs. In addition to bathroom and kitchen nonporous surfaces, also spray doorknobs, telephones, light switches, toys, etc.

ANXIETY

When a person gets excited there are several adrenal hormones that are released to combat the stress. When these hormones are either set off randomly or they do not return to normal after stimulation, it creates a condition known as anxiety. Menopause or PMS can induce anxiety in some women. While adequate exercise and rest are vital, nutritional supplementation can also be beneficial.

* Good nutrition should include the *Vitality Pack* with *Oligofructose Complex* and *CellWise*, along with *ProVex* and/or *ProVex-Plus*. Taking *ProvexCV* may also be wise, depending on your age. *Luminex* and *Sustain Sport* taken as directed can be very helpful as well. Hormonal fluctuations resulting in anxiety during times of PMS or menopause might improve when *EstrAval* is taken daily.

Recent studies have shown that anxiety disorders can also have a real physical basis. Experts believe that brain chemistry may malfunction so that

HEALTHY BODY

some areas of the brain become hyperactive and release norepinephrine, which causes blood pressure to rise with rapid pulse and breathing—the classic symptoms of panic attack. The *Vitality Pack* is essential, and it may help to throw in an extra *Vitality Calcium Complete* since the calcium and magnesium will do a lot to relieve anxiety, tension and nervousness and promote a sense of calm. *RestEZ* can also be a tremendous benefit and can be taken during the day to help relieve severe anxiety.

ARMS/LEGS ASLEEP

Loss of feeling in the arms or legs (paraesthesia) can be caused by pressure on muscles, which temporarily cuts off the blood supply. It also can be progressive due to peripheral circulatory problems where the sensory nerves in the extremities do not receive enough blood. Some people who have handled toxic solvents, paints, cleaners, pesticides, or herbicides experience extremity paraesthesia soon after.

* Use *Pain-A-Trate* on any tender muscles in your neck and upper back. If you are susceptible to paraesthesia, do not try to sleep in a moving vehicle without an inflatable cushion behind your neck. Trade legs often when holding someone on your lap. Be checked by a doctor or chiropractor when you have any kind of traumatic accident to your neck or back. Always have adequate ventilation when using volatile solvents or paint. Remember, at first your nose will alert you to the danger. If unheeded the signal will diminish until you "get used to it." Use only environmentally safe sprays.

ProVex and/or *ProVex-Plus* should be taken daily. Take the *Vitality Pack* with *Oligofructose Complex* and *CellWise* as directed, to offset the destruction of nutrients by these toxic substances in your liver. Take *FiberWise* drink or bars to carry the substances out of your digestive tract quickly. Drink extra water, *Melaleuca Herbal Tea* and *Sustain Sport* to maintain blood sugar during environmentally stressful times. Exercise after an exposure to harsh volatile chemicals to flush the lungs. Sweat from exercise or in a sauna or steam bath to wash out as many toxins as possible. If symptoms persist longer than 24 hours, see your health care provider if you haven't already.

ARTHRITIS

Hot, red, painful, stiff and swollen joints of the hands, wrists, elbows, neck, back, hips, and knees are common symptoms of arthritis. It can be caused by old injuries, allergies, gout, mineral deficiencies, hyperactive immune response, toxicity, poor circulation, handling of cold things, or prescription drug side effects.

It may start as a vitamin deficiency. Studies show that cartilage cannot grow without sufficient levels of the vitamin known as pantothenic acid. Without the production of new cartilage to replace damaged or worn spots in your joints, deterioration occurs. This condition is known as osteoarthritis.

Osteoarthritis is probably the most common form of arthritis. It afflicts millions and is characterized by chronic inflammation occurring in usually more than one joint. According to the Arthritis Foundation, most people over sixty show to have it on X-ray but may not have actual symptoms yet. Knees, hips, feet, hands, the spine and shoulders can all be affected. Osteoarthritis is known as the joint's cartilage degeneration. Some believe it affects weight-bearing joints such as those mentioned—hips, feet and knees—and they are partially correct. However, it also brings devastatingly harmful movement impediments to the hand, wrists, and fingers. Osteoarthritis is chronic and found primarily in adults older than their mid-30s.

Rheumatoid Arthritis is caused by inflammation of a joint membrane lining. Not only are joints swollen and painful, but they are also "red" and "hot." Common areas affected are wrists, hands and feet. It is characterized by a pain that is ongoing and never seems to be adequately relieved or alleviated. Women from their 30s to their 50s have a greater likelihood for developing this form of arthritis.

* More remedies are sold to treat arthritis than any other common condition. The best long-term treatment is the one that gets at the cause. Some cases of arthritis respond to reducing white sugar, white flour, nicotine, caffeine, and alcohol. Generally avoid cold temperatures to the affected joint. For osteoarthritis, take **Replenex** or **Replenex Extra Strength** to help rebuild cartilage and restore normal joint function. For all forms of arthritis, take **ProVex** and/or **ProVex-Plus** to help reduce inflammation. There are those that say **ProvexCV** has made a remarkable difference for them.

Some forms of arthritis respond well to resting the joint, while other forms, such as osteoarthritis, respond to motion such as knitting. **Pain-A-Trate** and **T36-C5** can be applied to the affected area to achieve rapid relief of pain and stiffness. Taking the **Vitality Pack** with **Oligofructose Complex** and **CellWise** as directed provides essential trace nutrients for reducing further injury and increasing healing. Since dehydrated joints ache, drink more liquids, including 2 to 4 cups of **Melaleuca Herbal Tea** per day.

ASTHMA

Congestion and restriction of the lungs causes labored breathing and wheezing, and affects one out of every twelve people. Many are small children. Although it is associated with airborne allergies and occasional food sensitivities, improvement can occur by following a few simple suggestions.

* Identify and restrict all sensitizing substances (*see Air Purification*). Rid your home of all toxic personal care and home care products. Convert your home to Melaleuca products, beginning with

the *EcoSense Laundry System*. As you convert your home to the safer products, remember to shampoo your carpets with *MelaMagic* or one of the other effective Melaleuca products. See the *Carpet Cleaner* section in this book.

Adults and teenagers should take the *Vitality Pack* with *Oligofructose Complex* along with *CellWise*, and children should take the *Vita-Bears*. *ProVex* and/or *ProVex-Plus*—1 capsule for each 25 lbs of body weight per day should be taken to increase resistance to attacks. Get enough rest. If congestion exists, increase the amount of *ProVex* and/or *ProVex-Plus* until you find the level that provides relief. *ProVex* and/or *ProVex-Plus*, as well as the *Vitality Pack* or *Vita-Bears* have given many asthma sufferers much relief.

Further relief may come from a humidifier or vaporizer with water plus 10 drops of *T36-C5* and 2 capfuls of *Sol-U-Mel*. Use in the bedroom each night for best results.

Adults can try adding 10 to 20 drops of Tabasco sauce (capsicum) in a few ounces of water and drinking it immediately before a meal to reduce congestion and thin mucous in the lungs.

One drop of *T36-C5* on a cotton swab, gently used to clean pollen and dust from each nostril before bed, has helped many children.

ATHEROSCLEROSIS

Hardening of the arteries can lead to high blood pressure, strokes, shortness of breath and cold hands and feet, as well as senility and premature aging. Cholesterol (LDL—the bad kind) and ionic calcium make up part of the "cement" that lines arteries of the liver, bowel, lungs, brain, kidneys, legs and arms. Several common-sense suggestions can help.

* Begin taking *ProvexCV*, *Phytomega*, the *Vitality Pack* with *Oligofructose Complex*, and *CellWise*. Every adult should be on this regimen for prevention of atherosclerosis. The probiotics in *Florify* have also been found to lower cholesterol levels. All of these supplements make up the *Vitality 6* pack which should be taken regularly by every person who wants to avoid cardiovascular disease and other health problems.

Stop smoking and avoid smokers. Avoid animal fats and cooked vegetable oils. Reduce total fat to less than 20% of your total diet. Eat a good variety of raw fruit and vegetables each day. Begin a gradual daily exercise program. Eat an *Access Performance Bar* 15 minutes before exercising and drink a *Sustain Sport* one half hour after exercising to speed up the fat-burning process. *FiberWise* bars contain 5 grams of fiber and are an excellent quick snack, and fiber is an important heart health. Drink 3 to 4 cups of *Melaleuca Herbal Tea* daily.

ATHLETE'S FOOT

Athlete's foot is a fungus known as tinea pedis. When the fungus infects the upper body, this is known as tinea corporis, or ringworm, causing raised and reddened rashes with clear centers. Athlete's foot is commonly found in athletic showering areas and long-term athlete's foot often involves the toenails and can totally destroy the nail plate and/or enter the bone. Blistering can occur when the immune system becomes sensitized to the fungus. It can usually be found between the toes where the skin has a greater tendency to crack, blister, or become sore and itchy. The infection will persist indefinitely until treatment is effective. The general health of the individual tends to determine the magnitude of the infection and extent of the symptoms. The good news is that athlete's foot rarely develops in young children or in those who go barefoot or wear sandals.

Products with Melaleuca oil are highly effective in the treatment of foot and toenail fungal infections. It is much more effective than griseo-fulvin, which has been commonly used. If the two are used together, the griseofulvin may lessen in effectiveness. It is also important to note that griseofulvin may be toxic to the liver and liver enzyme functions must be monitored during therapy with this drug.

Several years ago in a report issued by *The Physician and Sportsmedicine* it was stated that in some instances irritation was misdiagnosed as athlete's foot when it is really an allergic reaction to a chemical in sneaker insoles. This "contact dermatitis" can be differenti-ated from athlete's foot because the reaction occurs mainly on the ball, outer sides and top of the foot where it comes in contact with the shoe. Athlete's foot usually appears in the cracks between the toes.

If you have contact dermatitis, an entirely different method of treat-ment is required. With contact dermatitis, you must not use any pure Melaleuca alternifolia oil. To be safe, avoid every product that has the pure oil as an ingredient. For additional information, please read the information under *Dermatitis*.

*As in most infections, prevention is the best treatment. Always wear shower sandals when in public showers, such as athletic locker rooms and swimming pools. Spray feet with *Body Satin Foot Spray* and apply *Dermatin Antifungal Creme* between toes and to bottoms of feet immediately after showering. *Body Satin Foot Scrub* and *Body Satin Foot Lotion* can also be used to cleanse and stimulate circulation. Direct sunlight and air-drying the feet after showering or swimming is also a helpful preventive measure. Take the *Vitality Pack* with *Oligofructose Complex*, *CellWise*, and a *ProVex* product daily, to optimize trace nutri-ents. Drink 2–3 cups of *Melaleuca Herbal Tea* daily.

To eliminate athlete's foot, clean the affected area well with *Antibacterial Liquid Soap* and water. A great foot soak for athlete's foot

---

*The information presented in this book is in no way intended as a substitute for medical counseling. Always consult your physician before starting any course of supplementation or treatment, particularly if you are pregnant or currently under medical care. Always read and follow product packaging directions and warnings.

is to combine **Tough & Tender, Liquid Pain-A-Trate,** and **Renew Bath Oil** in a pan of hot water. An alternative would be to use just **Tough & Tender** or add a little **Sol-U-Mel** or **Renew Bath Oil** and soak your feet for about 30 minutes. For a severe case of athlete's foot, put 4 tbsp of **Sol-U-Mel** in hot water and soak for 20-30 minutes, morning and night for one week. After soaking, apply **Dermatin Antifungal Cream** as directed. It will kill fungus and bacteria. **T36-C5**, followed by **Renew Intensive Skin Therapy** or **MelaGel** could also be used each morning and night. If there is no improvement after one week, discontinue use and consult your health care provider if you haven't already.

Be sure to wear clean white cotton (if possible) socks daily. These should be washed only using **EcoSense Laundry System.** Don't use store-bought laundry products because too often they contain harmful chemicals. Each time you change socks, dribble a few drops of **T36-C5** on the clean socks. Rub them together before putting them on. You might even spray the inside of your shoes with a mixture of one-half ounce of **Sol-U-Mel** with four ounces of water.

To avoid reinfection, always wear bathing slippers in public swimming pools, saunas, and showers, as well as in dorms and hotels. Dry your feet carefully after washing. Avoid wearing polyester socks and shoes not made of leather. Don't wear rubber boots or tennis shoes the entire day and change your socks every day.

To help avoid infecting other family members, spray shower and bathtub surfaces, as well as bathroom floors, with **Sol-U-Guard Botanical** disinfectant. **Never use Sol-U-Guard on natural stone surfaces.**

ATHLETIC INJURIES

The human body is designed for motion. Actually, everyone is an athlete—you are either actively practicing or you are not. More middle-aged and elderly people are enjoying the benefits of regular exercise than ever before. Typical athletic injuries in all ages include pulled muscles, strained ligaments and tendons, bruises and muscle cramps. Common sense tells us that a proper warm up and cool down before and after exercise is essential.

* Take the **Vitality Pack** with **Oligofructose Complex** as well as **ProVex** or **ProVex-Plus** to optimize tissue-strengthening nutrients. **CellWise** should also be taken. Of course all adults should be taking **ProvexCV** as well to support a healthy cardiovascular system. Take more **Vitality Calcium Complete** if you have muscle cramps after a workout. Eat an **Access Performance Bar** 15 minutes before exercise to inhibit adenosine and open fat stores in the body for energy. **ProFlex** helps restore, repair, and strengthen muscle tissues, and helps provide energy. **Sustain Sport** can be mixed in your water bottle for continual replenishment of waning blood sugar.

Joints are repeatedly stressed as we go about our daily activities, and the body must constantly work to repair them. With age, the body becomes less efficient. **Replenex**, with 1500 mg of the purest glucosamine available, plus ginger, bromelain and green tea extracts to reduce inflammation and discomfort, helps preserve the health of joints, thereby promoting ease of movement.

Pain-A-Trate should be in the equipment bag of every athlete. Immediate application of **Pain-A-Trate** to any closed injury will start the healing process. Regular application of **T36-C5** stimulates circulation to injured tissues as well. Ice is good for injured joints, muscles, tendons and ligaments. Apply ice for no more than 5 to 10 minutes at a time. Longer treatment periods can actually cause frostbite or reverse the anti-inflammatory effect. Heat can cause problems so it should be avoided, in most cases, for the first 24 to 48 hours after an injury to bruised or pulled muscles. A health care provider, trained to treat sports injuries, should see chronic or untreated injuries.

BABY TEETH

All 20 baby teeth are usually present by the age of 3. Children will lose these teeth between the ages of 5 and 12, as the size of the growing head and mouth require larger teeth. Care and protection of these teeth is important to ensure a healthy environment for the permanent teeth, which may need to last 75 to 100 years.

* Do not put a child to bed with a nursing bottle of fruit juice or formula. This is the most common cause of dissolved baby teeth and the need for capping. As soon as the baby teeth appear, brush with **Koala Pals Sparkling Tooth Gel** or **Classic Tooth Polish**, after every meal. Give your child **Vita-Bears** to insure strong healthy teeth. Children should start seeing their dentist regularly by the age of four unless there are obvious cavities prior to that age.

BACK PAIN

More than one half of the adult American population suffers with back pain. Our sedentary lifestyles, motorized transportation, and poor diets cause a large portion of our discomfort. Stretching and strengthening exercises, eating a healthy diet, maintaining a healthy weight, supplementing calcium, magnesium, and micro-nutrients, and correcting spinal injuries before they become chronic can go a long way toward reducing back pain.

*Apply **Pain-A-Trate** to over-worked muscles. Apply moderate heat (use cold immediately after injury or acute pain 5 to 10 minutes each hour for the first 6 to 24 hours before using heat). Massage **T36-C5** over spastic back muscles to promote the relaxation reflex. Take **Replenex**. Drink 2 to 4 cups of **Melaleuca Herbal Tea** each day.

Take **ProVex** and/or **ProVex-Plus**, in addition to the **Vitality Pack** with **Oligofructose Complex** and **CellWise**, to help heal collagen structures in your back.

BAD BREATH

Bacteria that live inside the mouth create most bad breath. Sometimes it is caused by foods such as onions and garlic. Some find a coffee drinker's breath offensive, especially after several cups have been swallowed and digested. Alcohol and especially beer breath can be very offensive. Smokers generally have bad breath. The residues of digestion caused by sulfur compounds such as certain cheeses, cabbage, beans, some other milk products, and sausages may create bad breath. Another culprit can be medications such as tranquilizers, cough and congestion medicines, and other pharmaceuticals used to control angina and hypertension.

Breath-Away Mouth Rinse is an excellent start in improving one's bad breath regardless of the reason. Another way to improve is to change to *Melaleuca's Dental Care* products. This will include adopting the regular use of products such as the *Classic Tooth Polish*, the *Classic Dental Floss, Hot/Cool Shot Sugarless Gum*, and *Hot/Cool Shot Breath Spray*. In addition, *Melaleuca's Dental Care* products clean and stimulate taste buds, thus improving your ability to taste food.

Drinking a sufficient amount of water each day can help improve your breath, too. When you do this, include several cups of *Melaleuca Herbal Tea*.

Keep your toothbrush germ-free by soaking it in a solution of 5-10 drops of *T36-C5* and ½ cup of water for ten minutes and then rinsing. *Using Breath-Away Mouth Rinse* is also very effective, as is the simple process of applying a couple of drops of *T36-C5* directly to your toothbrush once or twice each week. (It is not advisable to use peroxide, as it will disturb the oral flora. *T36-C5* will not do this.) Replace your toothbrush at least once each month and immediately after any illness.

Breath-Away Mouth Rinse concentrate is an excellent choice in that you can determine the strength and flavor of your gargling or rinse solution. Gargle daily after meals and before bedtime. Bacteria in your mouth are the principal causes of mouth odor. To help kill serious odors caused by bacteria, add 2 or 3 drops of *T36-C5* to the *Breath-Away Mouth Rinse* before gargling. This aids in relieving odors, which arise from the intestinal tract.

Most commercial mouthwashes use alcohol as their antiseptic, which is found in concentrations as high as 30%. Studies suggest that this alcohol content is toxic to the mucous membranes, particularly those of the oral mucosa and that regular use of alcohol-based mouthwashes significantly increases cancer risks. This is another great reason to use *Breath-Away Mouth Rinse*.

BARBER'S ITCH

This is caused by a fungus from an improperly cleaned razor, shaving cream brush, or electric shaver. Fortunately, the use of disposable razors and canned shaving foam and gel has made this fungus much less common. The rash leaves the skin slightly flaky and (looking) sore. See the sections on *Athlete's Foot* and *Acne* in this book.

* Three things that you might try: the *Zap-It!* products and the *Dermatin Antifungal Creme*. Follow the directions on each of these products. Also periodically add a drop of *T36-C5* to your razor before using it. Use *Alloy Shave Gel* and *Alloy After Shave* for a close, safe shave and avoid this problem altogether.

BATHING

One of the most self-pampering events of life is taking a hot bath. Getting the most out of your time and effort is essential. Showers expose people with respiratory or skin sensitivities to 8 to 10 times the amount of chlorine as bathing. Chlorine-sensitive people should run hot bath water and allow it to de-gas for about 5 minutes with the window open or the vent fan running before plunging in. Never take long baths (30 minutes or more) with a breeze in the room, as the lungs are susceptible to infection from cool air when the body is heated above 100 degrees.

* Put *Sol-U-Mel* (1 oz per tub) in the water to thoroughly sanitize and disinfect the skin. The *Renew Bath Oil* is real therapy for the pores of the skin. It is also very relaxing to simply soak for ten minutes or so in a warm bath to which 8-10 drops of *T36-C5* have been added.

For alternate bathing suggestions, see the section on *Sitz Bath*.

BED SORES

Also known as decubitus ulcers, bedsores occur when people are bedfast or confined to a wheelchair. A lamb's wool or "egg carton" foam pad can be placed under the person to prevent the deep crater sores from forming. Daily inspection is important to identify the blanched skin heralding the onset of a bedsore. Once started, bedsores can lead to infections and delayed healing. Prevention is the best treatment.

* Healing begins at the outer edges and works inward when pressure is removed from the area. Apply *T36-C5* to any blanched skin areas before the sore begins. It can often be halted at this stage. If a sore is present, gently wash the area with *Antibacterial Liquid Soap* enriched with one capful of *Sol-U-Mel* in 1 qt of warm water. Apply *Triple Antibiotic Ointment* or *MelaGel*. Cover with loose gauze. Use a minimum amount of tape. Repeat washing and *Triple Antibiotic Ointment* every 8 hours until the wound heals. This can take from one day to several weeks depending upon the overall health of the individual. Some health care facilities will not allow the *T36-C5* to be brought in without a physician's orders. In such cases, *Renew Intensive Skin Therapy* or *Moisturizing Hand Creme* has been used very effectively. They can also be used as covering lotion after the bedsore has been treated.

HEALTHY BODY

It is important to couple treatment with preventive actions that will help prevent future bedsores from forming. Minimizing pressure on areas prone to develop sores is crucial. Placing pillows, cushions and ripple types of pressurized mattresses under the patient will help decrease the chances of the patient developing future sores. Sheepskin wraps for the heels and buttocks may also be helpful. A growing list of long-term care-staffs are now using Melaleuca alternifolia oil and products containing the oil, having discovered the oil's effectiveness in accelerating healing and alleviating patient discomfort.

WARNING: Bedsores should be taken very seriously in diabetics, persons on immune-suppressive drugs, and those with leg ulcers due to poor circulation.

BEE AND WASP STINGS

Bees are territorial creatures. They defend their territory by injecting a powerful chemical, formic acid, into the intruder. This injection also contains traces of immune reactive agents that can provoke violent reactions in humans.

*Grab and yank out the stinger as fast as you can. Wash the area with *Antibacterial Liquid Soap* and cold water. Immediately apply *T36-C5* or *MelaGel* to stop pain and prevent secondary infection. Do not use any other home remedies, such as baking soda, with the Melaleuca products for this. Reapply every 15 minutes until all signs and symptoms are gone. Four to six applications may be necessary. Take *ProVex* or *ProVex-Plus* immediately and continue for 24 hours.

WARNING: When a person is allergic to bee or wasp stings, this can be life threatening. The allergic person should carry an antidote kit containing adrenaline and benadryl. Administer this according to the directions before any other therapy. Shortness of breath or difficulty breathing, puffy or swollen throat or eyes, rapid heart rate, dizziness, or profuse sweating are signs of an allergic reaction and can appear within 10 to 30 minutes after being stung. **DO NOT DELAY! GET EMERGENCY HELP!**

BENIGN PROSTATIC HYPERPLASIA (BPH)
(Prostate Health)

As men age, and especially after "male menopause," testosterone is inefficiently utilized in the prostate gland. Physical trauma (sitting), stress, excessive animal fat intake, and nutrient deficiencies transform testosterone into dihydrotestosterone. This causes the prostate gland to enlarge and become less functional. Slow or dribbling urination, difficulty starting urination, incomplete emptying of the bladder, getting up multiple times at night, and reduced sexual function accompany this condition. After the age of 50, approximately one half of all men experience symptoms of BPH. BPH does not indicate cancer and should

---

be differentiated from this more severe condition.

* Get an annual prostate exam after the age of 50 including the sensitive blood tumor marker for prostate cancer called PSA. Prevention is the best treatment. Regular hot baths seem to reduce the incidence of BPH. Native Japanese men have a lower incidence of BPH and other prostate challenges due to their custom of very hot baths. Americans tend to shower and have a statistically higher incidence of prostate challenges. The ingredients in **ProstAvan** have a proven effect in helping prevent BPH and should be taken every day by men over the age of 40. One extra tablet for every decade past 40 is advised. **Luminex** is advised to maximize cerebral circulation and hormone regulation. The **Vitality Pack** with **Oligofructose Complex** and **CellWise** are vital. Men with higher levels of vitamin E in their systems have been found to have a 41% less incidence of fatal prostate cancer.

ProVex and/or **ProVex-Plus** should also be included in your daily routine. Of course, **ProvexCV** should always be taken for cardiovascular protection. The recommended dosage is 1 capsule per each 35 lbs of body weight taken daily. Drinking 3–4 cups of **Melaleuca Herbal Tea** each day is also very helpful.

BLACK EYE

Bruising almost anywhere on the head resulting from an automobile accident, sports accident, bump, fall, or even dental work, can cause a black eye.

*Apply an ice pack as soon as possible to the affected area, to slow down facial swelling. Do not use any Melaleuca products that contain Melaleuca oil near the eye, as its aromatic vapor is drying to the eye and may cause pain. Take the **Vitality Pack** with **Oligofructose Complex** as well as **ProVex** and/or **ProVex-Plus** to speed healing and prevent easy bruising.

BLADDER INFECTIONS

Bladder infections, most often in women, can be bothersome at best, and a potential full-blown illness at worst. Underwear made of synthetic fabric causes excessive perspiration, which leads to bacterial growth at the opening of the urethra. Some even think that getting too cool can aid in the development of a bladder infection, which can possibly be traced back to reasons related to fashion. Not drinking enough water encourages bacteria to grow within the urethra and bladder. Repeated infections are a cause for alarm.

WARNING: Recurrent infections treated with antibiotics can lead to highly resistant strains of bacteria and yeast infections.

*As a preventative, take **CranBarrier** daily. The ingredients in **CranBarrier** have been shown to prevent bacteria from adhering to the cells lining the bladder, and thus harmful bacteria is flushed harmlessly out of the urinary tract.

Drink 2 to 6 cups of **Melaleuca Herbal Tea** along with 2–4 quarts of pure water each day. Wear cotton underwear. Douche with **Nature's Cleanse** weekly to reduce bacteria in the area. Add 1 oz of **Sol-U-Mel** in the rinse water of washing cycles when laundering undergarments. Use the **EcoSense Laundry System** to avoid harsh chemicals.

Use white toilet paper since many colored or printed toilet papers contain formaldehyde, which should be avoided if at all possible. Wiping from the front to the back prevents the possibility of introducing bacteria into the urethra. When treating a bladder infection, add 10 drops of **T36-C5** to a quart of distilled water and dab the external urinal tract after each urination with a cotton ball soaked in this mixture. Keeping the abdominal area warm is very comforting, as is massaging the lower back with **Pain-A-Trate**.

There is some indication that baths can contribute to bladder infections, probably due to the harsh chemicals in most bath soaps. If you prefer to bathe rather than shower, bathe with **The Gold Bar** and/or add 3 to 10 drops of **T36-C5** to your bath water.

BLEEDING GUMS

Plaque or periodontal infections can cause bleeding gums, swollen gums or dental pain. Brushing too hard is a common cause. Chronic vitamin C deficiency, alveolar (jaw) bone loss, or chemical poisoning are other possible causes. The mouth is the literal window to overall health of the body.

Diabetics and pregnant women both tend to suffer from bleeding gums as they experience changes in hormone levels. When noted in youngsters, it is oftentimes seen in a milder form.

Bleeding without cause such as from injury or infection should be investigated. It is not normal to have bleeding gums.

* Switching to the **Melaleuca Dental Care** products often gives relief from bleeding gums. Regular brushing with **Classic Tooth Polish** and rinsing with **Breath-Away Mouth Rinse** is a good way to control the buildup of bacteria-causing plaque. Daily flossing with **Classic Dental Floss** and chewing **Hot/Cool Shot Sugarless Gum** can clean between teeth where a brush cannot reach. Just before bedtime, dip a pixel brush into the **T36-C5** and "brush" in between your teeth at the gum line. It will provide a "deep cleaning" to help alleviate pockets and sore gums.

Drinking 2 to 4 cups of **Melaleuca Herbal Tea** per day helps promote a healthy environment in the mouth. Take the **Vitality Pack** with **Oligofructose Complex**, **CellWise**, **ProVex** and/or **ProVex-Plus** while eating a healthy diet.

Using a cotton swab or your fingertip, apply **T36-C5** to affected gums. Most people do not enjoy the taste of pure Melaleuca alternifolia oil, however, a product does not have to taste good or sweet to accomplish healing. A Melaleuca mouth is far better than one harboring sore or bleeding gums. Get professional dental care if bleeding, pain or swelling of gums persists. Regular checkups can prevent dental problems.

BLISTERS

They are frequently caused by friction or by chemical or burn injuries, such as sunburns. Blisters can also be caused by skin conditions such as eczema, impetigo and dermatitis. Sometimes they occur when an area is scratched repeatedly. They appear as oval-shaped, raised areas of skin holding collections of fluid beneath the outer layer. They should not be punctured. Blisters can lead to blood poisoning if not properly treated.

* Blisters diminish rapidly after gingerly applying **T36-C5**. Dab the oil on the blistered area, and then leave it alone until the next application. The blisters will heal over quickly without itching or burning.

If the blister is small and closed, leave it alone. It already has its own natural covering bandage. If it needs protection from further damage, fit some sort of loose bandage about it. If the blister is in a weight-bearing area (big toe, little toe or heel), consider some sort of donut-shaped mole-skin pad to help assure the blister will not break and become worse.

When blisters break, all sorts of potential problems occur. Avoid these if possible. Protect the broken blister from further rubbing with a loose bandage, and avoid the activity that originally caused it. **Triple Antibiotic Ointment** may help, when used as directed. It is the strongest antibiotic ointment you can buy. It kills staph, strep and pseudomonas bacteria, which helps prevent infection in minor burns, cuts and scrapes.

For other types of blisters, see the section on *Cold Sores*.

BODY ODOR

Bacteria, yeast, bowel putrefaction, dental disease, vaginitis, chronic tonsillitis, kidney or liver failure, as well as a number of chronic degenerative disorders and chemical exposures, can lead to a foul body odor. Perfume was invented in Europe during the Dark Ages when the prevailing theory was that bathing and exposing the body to the air was the cause of infectious disease. WRONG! However, body odor may prevent people from getting close enough to you to give you a disease. Foul-smelling sweat (bromhyperhidrosis) is observed in some diabetics, nervous individuals, chronic smokers and people on certain prescription medications. People who have a bad odor become desensitized to it and need to be told by someone who cares. Read the sections on *Bathing* and *Yeast Infections* in this book.

* Drink 2 to 4 cups of **Melaleuca Herbal Tea** each day for detoxification. Take the **Vitality Pack** with **Oligofructose Complex** as directed. Brush regularly with **Classic Tooth Polish**, floss with **Classic Dental Floss,** and use **Breath-Away Mouth Rinse** after meals. Use **Hot/Cool Shot Breath Spray** before going out in public, and chew **Hot/Cool Shot Sugarless Gum** frequently. If you are a smoker, STOP! Bathe instead of showering. Use **Antibacterial Liquid Soap** and **The Gold Bar** lavishly.

A deodorant such as **Alloy Antiperspirant & Deodorant** or **Body Satin Deodorant** should be used after bathing and frequently during warm weather. Women can use **Nature's Cleanse** douche weekly if needed. Often body odor comes from the groin or feet and is caused by a fungus. That's why Melaleuca's extraordinary **Dermatin Antifungal Creme** works so well. It is soothing and healing and contains **T36-C5** as well as clotrimazole. Take **ProVex** and/or **ProVex-Plus** daily.

Pass the "odor test" from someone in your family before you use perfumes and colognes. When serious health concerns are causing the body odor, consult your health care provider.

BOILS

Staphylococcus organisms can cause raised, red, hard, hot and extremely painful pus-filled skin abscesses. They may appear anywhere on the body. Ears, nose, fingers and scalp are the most painful sites due to thin skin and constant pressure. The boil may start very small and then become red as it grows into a painful, pus-filled lump. The staphylococcus organism may be contracted from farm animals and it can remain dormant in the body for years before erupting, usually when the person is run-down, tired and overly stressed. Those with depressed immune systems and those with diabetes are more likely to develop boils.

WARNING: Staphylococcus is very infectious, and many strains are becoming resistant to prescription antibiotics. If fever is present, consult your health care provider immediately.

*Apply **T36-C5** every hour to a developing boil. Some boils can be stopped at this stage. Leave exposed to the air if possible. When a focal head begins to appear, usually after a couple of days, use a sterilized needle to lance the boil and allow drainage. The release of pressure usually provides immediate relief of pain. Continue applying **T36-C5** as long as drainage lasts. Soaking the site in a solution of 1 oz **Sol-U-Mel** and 1 tbsp Epsom salts in a quart of hot water can speed drainage. Apply **Triple Antibiotic Ointment** to a soft gauze bandage and cover. Drink 2 to 6 cups of **Melaleuca Herbal Tea** each day. Take the **Vitality Pack** with **Oligofructose Complex** as directed. If redness and swelling does not disappear after 7 days, see your health care provider if you haven't already. Take **ProVex** and/or **ProVex-Plus** daily.

BROMHIDROSIS (FOOT ODOR)

Excessively sweaty feet can occur in people of all ages. While it is often attributed to nervousness, it can be caused by other factors.

* Use **The Gold Bar** or **Antibacterial Liquid Soap** to wash the feet, including the areas between the toes. Rinse and pat day. Apply **T36-C5** to the soles of the feet and between the toes. Repeat this process at least twice daily. Change socks after each application to help eliminate odor.

Place several drops of Melaleuca oil on your clean socks and rub them together. A few drops inside your shoes may be helpful as well.

An alternative treatment is to use the **Body Satin Foot Scrub**. Be sure to dry the area between your toes carefully before you follow up with the **Body Satin Foot Lotion**. It is amazing how wonderful your feet can feel.

BRONCHITIS

Irritated bronchial membranes in the lung can swell and restrict airflow, resulting in a condition known as bronchitis. Chronic cases can lead to asthma. Possible irritants include: low-grade bacterial, yeast, or viral infections, allergies, household cleaning chemicals, and irritation from cigarette smoke. See the sections on *Asthma*, *Sinus Congestion* and *Coughs* in this book.

* Treat the cause. Protect your air quality by converting your home to Melaleuca home care and personal care products. Drink at least 7 to 10 glasses of water daily. Avoid forced air heat and over-the-counter medicines that dry coughs, suppressing the beneficial coughing action that brings up phlegm. Take the **Vitality Pack** with **Oligofructose Complex**, **CellWise**, **ProVex** and/or **ProVex-Plus** daily. Drink 2 to 6 cups of **Melaleuca Herbal Tea** each day.

Breathe the enriched steam from a vaporizer or bowl of steaming water each morning and night before bed. To do this, add 5 drops of **T36-C5** directly to the water. Form a tent over your head and vaporizer or bowl, breathing the aromatic vapors through your nose and mouth gently into your lungs. Keep your eyes closed. Add 1 or 2 drops of **T36-C5** every 5 minutes for 15 to 20 minutes. (*NOTE:* Do not use **Sol-U-Mel** for this breathing treatment as it can cause irritation to the lungs.) Many people find additional relief when sleeping in a room with a vaporizer or cool mist humidifier. Add two capfuls of **Sol-U-Mel** and 10 drops of **T36-C5** to the tank's water. For acute attacks, put 1 or 2 drops of **T36-C5** on a cotton swab and swab the inside of each nostril. It will also help to steam your chest by placing 5 drops of **T36-C5** on a warm, wet cloth and applying to the chest area.

Try these simple dietary tips: eliminate milk and milk products, substituting other sources of calcium; eat garlic regularly for its antibiotic effects; and eat fresh horseradish and hot mustard regularly to liquefy bronchial secretions.

WARNING: Consult your health care provider, especially if any of these conditions are present: fever, intensified attacks or coughing up blood. A health care provider should always be consulted if the person suffering from bronchitis has other underlying medical or lung problems.

---

* The information presented in this book is in no way intended as a substitute for medical counseling. Always consult your physician before starting any course of supplementation or treatment, particularly if you are pregnant or currently under medical care. Always read and follow product packaging directions and warnings.

BRUISES

Ruptured blood vessels near the surface of the skin or in muscles can occur from injury, infection or blood disorders. Discoloration is at first red, then black and blue, and finally green as healing takes place. Bruises can accompany other injuries such as sprains and strains, fractures or a more serious injury. The elderly and those with more sensitive bodies seem to experience bruises more frequently than does the typically healthy young adult.

* The immediate application of ice to a traumatized area helps reduce bruising. *Pain-A-Trate* has a deep penetrating effect and reduces swelling, increases circulation, and speeds healing. Apply as often as needed until pain, discoloration, and swelling disappear. In place of the *Pain-A-Trate*, *T36-C5* can be used on the bruise. Its penetrating qualities will start the healing from the inside out. This should be repeated at least twice a day. If the bruised injury is near the eye, use caution to not get the oil, or products containing the oil, in or too near the eye.

To prevent easy bruising and speed healing, take *ProVex* and/or *ProVex-Plus* on a daily basis. These improve the strength and elasticity of blood vessels and thus help to prevent bruising.

BUNIONS

Bunions are caused by the swelling of the second synovial joint bursa producing enlargement and displacement of the big toe, which eventually laps over the second toe. They are sometimes caused by misalignment in the spine, causing improper biomechanics in the foot. Some cases have been linked to improperly fitted shoes during childhood development. See the section on *Bursitis* in this book.

*Apply *T36-C5* or *Pain-A-Trate* generously to the affected joint as often as discomfort exists. Soak in a solution of 1 oz of *Sol-U-Mel* and 1 tbsp of Epsom salts per quart of hot water each night. Wear only well-fitting shoes, and see your chiropractor for a walking gait analysis.

Don't forget to pamper your feet with the *Body Satin Foot Scrub* and the *Body Satin Foot Lotion*. It feels so good!

BURNS

No burn is simple to treat! This is true for a first-degree burn that is red and swollen, a second-degree burn that produces a blister, or a third-degree burn that penetrates into muscle and deep tissue and occasionally chars the flesh. Infections, scars, and even shock can result if burns are improperly treated. Too much sun tanning damages skin cells. Ozone depletion in our atmosphere is increasing the amount of harmful ultraviolet rays from sunlight we are exposed to. There is an increase in melanoma skin cancer in those who are exposed to excessive ultraviolet radiation. Always protect your skin from sun exposure by using *Sun Shades Sunscreen*. Use *Sun Shades After Sun Hydrogel E*

HEALTHY BODY

after a day in the sun to instantly cool overexposed skin, reduce redness, and soothe dryness.

* Immediately flush a fresh burn with cold water and apply ice and continue until the area is cold. Pat dry and apply *T36-C5*. Then cover with a thin coat of ***Renew Intensive Skin Therapy***. Take ***ProVex*** and/or ***ProVex-Plus*** daily to speed recovery and reduce scarring. Most first-degree burns will subside very soon. Repeat the *T36-C5* and ***Renew Intensive Skin Therapy*** application every hour until pain is gone.

For second-degree burns, apply *T36-C5* and ***Pain-A-Trate*** each hour until pain and swelling are gone. If the burn does not show signs of healing, seek medical care if you haven't already.

Third-degree burns require professional care immediately, since deep blood vessels, nerves and lymphatic vessels in the skin are damaged. After cold applications, apply *T36-C5* and ***Renew Intensive Skin Therapy*** or ***Triple Antibiotic Ointment***. Cover with a sterile covering. Contact your health care provider immediately!

It is always wise to keep a bottle of *T36-C5* in the kitchen for treating grill and fryer burns. Melaleuca alternifolia oil provides an anesthetic-like action. It soothes and alleviates most pain on contact. It also will help prevent blistering and even scarring. Since infections nearly always develop in severe burns, frequent applications of *T36-C5* will help stop itching and accelerate healing.

For other types of burns, see the sections on *Radiation Burns* and *Razor Burns*.

BURSITIS

Small, fluid-filled, shock-absorbing sacs are present in some joints such as the elbow, knee, shoulder, hip, ankle or big toe. Inflammation of these sacs, called bursa, causes swelling and painful movement of the joint. Trauma, infections, allergies, or toxic accumulation are the usual causes. Gradual development from repetitive motion occupations can lead to chronic bursitis. Reducing coffee drinking curiously reduces bursitis of the shoulder. Acute bursitis can result from prescription drug reactions or sudden injury to the area. See the sections on *Bunions* and *Gout*.

* Take ***ProVex*** and/or ***ProVex-Plus*** to help reduce inflammation. Apply ***Pain-A-Trate*** generously to the affected area every 2 to 4 hours. Moist heat and limiting joint motion may be helpful during the healing phase. Do not exercise the joint until pain and swelling are reduced. If the pain does not subside in a few days, see your health care provider if you haven't already.

Of course, for overall better health, the ***Vitality Pack*** with ***Oligofructose Complex*** should be taken as well as ***CellWise***. ***Replenex*** may also be very helpful with bursitis.

---

*The information presented in this book is in no way intended as a substitute for medical counseling. Always consult your physician before starting any course of supplementation or treatment, particularly if you are pregnant or currently under medical care. Always read and follow product packaging directions and warnings.

CALLUSES

Thickening of normal skin caused by friction, usually on the hands or feet, is seen in people whose work causes repeated pressure on a particular area. Brick layers, musicians, runners, surfers, and dancers develop typical calluses. See the sections on *Corns* and *Warts*.

* Eliminate undue pressure to the affected site. Wear softer and better-fitting shoes. A moleskin or foam rubber protective bandage or arch inserts often help. *MelaGel* and *Renew Intensive Skin Therapy* applied regularly help to prevent friction at the active site. Use *Body Satin Foot Scrub* as directed, then apply *Body Satin Foot Lotion*. Massage this in until the lotion is fully absorbed. You will be amazed at how wonderful your feet feel.

CANCER PREVENTION

Cancer is the second most common life-threatening condition in North America next to heart disease. One of every two citizens will develop it. Most will die despite the best care available. Prevention is still the wisest strategy. While no clear cause for cancer is known, there appears to be a combination of circumstances that greatly increases the risk.

$$\text{Cancer Risk} = \frac{\text{Hereditary Tendency} + \text{Carcinogen Exposure}}{\text{Immune Weakness} + \text{Time}}$$

Each one of us is responsible for our own health. Applying a few simple facts can give us the advantage we need. Many scientists agree that this is a reasonable formula for preventing cancer as well as most chronic degenerative illnesses.

$$\text{Cancer Prevention} = \frac{\text{Optimum Diet} + \text{Exercise \& Rest}}{\text{Positive Attitude} + \text{Lifetime Practice}}$$

* Whether you have had cancer or not, these recommendations can give you a greater measure of future cancer prevention. Many cancer researchers now believe that a combination of approaches will prove to be the best treatment. Study your family tree for patterns of specific cancer types. Breast, colorectal, skin, prostate, uterine, and lung cancers seem to be more hereditarily linked. Tobacco (cigarettes, pipe, smokeless tobacco), fatty diet (animal or cooked vegetable oils), toxic chemical exposure (household cleaners and personal care products, food additives, pesticides, herbicides, etc.), electromagnetic radiation (x-rays, TV, ultraviolet, etc.), and putrefying food in our digestive tract are the greatest known risks.

Get an annual wellness checkup from a preventive health care provider. New blood tests (PSA for prostate, etc.) are being developed to detect antigens (immune sensitive chemicals) given off by early forms of cancer. Follow your doctor's recommendations.

Remove all sources of chemical exposure from your environment (especially household chemicals), and reduce your exposure to electromagnetic radiation as much as possible.

Eat as if your life depended on it, because it does!

Take *ProVex*, and/or *ProVex-Plus*, and *ProvexCV* to ensure adequate antioxidants, B vitamins and essential trace minerals, all of which are associated with cancer prevention. Research findings announced at the American Association of Cancer Research conference in 1998, stated that "a potent grape seed extract, currently available as a dietary supplement, has been shown to significantly inhibit and even kill cancer cells while increasing the growth and viability of normal healthy cells."

Take the *Vitality Pack* with *Oligofructose Complex* and *CellWise*. Researchers at the Arizona Cancer Center found that people who had high amounts of the trace mineral selenium had significantly less cancers.

To help prevent colon cancer, increase your fiber intake by eating a *FiberWise* bar for a quick snack or drinking the excellent *FiberWise* drink. Also, research indicates that the ingredients in *Florify* may help to prevent cancer of the colon along with all of the other healthful benefits of maintaining a proper balance of flora in the intestines.

Men should take *ProstAvan*, which contains lycopene. This has been found to reduce the risk of prostate cancer. Drink plenty of water and *Melaleuca Herbal Tea* to continually detoxify.

Apply *T36-C5* or *Triple Antibiotic Ointment* immediately to any suspicious skin lesion, mole, wart, skin tag, or discoloration. Continue application 2 to 4 times each day until it disappears (probably 2 to 3 weeks) or until seen by your health care provider.

Laugh, sing, and play at least 30 minutes each day.

CANKER SORES

Mouth ulcers, known as canker sores, form on the gums and on the inside of the cheeks. They are a localized bacterial infection characterized by a white scab appearance with a bright red border. The sores may form from pinhead size to lesions the size of a dime, and are very painful. They can originate from a number of causes such as damage from brushing your teeth, biting your cheek, wearing dentures, or eating hard foods. Food allergies are often linked to repeated outbreaks.

*See the section on *Cold Sores* in this book. Brushing with *Classic Tooth Polish* and then rinsing with *Breath-Away Mouth Rinse* reduces the bacterial count in the mouth.

At the first sign of a canker sore, apply *T36-C5* to the injured site. Repeat every four hours.

CARBUNCLES

Carbuncles are similar to boils. This painful condition is also caused by the staphylococcus organism. Sometimes a fever will accompany a carbuncle outbreak. Healing takes longer than when treating boils and may be more difficult as well. This is especially true when the person suffering is diabetic, older or has other contributing factors that may impede a more rapid healing.

WARNING: Staphylococcus is very infectious and many strains are becoming resistant to prescription antibiotics. If fever is present, consult your health care provider immediately.

* See the section on *Boils* in this book.

CARDIOVASCULAR DISEASE

In 1912, the first case of atherosclerosis was documented in an elderly man. It was called a disease of old age, and was a novelty that took up only one paragraph of a medical textbook. By 1960, cardio-vascular diseases were the number one cause of adult death in North America. The wars in Southeast Asia identified 19-year-old American soldiers killed in action who showed moderate to advanced plugging of the arteries in their hearts. In 1992, 485,000 Americans died from this disease. Researchers now suspect that dietary excesses and a sedentary existence may be the greatest contributors. Conditions such as diabetes, high LDL cholesterol, and those brought on by smoking and eating a diet low in roughage and containing over 30 percent fat seem to be the pattern of most of those affected. Hardening of the arteries can lead to high blood pressure, shortness of breath, strokes, and cold hands and feet, as well as senility and premature aging. Oxidized cholesterol (LDL, the bad kind) and ionic calcium make up part of the "cement" that lines arteries of the liver, bowel, lungs, brain, kidneys, legs and arms. Some new research indicates that heart attacks are caused not by high levels of cholesterol, but by low levels of a B vitamin known as folic acid. There is also a study of men over 50, which found that those who had the highest blood levels of bioflavonoids had the smallest risk of heart disease. Everyone needs a personal plan for prevention. See the sections on *Exercise* and *Cholesterol* in this book.

* *ProvexCV* is looking better all the time. It is difficult to understand why anyone who knows about this incredible, well researched, patented product, is not using it. Take *ProvexCV* as recommended to inhibit LDL cholesterol oxidation, regulate blood platelet activity, and maintain healthy blood pressure. If you are on Coumadin or other blood thinners, work closely with your doctor to phase in the *ProvexCV.*

Take *Phytomega* daily as recommended. The phytosterols and omega-3 fatty acids in *Phytomega* help to lower cholesterol levels and maintain healthy triglyceride levels for enhanced cardiovascular health.

Stop smoking and avoid smokers. Have a thorough physical examination performed to determine your risks. Follow the doctor's recommendations, and chart your progress. Avoid animal fats and cooked vegetable oils. Reduce total fat to less than 20% of your total diet. Eat two green, yellow, and orange-colored vegetables each day. Begin a gradual exercise program. A half hour of minimal exercise can give people with hardening of the arteries in their legs or arms a boost in protection from a heart attack or stroke. Eat an *Access Performance Bar* 15 minutes before exercising in order to speed up the fat-burning process. Take the *Vitality Pack* with *Oligofructose Complex* and *CellWise*, or choose the *Vitality 6* pack for easy-to-remember AM and PM packets with all the supplements you need to maintain a healthy cardiovascular system.

Twenty to thirty-five grams of fiber is recommended daily for good health. *FiberWise* contains 5 grams of fiber and the bars can easily be carried for a quick snack. *ProFlex 20* is an excellent high-protein meal replacement and can be used alone or mixed with *Attain* for a delicious shake.

Periodontal disease is linked to the development of heart disease and stroke, so practice good oral hygiene. Using the *Melaleuca Dental Care* products is an excellent place to start. See the *Dental – Gum Disease* section.

CARPAL TUNNEL SYNDROME

Those who use their hands with a continual repetitive motion, such as computer operators, may experience a thickening of the nerve sheath in their wrists, causing numbness, coldness, and often pain. Prevention is the best line of defense. B vitamins and trace minerals are needed.

* First, eliminate the repetitive motion that caused the problem until healing is completed (often 4 to 12 weeks). Take the *Vitality Pack* with *Oligofructose Complex* as directed and saturate with *ProVex* and/or *ProVex-Plus* by taking 1 capsule for every 25 pounds of body weight for two weeks. Then gradually reduce the dose until a maintenance level is reached. In addition, take *Replenex* or *Replenex Extra Strength* as directed. It has also been found to be helpful to saturate with *Replenex*, at least for a short time. Apply *Pain-A-Trate* to the inside of the wrist and outside of the elbow every 4 hours to reduce inflammation and control pain. Avoid cold water. Hot water gives temporary relief.

CATARACTS

Damage from ultraviolet (UV) light, pollution, or steroid drugs can lead to cataracts. Free radical damage causes clouding of the lens of the eye, slowly producing fuzzy vision and a halo appearance to lights at night. Nutrition and alternative therapy provide hope for those who are not able to have the surgery. A ten-year study showed that women with higher-than-average levels of vitamin C in their blood had almost no signs of cataracts or other vision loss. Prevention is the best treatment. See the *Eye* section in this book.

*Approved UV protection lenses should be worn by everyone who is exposed to sunlight or computer monitors. Avoid animal fats, antacids, and excessive sugar. Take Melaleuca's *NutraView* as directed. Also take the *Vitality Pack* with *Oligofructose Complex* and *CellWise* as directed. *ProVex-Plus* will give additional protection for both the treatment and prevention of cataracts.

CAT BITES AND SCRATCHES

Bites and scratches from all animals, and man, promote infection. Cat bites and scratches are among the worst. Because of the high population of bacteria growing on the claws, scratches can be particularly bad. See the section on *Disinfectants* in this book.

*Immediately wash the area with *Antibacterial Liquid Soap* or *The Gold Bar.* Apply a few drops of *Sol-U-Mel* to the wet washcloth for additional disinfecting. Apply straight *T36-C5* to deep and bleeding wounds to speed drying and to slow bleeding. Apply *Triple Antibiotic Ointment* to a sterile bandage and cover. Take *ProVex* and/or *ProVex-Plus* daily.

CHAPPED HANDS

Chapped hands are often caused by excessive exposure to cleaners, solvents, detergents and soapy water. This condition is characterized by small cuts or cracks in the skin.

People in the northern half of the United States and those who live higher in the mountains where there's snow and cold, as well as most people throughout Canada, experience chapped hands in the winter months. It is caused by the skin becoming excessively dry due to the lack of natural oils. In cold weather, the body's oil-secreting glands produce less oil, and what's left is often removed with hand washing.

* Wash hands with *Antibacterial Liquid Soap*. Apply *Renew Intensive Skin Therapy* or *Moisturizing Hand Creme*. Massage into the skin until the oil penetrates. If skin cracks still appear, repeat washing and apply *T36-C5* to all cracked areas. As the oil is drying, reapply the lotion or creme. Repeat this procedure as often as necessary.

By regularly using Melaleuca's *Moisturizing Hand Creme* throughout the day, you can frequently alleviate chapped hands and dry skin. In some cases, particularly where the hands are washed frequently or latex gloves are being worn, *Renew Intensive Skin Therapy* would be more effective.

See the section on *Dry Skin* in this book.

CHAPPED LIPS

Wind, cold and sun take its toll on mucous membranes of the lips. Fevers, medications and certain health conditions that lead to dehydration often cause chapped lips.

* Usually cracking and pain can be prevented and restored to normal within 1 to 2 hours by applying *Sun Shades Lip Balm* every 15 to 30 minutes. *MelaGel* can also be used to speed recovery. In extreme cases, apply the *T36-C5* directly to the lips with the fingertip, cotton ball or a cotton swab. It does not taste great, but it is very effective.

CHEMOTHERAPY

Chemotherapy is the use of chemical agents in the treatment or control of disease or mental illness.

* Chemotherapy and the accompanying treatments can frequently leave you with little or no energy. It has been suggested that cancer patients may find that after only a few weeks of the *Vitality Pack*, *CellWise*, and *ProVex-Plus*, their energy will "zoom through the roof." Nutrition is important, so the *Vitality Pack* with *Oligofructose Complex* and *CellWise* are excellent. *ProVex-Plus* and *ProvexCV* both contain gingko biloba, which is a mild blood thinner, and they should not be used during chemo due to lowering of platelet count and the potential for bleeding. After chemo, once the platelet count is back to normal, *ProvexCV* and *ProVex-Plus* are helpful. If you get to the point where swallowing pills becomes a challenge, you might consider crushing them in your juice or *Attain* in order to continue the level of nutrition.

When eating becomes challenging, try *Attain*. Some find it easier to tolerate when enduring chemo, and it has an excellent flavor. You might try freezing it, as sometimes it is easier to take things by mouth if they are frozen. *Sustain Sport* will also help with energy during periods of nausea.

During chemo, mouth sores are common, and there is a potential for gum infection. Try the *Classic Tooth Polish* because it has Melaleuca oil. The *Breath-Away Mouth Rinse* is also very helpful. Use *Sun Shades Lip Balm* for the cold sores in the corner of the mouth. It even works under lipstick. See the section on *Cold Sores* in this book. *T36-C5* used on the incision area following surgery seems to help with the deep aching.

Taking *Luminex* would be a good idea, as some depression during this sort of treatment is very common. If the cancer is breast cancer, especially estrogen-dependent breast cancer, estrogen cannot be used, but *EstrAval* is excellent. Depending on the age of the patient (if it is a woman), menopausal symptoms come on immediately, because the chemo knocks out the estrogen production, resulting in instant menopause with severe symptoms. *EstrAval* is excellent in this case.

Use *Renew Intensive Skin Therapy* and the *Moisturizing Hand Creme* on your hands regularly when taking chemo. It may help with fingernail loss.

HEALTHY BODY

Be sure to convert your home to the safer Melaleuca products. Having an environment without harmful products can help to prevent recurrent bouts of pneumonia and asthma, which can follow radiation damage to the lungs.

CHEST PAINS (ANGINA)

Chest pains can be quite harmless or quite dangerous depending upon the cause. Emotional stress can cause chest tightness and localized pain. Air pollution can cause lung irritation and related chest pains. Persons who eat late in the evening, overeat, or eat in a hurry tend to have frequent indigestion and experience chest pains due to a hiatal hernia. This condition occurs when the stomach pushes up through the diaphragm due to gas in the bowel. On the other hand, when chest pain is from an occluded blood vessel, a reflex pain is usually felt extending from the chest into the left shoulder and neck area. A thorough checkup including a resting electrocardiogram is recommended for active persons over 40 in an annual physical exam. Don't procrastinate! In over half of the cases of heart disease, there are no warning signs. A massive heart attack and death may be the only sign a doctor sees.

* See your health care provider if you have any chest pains! Listen to your body! Slow down when eating, and eat smaller portions. Decrease your dietary fat to 20% of your total calories. Begin a progressive exercise program to maximize circulation and oxygen to the diaphragm and heart. Minimize your sugar intake, since it is directly converted into fat within your body if you do not exercise enough. Maximize your lean body mass through weight training. Make sure you eat 2 fruit servings and 5 vegetable servings every day. Take the *Vitality Pack* with *Oligofructose Complex*, *CellWise*, *ProvexCV*, and *Phytomega* daily to ensure adequate nutrient levels. See the sections on *Cardiovascular Disease, Exercise,* and *Nutrition* in this book.

CHICKEN POX

This is a highly contagious disease caused by the herpes zoster virus. While chicken pox generally affects children, when it appears in adults and teenagers if can be far more serious. The incubation period is usually 14 to 21 days. The symptoms start with a skin rash. Often a fever, headache, and aching muscles are experienced. The rash changes into pimples and then blisters that enlarge and become filled with pus. The skin can become very itchy. Do not scratch the affected areas, as it could cause scarring. The blisters dry up in a few days and are covered with scales. After all the blisters have scabbed, the disease is no longer contagious.

* To help relieve symptoms, wash the affected area with *Antibacterial Liquid Soap*. Pat dry and liberally apply *T36-C5*. Allow the oil sufficient time to soak into the skin. After the rash has fully developed, usually within 2 or 3 days, soak in 1 oz of *Sol-U-Mel* and 1 oz of *Renew Bath Oil*

HEALTHY BODY

in a tub of warm water for 15 minutes to help with the itching. After soaking, pat dry and reapply the *T36-C5*. When the oil has started to be absorbed into the skin or is dry, apply either *MelaGel* or *Renew Intensive Skin Therapy*. Repeat the process several times a day. Drinking one to four cups of *Melaleuca Herbal Tea* each day may also be helpful.

CHIGGERS

These are described as tiny red larva having a bite that causes extreme itching. Walking through the grass in the summer in the southern, southeastern and southwestern areas of the U.S. occasionally results in painful, itching eruptions on the feet, legs, and thighs. The female mite digs into the flesh and lays eggs that cause a sore. The larvae hatch and then bore under the skin, causing an intense dermatitis. Read the section on *Scabies* in this book.

* Wash the bite areas with *Antibacterial Liquid Soap*. Rub *T36-C5* on the area of the bites each morning and evening. Follow by applying *Triple Antibiotic Ointment* to prevent a secondary infection. Large areas can be treated by soaking in a bath of warm water conditioned with 1 oz of *Sol-U-Mel* and 1 oz of *Renew Bath Oil*.

For prevention, apply *T36-C5* to the bottom of pant cuffs, or spray pants and socks with 1 oz of *Sol-U-Mel* diluted with 7 oz of water.

CHILBLAIN

Chilblain is a painful swelling or sore, especially on the fingers or toes, caused by exposure to cold or poor circulation. It resembles a mild case of frostbite or trench foot, but is characterized by an itching or burning dermatitis and probably a sensitization to recurring exposure to cold. The main contributing factors may be contact with wetness or metal and inadequate clothing. Alcoholism or an underlying vascular or systemic disease can also cause it. The young and the old are especially vulnerable. Vitamin and mineral deficiencies can also contribute to chilblain.

*A good nutrition program such as the *Vitality 6* pack can make a difference in almost any physical challenge, as can exercise and, in this case, warm clothing.

Keep your feet warm. Massage them daily with *Renew Bath Oil* or *Body Satin Foot Lotion* to stimulate circulation. Carefully apply *T36-C5* directly on the chilblain. See the section on *Frostbite* in this book.

CHOLESTEROL

Cholesterol is our body's own antioxidant protecting us against naturally occurring free radicals. It is needed for life. There is good cholesterol (made from balanced nutrition during exercise and play) and bad cholesterol (made during stress or from over-cooked animal fats). We need a certain amount of cholesterol to handle stress. We make about four times as much cholesterol in a day as we eat in our diet. Excess dietary fat (including margarine) tends to increase blood cholesterol. People who have high blood cholesterol and high stress cannot lower blood cholesterol by avoiding it in their diet. Adequate fiber and roughage in the diet carries fat and toxic substances quickly out of the body. Heat converts normal cholesterol found in animal products into oxycholesterol, which is unhealthy and toxic.

* Take *ProvexCV* and the *Vitality Pack* with *Oligofructose Complex* daily, as directed. Take *Phytomega* daily as recommended. The phytosterols and omega-3 fatty acids in *Phytomega* help to lower cholesterol levels and maintain healthy triglyceride levels for enhanced cardiovascular health. The ingredients in *Florify* have also been found to exert a hypocholesterolemic effect. Begin a regular exercise program, and eat an *Access Performance Bar* 15 minutes before your workout. Put *Sustain Sport* in your water while working out to maintain needed energy and electrolytes. Drink 2 to 4 cups of *Melaleuca Herbal Tea* each day.

CHRONIC FATIGUE SYNDROME (CFS)

Diagnosis of chronic fatigue and immune dysfunction syndrome (CFIDS—also known as chronic fatigue syndrome, or CFS) has only been possible in recent times. Previously the aches, pains, and tiredness that people with this condition suffered wasn't classified into a specific diagnoses, so treatment (if any) was often less than fully effective.

The outstanding symptom of CFIDS is extreme, even disabling fatigue lasting at least six months. Muscular pains, flu-like symptoms, and mood changes are also common and overlap with symptoms of fibromyalgia. The signs and symptoms of CFIDS vary from person to person and in severity.

The cause of CFIDS is unknown and therefore it is also not known whether or not it is contagious. Fortunately it is not progressive and does not lead to other serious diseases or destruction of body tissues. There is no known cure, and symptoms may come and go.

* Not much is known as to a definitive treatment for this condition; however, a healthy diet, rest, limited amount of exercise and good nutritional supplements seem to be the most effective. Stress seems to aggravate the condition appreciably.

It has been suggested that someone with chronic fatigue syndrome take the *Vitality Pack* with *Oligofructose Complex,* as magnesium supplementation has produced good results. This may be due to its importance in the serotonin function of the body. In addition take *CellWise* and *Replenex. Pain-A-Trate* is an excellent topical pain relieving cream. Taking a saturation dose of the *ProVex* and/or *ProVex-Plus* should also help the arthritic-type pain. (Take 1 capsule for each 25 pounds of body weight daily for approximately two weeks. Then begin to decrease the number of daily capsules until a maintenance dose is determined.)

HEALTHY BODY

Luminex may help the potential depression associated with CFIDS. See the *Immune System* section in this book.

Try the **Sustain Sport** as a "fatigue buster." It will not make you feel wired like caffeine or sugar. The **Access Performance Bar** can also be a tremendous help with energy.

Get a **Value Pack** to change your entire household to an environmentally safe atmosphere. Expect 12 to 16 weeks on the above regimen before any change is noted.

CIGARETTE SMOKING

Imagine a 747 jumbo jet filled with passengers crashing every hour of every day within the United States borders. How long would this tragedy be allowed to continue? Of all the plagues of man, cigarette smoking has probably caused more deaths and resulted in more disease than all other non-infectious causes combined.

Over 50 toxic or banned substances have been identified resulting from smoking; these include carbon monoxide, carbon dioxide, dioxane, arsenic oxide, biphenyls, and cadmium salts, just to name a few. Nicotine, after the Latin name of the plant meaning nightshade, is a powerful insect repellent, aphid killer on roses, and deadly poison, which is never eaten by animals in the wild.

Smoking one cigarette reduces the infection-fighting ability of the immune system by 50 percent for 1 hour. The March of Dimes has advised against it since 1974 for causing birth defects. Second-hand smoke has been linked to a 15 percent lower IQ among children of households where at least one parent is a smoker.

Nicotine is an addictive alkaloid drug related to codeine, morphine, and cocaine. Recently, cigarette companies have been accused of actually adding nicotine to their higher-priced brands to induce greater addiction and desire for their product. Many congressmen list financial holdings in the lucrative tobacco industry, which may account for the 30-year struggle to gain governmental bans of this deadly waste of human health.

*There is no greater single health measure you can take than to quit smoking and forbid the practice in your home or around your loved ones. Like any drug addiction, it must be faced with courage and compassion. If you have the personal strength to stop smoking, DO IT RIGHT NOW! If you need help, seek a health care provider who is trained in chemical addiction treatment with diet, herb, acupuncture and hypnosis.

Begin a lifestyle of wellness rather than self-destruction. Take **ProVex** and/or **ProVex-Plus**, as well as **ProvexCV** daily. Take the **Vitality Pack** with **Oligofructose Complex** and **CellWise** as directed. Drink 2 to 4 cups of **Melaleuca Herbal Tea** each day to help the body detoxify.

HEALTHY BODY

COLD

Cold viruses attack the moist, cooler regions of the nose, throat, sinuses, vocal cords, and larynx when our systems are run down. The virus has developed a way of avoiding destruction by the immune system and is present in a dormant state. Apparently, when we contact a cold from someone else (sneeze, handshake, kiss), the two viruses exchange fragments of genetic information to form a slightly new strain. Being a new strain, it is unrecognized by the immune system. It enters living cells undetected and begins to multiply until cell damage has taken place. The immune system drives the virus into seclusion until the next opportune time arises. Mucous membranes become swollen, red and irritated as the virus spreads from one cell to the next. Untreated colds can progress into more threatening conditions.

* The common cold usually gives a warning that it is about to develop. From the earliest signs of tiredness, sneezing, and hoarseness, you are given a few hours to launch an attack. Immediately take **Activate Immune Complex** during a cold or flu and take a hot bath. In recent studies the ingredients in **Activate** have shown to strengthen the immune system and reduce the duration and severity of symptoms of the common cold. Take **CounterAct** cold and flu medicines as directed. Rub **Renew Bath Oil** over the chest and back, as it will boost the immune system. Breathe the steamy vapor of five drops of **T36-C5** and water in a steam inhaler for fifteen minutes (air temperatures above 104 degrees kill the virus). Apply one drop of **T36-C5** to each nostril of your nose every four hours. Sip vegetable broth and/or Mom's chicken soup every couple of hours. Avoid any temptation to eat heavy foods as your digestive tract, including smell and taste, are on vacation for a while. If coughing is present, use **CounterAct Cough Relief Medicine** as directed. **CounterAct Cough Drops** are formulated with menthol and Melaleuca oil to reduce coughs and sore, dry throat, as well as vitamin C to help boost the immune system. Try a hot **Sustain Sport** drink to fight any fever you may produce. To reduce painful muscles, bathe with **Renew Bath Oil** frequently. "Drown the cold" with **Melaleuca Herbal Tea**, by drinking one cup per hour. Take the **Vitality Pack** with **Oligofructose Complex** and **CellWise**. You should also take **ProVex-Plus** each day. Get all the rest you can.

COLD SORES

Very painful, clear, fluid-filled eruptions on the border of the mouth form hard, oozing scabs resulting from an infection of either the herpes simplex or herpes facialis virus. Once thought to be more common in infants and children, adults are becoming more susceptible. The infection makes chewing difficult and may impede the appetite. Mild damage associated with exposure to the sun, stress, abrasions from a toothbrush, bad allergies to certain foods, the onset of menstruation, or any disease that produces a fever or increases metabolic rate may

HEALTHY BODY

produce a lesion. As a rule, the symptoms generally go away after 7 to 10 days. Dehydration and secondary infections give reason for concern. Those having secondary health problems where intake of food and liquid are essential (such as seniors, very young children, diabetics, or those with low blood sugar) need to be particularly careful that their cold sores don't interfere with any other medical problems they may be experiencing.

Since cold sores are a virus, they don't respond to antibiotics. Modern medicine appears sometimes to be at a loss as to how to "fix" the problem. Maybe that is one reason treatment will too often be centered on alleviating pain and preventing the spread of other infections rather than seeking the source of the problem and eliminating it. See the section on *Canker Sores* in this book.

* Since the virus feeds on an excessive intake of the amino acid arginine, diets avoiding citrus fruit and nuts should be followed. Supplementation with the amino acid L-Lysine, found in most health food stores, is advised to stop the early spread of the infection.

In 1991, a clinical study by Mayo and Shemesh, revealed the effectiveness of Melaleuca oil for the treatment of this difficult and recurring challenge. Dab *T36-C5* on the lesions immediately upon detection. Repeat every hour until the lesion either disappears or comes to a head. If it comes to a head, continue to apply *T36-C5* once every 2 hours followed by *MelaGel* or *Renew Intensive Skin Therapy*. For persistent or large surface sores, use *Triple Antibiotic Ointment* every 4 hours.

For sores in the mouth, gargle with 10 drops *T36-C5* blended with a half-cup of warm water. Repeat several times daily. Dab *T36-C5* onto your finger or a cotton swab and apply to the affected area. Regularly use *Breath-Away Mouth Rinse*, *Melaleuca's Classic Tooth Polish* and the *Hot/Cool Shot Breath Spray*.

COMPRESS

Compresses are made from sterile, folded pieces of bandage, cotton, or linen that can be put on wounds that are draining. They may be hot or cold. They are a proven remedy for infections, varicose veins, and many other ailments because they work slowly and deeply. The compress produces a unique healing component with *T36-C5*.

* Put 3 to 6 drops of *T36-C5* onto a wet cotton ball or a washcloth, depending on the size of the affected area, and leave it in place for at least one hour. See the section on *Poultice* in this book.

CONJUNCTIVITIS

An inflammation or infection of the membrane (conjunctiva) that covers the eye and lines the inner surface of the eyelid. It can be caused by a bacterial infection (often contagious), allergy (itching and burning), or chemical contact (red and painful). Children often get contagious "pink eye" from playmates.

* Consult your health care provider. Antibiotic eye drops may be prescribed for bacterial conjunctivitis. To prevent the spread of the infection to other people in the household, do not touch your hands to the infected eye. Wash hands frequently with **Antibacterial Liquid Soap**. Take **ProVex** and/or **ProVex-Plus** daily.

A child with conjunctivitis will have to be kept away from school for a few days to prevent the spread of infection to other children in school.

NOTE: Do not put any Melaleuca products directly on the eye. Use only products that are certified ophthalmologic grade.

CONSTIPATION

It is healthy and normal to have a bowel movement within one to two hours after eating. Wastes, including undigested fiber, pass out of the healthy body within 12 hours after eating the meal. Poor diet, lack of exercise, not drinking enough water, stress, and many drugs can cause constipation. We are a constipated society. Colorectal diseases are at an epidemic level. See the section on *Hemorrhoids* in this book.

* The following four things help most sufferers of constipation: eat enough fiber, drink enough liquids, get enough exercise to maintain bowel mobility, and don't worry so much. Specifically, get 20 to 30 grams of fiber each day. (*Note:* 1 medium apple + ½ cup of old-fashioned oatmeal + ¼ cup raisins + 2 carrots + 1 cup of broccoli + ½ cup of cooked beans = 10 grams of fiber). Eat *FiberWise* bars—2 per day to maximize fiber. *FiberWise* drink is also an excellent way to increase dietary fiber. *FiberWise* drink and bars contain 5 grams of fiber per serving and healthy biotics to help maintain digestive balance and keep you regular. Also take *Florify* to help maintain a healthy balance of flora in the digestive system. Drink 1 to 3 quarts of water including **Melaleuca Herbal Tea** each day. The **Vitality Pack** with **Oligofructose Complex** should be taken as well as **CellWise**. Take **ProVex-Plus** at the rate of 1 capsule for each 25 lbs of body weight each day. Run, walk, jog, bike, or swim, etc. for 30 minutes each day. Replace thoughts of fear or worry with happy, optimistic thoughts. This releases hormones in the bowel, which aids digestive juices and propels food along through the bowel and out of the body.

CORAL CUTS

Coral cuts are often jagged and irregular, and they harbor bacteria. This necessitates thorough cleansing and disinfecting. Some form of aggressive treatment should always be initiated whenever any coral cuts have been incurred. See the section on *Disinfectants* in this book.

* Thoroughly cleanse with pure water and **Antibacterial Liquid Soap** enriched with **Sol-U-Mel**. Remove particles of sand and coral. Apply **T36-C5** or **T40-C3** for maximum disinfecting. Suturing wounds that cut through the skin and into muscle speeds healing and reduces secondary infection. Apply *Triple Antibiotic Ointment* over the stitches, if applicable, and cover with a gauze bandage. Inspect the wound daily for redness or swelling, which gives indication of the spread of infection.

When sutures are not needed, soak affected areas in a solution of 1 oz of *Sol-U-Mel*, 1 oz of *Renew Bath Oil*, plus ¼ cup of Epsom salt in 1 quart of hot water. Rinse open wounds daily with 1 oz of *Sol-U-Mel* in 1 pint of water. Change the dressing daily and reapply *Triple Antibiotic Ointment*.

CORNS

Corns are raised areas of hyperkeratosis or thick, callused skin that are caused by friction or pressure over a bony extension of the foot, such as the ball or the toe joints. Hard corns occur over the toes, and soft corns occur between the toes. Corns may ache spontaneously or become very tender upon pressure. Properly fitting shoes will help prevent corns. See the section on *Calluses* in this book.

* Soak your feet in a solution of 1 oz of *Sol-U-Mel* and 1 oz of *Renew Bath Oil* in 1 quart of hot water for 15 minutes. Dry them thoroughly and apply *T36-C5* followed by *MelaGel* or *Renew Intensive Skin Therapy*. Repeat twice daily until the corn softens enough to painlessly remove with tweezers. Apply *Triple Antibiotic Ointment* or *MelaGel* and cover the area with a small bandage. *Body Satin Foot Scrub* and *Body Satin Foot Lotion* can also be used to cleanse and stimulate circulation. Wear only shoes that fit properly.

A 1972 study by Dr. M. Walker indicated a significant degree of success using tea tree oil to treat corns and other problems related to health conditions of the feet.

WARNING: Long-term diabetics often suffer from poor circulation to areas furthest from the heart. Because of the delicacy of their condition, diabetics especially should consult a health care provider before initiating any idea—including any of the ones mentioned in this book.

COUGHS

Our bodies produce phlegm and mucous in the throat and lungs when exposed to severe temperature changes, chemical irritation, or allergens. We instinctively cough to remove this phlegm and foreign substances. Smoking is the most common cause of chronic coughs.

Severe coughs can cause bleeding in the throat or even an inner ear infection. They can also be one of the body's early warning signs. Persistent coughs may indicate a potentially serious medical problem. Contact your health care provider, particularly if there are other medical problems present. If coughing is caused by a common irritant, or by the flu or a cold, the following may help alleviate symptoms.

* Treat the cause and eliminate your exposure to the irritating substances. In mild cases, breathe the vapor of 5 drops of *T36-C5* in a bowl of steaming water for 15 minutes while holding your head over the

bowl. Make a tent over your head and the bowl with a bath towel. Repeat morning and evening. Drink the *Melaleuca Herbal Tea* throughout the day. Use *CounterAct Cough Relief Medicine* as directed. *CounterAct Cough Drops* are formulated with menthol and Melaleuca oil to reduce coughs and sore, dry throat, as well as vitamin C to help boost the immune system.

For a more serious cough, apply *T36-C5* followed by *Moisturizing Hand Creme* on your upper chest and around your throat. Dab *T36-C5* under each nostril, as this will help you breathe easier.

Placing a cool mist humidifier by your bed each night with 10 drops of *T36-C5 Melaleuca Oil* and 2 capfuls of *Sol-U-Mel*, added to the water will help with your breathing and thus your cough. Also, try placing a few drops of *T36-C5* on your pillow at night.

Try these simple dietary tips: eliminate milk and milk products, substituting other sources of calcium; eat garlic regularly for its antibiotic effects; and eat fresh horseradish and hot mustard to help liquefy bronchial secretions.

CRADLE CAP

Cradle cap is a yellowish scaling and crusted area on the top of the scalp of an infant during the first month of life. The scales may pile up because the mother is afraid to wash the baby's scalp thoroughly. The face may also be affected. Cradle cap is more extensive in chubby infants. Susceptibility to bacterial infection and candidiasis is increased.

* Make a very diluted mixture of *T36-C5* blended with olive oil. Combine thoroughly and apply to the affected area. Leave it on for several minutes before shampooing with the *Koala Pals Tear-Free Conditioning Hair Wash*.

CRAMPS

Sudden decreases in tissue oxygen, decreases in muscle or nerve calcium levels, or hormonal changes before menstrual flow can trigger muscle cramps. Side aches during or after strenuous exercise are due to diaphragm spasms caused from low oxygen and low calcium levels in that muscle.

*After eating a meal, wait 45 minutes before exercising. Properly stretch and warm muscles before exercise. *Vitality Calcium Complete* taken at bedtime can prevent sub-optimum levels of calcium in the blood and prevent cramps. Eat an *Access Performance Bar* 15 minutes before exercise. Drink *Sustain Sport* during and immediately after exercise. A warm bath and a good massage can help reduce pain greatly. Massage *Pain-A-Trate* into muscles that cramp easily. The therapeutic dose of *ProVex* (1 capsule for every 25 pounds of body weight per day) can also give good relief, as can *CounterAct Extra-Strength Acetaminophen* or *CounterAct Ibuprofen*. See the section on *Leg Cramps* in this book.

HEALTHY BODY

---

*The information presented in this book is in no way intended as a substitute for medical counseling. Always consult your physician before starting any course of supplementation or treatment, particularly if you are pregnant or currently under medical care. Always read and follow product packaging directions and warnings.

CUTICLES

The rolled skin at the edge of the fingernails and toenails can give evidence of your general health. Dry cuticles, which split and become infected, are often due to exposure to harsh soaps or solvents such as gasoline or paint thinner. See the section on *Dry Skin* in this book.

*After washing your hands with *Antibacterial Liquid Soap* or *The Gold Bar*, apply *Moisturizing Hand Creme* and work it into the cuticles to prevent dryness. Apply *Triple Antibiotic Ointment* or *MelaGel* to the infected cuticles. See your health care provider for further advice.

CUTS

Cuts are narrow slices or slashes that break the skin's surface. When skin is cut the immediate area becomes red and inflamed. White blood cells, which fight infection, rush to the site. As cuts heal, scabs form natural bandages that protect the injured site.

If the object that caused the injury was dirty or exposed to disease-causing organisms, extra care must be taken in thorough cleaning. Cuts should be treated soon after injury. Serious cuts can lead to further complications and should be treated by a health care provider immediately.

*Clean the affected area with a washcloth, warm water, and *Antibacterial Liquid Soap* and/or *Sol-U-Mel*. Pat dry and apply *T36-C5*, followed by *Renew Intensive Skin Therapy*, *MelaGel* or *Triple Antibiotic Ointment*. Cuts heal faster and have less opportunity to develop infection if this suggestion is used as soon as an injury occurs. Keep the cut clean with a bandage and check the healing progress daily. Reclean and apply new bandages as often as needed. Deep or wide cuts may require a visit to your health care provider for suturing.

WARNING: Tetanus can occur when cuts are deep or contaminated. If it has been more than five years since your last tetanus shot, immediately contact your health care provider. The majority of victims dying from tetanus are older adults who have not kept current on their booster shots.

DANDRUFF

This dry flaking of the scalp is one of the most common conditions affecting nearly one half of Americans. White, scaly skin sloughs off of the head in a "snow storm" fashion to disgrace the victim. At one time, it was believed that dandruff was caused by poor personal hygiene. Occasionally it is an indication of extremely dry skin. Home remedies usually consist of trying to increase the scalp's oil, which just creates more dandruff.

Many dermatologists believe that dandruff is another form (albeit a mild one) of seborrheic dermatitis, which can be caused by a yeast-like fungus. Seborrheic dermatitis is an inflammation of the skin that can appear on the scalp and eyebrows. It is characterized by flaky, white,

---

*The information presented in this book is in no way intended as a substitute for medical counseling. Always consult your physician before starting any course of supplementation or treatment, particularly if you are pregnant or currently under medical care. Always read and follow product packaging directions and warnings.

scaly skin that sloughs off, leaving a dry or greasy scalp that produces the itching so common with dandruff.

There are others who believe dandruff is caused by using harsh detergents, soaps, and chemical-laden shampoos that challenge normal skin bacteria. Other factors may include Candida albicans, stress, inadequate blood circulation to hair sites, and even inadequate diets.

*Avoid harsh soaps, shampoos, and chemical-laden hair care products. Shampoo with **Melaleuca Original Shampoo** once or twice a day while dandruff is present. Leave the **Melaleuca Original Shampoo** on the scalp for at least three minutes before rinsing. It contains an abundance of healing **T36-C5 Melaleuca Oil** and works particularly well in the treatment of common scalp conditions such as dandruff. Since this shampoo contains conditioner, do not use an extra conditioner, as it could be a scalp irritant.

Also, check your diet and make sure that you are getting an adequate supply of balanced nutrition. The **Vitality Pack** with **Oligofructose Complex**, along with Melaleuca's other nutritional supplements, are worth a closer look.

DENTAL – DECAY

Dentists have done an admirable job in helping prevent tooth decay. Brushing, flossing and washing after eating have become a way of life for most of us. Nonetheless, some decay still takes place. Some dentists and scientists argue that the use of fluoride, while definitely reducing tooth decay, may pose a greater long-term risk to the general health of the body.

Refined foods (mainly sugar in its many forms) promote rapid yeast, bacterial, and other microorganism growth in the many cracks and crevices in and around the teeth. These microbes secrete acids, which erode the calcium-rich enamel of the teeth. Proper brushing and flossing habits are essential to reduce the microbial population.

*Gently brush the teeth and tongue after every meal with **Classic Tooth Polish**. Swish your mouth with **Breath-Away Mouth Rinse** to reduce mouth microbes as well as to control jungle breath. Floss frequently with **Classic Dental Floss** and chew **Hot/Cool Shot Sugarless Gum**. Take **ProVex** and/or **ProVex-Plus** to help prevent plaque buildup. Have regular checkups with your dentist to maintain healthy teeth.

For a painful tooth, apply a small amount of **T36-C5** to the gum surrounding the tooth. It will help with the pain until a dentist can be contacted. See the section on **Toothache** in this book.

DENTAL – GUM DISEASE

Also known as periodontal disease, gum disease is the plague of modern times. Over 90% of Americans have it, and some reports indicate that every one of us suffers with it to some degree. It should be of concern to everyone.

Conditions range from a mild inflammation to severe gum recession and bone loss. Inflammation of the gums, or gingivitis, is the most common gum disease and is due primarily to infection within the tissues. See the section on *Gingivitis* in this book.

We should be very aware of periodontal disease, as it is linked to the development of adult onset diabetes, heart disease, and stroke. In addition, pregnant women with gum disease have seven times the normal risk of delivering pre-term, low birthweight babies.

* Use a cotton swab or your finger to apply *T36-C5 Melaleuca Oil* directly to the affected region of the gums. Melaleuca oil soothes inflamed gum tissues and, while it does not have one of the greatest tastes in the world, it does taste like it is working and accelerating the healing process. Not only for the benefits of healing, but for prevention as well, use the entire *Dental Care* system. There are four toothpastes including a berry-flavored one for children. Any one of them will prove to be better than most store-bought brands, but *Classic Tooth Polish* is the one usually recommended for overall oral health.

Take the *Vitality Pack* with *Oligofructose Complex* for vital nutrients along with *CellWise* to help repair connective tissue around the teeth. Take *ProVex* or *ProVex-Plus* to help reduce inflammation of the gum tissues, and to help prevent plaque buildup.

Taking good care of your teeth not only provides good oral hygiene, but also may help you to avoid disease you probably don't associate with your teeth and gums. Be sure to get adequate calcium and vitamin C to keep teeth and gums healthy. The *Vitality Pack*, which includes *Vitality Calcium Complete*, is an excellent place to start. Also, brush your teeth with a soft-bristled brush for at least two and a half minutes and then floss. Use a fine bristled rotary brush, if possible. Change your toothbrush once a month and get regular dental checkups.

DEPRESSION

One of the most common conditions experienced by adults and young people is occasional depression. This is exemplified by an attitude that "I don't feel like doing what I normally would like to do." It is normal for someone to feel blue or have an attitude of melancholy from time to time due to undesirable situations. It is another thing to see a black cloud cast over the future. Some people actually develop a sort of regular "gloom and doom" attitude if depression is allowed to persist. Nutritional deficiencies or fast foods often provoke such feelings. Exposure to household chemicals and food additives may also contribute. If a cause for the depressed mood can be identified, then the cause should be treated. Menopause can also increase the need for estrogen stabilization to control mild depression.

Fortunately mild depression is one of the most treatable mental conditions. The first step toward a cure is to recognize the symptoms:

A sullen mood
Feelings of hopelessness, guilt and anxiety
Loss of interest in things that used to be pleasurable
Change in appetite
Change in sleeping patterns
Inability to concentrate
Lack of energy or feeling run down

* Having a positive support group during times of depression is of great benefit. Take *Luminex* along with the *Vitality Pack* with *Oligofructose Complex*, *CellWise*, and *ProVex* and/or *ProVex-Plus*. *EstrAval* can be taken as directed to reduce mild depression during menopause. A good nutritional system is essential to good health. Minerals are like catalysts; they are involved with almost all reactions in the body. Getting balanced minerals into the cells is critical. Studies have shown that these products can make a remarkable difference in not only mild depression, but also schizophrenia, bi-polar affective disorders, and even fibromyalgia.

Nutritional research indicates that low levels of omega-3 fatty acids in the nervous system correlate with a higher risk of depression. Try adding a good omega-3 supplement like *Phytomega* to the diet, and/or eat cold water fish three times a week.

Drinking 1 to 2 cups of *Melaleuca Herbal Tea* daily and eating and exercising regularly each day can be very helpful. Allow approximately 2 to 4 weeks before you expect to see results.

Harmful household chemicals should be eliminated and replaced with Melaleuca's biologically safe ones.

DERMATITIS

Dermatitis is an inflammation that can be caused by an outside irritant that can produce itchy, red skin. It can, when irritated, ooze, crust, scale, and develop vesicles. These can develop suddenly and be short-lived or can become chronic in nature. In the chronic stages, dermatitis is evidenced by dry, scaly and thickened skin patches. Chronic dermatitis is commonly known as eczema. See the section on *Eczema* in this book.

Healthy skin is able to withstand exposure to many natural substances and some synthetic chemicals without harmful effects. It is designed to be our first line of defense against the outside world. Substances that irritate the skin include plants such as poison ivy or poison oak, some trees, fruits and vegetables. Other irritants include fabrics such as wool and synthetics, as well as toxic household cleaners and chemicals. In addition to these external sources, there are internal conditions such as allergies, sensitivities to foods, prescriptions, and over-the-counter drugs.

* Reduce the amount of toxins in the air in your home by converting your home to Melaleuca cleaning and personal care products. Many cases of dermatitis are greatly reduced by switching to the *EcoSense Laundry System* and laundering all clothing, linens, and towels. Try to identify the cause of the dermatitis before aggressively treating the symptoms.

As soon as possible after the symptoms begin, wash the area with *Antibacterial Liquid Soap* or *The Gold Bar*. Additional soaking in a warm tub with 1 oz of *Sol-U-Mel* and 1 oz of *Renew Bath Oil* once daily is advised. Use *Renew Intensive Skin Therapy* twice daily. *Triple Antibiotic Ointment* is also effective. *Melaleuca Oil Shampoo* is highly recommended for a dry and scaly scalp.

CAUTION: Avoid using pure Melaleuca oil to treat any dermatitis condition.

DETOXIFICATION

To detoxify is to cleanse your body of toxic chemicals.

* There are many ways to detoxify your body. Some are very unpleasant. Using the Melaleuca products to detoxify is a much more pleasant experience and in many cases works just as well.

One suggestion is to drink eight glasses of *Melaleuca Herbal Tea* each day for two weeks, in addition to using your favorite detox diet. The kidney and liver are involved in processing vitamins, so it is recommended to stop taking all vitamin supplements during the detox. It is important to exercise regularly and drink plenty of water.

FiberWise drink and bars are very effective at detoxification because of the high level of fiber. A high-fiber and low-fat diet is a good place to start. Using the *Attain* will certainly help with the 20-35 grams of fiber you need daily. Adding fiber to your diet will not only remove the toxins, but also it will bind, dilute, and deactivate the carcinogens.

DIABETES

Juvenile-onset diabetes appears to be due to a defective gene that causes self-destruction of insulin-producing cells in the pancreas. Insulin must then be taken regularly to support life.

Adult-onset diabetes, on the other hand, appears to be due to suppression or inhibition of normal pancreas production. Being over 55 years of age, overweight, lacking exercise, and consuming large amounts of refined sugar and dietary fat (more than 20% of daily calories), is the typical picture. Usually, insulin is unnecessary but a pancreatic stimulant drug is often prescribed.

* Drink 2 to 4 cups of *Melaleuca Herbal Tea* each day, and take the *Vitality Pack* with *Oligofructose Complex* and *CellWise*. Take *ProvexCV* at the therapeutic dose level (one capsule per 35 pounds of body weight daily). This increases circulation and reduces the incidence of many diabetic symptoms. Heart disease has been shown to be one of the most serious possible side effects of diabetes. These supplements are very important to protect the eyesight of diabetics and should be taken by any diabetic suffering from neuropathy, retinopathy, kidney problems, or circulation problems.

The *American Journal of Clinical Nutrition* reported when working with insulin-dependent diabetics that 45% of all insulin-dependent diabetics tested significantly reduced their insulin requirement after only 16 days on a high-fiber diet. Seventy-five percent of all insulin-dependent diabetics significantly reduced their insulin after only a few weeks. *CAUTION:* Monitor your blood sugar carefully. You may have to adjust your insulin accordingly.

NOTE: Be careful to work *FiberWise* into your food exchange because it does have some sugar.

Blood sugar levels can be somewhat regulated using the *Access Performance Bars* and/or *Sustain Sport*. (Try a small amount at first and adjust to fit your personal needs and tolerance level.) Make exercise and a low-fat, low-sugar diet a way of life. A healthy nutritional program is important no matter what the challenging condition.

For the best mouth health, use *Classic Tooth Polish*, *Classic Dental Floss*, and *Breath-Away Mouth Rinse* at least twice daily. For the quickest healing of wounds, use *MelaGel* and *T36-C5*. *NutraView* should be taken as directed to safeguard your vision. Some find that taking *Luminex* three times each day and *ProVex-Plus* four times each day is also very helpful.

See the sections on *Dental – Gum Disease*, *Diabetic Foot Ulcerations*, and *Diabetic Gangrene* in this book.

DIABETIC FOOT ULCERATIONS

Ulcerations frequently occur in those who are over the age of 40 and have had diabetes for more than 10 years. Other contributing factors include obesity, lack of exercise and improper care of the feet. Diabetes causes blood vessel walls to thicken. This decreases the blood flow to the feet and lower legs. Some diabetics suffer from neuropathy and poor circulation. Neuropathy is a condition that causes damage to the foot and leg nerves. It makes feet numb and unable to feel heat, cold, pressure, cuts or bruises. These conditions can combine to create a situation where even routine cuts, blisters and scrapes can develop into gangrene. If not treated aggressively, gangrene will result in limb amputation.

* Soak your feet in a tubful of warm water to which you have added 1 tbsp of *Renew Bath Oil* and 1 capful of *Sol-U-Mel*. After soaking for 10 to 15 minutes, dry and liberally apply *T36-C5* to any sores or lesions. As this is drying, apply a thin coating of *Renew Intensive Skin Therapy*, *MelaGel* or even *Moisturizing Hand Creme*. Taking time to soak your feet will give you an opportunity to conduct your requisite daily foot inspection. See also *Diabetic Gangrene*.

DIABETIC GANGRENE

Diabetic gangrene is a complication of diabetes, causing the tissue to die. As the condition progresses, amputation of the affected limb is the traditional course of action.

* Dr. A. Penfold was successfully using tea tree oil on severe cases of diabetic gangrene as early as 1936. It is recommended that *T36-C5* or *T40-C3* be massaged into the affected area and the surrounding tissue for as long as needed. The area can also be treated with *MelaGel* or *Triple Antibiotic Ointment,* preferably on top of the oil. Frequently, the longer the condition exists, the longer it may take to get results. Coordinate this with your health care provider.

DIAPER RASH

Diaper rash is caused by friction and irritation in the presence of moisture. It is a common skin irritation affecting babies, who have otherwise healthy skin. It triggers yeast to grow. This occurs naturally when wet diapers are not changed promptly. Babies will vary in their susceptibility to developing diaper rash. Keeping the skin as dry as possible is one of the best methods of prevention. Hospital nurseries often harbor resistant strains of these organisms, and you may bring them home in your new bundle of joy. Elderly or incontinent adults must also be aware of this challenge.

* Proper laundering of all baby clothing as well as diapers in *MelaPower Laundry Detergent* enriched with 1 capful of *Sol-U-Mel* and 1 to 2 tsp of *MelaBrite*, will ensure that both colors and whites will be bright and clean-smelling.

Antibacterial Liquid Soap or *The Gold Bar* should be used to bathe your baby. After towel drying, allow the skin to air dry (in direct sunlight if possible) for a few minutes. Apply *Renew Intensive Skin Therapy* or *Moisturizing Hand Creme* to form a natural moisture barrier on the skin before diapering.

NOTE: *Sol-U-Mel* should not be used in a baby's bath water as the green soap in it may irritate sensitive skin (newborns lack active sweat glands).

DIARRHEA

A sudden increase in stool volume, fluidity, or frequency of fecal excretion is seen with microbial infections, flu viruses, stress, food poisoning, laxatives, certain genetic and malabsorption problems, and electrolyte loss from vomiting or drugs. The greatest concern is depletion of body fluids resulting in vascular collapse (the heart has nothing to pump). Children under the age of 4 can dehydrate quickly and die from uncontrolled diarrhea.

* Determine the cause, if possible. If there is abdominal pain, fever, or if the diarrhea does not resolve rapidly, seek emergency help without

HEALTHY BODY

delay. Otherwise, begin drinking **Melaleuca Herbal Tea,** 4 to 16 ounces every hour along with **Sustain Sport** for energy and nutrient replacement. The probiotics in **Florify** have proven to be an effective treatment for diarrhea in children, travelers' diarrhea, lactose intolerance, and irritable bowel syndrome. Take as directed.

DISINFECTANTS

Disinfectants work by selectively reducing the population of disease-causing germs to make room for the friendly germs without harming humans or household plants and animals. Sanitation engineers have taught us that in order to control the spread of disease, we must control the number and transportability of disease-causing germs. Several products are effective and especially stand out for their use in disinfecting toys, furniture, clothing, and bodies. See the *Appendix* in the back of this book for a comparison of the disinfectant properties of *T36-C5* to other agents.

* Sponge bathe a sick person with **Antibacterial Liquid Soap** or **The Gold Bar** on a washcloth to reduce surface germs transported through perspiration. Rinse well. Disinfect the air by running a steam vaporizer with 10 drops of **T36-C5** and 2 capfuls of **Sol-U-Mel** in the sick room. For preventing the spread of germs through the skin, use **Clear Defense Hand Gel** or **Wipes** throughout the day to sanitize and kill germs on your hands without the need for soap and water.

To help prevent the spread of germs in the home or office, spray surfaces with **Sol-U-Guard Botanical**, a broad-spectrum disinfectant that is 99.99% effective against common kitchen and bathroom germs. In addition to bathroom and kitchen nonporous surfaces, also spray doorknobs, telephones, light switches, toys, etc. **Sol-U-Guard Botanical** is also EPA-approved for use in hospitals, day cares, schools, and nursing homes.

DOG BITE

As incredible as it may seem, over a million people are bitten by dogs every year. Any animal bite can readily become infected. This is because bites are a type of puncture wound where contaminated secretions are injected deep into the tissues. Dog bites are notorious for becoming infected, and the rule of thumb is that any dog bite that breaks the skin, no matter how superficial, will become infected.

* Wash the area with **Antibacterial Liquid Soap** and water and then apply **T36-C5**. Repeat three times each day for several days. Then apply it once each day until the wound is healed. **See your doctor immediately if you cannot verify whether the animal has had a rabies vaccination.**

DOUCHE

A douche is a jet of liquid applied externally or internally to the body. It is used for cleansing and for treatment of infections.

* *Nature's Cleanse* is by far the most effective douche on the market for fighting irritating gynecological conditions including yeast infections, vaginal itching, burning, and feminine discomfort. If *Nature's Cleanse* is not available, 3-6 drops of *T36-C5* added to a bowl of water can be used. Mix it thoroughly and use as a douche or to bathe the affected area. See the *Sitz Bath* section in this book.

DRUG POISONING

Three out of every ten hospital admissions are due to either prescription or over-the-counter drug reactions. Sixteen hundred people die each year from aspirin poisoning alone. Be certain that your drug-oriented health care provider communicates all possible side effects from any needed medications. Eli Lily, pharmacist and founder of Lily Pharmaceuticals, is quoted as saying, "A drug without side effects is no drug at all." Dermatitis, nausea, accelerated heart rate, excessive sweating, stomach pains, and diarrhea are some of the milder reactions. Tumors, kidney failure, diabetes, ulcers, and sudden death are the more common severe reactions. It is estimated that only one third of prescriptions are taken in the proper dosage or for the length of time that they are prescribed. Authorities state that the overuse of prescription antibiotics has resulted in super-resistant strains of bacteria, which defy all known treatment and killed over 13,000 hospitalized patients in 1992 alone.

Some drugs react with others to provide baffling symptoms. When several health care providers are treating the same patient for different conditions, the risk of drug interactions increases. The most recent *Physicians Desk Reference* lists over 2,300 reactions from drugs. Most of these reactions were from the misuse of the drug. Be informed and realize that the majority of drugs are for "treating symptoms" only and do not offer a cure. If your health care provider says you will need to take the drug for the rest of your life, he or she is often referring to this philosophy. Only the body can cure. Prevention and common sense can reduce the need for many drugs and their potential side effects on us and on our environment.

* Always ask your health care provider or pharmacist to list the possible side effects of the prescription drugs you are asked to take. The speed of detoxification can be increased by drinking *Melaleuca Herbal Tea* every hour. Take the *Vitality Pack* with *Oligofructose Complex*, along with *ProVex* and/or *ProVex-Plus* daily for additional detoxification.

See the section on *Detoxification* in this book.

DRY HAIR

Whether your hair is dry, greasy or you simply have an itchy scalp condition, Melaleuca oil, and the hair products that are made with Melaleuca oil, will make you hair healthier and more manageable. It is an excellent conditioning treatment for the hair due to its fresh scent, gentle action, and powerful antiseptic properties. It helps to regulate the activity of the sebaceous glands, cleanses the scalp of bacterial fungal infection, and helps disperse dead skin cells.

* Shampoo your hair daily with **Envia Nature's Salon Shampoo**. Work up a rich lather with a small amount of the shampoo and then rise and shampoo again. Shampooing with the **Envia Nature's Salon Shampoo** designed for your particular type of hair is very effective. These shampoos contain hair-healthy ingredients to nourish your hair while delivering a superior clean. They are very concentrated, so be sparing in your use.

For exceptionally dry hair, 5-10 drops of **T36-C5** can be applied directly to the hair strands or massaged into the scalp. See the sections on **Cradle Cap**, **Dandruff**, **Lice**, and **Ringworm** in this book.

DRY SKIN

Some people have dry skin due to hormonal or nutritional deficiencies, prescription medications or a deficiency of essential fatty acids in their diet. Dry skin can also be caused by aging, the sun, or environmental stress. Hands that work in caustic or cold environments or those that are washed frequently (food handlers or health care workers) can develop excessively dry, cracked skin. Women who are going through menopause are very prone to dry skin and chapped hands. The decreased production of natural oils reduces moisture in the skin.

Dry skin is usually found on the heel of the foot and around the ball by the big toe. On the hands, it is found primarily on the palms, whereas on the elbows it is on the unprotected outside skin. Sometimes cracked and dried skin is the result of psoriasis. It can be traced to frostbite. There is a fungus that may contribute to it as well. It could be a viral skin infection. In short, there are many opinions when it comes to figuring out what causes cracked and dried skin.

* Wash the dry skin area in **Antibacterial Liquid Soap**, and then liberally apply **Renew Intensive Skin Therapy**. Apply **Triple Antibiotic Ointment** or **MelaGel** to the cracked or infected areas. **Moisturizing Hand Creme** should be used on your hands after washing to help restore moisture. When hand chapping has begun, apply **Renew Intensive Skin Therapy** every 4 hours until normal skin moisture is restored. Skin dryness that has invaded deeper tissues or caused swelling will require treatment with **Triple Antibiotic Ointment** every 4 hours. This will help to control the infection until healing is accomplished. **Pain-A-Trate** has been used by some patients with poor circulation. Take the **Vitality Pack** with **Oligofructose Complex** as directed, as well as the **ProVex** and/or **ProVex-Plus** to help improve skin suppleness and elasticity.

When it is possible, protective gloves should be worn to prevent contact by water, chemicals and so on, with the skin.

---

* The information presented in this book is in no way intended as a substitute for medical counseling. Always consult your physician before starting any course of supplementation or treatment, particularly if you are pregnant or currently under medical care. Always read and follow product packaging directions and warnings.

EARACHES

Unlike adults, the ear canal in infants and small children inclines upward from the inner ear toward its exit in the throat. This anatomical uphill climb makes children more susceptible to earaches and inner ear infections.

You do not have to have an infection to have an earache. Milk drinking after weaning, allergies, the common cold, and even teething can cause this problem. A cool breeze can set off ear canal muscle spasms. Many foreign substances have been removed from children's ear canals including beans, beads, blueberries, a live moth, and rocks. Using cotton swabs to clean the ears can push wax and other materials to the back of the ear canal against the eardrum, causing damage. Rapid changes in air pressure (such as landing in an airplane) quickly identify the children and adults who have Eustachian tube congestion.

We should also be aware that the American Medical Association has stated that formaldehyde in shampoos and air fresheners causes earaches. As a result, a serious consideration should be made to convert your home to safer products such as those made by Melaleuca.

* Determine the cause of the pain, if possible. Cover a child's ears when out in cold or windy weather to prevent earaches. Loose cotton pushed into the outer ear canal can help protect sensitive ears. Holding the open end of Styrofoam cups firmly over the ears when landing in an airplane has a dramatic effect on preventing earaches in adults as well as children.

A drop of warm *T36-C5* or *T40-C3* can be mixed with 5 to 10 drops of olive oil or other neutral oil. Insert the oil mixture directly into the outside ear canal with a dropper 3 to 4 times daily. *Renew Bath Oil* can also be used. Symptomatic relief is often given with antihistamines, *CounterAct IB*, *CounterAct Pain*, or *CounterAct Kids Pain Reliever*.

NOTE: For children the mixture should be much weaker. Allow only one drop of *T36-C5* or *T40-C3* to 15–20 drops of pure virgin olive oil. The Melaleuca oil is very strong and if too strong a mixture is used, it creates irritation to sensitive tissues within the ear. **NEVER use straight Melaleuca oil in the ear.**

EAR INFECTIONS

Repeated ear infections with fever and pain, requiring cycles of antibiotics, are a sign of continual blockage of the ear canal. (See the section on *Earaches* in this book.) Infections of the outer ear (pinna) can travel into the ear canal where severe pain is produced. Permanent hearing loss or meningitis can result if treatment is delayed. If antibiotics are unsuccessful, fine Teflon tubes are often surgically inserted through the eardrum, which allows accumulating fluid and pus to drain outward from the ear. The tubes are occasionally expelled within a few days or weeks and constitute a major part of some pediatricians' practices. Other pediatricians refuse to use this technique because of questionable results and the rare chance that the tubes may travel deeper into the middle ear to create new problems. Swimmers, bottle-fed infants, and recently immunized children frequently experience ear infections.

* Don't overlook allergies as a cause of the ear infection. Identify the cause, if possible. See your health care provider for further advice. Never send a child with an ear infection outdoors if the air is cool.

To treat an ear infection, use a drop of *T36-C5* or *T40-C3* mixed with 15 to 20 drops of warm olive oil. Insert the oil mixture directly into the outside ear canal with a dropper 3 to 4 times daily. Avoid using full strength *T36-C5* in ears as local irritation can result. A hot water bottle or heating pad set on low should be put over the ear. Drink 4 to 16 ounces of *Melaleuca Herbal Tea* every hour to prevent dehydration from the fever.

In addition, many have found that chronic ear infections can be significantly helped by consistently taking the *Vitality Pack* with *Oligofructose Complex* (*Vita-Bears* for children) and *Provex*.

NOTE: The American Lung Association cites formaldehyde as a possible major cause of chronic ear infection in children. Formaldehyde is an ingredient in many cleaning and personal care products commonly found in the home.

EAR INFECTION (OUTER)

Outer ear infections primarily afflict young adults and teenagers, and are a common compliant among swimmers. Bacteria, present in rivers, lakes, pool water and the ocean often affects the outer ear canal. Some researchers believe that an increased risk of developing a fungal ear infection may be related to long-term use of antibiotics or birth control pills.

* Dab several drops of *T36-C5* on a cotton swab and apply to the outer ear twice daily. **NEVER drip pure oil into the ear canal.** This cotton swab can be used in the same manner as the cotton earplug under *Ear Infections*.

See the section on *Ear Infections* in this book.

EARRING INFECTION

Earring infections result from the invasion of bacteria at the piercing site.

* Wipe earring posts with *T36-C5*. Rub *T36-C5* on the front and back of the piercing hole. Repeat daily until the piercing site is healed. *MelaGel* or *Triple Antibiotic Ointment* applied around the earring will make it easier and safer to turn as the healing progresses.

HEALTHY BODY

ECZEMA

Eczema is an inflammation of the skin where a known cause may not be readily apparent. It may be attributed to sensitivity, toxicity or an allergy. Eczema is characterized by an outbreak of papules that frequently cause considerable itching. See the section on *Dermatitis* in this book.

* Those with eczema recommend that you use only *Renew Intensive Skin Therapy*. Avoid using the pure Melaleuca oil on the eczema sensitive skin. In addition to *Renew Intensive Skin Therapy*, some have found that washing with *Antibacterial Liquid Soap* and applying Melaleuca's *Moisturizing Hand Creme* works just as well.

Some have also found that washing the area with *The Gold Bar* and then applying *Renew Intensive Skin Therapy* and/or *Renew Bath Oil* is very effective, even for children.

Of course, nothing stops the itching like *DermaCort*. It contains the maximum strength itch-stopping power of hydrocortisone to help soothe irritated skin.

If you have eczema on your scalp, try washing your hair with *Melaleuca Original Shampoo*. Let the shampoo remain on your scalp during your entire shower. After you have dried your hair with a towel, work *Renew Intensive Skin Therapy* into your scalp. The next morning, wash your hair with *Melaleuca Original Shampoo* again. The itching and bleeding should stop within a couple of days and if you continue with this program for another week, you should eliminate your challenge. Continue to use the *Melaleuca Original Shampoo* on a regular basis.

EDEMA

Hot weather, lack of exercise, kidney, liver, or heart problems as well as drug toxicity can cause swelling due to excessive sodium and water retention. A sudden weight gain of 2 to 15 pounds in a few days may be the first signal. Obesity, fatty diet, salty foods, carbonated beverages, and excessive sugar tend to increase edema. Lower legs, ankles, and feet are the most often affected. Facial puffiness usually denotes kidney disease. One way to test for edema is to press on the inside of the ankle with moderate finger pressure. If a "pit" is seen when the pressure is released, this means there is excessive fluid trapped in the space between the cells. Edema that develops only toward the end of the day most often responds to diet, exercise, and stress control.

*Exercise regularly. Drink 2 to 6 cups of *Melaleuca Herbal Tea* each day and take the *Vitality Pack* with *Oligofructose Complex*, *CellWise*, *ProVex* and/or *ProVex-Plus* as directed. Elevate the legs for 15 minutes in the mid-afternoon and evening. Wear support hose when standing or walking for prolonged periods.

HEALTHY BODY

EMPHYSEMA

Mature adults who have been exposed to air pollutants or who have smoked may develop emphysema. The germ and pollution digesting enzymes that are released by the white blood cells cause permanent damage to the tiny air sacs in the lung. The person has trouble exhaling and develops an enlarged or over-extended chest. A simple spirometry test (lung volume) and history usually tell a story of hard work and an abused life. If the person also has allergies, further development of asthma is common. See the sections on *Air Purification*, *Asthma*, and *Bronchitis* in this book.

* To prevent further damage stop smoking, get moderate exercise unless the heart is also damaged, drink 2 to 4 cups of **Melaleuca Herbal Tea** daily, and take the **Vitality Pack** with **Oligofructose Complex**, **CellWise**, **ProVex** and/or **ProVex-Plus** as directed. At night use a vaporizer, steamer or humidifier that has had 8 to 10 drops of **T36-C5** added to the water. The warm and moist air can be very healing. (Adding the **T36-C5** to the water will help to prevent infections from bacteria, yeast and fungus.) Also try rubbing the chest with **T36-C5** followed by **Pain-A-Trate**. If congestion exists, use **CounterAct** cold and flu medicines as directed.

It is most important to remove toxins from the home by converting to Melaleuca personal care and home care products. Use **Sol-U-Mel** to clean all of your equipment.

EXERCISE

Why should we exercise? We should exercise because we are designed to be physical creatures as well as emotional and spiritual ones. A better word for this activity is play. Children expend more daily calories per kilogram of their body weight than adults because of their attitude about play. The purpose of exercise is to improve the efficiency of combining oxygen with fuel to produce energy. In the clinical laboratory this is measured as the VO_2 max, (maximum volume of oxygen used per unit of time). The word aerobics (done with oxygen) describes exercises that tend to improve or condition the body to do this more efficiently. In order to achieve the greatest benefit, an exercise must be chosen that is enjoyable, comfortable, and ideally performed at a level of exertion at which a casual conversation can be maintained. Physically exhausting activities should be avoided if better health is the goal.

Having an exercise target helps you to get the most from your activity. Your target heart rate is based on an equation developed by exercise scientists. You must have a watch with a second hand and be able to take your pulse in your wrist or feel it in your neck.

220 – Your Age x 0.8 = Your Target Heart Rate

Example: If you are 50 years old:

220 – 50 x 0.8 = 136 beats/minute
(about 14 beats in 6 seconds)

This is 80% of your maximum attainable heart rate (at 100%, your heart is put under too much stress). Exercise helps to reduce the resting heart rate. The most complete body exercises are swimming, jumping on a trampoline, and cross-country skiing, because they use so many muscles. The next best exercises are walking, hiking, jogging, soccer, bicycling, aerobic dancing and skating. Court sports, such as tennis, racquetball, handball, basketball and volleyball are good, but do not keep the heart rate even enough to sustain the conditioning effect. Other activities usually need to be included in your weekly workout schedule if you want better overall health. Weight lifting, bowling, archery, baseball, and horseback riding are more anaerobic (done without oxygen) and are great sports, but they cannot provide the kind of activity to keep the blood and oxygen adequately supplied to all organs of the body. Always make sure that you have adequate hydration before your start to exercise (drink 1 quart of liquid before each daily workout).

* Take the *Vitality Pack* with *Oligofructose Complex*, *CellWise*, *ProVex* and/or *ProVex-Plus* as directed. Mature adults should also be taking *ProvexCV* and *Phytomega* as a preventive measure. Eat an *Access Performance Bar* preferably two hours after a meal and 15 minute before exercising. It should be eaten on an empty stomach. Do not drink sugar drinks or milk products with the *Access Performance Bar*. Drink water throughout and after exercise. *Sustain Sport* can be added to your water to help maintain a better blood sugar level. Take *ProFlex* to help repair, restore, and build muscle tissue.

EXERCISE STRAIN

There are several levels of muscle strain. Mild strain occurs regularly with all forms of exercise. Severe muscle strains can cause tearing and bruising. See the section on *Bruises* in this book.

* Overused muscles, tendons (connecting muscles to bones), and ligaments (connecting bones to other bones) are helped by immediately applying ice to prevent swelling. Keep the ice on for 5 to 10 minutes each hour, until the swelling is reduced. *Pain-A-Trate* gives dramatic relief from athletic strains.

EYE

The eye is the organ of sight.

* A major contributor to eye challenges is the typical high-fat, high sugar, preservative-laden American diet. Since the deficiency of just

HEALTHY BODY

one vitamin or mineral can lead to a variety of eye challenges, the **Vitality Pack** with **Oligofructose Complex** and **ProVex-Plus** along with **NutraView** are necessary to protect the eyes not only from macular degeneration, but can often help with blurred vision, cataracts, eyestrain, floaters, itchy or tired eyes, thinning eyelashes, or vascular retinopathy. In addition, the glucosamine found in **Replenex** has shown to prevent some diseases of the eye. People who are near-sighted (myopic) usually have much less glucosamine than people with normal vision.

See the sections on *Allergic Reactions, Cataracts, Eye Injuries,* and *Macular Degeneration* in this book.

EYE INJURIES

Never put T36-C5, Triple Antibiotic Ointment, or Mela Gel in the eye, as they can cause pain and dryness of the eyeball. None of the medicine chest products are approved for use in the eye. For black eye, see the section on *Bruises* in this book.

* None of the Melaleuca products are approved for use in or near the eye. If the injury is due to caustic chemicals splashing in the eye, you should immediately wash the eye with fresh water for several minutes. Contact your eye doctor without delay. Foreign matter in the eye can scratch or even penetrate the cornea. Avoid rubbing the eyes, so as not to cause further irritation. Use only products that are certified ophthalmological grade.

FATIGUE

Fatigue is the second most common complaint doctors hear. Fatigue is more than tiredness; it is an inner feeling of difficulty in performing the most basic physical tasks and usually leads to a "bad attitude." It can be caused from serious disorders such as anemia, cancer, chronic viral infections, low thyroid, hormone production, hypoglycemia, diabetes, allergies, premenstrual syndrome, and the near-exhaustion phase of stress or emotional crisis. It can also be due to correctable factors such as inadequate sleep, malnutrition, or habitual sedentary lifestyle. Clinical depression is often associated with fatigue. See the sections on *Allergic Reactions* and *Anemia* in this book.

* Faithfully take the **Vitality Pack** with **Oligofructose Complex** and **CellWise** as well as **ProVex-Plus** at the rate of 1 capsule for each 25 lbs of body weight per day. Balance exercise with rest. Identify and avoid possible allergic foods in your diet. Periodically see your health care provider for a good checkup.

FEVER

Consult your health care provider whenever a fever is present, and use the information below in conjunction with your doctor's advice. Fever is not an illness, but simply our body's healthy response to an infection. It increases the metabolism and strengthens the immune system. It signifies that you should rest your body and give it the time it needs to fight the cause. Melaleuca oil helps to support the immune system and thus the healing process because it promotes increased sweating (a process that causes the fever to go down on its own) and fights viruses and bacteria.

A rise in body temperature to 100.4 degrees (2 degrees above normal, the normal body temperature being 98.6 degrees) is considered a fever. A portion of the brain known as the hypothalamus measures the temperature of the blood. It stimulates hormones to increase the rate of burning fuel and directs blood flow away from the skin, causing chills. In this way, the body has its own internal thermostat. Bacteria and viruses give off hormone-like substances, known as pyrogens, which trigger the same body reaction.

A fever that comes and goes or lasts over two weeks may involve the "resetting" of the hypothalamus to a higher temperature. Certain types of cancer and brain tumors can cause this. Remember, however, that scientists generally agree that a fever, up to a point, is healthy and is the body's attempt to "burn" the foreign substance or organism out of the body.

* Consult your physician whenever a fever is present. If a fever is less than 103°, drink liquids, including **Melaleuca Herbal Tea**, every 1 to 2 hours and restrict activity. This will help to detoxify the body and prevent dehydration. Since fevers tend to reduce appetite, restrict solid foods. If a fever is above 103°, a tepid enema is helpful to bring the temperature down. Wrapping the legs in cold cloths with a few drops of *T36-C5* on them can also help. If the fever is above 105° for more than 2 or 3 hours, emergency measures should be taken to reduce it and prevent brain damage.

Fever may also be reduced using: *CounterAct Pain*, *CounterAct PM*, *CounterAct IB*, *CounterAct Kids Pain Reliever* or *CounterAct Kids Multi-Symptom Cold Plus Cough*.

Taking a lukewarm bath with three to ten drops of *T36-C5* (depending on your age) can help with the fever. Sponging is also effective if you are too weak to bathe.

FIBROMYALGIA

Fibromyalgia is not a form of arthritis but a medical condition that causes widespread pain and tenderness (soreness to the touch) at specific body sites. Some attribute its cause to an overload of toxic chemicals in the body. Others think it is caused by chronic fatigue syndrome or injury. What is known is that it results in pain, muscle aches, headaches, depression, bladder trouble, insomnia, anxiety, and sometimes numbness or tingling. The discomfort can be located in such unusual places as the neck, outside of the hip joints, upper buttocks, top of the shoulder and inside of the knee. Fortunately, fibromyalgia is not progressive and does not lead to other serious diseases or destruction of body tissue.

People with fibromyalgia have been found to have low serotonin and tryptophan levels. It has been suggested that 5-HTP might be useful, such as is found in Melaleuca's *Luminex*. A larger dose may be even more useful. *Luminex* may also help the depression associated with fibromyalgia, as will moderate exercise. Do simple stretches and flexing.

* Not much is known as to a definitive treatment for this condition; however, a healthy diet, rest, and good nutritional supplements seem to be the most effective. Diet, exercise, and nutritional supplements will be more likely to relieve your pain than painkillers.

Start with a high-fiber, low-fat diet. Eat as many raw fruits and vegetables, whole grains, raw nuts and seeds as you possibly can. Eat skinless chicken, turkey, or deep-water fish. Drink fresh juices, herbal teas, such as *Melaleuca Herbal Tea*, and lots of water. These foods create energy and immunity. Eat four to five small meals a day. *Sustain Sport* is the ultimate "fatigue buster," and the *Access Performance Bar* is a tremendous energy booster as well.

One of the best and most convenient sources of fiber on the market is Melaleuca's *FiberWise* drink and bars. Fried foods, animal fats, soft drinks, caffeine, sugars, and alcohol—all of these have to go. Be aware that stress seems to aggravate fibromyalgia appreciably.

It has been suggested that someone with fibromyalgia take the *Vitality Pack* with *Oligofructose Complex*, which will increase the magnesium level, *CellWise*, and *Replenex*. Magnesium supplementation has produced very good results, which may also be due to its importance in serotonin function. Take the *Vitality Calcium Complete* part of your *Vitality Pack* at night to facilitate deep tissue repair, which is largely accomplished while you are sleeping. Be sure to get sufficient rest—at least eight hours of sleep each night. *RestEZ* is an excellent choice if you need a sleeping aid. For those really rough times, you can add *CounterAct PM*.

ProvexCV is an outstanding supplement that contains certain nutrients that are essential for your wellness. It is also recommended that the body be rubbed with *Renew Bath Oil*.

Taking a saturation dose of the *ProVex* and/or *ProVex-Plus* should also help the arthritic pain. (Take 1 capsule for each 25 pounds of body weight daily for approximately two weeks. Then begin to decrease the number of daily capsules until a maintenance dose is determined.)

Alternate between hot and cold water while showering. Studies have shown cold showers to be beneficial for relieving the pain of fibromyalgia. Massage therapy can also be beneficial. A bath in Melaleuca's *Renew Bath Oil* will relieve muscle aches to an amazing degree because of the Melaleuca oil. Also, the patented *Pain-A-Trate* will help significantly with muscular pain.

---

*The information presented in this book is in no way intended as a substitute for medical counseling. Always consult your physician before starting any course of supplementation or treatment, particularly if you are pregnant or currently under medical care. Always read and follow product packaging directions and warnings.

If you feel that you are coming down with a cold or the flu, take *Activate* at the first symptom. If you really feel you are going downhill, make sure to get as much rest as possible, and double up on your *ProVex*.

Get a *Value Pack* to change your entire household to an environmentally safe atmosphere. Expect 12 to 16 weeks on the above regimen before any change is noted.

FROSTBITE

Exposure to freezing temperatures can cause ice crystals to form in and between cells, which causes cell damage. The skin stings, itches, burns, and sometimes turns red and/or numb. Peeling or blistering may occur in 24 to 72 hours. Lifetime sensitivity to temperature may develop.

* Protecting the body with warm, dry clothing can usually prevent frostbite. Pay close attention to the hands and feet. When frostbite is suspected, immediate action must be taken to warm the affected area.

Since numbness can be an advanced symptom, care should be taken to not overheat the area. Soaking for 30 minutes in water 100 to 110 degrees Fahrenheit is advisable. Then apply *Pain-A-Trate* to maintain microcirculation. Repeat the soaking and application of *Pain-A-Trate* every hour for four hours. *Body Satin Foot Scrub* and *Body Satin Foot Lotion* can also be used to cleanse and stimulate circulation. In addition to following these conservative measures, be sure to check with your health care provider.

The affected body part can become sensitive to cold after one attack and can easily suffer other attacks. Regular exercise and massage can help improve circulation in the area.

FUNGAL INFECTIONS

Several considerations are involved in understanding fungi. These organisms belong to the plant kingdom and are found on all healthy skin. Opportunistic forms of fungi that take advantage of a person's weakened immune system cause many infections. As such, fungal infections are common in people receiving x-ray therapy, taking birth control drugs, steroids, or antibiotics, diabetics, burn victims, and people with tuberculosis or emphysema. Many infections develop during tropical vacations or military service.

Severity can vary from a mild rash on the skin to fatal overgrowth in the lungs. When the infection is localized, it is more easily treated than if it has invaded a major organ. Because of the many forms of fungal infections, microscopic examination of the affected tissue, hair shaft, or sputum is helpful in making a diagnosis. Fungal infections fail to respond to antibiotics and can successfully be treated with Melaleuca oil.

Fungal infections have different names depending on the area of the body affected:

Face and Neck (Tinea barbae)   See the section on *Barber's Rash*
Feet (Tinea pedis)   See the section on *Athlete's Foot*
Groin (Tinea cruris)   See the section on *Jock Itch*
Nails (Tinea ungium)   See the section on *Paronychia*
Scalp (Tinea capitis)   See the section on *Ringworm*
Skin (Tinea corporis)   See the section on *Ringworm*

*For common fungal infections, wash the affected areas with **Antibacterial Liquid Soap**. Dry the area and apply **Renew Intensive Skin Therapy** or **Moisturizing Hand Creme**. For acute outbreaks apply **T36-C5** followed by **MelaGel** or **Triple Antibiotic Ointment**. Repeat at least 2–3 times daily for 7–10 days.

An alternate choice would be to use **Dermatin Antifungal Creme** with clotrimazole and Melaleuca oil. Consult your health care provider for further advice.

GANGRENE

Gangrene is a medical term for the death of tissue resulting from loss of blood supply or a diminished blood supply caused by the narrowing of arteries and vessels. It is a progressive bacterial infection that if, untreated, will require amputation. While it can affect any area of the body, gangrene generally appears on the feet, legs, fingers and arms. The majority of the estimated 50,000 non-traumatic amputations annually in America are performed on diabetics. Amputation is not always required, particularly if aggressive treatment can be initiated immediately.

If caused by the clostridium bacteria, moist gangrene causes blisters, oozing fluid, and putrid odors; thus the term gas gangrene. It also has the symptoms of dry gangrene where the affected area turns black, loses feeling, and has red, inflamed surrounding tissue.

Some of the causes of gangrene are bad wounds and infections, reduced blood supply to an extremity, diabetes, frostbite, drug reactions and swelling from large burns. Sclerosis of the arteries, thrombosis, and embolisms can also cause it. Warning symptoms include pain in the area when at rest and black, blue, or purple colored skin surrounding the affected area. See the sections on *Disinfectants, Diabetes,* and *Frostbite* in this book.

*See your health care provider if symptoms are suspicious. Depending upon the location and advanced state of the infection, antibiotic therapy may be ineffective and often fails to stop the disease. If caught in the early stages, soak the body part in a solution of 1 oz of **Sol-U-Mel** and 4 tbsp of Epsom salts in one gallon of very warm water (106 to 110 degrees) for 20 minutes, every 2 hours. The wound should be allowed to drain as much as possible. Keep the area warm, since the tissue usually feels hot and swollen. Apply **T36-C5** or **T40-C3** every 2 hours to the affected part. **Pain-A-Trate** can increase local blood circulation to the area and should be applied immediately after *T36-C5* or *T40-C3*.

Of course, a good nutritional program is always recommended. The *Vitality 6* pack, (the *Vitality Pack* with *Oligofructose Complex*, *CellWise*, *Florify*, *Phytomega* and *ProvexCV*), is a good start.

GARGLING

Gargling is a very useful treatment for mouth ulcers, sore throats, bad breath, or other mouth and gum infections.

*Use *Breath-Away Mouth Rinse* as directed or as strong as you can tolerate it. "As directed" is too strong for some people. Another excellent gargle is to combine 5–10 drops of *T36-C5* in half cup of warm water. Mix this solution well and then use for a mouth rinse and/or gargle.

GASTRIC ULCERS

Stress, aspirin, or spinal nerve irritation, as well as a poor diet, can lead to ulcers by stimulating the Vagus nerve, which controls production of stomach hydrochloric acid. Some scientists insist that the taking of antacids, while giving temporary relief from stomach acid, in the long run actually elevates production of stomach acid. Statistics show that while antacids are being taken at ever-increasing frequency, ulcers continue to be one of the most frequently treated conditions. Starting as indigestion and stomach pain, this condition can lead to referred back pain, anemia, and fatigue if uncorrected. Our high-stress lifestyle appears to be the most contributing factor.

* For people who have had ulcers for several years, lifestyle should be closely evaluated. The flavonoids in *ProVex* and *ProVex-Plus* help heal ulcers by reducing histamine secretion and by binding to and protecting connective tissue in mucous membranes of the stomach, so take as directed. Drink 2 to 4 cups of *Melaleuca Herbal Tea* each day. Begin an exercise program. Practice relaxation breaks for 20 minutes each day. For acute attacks, drink one cup of *Melaleuca Herbal Tea* every hour. Eat one half of a *FiberWise* bar every two hours between meals. *FiberWise* drink and bars are excellent ways to increase dietary fiber. Eat cole slaw or have boiled cabbage every four hours (compound U in cabbage stops production of stomach acid). Avoid alcohol, caffeine, smoking, and rich or fatty foods, as these stimulate the production of stomach acid.

GENITOURINARY INFECTIONS

Genitourinary infections are a general classification for infections of the genital and urinary organs. The antiseptic, bacterial, anti-itching, anti-fungal, anti-viral, and immune system stimulating properties of *T36-C5* make it an excellent agent for dealing with genitourinary infections.

* See the *Bladder Infections* or *Thrush* sections in this book.

HEALTHY BODY

GINGIVITIS

Gingivitis is an inflammation of the gum tissues that affects nine out of ten people to some extent. It is usually caused by a buildup of plaque. Some believe that toxins within the plaque irritate the gums and cause gingivitis. It often leads to infection and swollen gums that bleed easily during or after even gentle to moderate brushing and flossing. If not checked, this condition may lead to inflammation of the connecting bone tissue and possible tooth loss.

According to a study at the State University of New York at Buffalo, adults who consume less than the recommended 60 mg per day (about one orange) of vitamin C have nearly one and a half times the normal risk of developing severe gingivitis as those who consume three times the RDA (more than 180 mg).

* Brush your teeth a minimum of twice a day with *Classic Tooth Polish* and floss with *Classic Dental Floss*. If the condition is severe enough, apply *T36-C5* to your finger or a cotton swab and dab it on the affected gum areas. Rinsing with *Breath-Away Mouth Rinse* and using *Hot/Cool Shot Breath Spray* may also help alleviate gingivitis. Swishing several times each day with 3-5 drops of *T36-C5* in water or *Breath-Away Mouth Rinse* can be very effective.

Take the *Vitality Pack* with *Oligofructose Complex* for vital nutrients along with *CellWise* to help repair connective tissue around the teeth. Take *ProVex* or *ProVex-Plus* to help reduce inflammation of the gum tissues, and to help prevent plaque buildup. See your dentist for regular checkups.

GLOSSITIS

Inflammation of the tongue is a sign of a local irritation or, more often, a disease elsewhere. Local causes can include mechanical trauma from jagged teeth, ill-fitting dentures, or repeated biting during convulsive seizures. Other irritants include alcohol, tobacco, hot foods, and spices, or sensitization to chemicals in toothpaste, mouthwashes, breath fresheners, candy dyes, or dental materials. The most common general cause of glossitis is malnutrition or avitaminosis (a deficiency in specific B vitamins). A few rare disorders produce tongue inflammation but are determined by first ruling out these common causes.

* Take the *Vitality Pack* with *Oligofructose Complex* as directed. Also take *ProVex* and/or *ProVex-Plus* to help reduce inflammation. Stop smoking. Use only safe dental hygiene products such as *Classic Tooth Polish*, *Breath-Away Mouth Rinse*, and *Classic Dental Floss*. Drink 2 to 4 cups of *Melaleuca Herbal Tea* each day. Have dental checkups regularly.

GOUT

A condition with painful joints of the toes, fingers, or other areas, along with elevated blood uric acid, is typically known as gout. Sharp

---

*The information presented in this book is in no way intended as a substitute for medical counseling. Always consult your physician before starting any course of supplementation or treatment, particularly if you are pregnant or currently under medical care. Always read and follow product packaging directions and warnings.

crystals cause physical damage to the cartilage. Once known as a "rich man's disease," gout affects those who are usually overweight and consume alcohol, large quantities of red meat, and rich foods. It is frequently characterized by a sudden onset of extreme pain with the big toe swelling and becoming highly inflamed. While there sometimes is a headache and other times a fever that accompanies it, the most pronounced symptom is that huge, painful swollen big toe. Have a thorough physical examination performed and begin following the recommendations of a health care provider.

 * Start a low-stress diet consisting of more vegetables (a "greens and beans" diet) and fewer animal products. Take **Replenex** to help rebuild damaged cartilage. Drink 2 to 4 cups of **Melaleuca Herbal Tea** each day. Apply **Pain-A-Trate** to any affected joint 2 to 4 times each day at first, then each morning and evening until painless mobility is achieved. Take a hot soak with 1 capful of **Sol-U-Mel** in 1 quart of water 30 minutes each morning to minimize damage to cartilage.

It has been suggested that someone with gout take the **Vitality Pack**, **CellWise**, **Replenex** and **ProVex-Plus**. It is important to decrease uric acid levels in the blood. When the body is deficient in certain vitamins (such as B5, A and E) excessive amounts of uric acid may be produced. The **Vitality Pack** with **Oligofructose Complex** will help to prevent these deficiencies. Candida infections will also increase a uric acid blood level, which is why adding **Melaleuca Herbal Tea** to your diet each day may help.

GROWING PAINS

Growing pains are usually associated with a child complaining about leg pains at night. It is generally thought that growing pains are not severe even though they make the leg muscles tighten-up to a degree where one thinks they are severe. However, if you have any doubts about this, be sure to check with your child's pediatrician or health care provider for guidance. See the section on *Osgood-Schlatter's Disease* in this book.

 * Be aware of your child's overall nutritional needs. Be sure she/he is taking the **Vita-Bears**. For the actual pain, try the **CounterAct Kids Pain Reliever** and/or massage the legs with **Renew Intensive Skin Therapy** or **T36-C5**. Mixing **Pain-A-Trate** with one of the other Melaleuca lotions makes a very pleasant massage as well.

HAIR LOSS

One cause of hair loss can be an inherited trait seen in middle-aged men. A receding hairline is caused by an accumulation of male hormones, which alters the natural fats secreted in the scalp and stunts hair growth. The characteristic pattern is thinning and baldness beginning in the front and progressing backward over the head. Research has

HEALTHY BODY

recently shown that men who begin this pattern in their 20s or early 30s instead of the mid-40s have a greater risk of developing heart disease early in life. Male pattern baldness or slow hair loss due to aging has no known proven treatment. It appears to be nature's conservative desire to reduce unneeded plumage as we get older. We do know that protein metabolism (hair is pure protein) slows down by about one-half after the sixth decade of life. We also know that maximizing our nutrition in youth helps avoid or postpone many genetic weaknesses called inborn errors of metabolism.

In conditions other than male pattern baldness, we find quite an array of causes. Doctors have seen partial hair loss in children who were malnourished; patched hair loss due to heavy metal poisoning such as lead; thinning or splitting and lifeless hair due to harsh chemical hair care products; total body hair loss due to stress; and intermittent hair loss in people experiencing bowel parasitic infections. After giving birth, some women will lose up to one-third of their head hair but will quickly grow it back within a year if properly nourished. There have been a few cases of head lice and dog and cat fleabites that have produced immune reactions in the scalps of children, causing temporary hair loss. Dandruff sufferers, due to scratching, often have mild to heavy hair loss. See the section on *Dandruff* in this book. Your health care provider should evaluate complicated or unresponsive hair loss.

*After ruling out the pathological conditions causing hair loss, many people slow down or stop hair loss when simple steps are taken. A daily scalp massage with *T36-C5* or *Renew Intensive Skin Therapy* is often helpful. Use *Melaleuca Original Shampoo* to maintain healthy hair and scalp. Above all else, get adequate nutrition including protein. *ProFlex20* is an easy and delicious way to add protein to your diet. Take the *Vitality Pack* with *Oligofructose Complex* as directed. Adequate rest to prevent stress is essential. Include moderate exercise in your daily schedule to keep the pores of the skin clean and circulation optimal. It has even been suggested that you try rubbing your scalp with *Nature's Cleanse*. Drink *Melaleuca Herbal Tea* on a daily basis.

After an extensive study of about one thousand plant extracts, researchers in Japan discovered that proanthocyanidins extracted from grape seeds "promote proliferation of hair follicle cells isolated from mice by about 230% relative to controls (100%)." And that proanthocyanidins "possess remarkable hair-cycle-converting activity." So consider taking *ProVex*, *ProVex-Plus*, or *ProvexCV* for possible hair growth benefits along with all the other health benefits of these supplements.

HAY FEVER

Hay fever is one of the most commonly seen conditions. It is seasonal symptoms of tree, weed, and grass pollen hypersensitivity. Symptoms include runny, red, and itching eyes and a runny, stopped-up nose.

When possible, avoid exposure to the pollens to which you are allergic. Due to cross-sensitivity, food allergies may reinforce pollen allergies. For example, eating wheat may aggravate a wheat pollen allergy. In that case, avoid eating wheat, oats, rye and barley from May until August.

* The flavonoids in **ProVex** have been shown to have an anti-histamine action as well as anti-allergic action, so take **ProVex** and/or **ProVex-Plus** at the rate of one capsule for every 25 pounds of body weight daily. This should be in addition to your daily **ProvexCV** intake. Each night before retiring, swab each nostril of your nose with a cotton swab containing **Renew Intensive Skin Therapy**. This will reduce the accumulated pollen from the day and moisten dry mucous membranes. Take the **Vitality Pack** with **Oligofructose Complex** as directed to boost your immune system. Drink 2 to 4 cups of **Melaleuca Herbal Tea** each day.

A cold mist humidifier with ½ capful of **Sol-U-Mel** will have an almost immediate affect on breathing and coughing due to allergies and hay fever. During allergy and hay fever season, it is advisable to use it at night in the bedroom of the person who is affected. Some use as much as two capfuls of **Sol-U-Mel** combined with 10 drops of **T36-C5** in the humidifier.

HEADACHES

There are many types, degrees of severity, and locations of headaches. About 80% of all headaches are due to muscle tension or nerve restriction from stress or injury, which inhibits blood flow out of the brain. These respond well to chiropractic adjustments of the vertebral spine and massage of tense muscles. Allergies, eyestrain, sinus or dental infections, viruses, high blood pressure, reduced blood oxygen, low blood sugar, or toxemia (constipation, alcohol, chemical fumes, caffeine addiction, etc.) are other common causes. Brain tumors can also cause slowly developing, continual headaches. Migraine headaches usually are one-sided and can be severe enough to cause nausea and reduced vision. Migraine sufferers get dramatic relief from identifying and eliminating specific sensitized foods from their diet.

* For a tension headache, a gentle massage for 2 to 5 minutes to the back of the neck, on the temples, and on the sinuses over and under the eyes using **Pain-A-Trate** often relieves local muscles and promotes blood circulation. Special care should be taken to keep **Pain-A-Trate** away from your eyes. Apply a hot moist pack to the back of the neck or over the eyes afterward. Most tension headaches are relieved within 10 to 15 minutes with this technique. If symptoms do not improve, keep a log of the frequency, severity, and duration of your headaches and see your health care provider.

Remember, do the simple things first! Begin an exercise program to reduce tension. Take the **Vitality Pack** with **Oligofructose Complex** and **CellWise** as directed. Drink 2 to 4 cups of **Melaleuca Herbal Tea** each day. Take a **FiberWise** drink or bar to maximize bowel elimination.

Drink *Sustain Sport* between meals to maintain blood sugar. Drink water and get plenty of rest. If congestion exists, use *CounterAct* cold and flu medicine as directed. *ProVex* and/or *ProVex-Plus* have been found to be effective in relieving or reducing migraine headaches. *Luminex* often reduces the incidence of migraine headaches, as it boosts the level of 5-HTP, which has been shown to be very helpful in decreasing the number of attacks.

HEARTBURN

Heartburn, also known as acid indigestion, is characterized by a burning sensation in the upper chest. It occurs after eating, bending over, or lying down. Normally the lower esophageal sphincter (a muscular valve) opens just to allow food to pass into the stomach, however when it opens too often or does not close tightly enough, heartburn is experienced because the stomach acids seep into the esophagus.

* Heartburn relief can be achieved through lifestyle changes. Eat dinner earlier; wait at least two to three hours before going to bed after eating. Eat smaller meals more often during the day. If you are overweight, losing weight may have a significant effect on your heartburn. Keep a diet diary/heartburn log to identify your trigger foods.

Upon experiencing heartburn pain, take *Calmicid* as directed.

HEMORRHOIDS

Hemorrhoids are varicosities of the veins of the hemorrhoidal plexus in the anus, often accompanied by inflammation, reddening, and bleeding. Seldom are they painful unless accompanied by more advanced conditions such as fissures (tears) or fistulas (burrow-like tracts from the inner anus to non-healing sores around the anal area). Hemorrhoids bother over 50% of all adults. There are Biblical accounts of piles (hemorrhoids). Hemorrhoidal veins contain blood that is not emptying properly into the portal circulation to the liver. Constipation, laxative-induced diarrhea, pregnancy, and occupations requiring long periods of sitting on hard or cold objects tend to cause this itching, burning irritation.

Constipation causes excessive lower bowel pressure and can cause the external hemorrhoid veins to enlarge suddenly. Thin or flat-on-one-side stools or a full feeling immediately after a bowel movement is a good indication of internal hemorrhoids.

* Preventing this condition is best. Get adequate exercise and water each day. Take *ProVex*, and/or *ProVex-Plus* each day as recommended. *FiberWise* drink or bars are excellent fiber supplements and should be taken every day to prevent constipation. A cotton ball or a 2x2-inch gauze pad soaked with *T36-C5* or *Pain-A-Trate* held in the anal opening can quickly reduce the itching and burning. *MelaGel* applied to the area can also bring quick relief.

Chronic hemorrhoids are best treated as follows: Add 1 oz of *Sol-U-Mel* and 1 oz of *Renew Bath Oil* to 1 quart of warm water. Sponge the solution onto the hemorrhoidal area. Leave for several minutes. Pat dry. Apply *MelaGel, Renew Intensive Skin Therapy*, or *Triple Antibiotic Ointment*. Repeat the procedure morning and night for seven days. A hot sitz bath each evening with the above solution may be very helpful in shrinking any external hemorrhoids.

Stubborn hemorrhoids may require conservative therapy beyond the use of Melaleuca products. Contact your health care provider about non-surgical hemorrhoid treatments.

HIGH BLOOD PRESSURE

No single cause is known for hypertension. Whatever the cause, it will lead to either a restriction of blood flow in the blood vessels or increased heart pumping. Family tendencies are often seen as the most common trait. Lifestyle factors such as type "A" personalities (high stress), smoking, high blood cholesterol and triglycerides, alcohol consumption, and caffeine consumption predominate. Contrary to popular belief, salt consumption in healthy people does not increase blood pressure. (Low blood pressure, however, is often due to a deficiency of salt.) Those who are experiencing high stress and have high blood pressure benefit from restricting salt intake. Actually, deficiencies in many other essential nutrients including magnesium, potassium, and B vitamins are known to be present in people who have high blood pressure, and they are helped by supplementation. See the section on *Cardiovascular Disease* in this book.

* Progressive exercise helps high blood pressure by reducing stress hormones and increasing the efficiency of the vascular system. Take *ProvexCV* to maintain healthy blood pressure, regulate platelet activity and increase vascular integrity. Take the *Vitality Pack* with *Oligofructose Complex* and *CellWise* as directed. Take *Phytomega* daily as recommended. The phytosterols and omega-3 fatty acids in *Phytomega* help to lower cholesterol levels and maintain healthy triglyceride levels for enhanced cardiovascular health. Drink 2 to 4 cups of *Melaleuca Herbal Tea* each day.

HIVES

Hives are a form of skin rash that consists of raised white welts mixed with red patches on the skin. Burning, itching and the formation of smooth patches characterize it. The cause of hives is an allergic or hypersensitive reaction to drug allergies, severe stress, insect stings or bites, exposure to weeds or weed venom, and ingestion of certain foods (particularly eggs, shellfish, nuts or fruits). Desensitization injections can cause hives due to a hypersensitive reaction. Certain virus infections such as hepatitis, mononucleosis, and measles can be announced by the sudden appearance of hives. Hives lasting two weeks or longer can be caused by an allergic reaction to drugs or chemicals such as penicillin in milk, non-prescription drugs, food preservatives, dyes or other food additives. Hives can also result from animal dander. Determine the source and avoid it in the future.

*The flavonoids in **ProVex** have shown to have an antihistamine action as well as an anti-allergic action, so take **ProVex** and/or **ProVex-Plus** at the therapeutic dose of 1 capsule for every 25 pounds of body weight per day until relief is found. This can be in addition to taking your **ProvexCV** every day as recommended. Application of **T36-C5**, **MelaGel**, **Pain-A-Trate**, or soaking in a warm bath with 4 oz of **Sol-U-Mel** and 4 oz of **Renew Bath Oil** usually returns normal circulation to the affected area. Drink **Melaleuca Herbal Tea** 2 to 4 times each day to assist in detoxification. Chronic hives can be due to an underlying disease and should be brought to the attention of your health care provider.

Use **DermaCort** to take the sting out of poison ivy, hives, and rashes. Its unique formula includes pharmacist-recommended hydrocortisone for itch relief plus naturally soothing Melaleuca oil.

Obviously one should determine the source that causes the hives and then avoid it. This might be a good time to consider making the necessary changes to turn your home into an environmentally safe, Melaleuca household.

HOARSENESS

Hoarseness is due to inflammation of the voice box (larynx) and can simply be caused from overuse, such as yelling at an athletic event, or other disorders such as viral or bacterial infections.

*Inhale steam made from adding 10 drops of **T36-C5** and 2 capfuls of **Sol-U-Mel** to the water in a steam vaporizer. Drink hot **Melaleuca Herbal Tea** 2 to 6 times each day. Resting the voice usually reduces the symptoms within a few days and prevents further inflammation. For serious cases see your health care provider.

HOT FLASHES

Not to be confused with a fever, hot flashes can appear suddenly with a stiflingly stuffy hot feeling and reddened sweaty head, face, and neck skin lasting from a few seconds to several minutes. Chills often follow them. Hot flashes occur in over 75% of women at menopause and may occur for more than 5 years. Pregnant women may also experience hot flashes. Menopausal-aged women frequently experience these sudden hot spells with profuse perspiration during the day or night.

Adrenal-pituitary "storms" create an unstable hypothalamus, which brings about inadequate thermal regulation. Insomnia and resulting anxiety can be a complication. Apparently, the hypothalamus of the brain becomes unable to coordinate with other hormone fluctuations and body temperature changes, due to declining estrogen levels. Busy lifestyles and inadequate rest may intensify the general symptoms. Stress also can play a moderate part.

* Reduced stress is vital for control of hot flashes. Avoid sugar, caffeine, red meat (arachadonic acid), and chocolate. Use cold-pressed olive oil as a salad dressing. Get enough rest (night sleep and mid-day nap) and aerobic exercise. Take *EstrAval* and *Luminex* as directed. Maintain proper nutrition including the *Vitality Pack* with *Oligofructose Complex*, *CellWise*, and *ProVex* and/or *ProVex-Plus*. Also enjoy 2 to 4 cups of *Melaleuca Herbal Tea* each day.

HYPOGLYCEMIA (LOW BLOOD SUGAR)

Low blood sugar accounts for more behavioral symptoms than any single condition. Afternoon fatigue, forgetfulness, dull headaches, multiple food allergies, anti-social behavior, difficulty losing weight, bad dreams, sweet or alcohol cravings, sudden loss of energy, eating disorders, fits of anger or depression, body aches, poor protein digestion and slow physical reflexes are the more common symptoms.

Stress, overconsumption of refined sugar, and nutritional deficiencies of minerals and B vitamins appear to be the causes of hypoglycemia. Up to 50% of Americans randomly tested with a 6-hour glucose/insulin tolerance test had an abnormal response. Since the nervous system cannot store fuel, it must constantly be bathed in glucose for normal function. (One judge in California is known for not granting a divorce to couples until they have both taken a glucose tolerance test.) Children experiencing hyperactive behavior following a sugary holiday are well documented by teachers. In adults, sudden drops in blood sugar or low fasting levels (before breakfast) stimulate an instinct to eat something or somebody! Many convicted criminals have a story of sugar abuse. Alcohol is the simplest form of sugar. Untreated, hypoglycemia in some people tends to produce adult-type diabetes.

* Eat nourishing meals with the insurance of the *Vitality Pack*. Eating smaller, more frequent meals is also very helpful. Start with a high-fiber, low-fat diet. Lots of fiber cleanses the body, removes toxins and helps to dilute, bind, and deactivate many carcinogens. It removes excess bile from the stomach and intestine, prevents obesity, lowers cholesterol, stabilizes blood sugar, and increases energy. Avoid refined sugar, caffeine, and cooked fats. Exercise moderately after eating an *Access Performance Bar*. Drink *Sustain Sport* between meals to prevent sudden blood sugar drops.

IMMUNE SYSTEM

The immune system is what protects the body from damage due to infection, disease, or other traumas that can harm the body. Many things,

HEALTHY BODY

including environmental influences and stress, can weaken the immune system. Once it is damaged, viruses, bacteria, or fungi easily access it.

T36-C5 is a valuable and effective way to support the body's defense against infection because it directly influences the microorganisms that attack the body. It also stimulates and improves the activity of the impacted body cells, thereby improving the entire immune system. Using Melaleuca products containing *T36-C5* is an excellent way to strengthen the entire body before surgical procedures and during long-term debilitating illnesses such as glandular fever, hepatitis, and chronic fatigue syndrome. The value of *T36-C5* in slowing down the development and furthering the treatment of AIDS is also undergoing investigation with some success.

* Entirely converting your home to safer products such as those available through Melaleuca can provide a more conducive environment for a healthy lifestyle. Order a Value Pack to convert your entire household at a great price.

In addition, there are several specific things that can be done to help build up resistance levels: 1. Take a bath at least once a week with 8-10 drops of *T36-C5* in the water. 2. Massage the palms of the hands and soles of the feet once a day with *Renew Bath Oil*. 3. Use *T36-C5* in a cold air humidifier at night, put a few drops on your pillow, or leave some to evaporate in a dish. 4. Take the *Vitality 6* pack as directed. (Vitamins should be taken not because we are sick, but to move us from not being sick to being really healthy.) 5. Drink several cups of *Melaleuca Herbal Tea* each day. (It is also delicious as iced tea.)

It has been found that any illness that ends in "itis" (which means inflammation) such as sinusitis, bronchitis, arthritis, and so on, responds well to *ProVex-Plus*. Take a saturation dose of 1 capsule for every 25 lbs. of body weight for the first two weeks and then begin to taper off every few days until a maintenance level is reached.

Take *Activate Immune Complex* at the onset of symptoms. Then discontinue use when the illness has run its course. Take as directed.

One other point of interest: if you or anyone you know is susceptible to infection, they should be discouraged from using commercial furniture polish. Most commercial furniture polishes have a two-week half-life, which means that two weeks after you have used the polish, the toxic chemicals are still half as strong as they originally were. By that time, you have probably used it again! Use *Rustic Touch* instead.

IMPETIGO

This highly contagious skin disease is recognized by eruptions of pustules or blisters. Caused by the streptococcus or staphylococcus bacteria, the infection primarily affects children. Spots or inflamed patches break out on the scalp, neck and face. Blisters that sometimes crust over will appear on the knees and on the hands.

> *Use a cotton ball to apply *T36-C5* to all pimple and blister areas. When dry, treat the area carefully by applying *MelaGel*, *Renew Intensive Skin Therapy*, or *Pain-A-Trate*. Repeat several times each day.

Since impetigo is an extremely contagious infection, steps must be taken to assure that others in the household aren't infected. Wash the affected person's clothes and bedding separately using *MelaPower* and a capful of *Sol-U-Mel*.

INDIGESTION

Gas, belching, or a bloated feeling is a sign of inadequate digestion in the stomach. Eating on the run, inadequate chewing, dilution of digestive juices with copious amounts of liquids, and stress all play a great part in causing indigestion. Many antacids make the problem worse. Malabsorption, ulcers, constipation, and low bowel conditions including hemorrhoids and cancer are seen frequently in people who have a history of indigestion.

> *Sit down. Give thanks. Surround yourself with people you love as often as you can. Savor each bite. Use just enough seasoning to bring out the natural taste. Use *Calmicid* for fast relief of acid indigestion, heartburn, and gas. Take the *Vitality Pack* with *Oligofructose Complex*, *CellWise*, *Florify*, *ProVex* and/or *ProVex-Plus* for overall good nutrition. Drink 2 to 4 cups of *Melaleuca Herbal Tea* each day between or after meals. For more serious digestive challenges, consult your health care provider.

INFLUENZA (FLU)

Influenza is an infectious disease caused by a virus. Its many symptoms may include chills, fever, coughs, headache, and aches in the joints, weakness, and stomach distress. Much more severe than the common cold, the flu can progress to total exhaustion, acute bronchitis, pneumonia, and sometimes death. Since the virus is spread from one person to another, controlling the environment is important. Keeping one's immune resistance up is the best prevention.

> * Upon the first signs of the flu, immediately take *Activate Immune Complex*. Start drinking a cup of *Melaleuca Herbal Tea* every hour. Drink hot *Sustain Sport* to prevent exhaustion. To reduce painful muscles, frequently bathe with *Renew Bath Oil*. Use *CounterAct Cough* medicine as directed. Use *CounterAct Cough Drops* to reduce coughs and sore, dry throat. Use *CounterAct* cold and flu medicines as directed. Go to bed and get all the rest you can.

Use *Calmicid* if indigestion or gas is present. Begin a steam vaporizer with 10 drops of *T36-C5* and 2 capfuls of *Sol-U-Mel* in the infected person's room. Take the *Vitality Pack* with *Oligofructose Complex* as well as *CellWise* and *ProVex-Plus* for an antioxidant effect, which reduces pain of muscles, chest and abdomen.

INGROWN HAIR

When a hair that has not grown beyond the skin's surface folds back under the surface and begins to grow inwardly, it is known as an ingrown hair. Bacterial growth around the hair shaft can cause a painful eruption below the skin.

*Apply *T36-C5* to the specific area of the infection. Continue applications every two hours until the infection has disappeared. Consult your health care provider if the condition persists.

INGROWN TOENAILS

Ingrown toenails are usually due to poorly fitting shoes. One method of preventing a recurrence is to file a V notch on the middle of the nail so that the point nearly touches the quick. This will cause the nail to draw towards the center and prevent the embedding of the edges of the nail. Trimming in a rounded fashion is not recommended, as this actually causes further ingrown toenails. If possible, carefully remove the ingrown part of the nail.

* Soak the foot for 15 minutes in a solution of 1 oz of *Sol-U-Mel* per quart of hot water. Dry thoroughly. Apply *T36-C5* followed by *MelaGel* or *Triple Antibiotic Ointment*. Repeat morning and night. *Body Satin Foot Scrub* and *Body Satin Foot Lotion* can also be used to cleanse and stimulate circulation. If there is an infection, see the section on *Abscesses* in this book.

INSECT BITES

Most plagues and life-threatening communicable diseases have had biting insects (or other families of bugs) as carriers. From the fleas carrying black plague throughout Europe to the malaria-carrying mosquito that took the life of Alexander the Great, insect bites should not be taken lightly. Many unexplained itches and tiny sores on sleepers have been due to nocturnal flying and crawling bugs attracted by body heat. These insects can remain dormant in an unattended dwelling for years awaiting their next (or first) meal.

*When staying in a cabin or beach house, immediately fumigate the area with 10 drops of *T36-C5* in a pan of boiling water. The insect repellent properties of Melaleuca oil are international, thus this works anywhere. Apply *T36-C5* to children's clothing or spray with diluted *Sol-U-Mel* when going to natural parks or walking in the forest in the spring. Mix a few drops of *T36-C5* in *Renew Intensive Skin Therapy* or *Moisturizing Hand Creme* to spread over the skin.

Inspect your children and yourself daily for small breaks in the skin indicating bites. If you discover an attached tick, use curved forceps or tweezers to grasp the tick as close to the person's skin as possible and pull straight up. Wear gloves or have some kind of barrier on your hands to prevent transmission of Lyme disease. Do not apply anything to the tick before removal because of the risk of salivation back into the bite site and possible transmission of disease. Apply *T36-C5*, *MelaGel*, or *Triple Antibiotic Ointment* and cover with a bandage for 24 hours. Also see the section on *Ticks* in this book.

For simple insect bites, use *MelaGel*, especially if you have already started scratching. *Renew Intensive Skin Therapy* will also provide relief.

Also see the section on *Insect Repellent* in this book.

INSECT REPELLENT

These are great alternatives to those awful toxic and poisonous insect repellents that you buy at the store. Melaleuca products are not pesticides and therefore will not stop the varmints from landing on you, but they will greatly reduce the incidence of bites and the reactions that accompany them. They also do not make you feel like you need to take a shower after you use them. Frequent use enhances their effectiveness and your skin will be healthier because of it. It is also important to note that different body types respond differently to the different formulas. Some even say that just taking Melaleuca vitamins has stopped mosquito bites. So don't be afraid to experiment, find your own solution and pass it on. It's important that you make the time to find your personal solution, as the danger of insect bites is often underestimated. Someone in the world dies every 30 seconds because of an insect bite.

* For humans, mix 1 tsp of *Moisturizing Hand Creme* and 5 drops of *T36-C5* and apply to any exposed skin.

Another very effective insect repellent is to mix ¼ cup of *MelaMagic*, ¼ cup of *Tough & Tender,* 2 capfuls of *Sol-U-Mel*, and 5 drops of *T36-C5*. This has been used effectively in the rainforest, so it should work well for most of us.

An alternate solution would be to combine 2 oz of *Renew Bath Oil* with 2 oz of *Sol-U-Mel*, 1 oz of *Tough & Tender* and 20 drops of *T36-C5*.

You might also try mixing 2 capfuls of *Sol-U-Mel* with 10 to 15 drops of *T36-C5* in 16 oz of water in a spray bottle.

Finally, save your used *MelaSoft Dryer Sheets* and carry one in your front pocket, tie it in your hair, or slip it through a belt loop. It really keeps the bugs away. Try it!

INSOMNIA

Insomnia is a condition characterized by the inability of a person to fall asleep or by wakefulness in the middle of the night. Approximately one third of all American adults at one time or another suffer from insomnia. The most common cause of sleeplessness is worry. A stressful lifestyle, indigestion, over-excitement, pain, discomfort, drugs, coffee or other stimulants are other possible causes. General good health is the best approach in preventing insomnia.

*Avoid caffeine, nicotine, alcohol, sugar, and a sedentary lifestyle. Regular daily exercise, deep breathing, drinking most liquids early in the day, and practicing a philosophy that lives life in one-day segments are good habits to ensure good sleep. A relaxing walk after dinner helps digestion and promotes good sleep. Take *Calmicid* if heartburn, acid indigestion, or gas is present. Taking the *Vitality Pack* with *Oligofructose Complex* and *CellWise* and using *Sustain Sport* before stressful activities will help you feel better overall. If insomnia is a habit, try enjoying a warm cup of the *Melaleuca Herbal Tea* at bedtime. Take your *Vitality Calcium Complete* and a *RestEZ*. Breathe slowly and deeply as you begin to relax. Massage your feet with the *Body Satin Foot Lotion.* Yawnnnnnnnnnnn.

ITCHING

For itching that is on the skin, see the appropriate section on *Athlete's Foot, Barber's Rash, Chiggers, Dandruff, Dermatitis, Dry Hair, Head Lice, Hives, Insect Bites, Itching and Flaking Skin, Lice, Mosquito Bites, Poison Ivy, Poison Oak, Poison Sumac, Prickly Heat, Pruritis Ani (Itching Anus), Psoriasis, Ringworm, Sand Flies and Ticks* in this book.

For itching that is due to sexually transmitted infections or in the genital region, see the appropriate section on *Jock Itch, Leucorrhoea, Pruritis, Genitourinary Infection,* or *Vaginitis* in this book.

ITCHING AND FLAKING SKIN

Itching and flaking skin can be caused by many different health conditions. Those suffering from psoriasis or allergies can experience this challenge with their skin. This condition may also be seen in people whose diet is deficient in essential oils and some who are post-menopausal. Also see the sections on *Allergic Reactions* and *Psoriasis* in this book.

* Regularly take the *Vitality Pack* with *Oligofructose Complex* and *CellWise. ProVex* and/or *ProVex-Plus* will help to restore skin suppleness and elasticity. Bathe with *Renew Bath Oil* or *The Gold Bar.* Apply *Moisturizing Hand Creme* or *Renew Intensive Skin Therapy* to the troubled areas. During the day be sure to use *Sun Shades* to protect your skin and keep it moisturized. Continue this at least twice a day for 10–14 days. See your health care provider for further instructions.

JOCK ITCH

Fungal infections of the groin, commonly known as jock itch, can form ring lesions around the sides of the crotch. Scratching of the area can cause secondary infections or chronic dermatitis. The lesions may be complicated by secondary bacterial or yeast infections such as candida. The occurrences are chronic since the fungus may persist indefinitely or may repeatedly infect susceptible individuals. It occurs more often during the summer or when humidity is high.

* Bathing in 1 oz of **Sol-U-Mel** and using the **Antibacterial Liquid Soap** or **The Gold Bar** is helpful in controlling the fungus. After patting dry, apply **Dermatin Antifungal Creme** as directed. **MelaGel, T36-C5**, and **Triple Antibiotic Ointment** are also effective.

It has also been suggested that **Nature's Cleanse** be used as a deterrent to jock itch, as it is very effective on yeast.

Reduce your chances for re-infection by cleaning the bathroom areas using a 16 oz spray bottle containing 2 capfuls of **Tough & Tender**, 10 drops of **T36-C5** and 2 capfuls of **Sol-U-Mel** in water. Wash all contact clothing in **MelaPower** and **MelaBrite** for additional protection.

LEG CRAMPS

Leg cramps are due to either a deficiency in circulating calcium or reduced oxygen to muscles. Muscle cramps tend to appear after unconditioned physical activity. Stretching a "crampy" muscle can prevent knotting.

* Exercise in three steps: warm up for 5 minutes to stretch muscles, do your workout, then cool down by moving slower or walking until the heart returns to its pre-exercise rate. Eat an **Access Performance Bar** 15 minutes before beginning exercise. Take the **Vitality Pack** with **Oligofructose Complex**. Drink **Melaleuca Herbal Tea** and **Sustain Sport** before, during, and after exercise to reduce stress on the body. Take **CellWise** to properly oxygenate muscle cells during exercise without free radical formation.

It is also recommended that **ProvexCV** be taken. Persons who are bedridden may need the assistance of external pneumatic compression boots to maximize circulation and prevent leg pains.

LEUCORRHOEA

Leucorrhoea is an inflammation of the vagina caused by an overabundance of unwanted bacteria or fungi. It can have a variety of causes. Symptoms often include a thick white or yellow discharge and severe itching of the vaginal area.

Pruritis or itching is an irritating condition, which generally accompanies any type of mild vaginal infection, such as trichomonal vaginitis or cervicitis.

* Bathe daily in a warm water bath to which you have added 8–10 drops of **T36-C5**. This will not only act as an antiseptic but will help with the itching and irritation. Sit in the warm water for 5–10 minutes.

Avoid tight clothing, nylon underwear, and harsh bubble baths. Keep tea, coffee, alcohol, and spices to a minimum. See the sections on **Bladder Infections, Pruritis and Thrush** in this book.

HEALTHY BODY

LEUKOPLAKIA

Leukoplakia is white lesions on the skin inside the mouth. They are occasionally pre-cancerous. While no certain cause is known, suspicion is aimed toward chemical irritations from smoking tobacco, chewing tobacco, food additives, food preservatives, food colorings, and dental materials, as well as toothpastes, mouthwashes, and oral medications that contain alcohol, which tends to dry the mucosa. This condition is seen in people of all ages.

* Discontinue contact of questionable substances with the oral mucosa. Use *Classic Tooth Polish, Breath-Away Mouth Rinse*, and *Hot/Cool Shot Breath Spray*. Drink 2 to 6 cups of *Melaleuca Herbal Tea* daily. Take the *Vitality Pack* with *Oligofructose Complex, CellWise, ProVex* and/or *ProVex-Plus* as directed.

LICE

Lice infestation (Pediculosis) involves the head (P. capitis), the trunk or extremities (P. corporis), or the genital area (P. pubis). The lice live directly off blood after biting and puncturing the skin. They live in hairy areas including eyebrows, eyelashes, or beards, where they lay grayish-white eggs (nits), which can be seen with a magnifying glass on the hair follicles. Head lice can live for about 30 days and lay about 100 nits each! The nit is glued onto the hair shaft and hatches in 7 to 10 days where the sluggish, overweight-looking insects seem eager for their first meal. Multiple families of lice cause excruciating pain, irritation and itching. Lice are transmitted by contact with objects such as combs, hats and shared garments. For this reason, head lice are common among school children. Scientists believe that 80% of lice are resistant to prescription and over-the-counter treatments which often contain dangerous pesticides. Fortunately, Melaleuca oil products are a safe alternative.

* Immediately upon suspecting or seeing evidence of lice, shampoo with *Melaleuca Original Shampoo* and bathe with 1 oz of *Sol-U-Mel* and 1 oz of *Renew Bath Oil* added to the bath water. Afterwards, massage *T36-C5* into the scalp and hair to soften and dislodge the nits (the eggs of the lice). Don't be stingy with the oil! Comb the oil through the hair. To fumigate the live insects, wrap your hair in a hot moist towel for 10 minutes. Repeat every other day for at least 5 treatments (10 days).

It has also been suggested to spray the hair with diluted *Sol-U-Mel*, followed by shampooing with *Melaleuca Original Shampoo*. Let it set for about 10 minutes before rinsing. Using a nit comb, the eggs should come out easily. Repeat this procedure to be sure that all the lice are gone.

To avoid re-infestation, wash all clothing and bedding with *MelaPower* plus *Sol-U-Mel* in hot water. Add 2 oz of *Sol-U-Mel* to 16 oz of water and spray the entire house, especially affected areas. Wash hair regularly with *Melaleuca Original Shampoo*.

LIVER DISORDERS

The liver is the master chemist of the body. Every bit of food, every ounce of non-food chemicals (Americans ingest more than 11 pounds per year), and every waste product of the cells in the body is processed through the liver. The liver is so vital to life that we have been given one that is seven times larger than needed. Yes, we could actually have six-sevenths removed surgically and still live. The liver would respond by regrowing to its original size, a feat that no other organ can do.

Besides genetic defects, two main types classify disorders of the liver: toxic and infectious. Liver toxicity occurs from alcohol consumption as well as storing substances in the liver that are unable to be detoxified. Infectious damage occurs from such conditions as mononucleosis, hepatitis, and parasites. Once the liver is damaged, it begins to affect every other function and system of the body. Protecting the liver is of vital concern in these days of environmental pollution and untreatable infectious diseases.

* Drink plenty of water. Prepare food in a safe manner and demand safe handling by food establishments. Drink 2 to 4 cups of *Melaleuca Herbal Tea* each day. Take the *Vitality Pack* with *Oligofructose Complex*, *CellWise*, *ProVex* and/or *ProVex-Plus* as directed.

NOTE: Allowing the liver to detoxify is essential for health. Our great grandmothers used to give the family sulfur and molasses, along with cod liver oil, each spring. Unless you are a child, pregnant, nursing or hypoglycemic, you may want to do the following spring and fall liver cleanse:

Eat only raw, steamed, or juiced vegetables, or vegetable soup and rice for one week. Drink one quart of apple juice along with 2 to 4 cups of *Melaleuca Herbal Tea* each day. On the sixth and seventh day, take one-fourth to one-half cup of olive oil followed by 1 tbsp of Epsom salt dissolved in citrus juice. Stay close to home those days. Some nausea may occur due to the release of bile. Consult your health care provider before beginning this regimen.

LONGEVITY

The human body and mind are designed to last one hundred and twenty years. Illnesses, stress, and accidents can shorten that span. Much of our ability to live a full and active life has to do with planning to be well and taking preventive measures against disease early in life. Using health-building Melaleuca products along with a healthy diet and exercise enhances wellness and enjoyment of life. We all will get older, but aging can be slowed significantly using these products.

* Drink plenty of water. Drink 2 to 4 cups of *Melaleuca Herbal Tea* each day. Take the *Vitality Pack* with *Oligofructose Complex*, *CellWise*, *ProVex* and/or *ProVex-Plus* as directed. The antioxidants in *CellWise* and the **ProVex** products are the best defense available against free radical activity, which causes aging and plays a large part in developing age-related diseases. Take **ProvexCV** as directed to maintain healthy blood pressure, help support normal platelet activity and thus give you superior heart protection. Take **Florify** to help maintain the proper balance of flora in the digestive system. Use **Access Performance Bars** daily to help burn stored fat and maintain muscle tone. Take **NutraView** to prevent macular degeneration and cataracts. If you are concerned about maintaining memory, recall or concentration, use **Unforgettables** for cognitive health. Use **Nicole Miller Skin Care** to fight aging and maintain healthy skin.

Convert your home to the environmentally safe Melaleuca products to stop the poisoning of you and your family by all the dangerous chemicals found in the grocery store brand products.

Be happy, smile, laugh and let the significant people in your life know how much you love them. Each day is a gift. Treat it as one. Attitude does make a difference.

LUPUS

Lupus is an immune system disorder of unknown origin occurring predominantly in young women but also in children and older adults. It may begin abruptly with fever simulating an acute infection or it may develop over a period of months or even years. It is characterized by inflamed connective tissue and skin lesions.

Nearly 1.5 million Americans have lupus. It is more common than muscular dystrophy, multiple sclerosis, or leukemia. Lupus can be mild to life threatening, depending on what organs are involved. There is no cure, but symptoms can be treated. It is often misdiagnosed until severe damage has been done. As a result, it is known as the "Great Imitator."

* Take the **Vitality Pack** with **Oligofructose Complex**, **CellWise**, and **Replenex**. Also, saturate with **ProVex-Plus** by taking one capsule for every 25 lbs of body weight for the first 2-4 weeks. Then decrease by one each day. Continuing decreasing until you reach the level of four per day. Never go below four. If you feel that you are slipping, increase the **ProVex-Plus** by one per day. This is not an exact science, so you will need to pay attention to your body and listen to what it is telling you it needs. Only you can determine your maintenance level.

Drink eight glasses of water each day and drink a cup of hot **Melaleuca Herbal Tea** before bedtime. Stay away from highly inflammatory foods, and stay away from all sugar. Give it time. It will take 14 to 21 days for this regimen to saturate the tissue.

Sustain Sport is the ultimate "fatigue buster" and does not make you feel wired like caffeine or sugar. The **Access Performance Bar** is also a tremendous help with energy.

MACULAR DEGENERATION

Macular degeneration is the deterioration of the central focal region of the back of the eye called the macula, and it results in impaired vision. The symptoms can be gradual or sudden, with objects usually appearing distorted in one eye. Upon examination, degeneration is often found in the normal-appearing eye as well. Both men and women, mostly elderly, contract this condition and seldom have any other eye problems. There may be a hereditary link. Since the condition involves lack of nurturing of this normally blood-rich tissue, some scientists believe that it is similar to brain tissue degeneration taking place in senility and atherosclerosis. Laser treatments are often used to treat advanced cases.

See the *Eye* section, as well as the sections on *Atherosclerosis* and *Cardiovascular Disease* in this book.

* Take **NutraView**, which promotes long-term macular health and visual acuity with lutein, bilberry, blueberry, and Vitamin C. Take the **Vitality Pack** with **Oligofructose Complex** and **CellWise**. Take **ProVex-Plus** to promote vascular integrity. Drink 2 to 4 cups of **Melaleuca Herbal Tea** each day. If you are older than 60, get a visual field evaluation test performed by your eye doctor every year.

MASSAGE

This is not a condition as much as it is a preferred treatment. It is a truly wonderful remedy for easing life's aches and pains. In addition, massage helps revive the flesh and motivates the circulation. It increases the production and release of the body's natural healing chemical called oxytocin.

Massage is one of the oldest and most widely practiced health-preserving therapies known. (See the section on *Bathing* in this book.) Part of its benefit is the mechanical effect of "rubbing" and "kneading" tensions from the body. Many times we are not aware of these tensions until we are actually being massaged. Often, we can massage certain muscles on our own bodies. However, the greatest benefit is generally received when a trained pair of gentle hands does it. There are several different techniques, each having certain advantages in specific situations. Massage is especially recommended for those who are bedridden or who are unable to exercise. Well-muscled people can usually withstand more vigorous techniques, while those with less muscle will be comfortable with more gentle techniques. Modern massage therapists are trained in multiple techniques to meet our level of need and comfort.

* Start by taking a hot bath with 1 to 2 oz of **Renew Bath Oil** for 20 to 30 minutes. Light a few Sun Valley Candles and put on some soft, soothing music. Relax. Feel the smoothness of your skin. The person receiving the massage must be in a comfortable position, usually face down. The person giving the massage must not feel hurried or uncomfortable when bending at the waist. Apply ample amounts of warmed *Moisturizing Hand Creme* to one extremity, neck, upper back, or lower back area at a time. Rub *Pain-A-Trate* into tender muscles and over stiff or painful joints. A few drops of *T36-C5* can be massaged into areas that feel cold and need better circulation. Massage the limbs toward the heart area, not away from the center of the body. When done gently, you can do no harm.

MEASLES

Rubeola, also known as red measles, is a highly contagious viral infection characterized by fever, bronchial cough, sneezing, and irritated eyes that are sensitive to light. A brownish-red rash starts around the ears, on the face and neck, and then spreads over the trunk and occasionally over the limbs. The primary symptoms usually last 4 to 7 days before the rash appears, and from 2 to 5 days after the rash disappears. In most cases, a person only has the measles once. Some people who are weakened by the measles suffer complications such as lung or middle ear infections. See the sections on *Rubella, Ear Infections* and *Disinfectants* this book.

* In well-nourished children and adults, measles usually pass without complications. In malnourished or unhealthy individuals, great care must be taken to prevent a weakened immune system. Preventing ear infections (see *Ear Infections*), bacterial infections (see *Disinfectants*), and pneumonia is a primary goal. To prevent respiratory complications, use a warm steam vaporizer in the person's room with 10 drops of *T36-C5* and 2 capfuls of *Sol-U-Mel*. Drink *Melaleuca Herbal Tea* 3 to 6 times each day.

MENOPAUSE

Menopause (stopping of flow) may be natural (average age 45–51), artificial (radiation or surgery), or premature (illness or stress-induced). In a state of health, natural menopause has mild symptoms, such as the ovaries ceasing to produce eggs and shriveling up like gray colored prunes. When a woman undergoes premature menopause, there are underlying causes that need specific attention. The greatest concern during and for about 5 years after menopause is the rapidly dwindling levels of estrogen to the cells of the body. Various lifestyle factors can have a great effect on estrogen production at this time of life, including stress vs. rest cycles.

Hot flashes, sweating, or light-headedness affect approximately 75% of menopausal women and last for about a year. (See the section on *Hot Flashes* in this book.) Approximately 25% to 50% of these women have these symptoms for 5 years or more. Other symptoms of tiredness, weight gain, headaches, irritability, insomnia, and nervousness may be related to both estrogen deprivation and the stress of aging and changing lifestyle roles. Lack of sleep due to disturbances from hot flashes makes the fatigue and irritability worse. Occasional dizziness, numb or tingling sensations, palpitations, and fast heart rate may occur. The risk of heart disease increases. Urinary incontinence and urinary tract infections increase. Nausea, lower bowel gas, constipation or diarrhea, and joint and muscle pains are also common complaints. The major health risk is osteoporosis at this time. (See the section on *Osteoporosis* in this book.) Preventing this challenge should be every woman's primary health concern.

   * See your health care provider and begin following his/her advice for controlling stress. Take *EstrAval Natural Support for Menopause*. Take the *Vitality Pack* with *Oligofructose Complex* and *CellWise* for nutritional support. Take *ProvexCV* for cardiovascular protection. Begin a daily exercise program using the *Access Performance Bar* and *Sustain Sport* drink to prevent low blood sugar and fatigue. Drink 2 to 4 cups of *Melaleuca Herbal Tea* each day and take *CranBarrier* to prevent urinary tract infections. Communication is very important during this time. Overwork and continued stress can prolong symptoms.

MONONUCLEOSIS

   The presence of fatigue, fever, sore throat, and enlarged lymph nodes signifies the illness known as "Mono," which is caused by the Epstein-Barr virus. About 50% of children contract the virus before the age of five and have mild or no symptoms. Recovery is rapid. When infection occurs in young adults, an immune system battle results. Damage is done to human lymphocytes, the spleen, and the liver. Relapses are common if activity is resumed too soon. Many high school and college students miss school because of not heeding the necessary "rest and recover" treatment. No medicines are known to treat this illness.

   The incubation time of the virus is not fully known, but one week to two months is common. The illness can take up to three months to run its course. Complications may occur if it is not properly treated. "Mono" can go on to cause seizures, meningitis, psychosis, chronic fatigue syndrome, respiratory disease, jaundice, and hepatitis. Blood testing can detect past infections for several years after the illness has passed.

   * Complete bed rest for the first several weeks is often necessary to ease symptoms and prevent complications. Mild activity with mid-day rest periods is recommended for the first 4 to 6 weeks. Drink 2 to 6 cups of *Melaleuca Herbal Tea* each day. Take the *Vitality Pack* with *Oligofructose Complex*, *CellWise*, *ProVex* and/or *ProVex-Plus* with juice or broth for the first 2 to 3 weeks, then with meals. Breathe *T36-C5* enriched steam vapor to prevent respiratory complications. Thirty-minute hot baths, with 1 oz of *Sol-U-Mel* and 1 oz of *Renew Bath Oil*, are helpful in the absence of a fever. Do not do heavy lifting, bending at the waist, or jumping for 3 months, as permanent damage to the liver or spleen may occur.

HEALTHY BODY

MORNING SICKNESS

On about the tenth day after conception, the developing placenta begins producing the hormones HCG and estrogen, which may cause mild to severe nausea and vomiting in susceptible mothers-to-be. This, along with tender breasts and no menstrual period, is strong (but not absolute) evidence of pregnancy. A self-administered pregnancy test can be performed on urine, and these tests are now sensitive enough to be accurate only a few days after conception.

*There are no FDA-approved medicines for morning sickness. Any anti-nausea drugs can cause damage to the developing baby. Drink and eat small amounts of bland food (steamed vegetables, baked potato, dry bread, etc.) throughout the day to not stretch the stomach and trigger the very sensitive gag reflex. The first food and drink should be before getting out of bed in the morning. *Sustain Sport* drink is a helpful supplement at this time. Small amounts of *Melaleuca Herbal Tea* taken throughout the day are very calming to the stomach. The need for vitamin B-6 and magnesium is great and can be supplied from the *Vitality Pack Prenatal* with *Oligofructose Complex* (they may need to be ground up and put in a drink or taken in the middle of the night). Ginger is a very good herb for controlling nausea and has no side effects. Take *Calmicid*, which contains a natural stomach-calming herbal complex which includes ginger and chamomile. Take as directed. The use of wrist straps fitted with acupressure beads help some women with morning sickness.

MOSQUITO BITES

In many parts of the country, summer is well known as "Mosquito Season." The pesky little creatures can not only ruin an evening on the porch, but your sleep as well. Prevention is the best method of control. Check the recipe for Insect Repellent and *Mosquito Spray* in this book.

*Apply *T36-C5* to bites and follow with *MelaGel* on any bites where the skin is broken. If the skin is itching significantly without a break occurring, use *Renew Intensive Skin Therapy* or *Moisturizing Hand Creme* to alleviate the itching and the pain. See the section on *Insect Bites* in this book.

MOSQUITO SPRAY

One of the most important things to remember when using Melaleuca products is that they are NOT pesticides and therefore will not stop the varmints from landing on you. They will deter them and greatly reduce the incidence of bites and the reaction that accompanies them. Melaleuca products also do not make you feel like you need to take a shower after you use them, but will actually enhance the healthiness of your skin. It is also important to note that different body types respond differently

HEALTHY BODY

---

to the different formulas. Some say that simply taking the vitamins has stopped mosquito bites. Do not be afraid to experiment and find your own solution and then pass it on! See the sections on *Insect Bites*, Insect Repellent, and Mosquito Bites in this book.

* Mix 4 oz of *Sol-U-Mel* with 4 oz of *Renew Bath Oil* and 5 oz of *Moisturizing Hand Creme*. This formula can be spread on the exposed body skin or over the entire body.

An alternate choice might be to blend 2 oz of *Renew Bath Oil* and 2 oz of *Sol-U-Mel* with 1 oz of *Tough & Tender*, 20 drops of *T36-C5* and 6 to 12 oz of water. Apply this frequently with a spray bottle.

Keep in mind that shampooing with *Melaleuca Original Shampoo* affords insect repellent protection as well.

MOUTH – FOUL TASTE

The human taste buds are highly developed in some people. Certain food tastes are pleasant to some and not so pleasant to others. Disorders of taste can be caused from sinus infections, reduction in smell due to nasal congestion, smoking, or facial nerve damage. Other conditions causing foul tastes are poor dental hygiene, chemical poisoning, heavy metal poisoning, viral infections or psychological depression. Reduced taste can be due to a zinc deficiency in the diet.

* If organic causes for the foul taste cannot be determined, begin a systematic treatment plan of your own. Proper daily dental care with *Classic Tooth Polish*, *Breath-Away Mouth Rinse*, *Hot/Cool Shot Breath Spray*, and *Hot/Cool Shot Sugarless Gum* can be very helpful in restoring normal taste. Have regular dental checkups. Take the *Vitality Pack* with *Oligofructose Complex*, *CellWise*, *ProVex* and/or *ProVex-Plus* as directed. Drink 2 to 4 cups of *Melaleuca Herbal Tea* each day. Avoid being around pesticides and herbicides as well as solvents, paints, or petroleum-based products. If you experience frequent nasal congestion, consult your doctor for allergy testing.

MOUTHBURN RELIEF

Biting something which is too hot can cause a burn inside the mouth.

* Immediately flush your mouth with ice water. Follow with a dab of *T36-C5* on the burned area.

MUCOUS

Thin, watery mucous is a product of healthy membranes in the body and is needed to protect soft tissues from damaging environmental substances. Thick, discolored or stringy sputum (phlegm), and vaginal, eye, stool, or nasal mucous are signs of irritation or infection. Mild bacterial growth, viruses, chronic yeast or fungal infections, digestive problems, stress, allergies and chemical sensitivities can produce this type of mucous.

HEALTHY BODY

* Drink 2 to 6 cups of *Melaleuca Herbal Tea* each day to reduce the number of harmful organisms in the bowel and urinary tract. Use *CounterAct Cough Relief Medicine* as directed. If congestion exists, use *CounterAct* cold and flu medicines as directed. Breathe steam and *T36-C5* to clear nasal and sinus mucous membranes. Douche with *Nature's Cleanse* as directed to reduce vaginal viruses, yeast, molds, fungus, and bacteria. Repeat any of the above to maintain healthy mucous.

MULTIPLE SCLEROSIS

Multiple sclerosis (MS) is an illness diagnosed in over 350,000 people in the United States today. Even now, much is to be learned. In brief, what is known about MS is that it is signified by more than one (multiple) area of inflammation and scarring of the myelin in the brain and spinal cord. Myelin is the tissue that covers and protects our nerve fibers. When this damage occurs, nerve "communication" is disrupted. Thus, a person with MS experiences varying degrees of neurological impairment depending on the location and extent of the scarring. Although there is no known cure for MS at this time, there is much that can be done to make your life easier.

* The following suggestion has been recommended for MS. Take the *Vitality Pack* with *Oligofructose Complex* and *CellWise* as directed. For the first 2-4 weeks, take a saturation dose of *ProVex-Plus*—1 per 25 pounds of body weight per day. Take half in the morning and half in the evening. After the saturation period, you should be able to decrease by one per day and gradually decrease until you are taking four each day. Never go below four. However, if you are decreasing and you seem to be "slipping" a little, increase the dosage by one each day. This is not an exact science, so you will need to pay attention to your body and listen to its needs. *Sustain Sport* is the ultimate "fatigue buster" and will not make you feel wired like caffeine or sugar. The *Access Performance Bar* is also a tremendous help with energy.

Dr. Roy Swank, head of the Department of Neurology at the University of Oregon, put 146 incurable MS patients on low-fat, high-fiber diets (approximately 30-40 grams of fiber per day), with a vitamin supplement and found that 90% of the early stage MS patients had a complete arrest of the progress of their disease. In fact, they showed improvement even over a twenty-year span of the illness. He then looked at the intermediate stage and had a 65% success rate in that it significantly slowed the progression of the disease. This regime was continued for seven years, and it arrested the progression of the MS in patients at the intermediate stage of this disease. In the advanced stages, Dr. Swank found that there was a 30% arrest of the progression

Adding fiber to your diet is easy if you use *Sustain Sport*, *Attain*, and *FiberWise* drink or bars provided by Melaleuca. It is not only easy to do, but they taste good as well!

MUSCLE STRAIN

There are several levels of muscle strain. Mild strain occurs regularly with all forms of exercise. Severe muscle strains can cause tearing and bruising. Overused muscles, tendons (connecting muscles to bones), and ligaments (connecting bones to other bones) are helped by immediately applying ice to prevent swelling. Keep the ice on for 5 to 10 minutes each hour, until the swelling is reduced.

* Pain-A-Trate gives dramatic relief from athletic strains and soreness. Soaking in a hot bath with *Renew Bath Oil* is very relaxing for aching muscles.

NASAL CONGESTION

Nasal congestion comes from a partial blockage of a nasal passage caused by an inflammation of the mucous membrane. Congestion can be caused by infection of the passageway as a result of a cold, an infection coming from the sinuses, or allergies. See the section on *Sinus Congestion* in this book.

* Place two caps of *Sol-U-Mel* and 10-12 drops of *T36-C5* in a cool mist humidifier in your bedroom and breathe deeply all night. A warm air vaporizer will work as well, but it will not last as long and thus is more expensive. Use *CounterAct Cough Drops*, which contain menthol and Melaleuca oil, to reduce coughs and help open nasal passages. If the blockage is severe, take a cloth and drip 4 to 5 drops of *T36-C5* on it and place it on or near your pillow. Placing a few drops of *T36-C5* or *T40-C3* in hot water and making a tent with a towel over your head is also very effective.

NASAL ULCERS

Nasal ulcers are open sores or lesions of the mucous membrane, which are accompanied by sloughing of inflamed tissue.

*Dab *T36-C5* onto the infected area with a saturated cotton swab. This will not only help with the infection, but will aid with the pain as well.

NERVOUSNESS

"A sound mind in a sound body" was the Greek ideal for a healthy person. We now know that what impairs one part of our being will affect the other. Nervousness (mild anxiety) can be due to worry about an unfounded or unlikely situation or event. Deprivation of sleep, clinical depression, and the aches and pains that often accompany tense muscles are typical with nervous people. Nervousness tends to be a learned behavior that depletes the body of valuable nutrients, which in turn perpetuates the condition. Chemical addictions, including nicotine (nervous stimulant) and alcohol (nervous depressant), as well as long-term prescription drugs, should be avoided and corrected before permanent improvement can take place. A healthy body makes its own

HEALTHY BODY

---

*The information presented in this book is in no way intended as a substitute for medical counseling. Always consult your physician before starting any course of supplementation or treatment, particularly if you are pregnant or currently under medical care. Always read and follow product packaging directions and warnings.

chemicals for awareness and response to real problems. Nervousness is one way the body responds to stress. Nearly all mental disorders include nervousness as a component of the diagnosis. See the section on *Exercise* in this book.

* See your health care provider and follow his/her recommendations for stress control, exercise, and diet. Take *Luminex*, which contains St. John's wort, Griffonia seed, folic acid and B-12, daily as directed. Take the *Vitality Pack* with *Oligofructose Complex*, *CellWise*, *ProVex* and/or *ProVex-Plus* as directed as well. Drink 2 to 4 cups of *Melaleuca Herbal Tea* each day. Practice relaxation and breathing exercises. Believe that you can train your body, with help, to be more calm.

NEURODERMATITIS

So far, not much is known about this illness except that the number of people suffering from it has been increasing continuously in the industrial countries of the world. The main symptoms range from severe itching and reddening of the skin to papules and pustules. Experts do agree that its causes are in some way connected to the immune system. It could be a result of overreaction similar to what happens to allergies. It has been observed that people who suffer from neurodermatitis are frequently affected by illnesses that are also caused by an overreaction of the immune system, like allergic asthma and hay fever.

In nearly 90 percent of all cases, neurodermatitis appears for the first time before a person is six years of age. The risk of getting the disease is increased by inheritance, the mother smoking during or before pregnancy, or such socioeconomic standards such as excessive hygiene, stopping breastfeeding sooner, or the stress of holding down two jobs.

Neurodermatitis occurs intermittently and can be triggered by synthetic materials that irritate the skin, rapid changes of temperature, showering or bathing too frequently, contact allergens, natural allergens, food allergens, and stress.

* People with neurodermatitis have very dry skin. Taking oil baths in body temperature water and *Renew Bath Oil* can be very helpful. *Renew Intensive Skin Therapy* as well as the *Renew Bath Oil* directly on the skin is very effective for dry skin.

One of the basic rules for dealing with neurodermatitis is "moist on moist and dry on dry." This means that if acute phases are accompanied by discharges, you should apply moist compresses and cooling ointments and lotions. Contrary to this, during healthy intervals, you should use, as needed individually, the oil, ointments and cremes.

Products with Melaleuca oil are very effective in treating neurodermatitis because they work as a local anesthetic and cool the skin. It can also fight the skin infections that are frequently caused by the damaged immune system.

NOTE: Some doctors have had excellent results using Melaleuca oil and are in favor of using it with neurodermatitis. However, others are critical of it and claim that it may cause a contact allergy. Discuss this with your health care provider.

NEUROPATHY

One of the complications of diabetes is neuropathy. In the early stages of neuropathy there is a tingling and numbness of the hands and feet. In severe cases, the tendon reflexes are decreased or absent. Vibration sense may be diminished or lost. A constant aching type of pain is frequent and is usually worse at night.

* It has been recommended that people with neuropathy take the *Vitality Pack* with *Oligofructose Complex* and *CellWise* for nutritional support. Also take *ProVex-Plus*—1 capsule for each 25 lbs of body weight per day. Diabetics must take very good care of their feet. See the section on *Diabetic Foot Ulcerations* in this book.

NICOTINE WITHDRAWAL

The question is often asked, "How can I quit smoking?" The answer is different for each individual. Some people make up their mind to quit and have no symptoms of withdrawal. Others have neurological and psychological symptoms typical of drug addition. Depression, anxiety, and behavioral changes are common. Since nicotine is of the alkaloid family, along with morphine and codeine, chemical detoxification and emotional support are important to recovery. The appetite-suppressive effects of nicotine are well known. Compulsive eating during recovery must be compensated for with exercise and adequate nutrition.

* See your health care provider and begin following his/her advice. Take the *Vitality Pack* with *Oligofructose Complex*, *CellWise*, *ProVex* and/or *ProVex-Plus* as directed. Drink 2 to 4 cups of *Melaleuca Herbal Tea* each day. Take one *FiberWise* bar or drink each day to speed detoxification. Exercise and drink plenty of water. If needed, do not hesitate to get professional guidance.

NUTRITION

Nutrition is more than just getting enough food. It is getting enough of the right food at the right time for the prevailing needs of the body. Nutrition is the miracle the body performs when changing the molecular structure of food into living human tissue. Everyone has slightly different needs for nutrition based upon genetics, lifestyle, temperament, geographic location, past illnesses, digestive and absorptive capacity, and stress effects. The best thing you can do (after choosing the right parents) is to determine your unique nutritional needs. Waiting until you have a health problem before getting concerned about nutrition is like waiting until your car engine runs out of oil before becoming interested in engine lubrication. Just do it!

Not getting enough of the right kinds of food causes malnutrition.

HEALTHY BODY

On the average, Americans are overfed and undernourished. Ninety-seven percent of Americans have some sort of nutritional deficiency. In any one day 47% of Americans do not consume even one fruit. Twenty-four percent have not chosen any milk products and 18% have avoided consuming even one vegetable. In addition, choosing "brands" that are heavily advertised in place of foods in their original state is often due to clever marketing and advertising techniques. An example is potato chips in place of a baked potato.

Why is the topic of nutrition so important to us? The Surgeon General's Report in 1990 disclosed that, "...eighty percent of all current diseases are due to chronic degenerative states in the body either directly or indirectly related to diet and nutrition." Twenty-five years ago, in spite of volumes of published clinical studies, medical scientists lacked "conclusive" evidence that heart disease and cancer (number 1 and 2 leading causes of death) were related to diet. More recently, only a few physicians would deny that diet and nutrition are the leading cause and the best prevention for these conditions. This sudden awakening of the public to the "new" nutrition has paved the way for fad diets, quick vitamin cures, and overnight experts who have had little training and often less experience in using nutrition as "the" first medicine of choice. As Hippocrates said, "Let your medicine be your food and let your food be your medicine." This should not be too difficult to understand.

*Consult your health care provider. Learn where your weaknesses are and design a plan to promote wellness. There is a big difference between preventing disease and promoting wellness, and we certainly want to work on the latter. So take the *Vitality Pack* with *Oligofructose Complex*, *CellWise*, *ProVex* and/or *ProVex-Plus* as directed. *ProvexCV* should be a regular part of your health care plan as well. Take *Florify* to help maintain the proper balance of flora in the digestive system which will help with nutrient absorption. Drink *Melaleuca Herbal Tea* daily. Get enough rest. Learn how to relax. Practice playful activities (those that make you talk, laugh and breathe deeply) every day. The desire for self-nurturing exists when body, mind and spirit are healthy. Some people may need a little help to get started.

OBESITY

The underlying causes of clinical obesity (being more than 20% above your optimum weight, or having more than 40% of your body weight as fat) often stems from boredom eating, stressful eating, childhood or sexual abuse, drug effects, or improper nutrition. See the section on *Nutrition* in this book. Less than 10% of obesity involves glandular conditions. The obvious problem is in storing more calories than are being burned through metabolic need and exercise. All chronic degenerative diseases are accelerated when obesity is present.

Obesity increases the chances of becoming seriously ill. High blood pressure, stroke, coronary heart disease, and other conditions are more common in an obese person than in someone who is lean. Diabetes is five times more likely in those who are obese. Women who are overweight show a corresponding increase in the risk of developing breast, uterine and cervical cancer. Osteoarthritis is aggravated by obesity. Obese men have a greater risk of developing cancer of the colon, rectum and prostate.

Our ancestors earned and burned 4,000 to 6,000 calories each day just in living, working and walking to school. Because of our automated lifestyle, we earn and burn between 1,200 and 2,000 calories each day. Our nutrient needs for vitamins, minerals and cofactors common to food remain the same. What is wrong with this picture?

Many people have lost hundreds of pounds over the years only to gain it right back. This is due to a physiological condition called "set point." The hypothalamus gland in the brain constantly monitors the temperature of the inside of the body compared with the outside surface of the body. The appetite center, also located in hypothalamus, is activated when factors begin to lower blood sugar. Our bodies are then conditioned or "set" to burn less when apparent reserves begin to drop. We actually slow down our rate of calorie burning to conserve fuel. This is why people can go on a water diet for a week and not lose more than one or two pounds. Fatigue is the most common complaint when total calories are restricted. The set point must be changed so that the body is satisfied with fewer intakes, while it is burning more of its reserves. Restricting dietary fats to less than 20% of daily intake decreases free radicals and hunger sensations. Continuing exercise establishes a new set point, which is the permanent way to control weight. See the section on *Exercise* in this book.

* See your health care provider and begin following his/her advice. Melaleuca's online tool to encourage, inform, and challenge you to meet your exercise and diet goals is *Vitality for Life* at *www.VFL.com*. There are step-by-step exercise and meal recommendations, as well as the community support of your peers in the online forums.

Start with a high-fiber, low-fat diet. Lots of fiber cleanses the body, removes toxins, and helps to dilute, bind, and deactivate many carcinogens. It moves excess bile from the stomach and intestine, prevents obesity, lowers cholesterol, stabilizes blood sugar, and increases energy. Use *FiberWise* drink or bars regularly to increase the fiber content in your diet. Take *Florify* to maintain a proper balance of flora in the digestive system.

Eat an *Access Performance Bar* 15 minutes before exercise. This will allow your body to actually burn stored fat. Plan your meals ahead of time. Remove all unhealthy snack foods from your home. Enjoy *Attain* as a healthy meal replacement. It is especially effective for weight loss when it is mixed with water or rice milk. *Attain* can also be mixed with

ProFlex30 for added protein. Protein helps lower appetite cravings and cholesterol while it increases strength and endurance. *Attain* is a great replacement for **Slim Fast** and **Ensure**. *Luminex* would be helpful in boosting the level of 5-HTP, which is known to help in obesity.

Use exercise, instead of eating, as a means of handling stress. If childhood stresses are present to any extent, contact Overeaters Anonymous and get involved. This non-profit group is an excellent source of free support. If necessary, see a counselor or a health care provider for appetite suppressive-herbs, acupuncture, or specific metabolic testing. Seeking help in getting started is far better than reading a "how to" book and doing it alone. They don't work for 99% of the people who buy them. The weight simply slips back, with interest!

OILY HAIR

Oily hair is often the body's reaction to overwashing. The more often the hair is washed, the more oil our body tends to produce. When the hair is frequently washed it removes much of the hair's natural oils, causing the oil glands to overact.

∗ Wash your hair daily with *Envia Nature's Salon Clarifying Shampoo*. If the oily condition persists after two weeks, cut back to washing your hair every other day. At first this may seem to exasperate the problem, but the body will slow down its oil production when there is an ample amount of oil in the hair. This is one condition which often gets worse before it gets better. Fortunately, a few days of abstinence will pay off in the long run.

OSGOOD-SCHLATTER'S DISEASE *(Growing Pains)*

Young athletes have muscles that are stronger than the actual bones to which they are attached. Heavy track and field events, especially broad jumping, puts an unusual amount of strain on the thigh muscles as they connect with the tibia just below the knee. Some young athletes develop this crippling disorder due to an avulsion (fracture), which tears away soft bone. This causes pain and swelling in the damaged area. This pain was once called "growing pains." Knee supports are often used to prevent injuries in 14 to 18-year-olds. See the section on *Growing Pains* in this book.

∗ Apply an ice pack for 5 to 10 minutes to acute pain areas. Take *Vitality Calcium Complete* with each meal, as well as before and after exercise to maximize bone development. *Vitality*, taken as directed, will enhance growth and healing of injuries. *ProVex* and/or *ProVex-Plus* will reduce pain and inflammation. Apply *Pain-A-Trate* directly to the affected area before and after exercise to minimize swelling and pain. Rub exercised thigh muscles with *Pain-A-Trate* to relax tension and stimulate circulation. Jacuzzi or whirlpool massage is excellent for reducing tension. Do not overtrain. You have a long life ahead of you.

OSTEOARTHRITIS

A degeneration of joint material, including cartilage and bone, takes place when complex systems of mechanical injury, biological stress, biochemical irritation, and enzymatic or nutritional deficiencies are upset. There is no single cause for osteoarthritis. Healthy joints have such little friction that without some precipitating condition, they will never wear out. Apparently the amount of friction in the joint increases after repetitive injury, taking drugs for other conditions (many drugs affect joint and bone metabolism), toxic reactions to environmental pollution (pesticides, herbicides, food additives, etc.) trace nutrient deficiencies, or dietary habits that promote nutritional deficiencies (excessive coffee drinking, alcohol, limited diet selection. etc.). Osteoarthritic joints have less flexible cartilage and more infiltrated bones, causing the telltale enlarged joints on fingers. Exercise tends to pump nutrients in and wastes out of healthy cartilage. See the section on *Arthritis* in this book.

* Exercise and movement are imperative. Some people who have complained of painful hands, especially in cold weather, have found relief by taking up knitting. Start each morning by washing the evening snack dishes by hand in hot water. Apply *Pain-A-Trate* to the affected joints. Take *Replenex* or *Replenex Extra Strength* for cartilage growth. *ProVex* and/or *ProVex-Plus* will help to reduce inflammation.

It has been suggested that someone with osteoarthritis take the *Vitality Pack* with *Oligofructose Complex*, *CellWise*, *Replenex*, and *ProVex-Plus*. Drink 2 to 4 cups of *Melaleuca Herbal Tea* each day.

OSTEOPOROSIS

There are two major types of osteoporosis, primary and secondary. The primary type occurs more often in women and progresses with age. Known as the "shrinking disease," it affects more women over the age of 65 than breast and uterine cancer combined. The loss of calcium prematurely is due to a combination of factors. Women who are slight of build, smoke cigarettes, consume caffeine and animal products, fail to exercise, and do not ingest enough usable calcium from vegetable sources are prone to develop fractures of large weight-bearing bones after menopause. The spine, pelvis, and femoral hip joint areas are most often affected. School-aged girls are often deficient in dietary calcium from vegetable sources. Most are at great risk of never attaining 100% of their expected bone calcium density. Since the expected life span of a woman born in the 1990s is 90+ years, more emphasis should be placed on teaching girls how to prevent this disease.

Secondary osteoporosis is less common and can be due to malabsorption of calcium, endocrine imbalances, prescription or other drug reactions, liver disease, or kidney disease. Recent studies indicate

HEALTHY BODY

that a deficiency of vitamin D is the real cause of osteoporosis. Vitamin D allows your body to absorb calcium. Without it, you can take all the calcium supplements in the world and it would not help.

* If you are having any of these challenges, see your health care provider and begin following his/her advice. Limit or eliminate all dairy and other animal products. Also eliminate soda pop from your diet. If you are a woman of menopausal age and have lost ½ inch or more of height since you were 18, begin a program to minimize osteoporosis. If more than 1 inch of height has been lost, consult your health care provider for a calcium metabolism evaluation.

Women of all ages can benefit from taking *EstrAval* daily as directed. Take the *Vitality Pack* with *Oligofructose Complex* and *CellWise* to ensure adequate trace nutrients. Drink 2 to 4 cups of *Melaleuca Herbal Tea* each day to detoxify. Take *ProVex* and/or *ProVex-Plus* daily as directed. The ingredients in *ProFlex20* are powerful stabilizers of collagen structures, which is the major protein structure in bone.

PARKINSON'S DISEASE

Parkinson's is an incurable neurological disorder. It occurs when brain cells that produce dopamine, an important neurotransmitter (message-carrying chemical), are destroyed by oxidative stress in a part of the brain known as the substantia nigra. Some symptoms include muscle tightness, tremors, and possible speech impediments. High risk individuals are those over 65 who have suffered brain trauma, or have been exposed to high levels of pesticides/herbicides, or who have a family history of Parkinson's.

* High risk individuals should convert the home to Melaleuca products, take a healthy nutritional supplement program such as the *Vitality 6 for 50+* pack, and add *Unforgettables* for cognitive health. This will provide at least four types of antioxidants. Studies show a blend of at least 3 to 4 antioxidants work best in the prevention or delay of Parkinson's Disease. Be sure to eat fresh fruits, nuts and vegetables each day, including walnuts and blueberries, because they are an important source of antioxidants. See *Insect Repellent* in this book for alternatives to chemical pesticides.

PARONYCHIA

Paronychia is an infection or inflammation of the tissues around a fingernail or toenail. Some researchers maintain that yeast such as Candida albicans or bacteria such as Pseudomonas or Proteus cause it. However, the most common cause is usually staphylococcus, with Candida as a secondary invader.

It enters through a break in the skin. It will usually first appear as white patches or a lifting or thickening of one edge of the nail plate. The infection may follow the nail margin and may extend beneath the nail where the infection penetrates more deeply into the finger or toe.

---

* The information presented in this book is in no way intended as a substitute for medical counseling. Always consult your physician before starting any course of supplementation or treatment, particularly if you are pregnant or currently under medical care. Always read and follow product packaging directions and warnings.

Tissue breakdown into the tendons and muscle in the finger or toe may result. Eventually the infected nail may become distorted and lose normal function if not treated promptly.

*Early detection and treatment is important. Wash the affected area with *Antibacterial Liquid Soap*. Soak for 15 minutes in 1 quart of warm water and 1 oz of *Sol-U-Mel*. Pat dry. Apply *T36-C5* to the fingernail or toenail morning and night, and then follow with *Triple Antibiotic Ointment* or *MelaGel*. Cover the area with a loose bandage. Chronic infections may require repeated applications for several months. If Candida albicans is the causative agent in a female, douching with *Nature's Cleanse* may be needed to reduce the fungus. Drink *Melaleuca Herbal Tea* 2 to 4 times each day.

An alternate choice would be to clean the affected area with *Antibacterial Liquid Soap* and then apply *Dermatin Antifungal Creme*.

PLAQUE

Bacteria in the mouth cause a thin, sticky film on the tooth enamel called plaque.

*Gently brush the teeth and tongue after every meal with *Classic Tooth Polish*. Swish your mouth with *Breath-Away Mouth Rinse* to reduce mouth microbes. Floss frequently with *Classic Dental Floss* and chew *Hot/Cool Shot Gum*. Take *ProVex* to help prevent plaque buildup. Have regular checkups with your dentist to maintain healthy teeth.

PLANTAR WARTS

This common wart, usually located on the sole of the foot, can become quite tender when pressure is applied. Plantar warts can be distinguished from corns and calluses by their pinpoint bleeding when the cap is shaved away.

*Apply *T36-C5* to the specific area daily. *Renew Intensive Skin Therapy* will help to decrease and soften cornified tissues around the wart.

POISON IVY, POISON OAK, POISON SUMAC

Complex chemical agents in certain plants are capable of producing acute dermatitis in sensitized individuals. Poison ivy, poison oak, or sumac's blistery rash is a result of coming in contact with the plant itself, or handling the clothing of someone who has been in contact with it. Some people are more sensitive to the oily plant juices than others. Many substances other than poison oak, poison ivy, or sumac cause this acute reaction, including ragweed and primrose. Shoe dyes, formaldehyde in clothing, penicillin, sulfonamides, neomycin, anesthetics, food stabilizers and cosmetics can also produce severe dermatitis.

When out of doors, be aware of these three plants. Poison ivy appears as a plant, bush or vine and has three shiny leaves on each stem.

---

*The information presented in this book is in no way intended as a substitute for medical counseling. Always consult your physician before starting any course of supplementation or treatment, particularly if you are pregnant or currently under medical care. Always read and follow product packaging directions and warnings.

The leaves turn red in the fall. In late summer, it has white flowers or cream-colored berries. Even in winter when the leaves have dropped, the plant can still be quite toxic.

Poison oak is commonly found in sandy soil and pinewoods along both the West and East Coasts. Poison oak has shiny green oak-like leaves clustered in groups of 3 or 5.

Poison sumac has the same characteristics of the two preceding plants. It is a short shrub or small tree having smooth gray bark and branches with 7 to 13 dull green leaflets. The leaves turn yellow in autumn. White berries distinguish it from the harmless sumacs. The poison variety predominantly grows in swampy areas or along streams.

* Immediate removal of the affecting agent is necessary for any treatment to be effective. Immediately wash the area thoroughly with *Antibacterial Liquid Soap* and warm water. Pat (don't rub) dry. Apply *Triple Antibiotic Ointment* and cover with a loose gauze bandage three times each day until resolved. If the rash or blistering has appeared before treatment can be started, soak gauze in cool *Melaleuca Herbal Tea* and cover the affected area. Re-soak the gauze and apply every 15 minutes until the pain subsides. Apply *Triple Antibiotic Ointment* three times each day until resolved. Draining the blisters can be done, but do not remove the covering skin. If pain does not reduce, apply *Pain-A-Trate*. Contact your health care provider, especially if improvement is not seen after four days.

Another solution would be to try *DermaCort*. It is designed to take the sting out of poison ivy, oak and sumac, as well as hives and rashes. This unique formula includes pharmacist-recommended hydrocortisone for itch relief plus the naturally soothing Melaleuca oil.

POULTICE

A poultice is a hot, soft, moist mass applied to a sore part of the body. It is designed to extract pus from an abscess or to remove an infected splinter. It will disinfect, soothe pain, and speed up the healing process. See the *Compress* section in this book.

* Mix a small amount of healing earth (from your health food store) with water and add 3-6 drops of *T36-C5*. Apply the mixture to the affected area and cover with a bandage.

PREGNANCY

Pregnancy is a natural process, yet one out of every eleven pregnancies produces an abnormal baby. External factors that are known to greatly affect a normal pregnancy include the nutrition of the mother and the safety of the environment. Exercise should be continued during pregnancy to maintain muscle tone and prevent back problems from the added 20 to 30 pounds of normal weight gain.

Since the baby is made from molecular building blocks, maximizing

HEALTHY BODY

nutritional needs and minimizing non-nutritional chemicals is vital. Nutritional needs for the expectant mother increase for all of the known nutrients. A lack of folic acid is now known to cause spinal cord defects in babies of deficient mothers. It is estimated that 85% to 90% of all pregnant women take prescriptions or over-the-counter drugs during their pregnancy, with 3% to 12% of abnormal pregnancies resulting from their side effects. Drugs and babies do not mix well. Other dangerous substances include carbon monoxide from cigarette smoke, alcohol, and fumes from paint or toxic household cleaners. Actually, common sense gives us good direction in avoiding these things. The heightened sense of smell and taste during pregnancy gives a woman a great defense for her baby. Remember, if it bothers you, it will bother the baby. See the sections on *Nausea* or *Morning Sickness* in this book.

*Plan for your baby at least one year before you intend to get pregnant. Begin taking the **Vitality Pack Prenatal** with **Oligofructose Complex** as directed. The **Vitality Pack Prenatal** satisfies all of the minimum recommendations for 18 vitamins and minerals, including folate, during pregnancy.

Melaleuca also offers **Prenatal Omega-3**, designed to support healthy fetal brain and eye development. It provides an optimal blend of DHA and EPA to support prenatal cognitive health, and it has a lemon flavor to help mask the fishy aftertaste some pregnant women experience. Also, if a pregnant woman consumes too few omega-3s, the developing fetus will take all that's available, possibly setting the stage for post-partum depression in the mother.

See your health care provider and follow his/her advice. Excercise for 30 minutes daily. Walking is the best exercise prior to the birth of the baby. Eating low on the food pyramid automatically gives adequate roughage to prevent constipation and water retention. Minimizing stress while balancing activity with rest is the best way to prevent toxemia during pregnancy.

PRICKLY HEAT

Prickly heat is a skin eruption caused by inflammation of the sweat glands. Some factors that can cause or worsen the challenge are personal hygiene, nutritional deficiencies, clothing that does not breathe, emotional or physical stresses, detergents, underarm deodorants, cosmetics, and allergic reactions. It is important to identify and remove the cause of this inflammation.

*Massage **T36-C5** into the affected area. It will help to reduce the inflammation and speed the healing. For general care of the inflamed areas, wash your face with **The Gold Bar** and bathe with **Renew Bath Oil**. Dry the skin gently and then apply **T36-C5** followed by **Renew Intensive Skin Therapy**. By using products that contain **T36-C5**, you can continue the healing process.

HEALTHY BODY

PRURITIS

Itchy skin is certainly annoying, yet it can also be an indication of serious disease. However, it is usually a manifestation of a relatively minor ailment such as an allergic reaction or dry skin.

Some of the illnesses and diseases that may cause pruritis include: hepatitis, cancer, kidney failure, kidney infections, liver failure, food allergies, contact allergies due to poisonous plants, soaps and metals, internal fungal infections, skin fungal infections, essential fatty acid deficiency, and vitamin A deficiency.

* Melaleuca's products that contain Melaleuca oil are excellent for pruritis, as the oil is one of nature's finest anti-itch remedies. Some conditions warrant the direct use of *T36-C5*, while others will respond more readily to *DermaCort* or *Dermatin*. See the particular section in this book that applies to the condition you are experiencing, such as *Leucorrhoea* or *Candida Albicans*.

PRURITIS ANI

Pruritis ani is Latin for "itching anus." This area of the body tends to have an almost built-in "readiness to itch." Itching around the anus can be caused from something as simple as pinworms in children, or as complicated as rectal cancer in adults. Internal hemorrhoids are often discovered as a cause in adults.

Many causes stem from chemical irritation with perfumed soap or toilet tissue. Food allergies (particularly eggs or milk) are frequently associated with this condition and often produce a red ring around the anal opening. Food additive sensitivities (colorings, flavorings, and preservatives) are among the most common causes in children. Other causes include fungal growths such as Candida albicans, psychological responses in anxiety patients, skin problems such as psoriasis or contact dermatitis, heavy coffee or cola drinking, poor hygiene, vitamin deficiency, and overly meticulous cleaning with soaps and perfumed powders.

* Try to treat the cause. Soaking in a warm bath with 1 cup of Epsom salt and 1 oz of *Renew Bath Oil* often reduces anal muscle tightness, which contributes to the itch. Avoid applying or consuming chemical conditioned substances. Take *Florify* to help maintain the proper balance of flora in the digestive system and combat Candida overgrowth. Drink 2 to 6 cups of *Melaleuca Herbal Tea* each day. Take the *Vitality Pack* with *Oligofructose Complex*, *CellWise*, *ProVex* and/or *ProVex-Plus* as directed. *Pain-A-Trate* can be dabbed around the anus during extreme cases to minimize itching. *Renew Intensive Skin Therapy* often gives lasting relief from pruritus ani while the true cause is being corrected. If itching persists, consult your health care provider for further evaluation.

PSORIASIS

Psoriasis is a chronic and recurrent disease of the skin that affects up to 3% of Americans. Dry, well-circumscribed, silvery, scaly patches of various sizes characterize it. The patches can vary in severity from one or two lesions to a widespread dermatosis. The cause is unknown, but it appears to be related to inadequate detoxification, possibly through the kidney or the alimentary tract. Thick scaling is probably due to an increased rate of epidermal cell growth. This cosmetic deformity proves socially embarrassing although it is not contagious.

Psoriasis usually involves the scalp and the upper surface of the extremities, particularly the elbows, knees, back, and buttocks. The nails, eyebrows, armpits, abdomen, or groin region may also be affected. Occasionally the illness is generalized.

The lesions are more sharply localized and usually heal without scarring. Hair growth does not appear to be affected. Extension of lesions sometimes produces large plaques up to one-half inch thick. Nail involvement may resemble fungal infections, causing a separation of the nail with thickening, discoloration, and debris under the nail plate. Allergies, stress, and environmental sensitivities should be evaluated. Nutritional needs tend to be elevated.

* Bathe using *Antibacterial Liquid Soap* and soak in *Renew Bath Oil* for 30 minutes each night. Pat dry. Do not rub. Apply *Renew Intensive Skin Therapy* to the scaly areas. Use *T36-C5* on newly inflamed or red areas. Cover the area with *MelaGel*. Daily sunlight exposure for 15 to 20 minutes is helpful. Practice relaxation. Eat healthy food. Take the *Vitality Pack* with *Oligofructose Complex*, *CellWise*, *ProVex* and/or *ProVex-Plus* as directed, and drink 2 to 6 cups of *Melaleuca Herbal Tea* daily to help detoxify. It has also been suggested that you dab straight *Nature's Cleanse* on a small area of the psoriasis. If it does not turn red, repeat several times. Consult your health care provider for further advice.

RADIATION BURNS

Radiation burns can occur to skin that has been exposed to prolonged doses of radiation, such as is frequently used in the treatment of cancer.

* There are many prescriptions that are recommended to aid in this painful condition. However, it has been found that simply using *Renew Intensive Skin Therapy* has proved just as effective.

RASHES

Rashes can be caused by many things. They should be treated to prevent secondary infections and reduce any stinging or itching. See the section on *Dermatitis* in this book.

* Take a hot bath with 1 oz of *Renew Bath Oil*, plus 1 oz of *Sol-U-Mel*. Soak for 20–30 minutes. Pat dry and apply *Renew Intensive Skin Therapy*,

Triple Antibiotic Ointment or *Pain-A-Trate* to the affected area.

If you don't have time for a nice relaxing bath, try adding one capful of *Renew Bath Oil* to a cupful of water and dabbing it on the rash. Pat dry and then apply *Renew Intensive Skin Therapy*, *MelaGel* or *T36-C5*. Of course, nothing stops the itch of a rash like *DermaCort*. It is an anti-itch cream formulated with the #1 pharmacist-recommended itch-stopping ingredient, hydrocortisone, plus Melaleuca oil.

When outdoors, be sure to use *Sun Shades Sunscreen* and *Sun Shades Lip Balm* (SPF 15). If exposed to the sun for any length of time, use the *Sun Shades After Sun Hydrogel E* when you go inside to instantly cool overexposed skin, reduce redness, and soothe dryness.

Another suggestion is to mix *T36-C5* with olive oil and put it on the skin of someone with poison ivy, oak or sumac. This works particularly well on the skin of children. Within 24 hours they will usually start healing and they will feel better immediately. Mix a few drops of the oil with ⅛ cup of olive oil and apply it with cotton balls several times each day.

The preceding addresses treating the results of the condition rather than dealing with the cause of the condition. A program of regularly taking *ProVex* and/or *ProVex-Plus* along with the *Vitality Pack* with *Oligofructose Complex* has been suggested for allergies of all kinds. However, if you think you have too many rashes, you may want to talk with your health care provider about the possibility of having allergy tests done. Undergoing a series of allergy tests can point toward determining the challenge.

NOTE: Anyone with contact dermatitis should NOT use a Melaleuca alternifolia oil product. Even if a situation seems to be improving, it may grow worse.

For other types of rash, see the *Diaper Rash* and *Shaving Rash* sections in this book.

RAZOR BURNS

Razor burns can happen when the skin is not sufficiently protected before being shaved. This can be caused by not enough lubrication or ineffective lubrication.

*Alloy Shave Gel can protect your skin when you shave by moisturizing it. Its unique blend of aloe vera, vitamin E and green tea, and melaleuca oil forms a moisturizing film. Combined, your sharp razor will glide over your skin.

Women can use *Body Satin Shave Gel*. It does not contain melaleuca oil, but the "buttersilk" formulation does wonders for the prevention of razor burn in the bikini area.

RHEUMATISM

Soreness in the joints and muscles, red and swollen joints, backaches, a stiff knee, and many other ailments can identify rheumatoid conditions.

The term 'rheumatism' is used to describe a whole range of disorders, which involve these symptoms. Rheumatism refers to muscular pain, whereas arthritis and gout are associated with pain located within the joints themselves. To arrive at a more specific diagnosis and to find the remedies best suited to you, check with your health care provider.

* Because of pain-relieving properties, products with Melaleuca oil are very effective in treating rheumatism. They also improve blood circulation and flexibility. Since rheumatism, like arthritis, is aggravated by an accumulation of toxins in the system, your diet and lifestyle should be evaluated.

A warm bath can provide instant pain relief. Add 8 to 10 drops of **T36-C5** to your warm bath water and bathe with **Renew Bath Oil** as it, too, has pain-relieving properties. Massage the aching areas twice a day with **Pain-A-Trate** to increase circulation and dispose of pain-causing toxic substances.

Since rheumatism is worsened by an accumulation of toxic substances in the body, consider changing your diet. 1. Eat as little protein from animals and eggs as possible. 2. Eat a lot of raw vegetables and fruit. 3. Take the **Vitality Pack** with **Oligofructose Complex** as directed daily. See the sections on **Arthritis** and **Aches and Pains** in this book.

RINGWORM

A round, reddened, often bulls-eye appearing rash anywhere on the skin is evidence of ringworm. Dermatophytes fungi cause the superficial infection (those that invade only dead tissue of the skin, nails, or hair). At least three different strains of fungi can cause ringworm. Household pets such as cats and dogs carry these fungi on their fur and skin. Some cases produce only mild inflammation and often go unnoticed and untreated, then gradually reappear in hot weather. Other types cause a sudden outbreak of a violent-looking rash with vesicles and swelling of the tissue due to a strong immunological reaction of the body against the fungi.

Severe itching, especially in the groin area, provokes scratching, which tends to spread the infection by the fingernails or causes skin damage and produces a secondary infection from bacteria. (See the section on *Jock Itch* in this book.) Since differentiation of these types of fungi is difficult, these infections are approached according to the sites involved. Your health care provider can make a diagnosis after he/she scrapes a sample of skin and either examines it under a microscope or sends it to the lab for culture.

* As in most infections, prevention is the best thing to stop the spread of the infection. Family members must take precautions to not pick up the infection from other family members. Always wear shower sandals when in public showers such as athletic locker rooms or in swimming pools where the fungi grow readily and cross with other strains. Bathing is advised over showering. Always put 1 oz of **Sol-U-Mel**, along with

Renew Bath Oil, in the tub. Use a clean washcloth with *Antibacterial Liquid Soap* or *The Gold Bar.*

Cracking or oozing skin should receive a generous amount of *Renew Intensive Skin Therapy.* Apply *Dermatin, T36-C5, MelaGel,* or *Triple Antibiotic Ointment* on any suspicious areas of the skin immediately after showering or bathing. Direct sunlight and thoroughly air drying the body after showering or swimming is a great preventive act also.

Take the *Vitality Pack* with *Oligofructose Complex, CellWise, ProVex* and/or *ProVex-Plus* as directed to optimize trace nutrients. Drink 2 to 3 cups of *Melaleuca Herbal Tea* daily.

ROSACEA

Rosacea is a skin disease of the face that usually appears after the age of 40. Small, red veins and inflammation of the skin develop on the nose, cheeks, or forehead and are sometimes accompanied by papules, or small knots, with fine scales on up to festering pustules.

The cause of this disorder has not been fully identified, but it appears together with certain other complaints, such as gallbladder disorders, chronic infections, genetically caused vascular weakness, and high blood pressure.

*Avoid coffee, excessive alcohol or tobacco, and exposure to heat, as they can all intensify this skin disease. Treating the skin as though it has acne has proven to be quite effective. The *Zap-It!* skin care program certainly should be considered. See the section on *Acne* in this book.

Check with your health care provider for an accurate diagnosis.

RUBELLA (German Measles or Three-Day Measles)

Fourteen to twenty-one days from the time of exposure to rubella, susceptible persons will feel tired and may have slightly swollen lymph nodes under the eyes, behind the ears, and in the neck. Other symptoms of rubella include the development of a headache, moderate fever and runny nose, and a finely textured pinkish rash which starts on the face and neck, moves to the trunk and limbs, and lasts for about 3 days. The virus is spread through the air or by physical contact. See the sections on *Measles* and *Air Purification* in this book.

Rubella is much milder in children and adults than "red" measles, which not only differs in the color of the rash from rubella, but displays a painful cough and Koplik's spots on the inside of the mouth.

Women in their first three months of pregnancy who are susceptible to rubella, can contract the virus (usually from children) and naturally abort or give birth to developmentally defective and often mentally retarded (congenital rubella) infants.

In children up though teenagers, the illness is generally mild. Except for the risk of congenital rubella, some scientists question the risk/benefit ratio of immunizing children. An immunization offers about 15 years of protection and may pose risks.

Rubella may be difficult to properly determine without a trained health care provider using laboratory testing, as some of the symptoms can resemble other illnesses.

*Since the active virus can be spread from about one week before to one week after the eruption of the rash, epidemics of rubella sweep through susceptible children quickly. By then the virus has spread throughout the body. Only palliative care can be given to ease discomfort and prevent secondary infections such as pneumonia. Soaking in a hot bath with 1 oz of *Renew Bath Oil* and 1 oz of *Sol-U-Mel* for 20 minutes may help diminish the rash. Chicken soup, *Melaleuca Herbal Tea*, and *Vita-Bears* are the rations of choice. Solid food can be given upon request, which is usually after the rash subsides. See also *Measles*.

SAND FLEAS

Sand fleas are fleas found in sandy places. They are sometimes known as beach fleas.

*Applying *T36-C5* to the sting area can be very effective in not only the healing, but it will help with the pain as well. *Triple Antibiotic Ointment* or *MelaGel* can be used on larger areas.

SAND FLIES

Sand flies are a particularly irritating insect, generally found in sandy locations. Their small size allows them to easily get through most protective defenses one sets up. The itching and scratching they cause can create open wounds or sores.

* *T36-C5* gives fast relief for sand fly bites. It not only soothes the itching, but also prevents the possibility of infection. Apply *T36-C5* to the affected area every 4 hours as needed. It is also very helpful to add 8-10 drops of *T36-C5* to a warm bath and relax in the tub for at least 10 minutes. The use of *MelaGel* will protect the area and help with the itching as well.

T36-C5 applied directly to exposed skin, and clothing such as scarves, socks, collars, and cuffs on pants and shirts will serve as an effective sand fly repellent. Sand flies will also avoid your tent or home if you put *T36-C5* on a hanging ribbon or use it in a vaporizer.

See also *Insect Repellents*.

SCABIES (CRABS)

Scabies, or crabs, are transmittable parasitic infections characterized by intensive itching and secondary bacterial infections. They are caused by the itch mite known as Sarcoptes scabiei, which burrows under the skin to feed and lay its eggs. The itching is usually most intense when the person is in bed. The characteristic initial lesions of the burrow are seen as fine wavy dark lines a few millimeters to a half-inch long with a minute papule at the open end. A red lesion occurs on the finger webs, on the under-surface of the wrists, about the elbows and under arms, around the nipple area of the breasts in females, on the genitals in males, along the belt line, and on the lower buttocks. The face is not usually involved in adults but may be in infants. The burrow may be difficult to find, especially when the disease has been persistent for several weeks, because it is often obscured by scratching or by secondary lesions. Diagnosis is confirmed by seeing the parasite under a microscope after a scraping is taken from the burrow. The mites can remain dormant in infected bedclothes or blankets for months awaiting a warm victim to bring them back to life. Scabies are nothing to ignore. See the section on *Chiggers* in this book.

NOTE: Treatment of scabies with lindane-containing medications (Kwell) has multiple hazards to children. Nervous system disturbances have been observed and reported in scientific literature.

*Soak in a hot bath for 20 minutes each night with 1 oz of **Renew Bath Oil** and 1 oz of **Sol-U-Mel**. Apply **T36-C5** to the affected areas each morning and night. Apply **Renew Intensive Skin Therapy** or **Triple Antibiotic Ointment** to give long-term protection against infection. Apply **Pain-A-Trate** to extremely itchy areas. Consult your health care provider for further advice.

Be sure to wash all clothes, towels and bedding separately. Add 2 oz of **MelaPower Laundry Detergent**, two capfuls of **Sol-U-Mel** and 2 oz of **MelaBrite** to your wash water. Line dry rather than tumble dry, since these parasites are so easily transmittable.

SCALDS

Hot water, steam, liquid nitrogen, or liquid propane can produce scalds. Immediate blistering and light colored skin is characteristic. Care should be taken to not dislodge delicate superficial skin. Painful blisters may appear within a few minutes indicating second-degree penetration. Loose, swollen skin without blistering is evidence of third-degree penetration. See the section on *Burns* in this book.

* Immediately apply cold water to hot water scalds and warm water to cold scalds. Pat dry and apply **MelaGel**, **T36-C5**, or **Pain-A-Trate** to the affected area. Wrap the area with a sterile dressing. Begin treating as a second- or third-degree burn.

SEBORRHEA

This is a scaly inflammation of the skin that occurs around the scalp, face, and occasionally on other areas of the body. Seborrhea primarily affects adults and usually appears as dry or greasy scaling and is often misdiagnosed as thick dandruff. In the most severe cases, a yellow or red scaling with papules around the rash appears usually along the hairline

HEALTHY BODY

and behind the ears. If is often found in the ear canal, on the eyebrows, on the bridge of the nose, in the nasal folds, or on the upper chest. Seborrhea dermatitis does not cause hair loss.

Infants in the first month of life may develop seborrhea dermatitis, often called cradle cap, which results in thick yellow-crusted scalp. In severe cases, cracks and yellow scaling behind the ears and red facial papules may be present.

Nutritional deficiency is a contributing cause of seborrhea. Deficiencies of vitamin A, biotin, vitamin B-2 (riboflavin), vitamin B-6 (pyridoxine), essential fatty acids, zinc, sulfur and selenium have all been documented, and treatment with these nutrients invariably results in improvement. In particular, the development of seborrheic dermatitis is a sign of severe essential fatty acid deficiency. Zinc, B-2, B-6, and biotin are all required for optimal digestion and utilization of essential fatty acids.

Optimal results are achieved when antimicrobial treatment is combined with nutritional therapy. The diet should be high in natural fats and protein and low in sugar, particularly refined sugar. Daily doses of essential fatty acids, zinc, selenium, vitamin A, B-6, biotin, and riboflavin should be taken. Genetic and climatic factors, in addition to chemical and allergic sensitivities, seem to affect the incidence and severity of the disease. It is more prevalent in the winter when more time is spent indoors and household chemicals are more concentrated. Some cases of seborrhea miraculously improve with the avoidance of coffee.

*Take the *Vitality Pack* with *Oligofructose Complex*, *CellWise*, *ProVex*, and/or *ProVex-Plus* as directed. Drink 2 to 6 cups of *Melaleuca Herbal Tea* daily for detoxification. Bathe using *Antibacterial Liquid Soap* in a tub containing 1 oz of *Renew Bath Oil* and 1 oz of *Sol-U-Mel*. Shampoo with *Melaleuca Original Shampoo*. Continue the bathing procedure once a day, but apply *T36-C5* with either *Renew Intensive Skin Therapy* or *MelaGel* after each bath.

SHAVING RASH

A rash is an eruption of spots on the skin, in this case caused by shaving. It can lead to a bacterial or fungal infection or be compounded into an outbreak of acne.

*Avoid commercial aftershaves and harsh soaps. Use *Alloy Shave Gel* or *Body Satin Shave Gel*. Follow with *Renew Intensive Skin Therapy* or *Alloy After Shave*. Putting a drop of *T36-C5* on the blade of your razor occasionally will also help.

SHINGLES

The same virus that causes chicken pox in children causes shingles in adults. It manifests as small, very painful clusters of blisters, which form along a sensory nerve on the skin of the chest, neck, face, stomach or limbs. These pink or white blisters contain a clear fluid, which may later become pus. They dry up and disappear in about a week, but the irritation may remain for a longer period of time. See the section on *Chicken Pox* in this book.

   * Shingles can be treated similarly to chicken pox, except for the use of more *Sol-U-Mel* and *Renew Bath Oil*, detoxification, and satisfying the increased nutritional need for B vitamins. Take the *Vitality Pack* with *Oligofructose Complex*, *CellWise*, *ProVex* and/or *ProVex-Plus* as directed. Drink 2 to 6 cups of *Melaleuca Herbal Tea* to reduce virus growth. Add 2 oz of *Renew Bath Oil* and 2 oz of *Sol-U-Mel* to a warm tub of water. Soak for 30 minutes. Pat dry. Apply a drop of *T36-C5* to pustules, followed by *Triple Antibiotic Ointment*. If the pustules are particularly sensitive, apply the *T40-C3*, as it is a rarer, more gentle form of Melaleuca oil. Continue this once or twice a day for 6 days. Consult your health care provider for further advice.

SINUS CONGESTION

   Sinus congestion can be due to mild infections or generalized irritations caused from allergies, chronic airborne pollutants, dust, grasses, pollens, cigarette smoking, or other chemicals. Often, bacterial sinus infections are caused by repeated use of antihistamines, which dry mucous membranes and create opportunity for other infections. Inflammation from mold sensitivity or anemia can also be an underlying cause. When frontal sinuses, found above and behind the eyes, are affected, headaches may occur. Coughing is often associated with deeper irritations in the nasal pharynx and can lead to ear infections in children or nose bleeds in older children and adults. If repeated episodes of sinus congestion occur, your health care provider should determine the cause. If bacterial infections are present, the condition is termed sinusitis. When it is not properly treated, pneumonia can result. Prescription antibiotics are becoming less effective against these types of infections due to their overuse.

   * Drink 2 to 6 cups of *Melaleuca Herbal Tea* each day as a decongestant. (*Note:* For adults only: To ¼ cup of warm *Melaleuca Herbal Tea*, add ⅛ tsp of sea salt. From a cup, snort the mixture into your nose. Tilt your head back and hold it in your sinuses for 10 to 15 seconds. Expel the mixture through your nostrils into a sink. Blow your nose gently. Repeat morning and evening.)

   Use *CounterAct Cough Drops*, which contain menthol and Melaleuca oil, to reduce coughs and help open nasal passages. Dab *T36-C5* directly under each nostril. Breathe the enriched steam from a vaporizer or a bowl of very hot water. To do this, add 10 drops of *T36-C5* and 2 capfuls of *Sol-U-Mel* to the water. Form a tent over your head and the vaporizer, breathing the aromatic vapors through your nose and mouth deeply and gently into your lungs. Keep your eyes closed. Add 1 to 2 drops of *T36-C5* every 5 minutes for 15 to 20 minutes. Repeat each morning and

---

evening, or use the vaporizer all night.

Apply *Pain-A-Trate* on the temples and forehead to reduce pain from the congestion (keep away from eyes). Repeat every 2 to 4 hours for relief. As long as congestion exists, use *CounterAct* cold and flu medicines as directed. See also the section on *Sinusitis*.

SINUSITIS

Sinusitis is an inflammation of the mucous-lined air spaces often caused by an infection spreading from the nose. While often a bacterial infection, Mayo Clinic's Otorhinolaryngology Department published results that suggest fungi caused 96.6% of all chronic sinusitis. You may want to check your home for fungus growth. Also remember that Melaleuca alternifolia oil is excellent in opening closed respiratory passages as it kills both bacteria and microbes.

* Follow the directions under *Sinus Congestion* above.

SITZ BATH

A sitz bath is a therapeutic bath in which only the hips and buttocks are immersed. It is used to soothe itching sensations in the genital area, soothe hemorrhoidal discomfort, and produce healing effects on bladder infections. Some are used in conjunction with a douche to bathe the external genitalia. It will increase the effectiveness of the treatment, particularly in extreme or prolonged cases of infection.

* Put 6 to 8 drops of *T36-C5* into a bowl or bathtub containing warm water. Sit in the bath for 5–10 minutes. For genital itching, rinse the area with a mixture of 4 or 5 drops of *T36-C5* in a container of warm water. Let the mixture run slowly over the genital area.

SKIN CARE

Good skin care is important. Your personal appearance is your own best advertisement, and your overall health is reflected in your skin. The *Nicole Miller* skin care program does make a difference. Much like fructose compounding, *Nicole Miller* uses a delivery system called liposome encapsulation that delivers vitamin C and E to the epidermis. In addition, it delivers even greater amounts of vitamins A, B, C, D, and E to the second layer of the skin. This is important because the dermis is where the new cells are born. *Multi-Action Vitamin Complex* has every vitamin and antioxidant known to have a beneficial effect on the skin in a delivery system. *Timeless Age-Defying Serum* is a revolutionary breakthrough in skin care, as it is a powerful antioxidant blend which shields your face to protect it against damage caused by free radicals and harsh environmental elements.

Nicole Miller uses ingredients in her products that actually reduce lines and wrinkles or plump the cells as opposed to fillers, binders or preservatives. And, remember, good skin care is not just for women.

Men want it and need it just as much as women do.

*In addition to using a good skin care system, such as **Nicole Miller** provides, a proper nutritional program is essential. The **Vitality 6** pack is a good place to start. Add a positive mental attitude, sound sleep (with **RestEZ**), plenty of water and regular exercise, and you can enhance and enjoy that good skin that you inherited. See also the section on **Acne**.

SKIN WOUNDS

These are individual punctures, scrapes, scratches and cuts that break the skin's surface. The top layers of skin are damaged, causing nerves, blood vessels, and lymph vessels to be exposed to the air. This causes immediate pain and creates an opportunity for germs to enter the body. When an injury occurs, the immediate area can become red and inflamed. The infectious fighting white blood cells rush to the site and begin the healing process. A dry protective scab will usually form within a few hours, as nature's protection against infection. Unfortunately, scabs will occasionally obscure secondary infection, so treatment needs to continue as long as redness is present. See the section on **Abrasions** in this book.

*Wash the area gently, yet thoroughly, with **Antibacterial Liquid Soap** and cool water. Cool water quickly reduces the pain. (Warm or hot water increases nerve stimulation and thus pain in most people.) Allow the stream of water to wash off all visible particulates. Pick out any embedded material if possible. Pat dry and apply **T36-C5**. Because of its ability to kill bacteria, **T36-C5** will help treat the infection and the soreness created by the inflammation. As this dries, apply **Renew Intensive Skin Therapy**, **MelaGel**, or **Triple Antibiotic Ointment** and try to allow the wound to remain open to the air. If a bandage is necessary, saturate it with **Triple Antibiotic Ointment** or **MelaGel** to prevent sticking. Repeat this as needed until the wound is adequately covered with a scab and all redness has disappeared.

WARNING: If the skin wounds are deep or contaminated and if it has been five years or more since your last tetanus shot, immediately contact your physician. Older adults are much more susceptible to tetanus because they are not as likely to be current on their booster shots.

SNEEZING

Irritations in the nasal pharynx stimulate local histamine production that increases mucous secretion and triggers the central nervous response to expel the irritant. Food or chemical allergies, sensitivities such as hay fever, and viral infections provoke this response. A sneeze is the most efficient way to spread viruses and bacteria to your family, workmates, and friends. The velocity of air and atomized mucous exiting the nose and mouth approaches the speed of sound! Studies show that particles can be projected up to 20 feet across a room from a sneeze. See the section on *Air Purification* in this book.

* Take the *Vitality Pack* with *Oligofructose Complex*, *CellWise*, *ProVex* and/or *ProVex-Plus* as directed. A therapeutic dose of *ProVex* (1 capsule for every 25 pounds of body weight per day) may be helpful. Drink 2 to 4 cups of *Melaleuca Herbal Tea* each day. Launder handkerchiefs with *MelaPower Laundry Detergent* and rinse in a solution of 1 oz of *Sol-U-Mel* per gallon of rinse water. Air dry. For acute sneezing attacks, put 1 to 2 drops of *T36-C5* on a cotton swab and swab the inside of each nostril. If congestion exists, use *CounterAct* cold and flu medicines as directed.

SORE GUMS

Damage from rough foods, overzealous flossing, or from a toothbrush needs immediate attention to prevent secondary infections and canker sores. Poor dental hygiene or accumulated plaque below the gum line can lead to periodontal infections. See your dentist or dental hygienist without delay. Many health problems stem from improper dental health. See also the sections on *Bleeding Gums* and *Dental – Gum Disease*.

* Following an injury, immediately swish your mouth with *Breath-Away Mouth Rinse*. Follow the printed directions. Apply *T36-C5* to the sore area with your finger or a cotton swab to reduce the soreness. Take *ProVex* and/or *ProVex-Plus* to strengthen gum tissues, reduce inflammation, and to help reduce plaque buildup.

Use the *Classic Tooth Polish* which combines the antibacterial properties of propolis and myrrh with Melaleuca alternifolia oil. Not only does it fight bacteria, which often is the cause of sore gums, but it also works against plaque buildup.

Sore gums may also be caused by a mineral deficiency that can be alleviated by switching to products from the *Melaleuca Vitality for Life Nutritionals*. In addition to changing your oral care to the *Dental Care* line of products, be sure to have regular dental checkups.

SORE THROAT

The challenge to our body's immune system comes partly from the air we breathe, the fluids we drink, and the food we eat. Viruses, bacteria, allergens, pollutants, prescription drugs, and overusing our voice can produce a sore throat. Many people get a sore throat if they do not get enough rest. Sore throats are often the body's first indication of an oncoming cold or flu. In children, a sore throat can precede chicken pox, mumps, colds or measles.

Whatever the cause, proper treatment is necessary to prevent the condition from escalating. Cancer of the throat starts with a mild, chronic sore throat with or without a cough. If a sore throat continues for longer than several days, your health care provider should be contacted. See the sections on *Coughs* and *Hoarseness* in this book.

HEALTHY BODY

* Gargle with *Breath-Away Mouth Rinse* or *T36-C5* to reduce bacteria and viruses. When using *T36-C5*, add 10–12 drops of *T36-C5* to ½ cup of warm water. Gargle with this solution, then spit it out. Use *CounterAct Cough Drops* as needed to help relieve throat pain. Spray the throat with *Hot/Cool Shot Breath Spray* as often as needed. Drinking large amounts of *Melaleuca Herbal Tea* will help, along with getting plenty of rest. In a bedside vaporizer add 2 capfuls of *Sol-U-Mel* and 10 drops of *T36-C5*. Begin taking *Activate*, as directed, immediately.

STRESS

Ninety percent of all visits to health care providers are due to stress-related challenges. Disease, anxiety and the resultant stress in our fast paced society are taking their toll. But they don't have to. Stress isn't always bad, but it is always a choice. Simple things can make a difference. Things like:

Take a lunch break every day.
Make time for family and friends.
Listen to your body. Rest when it says rest.
Keep things in perspective.
Wear clothes that make you feel good.
Prepare the night before.
Live one day at a time.
Be sure the clock and telephone belong to you—not you to them.
Laugh, love and choose to be happy.

* Drink hot or ice-cold *Melaleuca Herbal Tea* each day. On a regular basis, take *Luminex*. It helps promote emotional health and is definitely important for anyone suffering from stress. Carefully consider a good nutrition program. The *Vitality 6* pack is a good place to start. A wholesome balanced diet and regular exercise can help you stay calm. Breathing and relaxation exercises are important stress relievers, too. Give yourself 15 minutes each day that belongs to no one but you. Do anything you want to do with it: read, walk, pray, or suck your thumb! It doesn't matter as long as you know that those 15 minutes are all yours. MAKE time for fun! Your body needs to be healthy both mentally and physically for peak performance. Remember, this is your life—your only life. It is not a practice run.

SWIMMER'S EAR

Swimmer's ear is a common type of outer ear infection. It affects mainly children and teenagers and occurs almost exclusively during the summer months. Water in swimming pools, lakes, or seas may become contaminated with pathogens. These water-borne pathogens readily infect the outer ear canal. They include viruses, bacteria, bacteria-like organisms, fungi, protozoans, amoebas, and parasitic worms. Bacteria and fungi cause the vast majority of outer ear infections.

In acute infections, symptoms include pain, aching, and discharge. With chronic infections, the symptoms are primarily fullness in the ear, excessive wax, irritation and itching.

* To treat these conditions apply one drop of *T36-C5* onto a cotton swab and wipe the outer ear region morning and night. **Do not drip Melaleuca oil directly into the ear.** Continue this twice a day until symptoms disappear. If no improvement is noted within 72 hours, discontinue and check with your health care provider if you haven't already.

See the section on *Ear Infection (Outer)* in this book.

THRUSH

Thrush is a fungal infection of the mouth or throat, caused by the Candida albicans organism. Oral yeast infections are common in persons who are on drug therapy. The condition causes the tongue, gums, inside of cheeks, and throat to have a white patched and swollen appearance. Repeated use of anti-yeast drugs tends to produce resistant strains.

* Use *Breath-Away Mouth Rinse* as directed every 2 hours. Brush with *Classic Tooth Polish*. Drink 2 to 6 cups of *Melaleuca Herbal Tea* daily. Take the *Vitality Pack* with *Oligofructose Complex*, *CellWise*, and *ProVex* or *ProVex-Plus* as directed. Avoid sugar, alcohol, yeast bread products, cheese, and vinegar products.

TICKS

Ticks are small, 8-legged bugs that attach themselves to human (or animal) skin where they feed on the blood. They thrive in a warm, moist environment and may be picked up when walking in rural or suburban yards, woods, in long grass and scrublands. They are often found on dogs, cats, deer, or livestock and may jump to a human host when given the opportunity. Some ticks attach themselves and go unnoticed for several hours; others can cause pain, bruising and even severe irritation. Ticks can carry diseases like Lyme disease or Rocky Mountain Spotted Fever. Certain ticks are known to be carriers of viral encephalitis. Ticks can be extremely harmful, particularly to the very young or the very old. In rare instances, they emit a dangerous toxin that can ultimately result in paralysis and death.

* Inspect your children and yourself daily when any outdoor activity takes place. If you discover an attached tick, use tweezers or curved forceps to gently grasp the tick near its mouthparts, as close to the person's skin as possible and pull it straight out, with no twisting motion. Wear gloves or have some kind of barrier on your hands to prevent transmission of diseases. Put the tick in a jar of rubbing alcohol for identification. Label it with the date, and watch for any symptoms of illness in the victim for two weeks. After you remove the tick, clean

the site with *Antibacterial Liquid Soap.* Then dry thoroughly and apply *T36-C5, MelaGel,* or *Triple Antibiotic Ointment* to the site and cover with a bandage for 24 hours. Disinfect the forceps or tweezers. If fever or any other conditions develop within two weeks of the bite, bring the victim and the tick sample to the doctor immediately. **NOTE:** Current recommendations from the *Center for Disease Control* indicate **not** to coat the tick with any substance prior to removal from the victim because of the risk that the tick will expel infected saliva back into the victim.

TINNITUS

Sufferers of this condition hear unexplained noises such as buzzing, ringing, roaring, whistling, or hissing. It can be in one or both ears. Tinnitus can be a symptom of almost any disorder of, or around, the ear. It may be caused by low-grade infections, anemia, trauma to the head, obstructions such as earwax, Eustachian tube obstruction, allergies, hardening of the acoustic arteries, tumors, toxicity from chemicals such as carbon monoxide, heavy metal poisoning, many drug reactions, and alcohol. See your health care provider.

* If an organic cause cannot be identified, decongestion is the next best approach. If congestion exists, use *CounterAct* cold and flu medicines as directed. See the section on *Sinus Congestion* in this book.

TOOTHACHE

Dental problems are more easily prevented than treated at home. A sensitive tooth, due to root exposure, thin enamel, or cavities can begin aching from things such as sweets, hot or cold foods, or an uneven bite plane. See the section on *Abscesses* in this book.

* For prevention, brush with *Classic Tooth Polish* and use *Breath-Away Mouth Rinse* after every meal. Use *Classic Dental Floss* at least once each day and chew *Hot/Cool Shot Sugarless Gum* frequently. Apply *T36-C5* directly to the sensitive tooth and surrounding gum with a cotton swab to achieve immediate relief, and see your dentist to determine the cause of your pain. Have regular checkups with your dentist to maximize the general health of your teeth.

ULCERS, TROPICAL

Tropical ulcers (also known as naga sores) usually occur in hot, humid climates. A large painless sore develops, often on the feet or legs. This is usually associated with a bacterial infection, poor nutrition or environmental factors.

*As a preventive measure massage the legs daily with *Renew Intensive Skin Therapy.* To treat the ulcer, bathe the sore gently with *Antibacterial Liquid Soap* and water. Cover the area with *Triple Antibiotic Ointment* or a surgical pad saturated in a 1:3 solution of *T36-C5* and olive oil. See the section on *Leg Ulcers* in this book.

HEALTHY BODY

---

*The information presented in this book is in no way intended as a substitute for medical counseling. Always consult your physician before starting any course of supplementation or treatment, particularly if you are pregnant or currently under medical care. Always read and follow product packaging directions and warnings.

ULCERS, VARICOSE

Open sores may form on the lower leg when the veins are not functioning properly. They are usually painless and are often a result of varicose veins. They frequently become infected and are very slow to heal. Elderly people and diabetics are particularly prone to this condition due to poor circulation.

* Wash the area carefully with *Antibacterial Liquid Soap* and then cover the affected area with a surgical pad saturated in a 1:3 solution of *T36-C5* and olive oil.

URETHRITIS

Urethritis is a bacterial infection of the urethra, which usually precedes an attack of cystitis. A sign of cystitis is the need to urinate frequently, accompanied by a painful burning sensation while urinating and sometimes feeling feverish. The urine may look cloudy.

*As a preventative, take *CranBarrier* daily. The ingredients in *CranBarrier* have been shown to prevent bacteria from adhering to the bladder and urethral linings, and thus harmful bacteria is flushed harmlessly out of the urinary tract.

Proper hygiene is an important preventive measure. Women should wipe from the front to the back. Drink *Melaleuca Herbal Tea* frequently throughout the day.

Frequent bathing with Melaleuca oil as a general disinfectant is a good preventive measure. Prepare a bath with 8–12 drops of *T36-C5* and soak for 5–10 minutes. See the section on *Bladder Infections* in this book.

URINARY TRACT INFECTIONS

Almost any normal skin organism is capable of living in the nutrient rich, moist, and dark environment found in the lower urinary tract. Women are more prone to UTIs because of the constantly moist environment of the urethral opening and its close proximity to the anus. If improperly treated, UTIs can progress to bladder infections (cystitis) or kidney infections (nephritis). Fewer than half of the women with UTIs have any symptoms of the illness. Tight-fitting clothes, prescription drug reactions, synthetic undergarments, warm weather, inadequate toilet hygiene, or a generally weakened immune system can lead to bacterial or yeast infections in the urinary tract. Drinking enough water can usually prevent or overcome many of these shortcomings.

* The best treatment is prevention. Take *CranBarrier* daily. The ingredients in *CranBarrier* have been shown to prevent bacteria from adhering to the bladder and urethral linings, and thus harmful bacteria is flushed out of the urinary tract. Use cotton undergarments. Dry your body well after showering or bathing. Drink enough water and drink 4 to 12 cups of *Melaleuca Herbal Tea* each day. Women should wipe from the front to the back when using the toilet. Take the *Vitality Pack* with

*The information presented in this book is in no way intended as a substitute for medical counseling. Always consult your physician before starting any course of supplementation or treatment, particularly if you are pregnant or currently under medical care. Always read and follow product packaging directions and warnings.

Oligofructose Complex, CellWise, Florify, ProVex and/or *ProVex-Plus* as directed. Douche as needed with *Nature's Cleanse*. Contact your health care provider for further advice. See the section on *Bladder Infections* in this book.

VAGINAL CLEANSING

Vaginal cleansing is cleansing of the vagina usually by means of a douche.

* Use *Nature's Cleanse* as directed. If that is not available, you might try using a mixture of 8 to 10 drops of *T36-C5* in one pint of distilled water.

Vaginal cleansing can also be accomplished by soaking for approximately 20 minutes in a warm bath to which 10 drops of *T36-C5* has been added.

VAGINITIS

Bacteria and yeasts can infect the nutrient-rich vaginal lining causing painful swelling, foul odor, colored discharge, and reduced libido.

* For acute infections, use *Nature's Cleanse Feminine Douche* morning and evening for 3 to 5 days. For recurrences or chronic infections, douche each night. Bathe instead of showering each night, soaking for 30 minutes in a solution of 1 oz of *Sol-U-Mel* and 1 oz of *Renew Bath Oil*. Avoid sugar. Drink 2 to 6 cups of *Melaleuca Herbal Tea* each day and 2 to 3 quarts of water per day, along with taking the *Vitality Pack* with *Oligofructose Complex, CellWise, ProVex* and/or *ProVex-Plus* as directed. This will help to build resistance to infections.

VARICOSE VEINS

Enlarged veins in the lower legs are common among civilized people because of standing and walking on flat, hard surfaces all day. Chronic constipation and pregnancy also tend to cause circulation backup in the legs, which leads to varicose veins. Occasionally there is leg pain or discomfort, but usually not. Valves in veins normally prevent blood from flowing backward or pooling. Sedentary lifestyles destroy this check-valve effect and lead to pooling. Varicose veins and hemorrhoids are often found together.

Toe action, like walking barefoot on a sandy beach, assists the pumping of blood back to the heart and keeps leg veins and their check-valves healthy. A clinical examination for venous circulation often finds the beginnings of blood clots blocking this natural flow. Some scientists feel that most blood clots plugging brain (stroke) and heart (heart attack) arteries originate in the oxygen-depleted veins of the legs. See the section on *Constipation* in this book.

* Elderly people may require specialized care beyond these suggestions. The bioflavonoids in *ProVex, ProVex-Plus* and *ProvexCV* have been known to greatly reduce the unsightly appearance of varicose

veins, so take them daily. Do not wear tight-fitting belts or girdles. Wear support hose ONLY when walking or standing for prolonged periods of time. Wearing them while sitting or driving can cause more circulation problems than it helps. Walk barefoot for 10 minutes each morning in the dew or on a sandy beach. *Body Satin Foot Scrub* and *Body Satin Foot Lotion* can also be used to cleanse and stimulate improved circulation.

Maintain healthy, regular bowel movements. You should not have to strain when making a stool. Drink 2 to 6 cups of *Melaleuca Herbal Tea* each day. Take one or two *FiberWise* bars or drinks each day. They are excellent ways to increase dietary fiber and promote regularity and bowel mobility. Also take *Florify* to help maintain the proper balance of flora in the digestive system.

WALKING

Walking is a wonderful exercise that can burn fat and improve your health. It is easily the most popular form of exercise for all ages. It is the only exercise in which the rate of participation does not decline in the middle and later years. Walking burns approximately the same amount of calories per mile as does running. It should be an important part of every wellness regimen.

* Make the effort to find good walking shoes that fit properly. Treat your feet well. Pamper them with *Body Satin Foot Scrub* to stimulate circulation and make them come alive with *Body Satin Foot Lotion*. Freshen them throughout the day with *Body Satin Foot Spray*.

If an injury should occur, carefully clean it with *Antibacterial Liquid Soap* and, after drying, apply *T36-C5*. This should be followed with *MelaGel* or *Renew Intensive Skin Therapy*.

WARTS

Common warts, also known as verruca, are non-cancerous tumors caused by pathoviruses. Under microscopic examination, the flat plates of the epidermis are seen to be tilted at ninety degrees, growing outward instead of lying flat with the skin surface. Otherwise, the skin cells appear normal. Viral warts most frequently grow on the hands or fingers of children. Warts on the elbows, knees, face, and isolated sites elsewhere on the body are less common. They appear most frequently on sites subject to injury. The appearance and size depends upon the location and on the degree of irritation they are subjected to. They can be round or irregular, and are usually firm and dry. Color varies from light gray, yellow, and brown, to grayish black. Size varies from ⅛ to ½ inch. They may come and go in the same individual in a haphazard way. Infections with the virus may appear as single or multiple growths and develop by spreading from one side of the body to the other. Complete regression is common, with or without treatment.

HEALTHY BODY

Warts can persist for years and may reoccur at the same or different sites.

Plantar warts are common on the sole of the foot. When they are flattened by pressure, they are surrounded by cornified tissue and may be very tender. They can be distinguished from corns and calluses by their tendency to pinpoint bleeding when the surface is shaved away. Filiform warts are long, narrow growths usually seen on the eyelids, face, neck, or lips. Flat warts are smooth, flat yellow brown lesions seen more commonly in children and young adults, most often on the face. Warts of unusual shape, which resemble cauliflower or other structures, are most frequent on the head and neck, especially the scalp and in the bearded regions. Around the moist genital area, they are often called venereal warts and may or may not resemble warts in other parts of the body.

* For isolated common warts, apply *T36-C5* each morning and night faithfully for up to 3 weeks. If the wart is thick and dry, shave the excess away before applying *T36-C5*. *Body Satin Foot Scrub* and *Body Satin Foot Lotion* can also be used to cleanse and stimulate improved circulation. For body warts, bathe in a hot tub with 1 oz of *Sol-U-Mel* and 1 oz of *Renew Bath Oil* for 30 minutes. Apply *T36-C5* or *MelaGel* afterwards. Some warts require the added strength of *T40-C3* to disappear.

An alternate solution is to simply use *Renew Intensive Skin Therapy* to remove the skin warts. It may be a slower process, but it can be just as effective. Remember, a few types of warts do not respond to Melaleuca oil. Also see the section on *Plantar Warts* in this book.

YEAST INFECTIONS

Yeast such as Candida albicans are naturally occurring in every human and do not tend to activate the body's immune defenses except in overgrowth situations. They are naturally kept from growing out of control by neighboring friendly bacteria that secrete anti-yeast chemicals. Broad-spectrum antibiotics given for other conditions innocently destroy these friendly bacteria. When these friendly bacteria leave the body unprotected, yeasts can have a picnic on the nutrient-rich protein found on the skin and sugar-enriched mucous membranes. Once yeast infections get started, they must be dealt with in an aggressive way for best results.

Yeast infections are a generalized term that includes a variety of challenges including vaginal infection, inflammation, and irritation. Parasites, viruses, fungi, or bacteria can cause infections. Inflammation and irritation may be attributable to chemicals in tampons, bubble bath and tissue paper. Sometimes excessive use of harsh soap will cause vaginitis.

Clothing contributes to yeast infections, particularly in those containing synthetic fibers such as polyester and nylon. Synthetic clothing retains moisture and encourages yeast growth. Bacteria can remain in synthetic fibers even after washing.

While yeast infections are common complaints by women, they are not limited to just females. Jock itch is a form of yeast infection as well. Symptoms include pain, itching, spotting, odor, irritation and discharge. Recurrent or chronic infections will develop in those who are diabetic, and in those taking birth control pills or antibiotics. Symptoms can be alleviated for many; however, the majority will not be cured by traditional treatments prescribed.

This is contagious; therefore, intimate partners should treat it together and should pay attention to the danger of becoming re-infected.

* Use **Nature's Cleanse** according to the directions. Melaleuca alternifolia oil is the only antiseptic capable of eliminating each of the major types of vaginal yeast infections while exhibiting virtually no toxicity to vaginal tissue. Take **Florify** to help keep yeast and harmful bacteria in the digestive system in check.

Drink **Melaleuca Herbal Tea** and take the **Vitality Pack** with **Oligofructose Complex**, **CellWise**, and **ProVex** or **ProVex-Plus** with each meal. Avoid sugar, yeast, or mold-processed foods. Apply **T36-C5**, **MelaGel**, or **Triple Antibiotic Ointment** to affected areas other than the vagina.

Wash your clothes in **MelaPower Laundry Detergent** and add 1–2 capfuls of **Sol-U-Mel** to each wash load. This will leave clothes as close to adverse organism free as possible.

See the sections on *Air Purification, Body Odor, Dental Decay, Diaper Rash, Emphysema, Jock Itch, Mucous, Paronychia, Thrush, Urinary Tract Infections,* and *Vaginitis* in this book.

ZONA

Zona is also called shingles and is the same virus as chicken pox—herpes zoster. This virus affects the sensory nerves, and causes clusters of blisters to appear, often in the form of a band around the torso. The condition can be accompanied by severe pain, usually before the rash appears, and there may be fever. See the sections on *Shingles* and *Chicken Pox* in this book.

* Wash the affected area with **Antibacterial Liquid Soap**. Pat dry and liberally apply **T36-C5** or **T40-C3**. (**T40-C3** is a rarer form of Melaleuca oil and is sometimes less offensive.) Allow the oil sufficient time to soak into the skin. After the rash has fully developed, usually within 2 or 3 days, soak in 1 oz of **Sol-U-Mel** and 1 oz of **Renew Bath Oil** in a tub of warm water for 15 minutes to help with the itching. After soaking, pat dry and reapply the **T36-C5**. When the oil has started to be absorbed into the skin or is drying, apply either **MelaGel** or **Renew Intensive Skin Therapy**. Repeat the process several times a day. Drinking one to four cups of **Melaleuca Herbal Tea** each day may also be helpful.

HEALTHY BODY

CHAPTER SEVENTEEN

Healthy Home Solutions

AIR FRESHENER

To make a fresh smelling and safe air freshener, combine 3 oz of *Sol-U-Mel* with water in a 16 oz spray bottle.

ANT KILLER

Spray concentrated *PreSpot* on areas where ants congregate. Be aware of the surface of these areas when using *PreSpot* as it can take the finish off of some wooden floors.

An alternate idea is to combine 1 oz of *MelaMagic* and 1 oz of *Sol-U-Mel* in a 16-oz bottle and fill with water. This works particularly well with large black ants.

Another simple solution is *Tough & Tender*. It will kill ants.

ANT PREVENTION

If you prefer to just prevent ants, simply spray the most likely areas with *PreSpot*.

APPLIANCES

Unplug all electrical appliances before cleaning them. Use 1 tsp of *Tough & Tender* and 1 capful of *Sol-U-Mel* combined in a 16 oz spray bottle filled with water to clean your kitchen appliances. Spray your appliance and allow it to set for a moment before wiping. Alternatively, try the *Tough & Tender Wipes.*

For heavier cleaning, add 4 oz of *MelaMagic* and 1 capful of *Sol-U-Mel* to a gallon of water. This is also an excellent grease cutter.

AUTOMOBILES

For dusting the inside, spray a solution of 1 tsp of *Tough & Tender* in 16 oz of water on a cloth. Wipe the area thoroughly. Alternatively, try the *Tough & Tender Wipes* for the dashboard and other surfaces. For the windows, spray on *Clear Power* (diluted to ½ the strength suggested on the bottle) and wipe them with a soft cloth or cheap paper towels.

Rustic Touch cleans vinyl and leather. It is also great for cleaning the dash of your car. **NOTE:** Spray it on a cloth to apply. If you spray it directly on the dash, you will get it on the inside of your windshield.

Always read and follow product packaging directions and warnings.

For cleaning the outside of the car, in a gallon warm water add 1 oz of *Tough & Tender*. Apply with a cloth or spray bottle, and rinse with clean water.

To clean under the hood of your car, mix 1 capful of *Sol-U-Mel* and 2 oz of *MelaMagic* in a 16 oz spray bottle and fill with water. After spraying it on, let set for 10 minutes and hose off the dirt and grime.

Add 4 to 5 drops of *Tough & Tender* to every 4 oz of water in your windshield washer. It works amazingly well. (Make sure you use non-freezing washer fluid in the winter.)

BABY WIPES

Combine 1 tsp of *Sol-U-Mel* OR 1 capful of *Nature's Cleanse* with 1 capful of *Renew Bath Oil*, ¼ tsp of *Tough & Tender* and 2 cups of water to make very effective and cost-efficient baby or travel wipes. Cut a roll of paper towels in half and remove the cardboard roll so that you can begin pulling the towels from the center. Place the towels in a plastic container and saturate with this solution. Replace the lid and cut a "star" in the center. You can then pull the towels through the lid.

An alternate solution would be to cut a roll of 1 ply (cloth like) Viva paper towels in half and place ½ of the roll into a 3 quart Rubbermaid Servin' Saver bowl with a lid. Add 2 cups of water, 1–2 tbsp of *Koala Pals Hair Wash* and 2 tbsp of baby oil. If you experience problems with mold developing, add 1–2 drops of *T36-C5* to the mixture. Cover and let them soak for 10 minutes or so before using. Remove the center cardboard core and pull wipes from center and tear off.

Another recipe for baby wipes would be to use white Bounty paper towels (because they are stronger), and cut the roll in half. Take out the cardboard core. Mix in a large bowl—2½ cups of warm water, 1½ tsp of *Tough & Tender*, ½ tsp of *Sol-U-Mel*, and 1 capful of *Renew Bath Oil*. Stir and then put the ragged edge of the paper towels into the water first. Let this set until all the water is soaked up. Put the towels into a large plastic container with a lid. Pull from the middle. This also makes wonderful hand and face wipes. Only half of a roll of towels is used, so make 2 bowls at once.

BALLPOINT PEN

Sol-U-Mel is very effective at removing ballpoint pen and many other difficult to remove items. Put a little *Sol-U-Mel* on the area and let it soak for a few minutes and then dab it with water.

BARBECUE GRILLS

Soak your barbecue grill in a solution of 1 oz of *MelaMagic* in ½ gallon of water. Clean it with a brush. For the outside of the grill, use ⅓ cup of *Tough & Tender* in a 16 oz spray bottle of water and scrub with a soft brush. For baked on areas, use the *Tough & Tender* solution and let soak for a few minutes before scrubbing and rinsing.

BATHROOM − CEILINGS

Mix 1 tsp of *Tough & Tender* with 16 oz of water in a spray bottle and apply to the ceiling. Wipe it with a damp cloth. For really dirty or greasy ceilings, use 1 oz of *MelaMagic* in a gallon of water.

BATHROOM − COUNTER

Use *Sol-U-Guard Botanical* disinfectant to treat your bathroom surfaces. This will kill any germs that may be on your counter. **Never use *Sol-U-Guard* on natural stone surfaces.**

PreSpot works great on laminated countertops for tough stains. Spray it on and let it soak for a few minutes before wiping.

BATHROOM − DISINFECTING

Sol-U-Guard Botanical is a broad-spectrum disinfectant that is 99.99% effective against common bathroom and kitchen germs.

BATHROOM − FLOOR

Combine 2 tbsp of *MelaMagic* and 1 capful of *Sol-U-Mel* in 16 oz of water. Spray or wipe it on the floor and mop thoroughly.

BATHROOM − HARD WATER SPOTS

Mix 1/3 cup of *Tub & Tile* and 1 capful of *Sol-U-Mel* with water in a 16 oz spray bottle. Sprayed on hard water spots this solution will clean and shine, but also will wipe out fungus, mold, and mildew. **Never use *Tub & Tile* on marble or granite surfaces.**

BATHROOM − MIRRORS

Use *Clear Power* (diluted to ½ the strength suggested on the bottle). Wipe the mirror with the *Clear Power* and **cheap** paper towels. It works great and at a very reasonable price.

BATHROOMS − MOLD AND MILDEW

Apply *Tub & Tile* full-strength. Spray it on and let it stand a few minutes before rinsing. This is also excellent when cleaning mold and mildew off bathroom shower curtains. **Never use *Tub & Tile* on marble or granite surfaces.**

BATHROOM − ODORS

Mix 3 oz of *Sol-U-Mel* and water in a 16 oz spray bottle to eliminate odors of all kinds. *Sol-U-Guard Botanical* has the great smell of thyme and will also kill bathroom germs that cause odors.

BATHROOM − SHOWER CURTAIN

Combine 1 capful of *Sol-U-Mel* and 1 oz of *MelaMagic* with water in a 16 oz spray bottle and thoroughly spray the shower curtain. Allow some time for the cleaning combination to work and then use the shower to rinse off the mixture before wiping off the remaining grime.

HEALTHY HOME

BATHROOM — SHOWER STALL

Use the *No Work Daily Shower Cleaner* as directed. With *No Work* you can keep your shower sparkling clean with a daily 15-second spray. Its dual action breaks up soap scum and hard water deposits and leaves behind a fresh smell.

As an alternative, combine 1 oz of *Tub & Tile* and 1 capful of *Sol-U-Mel* in a 16 oz bottle. Fill with water and spray on the shower stall. Wipe thoroughly with a damp sponge.

For an extra-challenging shower stall, increase the mixture to 1 capful of *Sol-U-Mel* and 3 oz of *Tub & Tile* in a 16 oz bottle with water. **Never use *Tub & Tile* on marble or granite surfaces.**

BATHROOM — SINK

Mix 4 tablespoons of *Tub & Tile* and 1 capful of *Sol-U-Mel* with 16 oz of water in a spray bottle. Spray the sink and wipe it with a damp cloth. For rust stains or mineral deposits, use *Tub & Tile* full-strength. You may need to use a soft bristle brush on stubborn stains. Rinse the sink with water. By the way, the *Whitening Tooth Polish* is a wonderful enamel cleaner. **Never use *Tub & Tile* on marble or granite surfaces.**

BATHROOM — TOILET

Pour 2 oz of *Tub & Tile* in the toilet. Let this set for a few minutes, and then clean the area with a toilet brush.

If you have a lot of buildup, turn the water off on your toilet and let it drain. Pour in 2 oz of *Tub & Tile* and let it set for a few minutes before scrubbing with a toilet brush. Use *Sol-U-Guard Botanical* to disinfect the seat and exterior surfaces.

BATHROOM — UNDER THE COUNTER

Mix 1 tsp of *Tough & Tender* with 1 capful of *Sol-U-Mel* with water in a 16 oz spray bottle. Clean thoroughly with a soft cloth or brush. The addition of *Sol-U-Mel* to the *Tough & Tender* mixture will take care of any mold or mildew problems under the counter.

BATHROOM — WALLS

Mix 1 tsp of *Tough & Tender* with water in a 16 oz spray bottle and apply this mixture to the walls. Wipe with a damp cloth. Alternatively, try the *Tough & Tender Wipes* for removing fingerprints from walls.

BATHROOM — WIPES

Use the recipe for the Bounty paper towel baby wipes (see *Baby Wipes* in this chapter) and instead of making two batches of baby wipes, use half of the recipe for bathroom wipes. Buy the Bounty "select a size," pull them apart and fold them. Make the baby wipes as directed. In the second batch, however, add an extra capful of *Sol-U-Mel* to the mixture. This is wonderful for quick bathroom clean-ups.

HEALTHY HOME

Always read and follow product packaging directions and warnings.

BATHTUB

Mix 3 oz of *Tub & Tile* with water in a 16 oz spray bottle. Spray on the tub and let it set for about 2 minutes. Wipe with a damp cloth. For rust spots, apply straight *Tub & Tile* to the area. Wait until the rust dissolves and then wipe with a damp cloth. For hard water or mineral deposits, use full-strength *Tub & Tile* with a soft scrub brush. Initially there may be strong fumes due to the quantity of build up being dissolved, so run the fan or open a window. This problem should disappear very soon if *Tub & Tile* is used on a regular basis. **Never use** *Tub & Tile* **on marble or granite surfaces.**

To maintain a cleaner tub, keep a bottle of *No Work* close by and spray the tub each time it is used.

For the chrome, try *Clear Power*. It is very effective.

BLEACH SUBSTITUTE – LAUNDRY

Use *MelaBrite 6x Color-Safe Brightener*. You may want to use 2 tablespoons in a white load for extra whitening as opposed to just 1 tablespoon, which is what you would normally use in a regular load.

BLINDS

Liberally spray the slats of your blinds with 1 tbsp of *Tub & Tile* in a 160oz spray bottle filled with water. Rinse well and repeat the process on the reverse side of the slats. NOTE: Do not use *Tub & Tile* on wood blinds. Wood blinds should be cleaned with *Rustic Touch*.

An alternate solution would be to mix 5 drops of *Tough & Tender* with ½ capful of *Sol-U-Mel* and in a 16 oz spray bottle filled with water. Close the blinds and spray on the solution. Wipe them with a soft cloth.

BLOOD STAINS – CLOTHING

Blood is a very challenging stain to remove, but here are a couple of ideas to try. Spray the stained fabric with full-strength *PreSpot*. Let it set for a few minutes and then rub out the stain with cold water. Repeat the procedure with *PreSpot* if necessary. Wash the fabric with *MelaPower Laundry Detergent* and 1 to 2 capfuls of *Sol-U-Mel*, if possible.

Antibacterial Liquid Soap rubbed into any fresh red stain seems to work very well. This applies to blood as well as catsup, spaghetti sauce, and bar-be-cue sauce. Then wash as usual.

BOATS

The bottom of your aluminum fishing boat can be readied for a new season with a mixture of 4 oz of *MelaMagic* with 1 gallon of water and 4 capfuls of *Sol-U-Mel*. Restore the interior with diluted *MelaMagic* or *Tough & Tender*.

Try cleaning your fiberglass boat with diluted *Sol-U-Mel*. It will even work on the seats.

Any wood areas can be beautifully restored with *Rustic Touch*.

HEALTHY HOME

BREAD BOX

If you spray the bread drawer or box with diluted *Tough & Tender,* your bread will not mold as fast.

BROILER

After baking or broiling anything, run some water on the broiler pan and add a couple of squirts of concentrated *Tough & Tender.* If it is particularly bad, add 1 part of *Lemon Brite* mixed with 8 parts of water for a spray. Of course, *MelaMagic* is the magic grease cutter and will work effectively on built up grease.

BUG SPRAY

A safe and non-toxic bug spray can be made from a combination of ¼ cup of *Sol-U-Mel*, 5 drops of *T36-C5*, 1 tsp of *Tough & Tender*, and 14 oz of water. It costs a fraction of commercial sprays. One medical study suggests that bug sprays may increase the risk of Parkinson's disease. Why take the chance?

BUMPER STICKER REMOVAL

Old bumper stickers should disappear by applying concentrated *Sol-U-Mel.* Let soak for a few minutes. It may take a couple of applications before the glue is dissolved.

CANDLE WAX STAIN

To remove wax stains from linens or carpeting, press a warm iron over a paper towel on the spot. Continue to iron until the wax melts and is absorbed into the paper towel. (Be careful not to set the iron so hot it could melt the carpet.) Then clean the area with ½ tsp of *Tough & Tender* in a 16 oz spray bottle of water.

CAR CLEANING

See *Automobiles*

CARPET CLEANER – MACHINE MIX

Check the color fastness of your carpet before using any cleaning product.

Clean carpets by mixing 1 oz of *Tough & Tender* and 1 capful of *Sol-U-Mel* for each gallon of water in your cleaning machine reservoir. This makes an excellent carpet cleaning machine solution.

If you have greasy or hard to remove stains, try 1 oz of *MelaMagic* and 1 capful of *Sol-U-Mel* per gallon.

If you have soft water, reduce the amount of ingredients by at least fifty percent.

NOTE: Rinse your carpets well after steam cleaning or shampooing, as any remaining product will attract dirt.

CARPET – DEODORIZATION

Mix 1½ capfuls of *Sol-U-Mel* with water in a 16 ounce spray bottle. Spray on the carpet and let it set for 5 minutes. Clean the carpet with a scrub brush and blot the area with a damp cloth.

CARPET – SPOTS

Clean spots on your carpet with 1 tsp of *Tough & Tender* and 1 capful of *Sol-U-Mel* blended in a 16 oz spray bottle filled with water. If the spot is greasy, try 1 oz of *MelaMagic* combined with 7–8 oz of water.

An alternate choice might be to mix 2 tbsp of *PreSpot* with ½ capful of *Sol-U-Mel* in a 16 oz spray bottle filled with water. Apply the solution to the soiled area. Let it set for 5 minutes and then clean it with a soft brush. Blot the spot with a damp cloth until it is clean.

For extremely difficult spots, try concentrated *PreSpot*. It may need to soak for a couple of hours before you rinse with warm water, but it usually does a good job and will not discolor the carpet.

CARPET – VACUUMING

Lightly spray the carpet with diluted *Sol-U-Mel* for the most effective vacuuming.

If you use a sweeper that runs in water, add 1 tsp of *Sol-U-Mel* to the water and it will refresh the air in your home while it cleans.

CEILINGS

For a very effective general cleaning disinfectant, mix 1 tsp of *Tough & Tender* in a 16 oz spray bottle of water or add 1 oz of *Tough & Tender* to a gallon bucket of water. If you need a stronger mixture, add 1 capful of *Sol-U-Mel* to either the spray or the bucket.

CEILING FAN

Mix 5 drops of *Tough & Tender* in a 16 oz spray bottle of water. Spray on the fan and wipe with a soft cloth. If the fan is wood, you may use the same technique followed by *Rustic Touch*, or simply use the *Rustic Touch* for the complete cleaning job.

CHEWING GUM

Remove all the chewing gum possible before applying concentrated *Sol-U-Mel*. Rub fabric against fabric or use a soft brush to clean the area.

ALWAYS check the color fastness of any carpet or fabric **BEFORE** applying *Sol-U-Mel* or any cleaning product.

CHINA STAINS

China that is seriously stained may have to be soaked overnight before washing. For soaking, dissolve ¼ to ½ cupful of *Diamond Brite* in a gallon of hot water. Following the soaking, wash and dry as usual.

HEALTHY HOME

CHOCOLATE STAINS – CLOTHING

Wet the chocolate spots with water and apply concentrated *Sol-U-Mel* with a damp cotton swab. Allow it to soak for a few minutes and then rinse out the *Sol-U-Mel*. Wash with *MelaPower* and *MelaBrite* as soon as possible.

An alternate solution would be to spray *PreSpot* on the chocolate and wash as soon as possible in *MelaPower* and *MelaBrite*.

CHROME

Clear Power is a wonderful product to use on chrome, or anything shiny. For best results mix it in distilled water and wipe with a soft cloth or cheap paper towels. Consider using ½ the amount indicated on the directions, especially if you have soft water.

CLAY FLOWER POTS

To clean moss or algae, spray clay flowerpots with 1 tsp of *Sol-U-Mel* mixed with 16 oz of water. Scrub them with a stiff brush or steel wool. Rinse with water and towel dry.

CLEANING BOOSTER

Offensive odors can be eliminated from your wash by adding 1 capful of *Sol-U-Mel* to each load. Bacteria causes odors and *Sol-U-Mel* eliminates bacteria while leaving clothes smelling fresh and clean. The same procedure is very effective if you have mildewed clothes, such as the ones you leave in the washer while on vacation.

COFFEE STAINS

Coffee stains on kitchen counters or tables can easily be removed by applying concentrated *Tub & Tile*. Rinse with a clean sponge before wiping dry. Formica or fiberglass counter tops should be rinsed immediately. Do not allow the *Tub & Tile* to dry on this surface before rinsing and wiping.

Never use *Tub & Tile* on marble or granite surfaces.

CONCRETE PATIOS

For general cleaning, mix 1 oz of *MelaMagic* in 1 gallon of warm water. Dump a small puddle of this solution on the floor and scrub with a brush. Spray the floor with water to rinse.

COPPER

Have you tried the penny test to see what *Tub & Tile* does to copper? Dip a copper penny in a capful of *Tub & Tile* and watch it clean that dirty, tarnished old penny in seconds. It will do the same for your copper pots and frying pans. Spray or wipe *Tub & Tile* on the copper and wipe the grit and black tarnish away. In most cases it is not even necessary to use it concentrated.

COUNTERTOPS

Use 1 tsp of *Tough & Tender* in a 16 oz spray bottle filled with water to clean countertop surfaces. Wait several moments before wiping with a damp cloth or clean sponge. Alternatively, try the *Tough & Tender Wipes* for a quick clean-up.

Disinfect all food preparation surfaces regularly with *Sol-U-Guard Botanical* disinfectant. Use as directed.

If you have dark Formica countertops, using *Rustic Touch* after cleaning makes them look like new. Use *PreSpot* to remove juice stains from countertops.

CRAYON

To clean crayon marks off of walls, use concentrated *Sol-U-Mel*. Gently try a small amount on the crayon mark, as this may also remove what is under the crayon mark—such as the paint.

For clothing, spray the affected area with full-strength *PreSpot*. Let it set for a few minutes. Scrub the mark to loosen the crayon from the fabric. If the spot still exists, repeat the procedure. When the crayon has been removed, wash the clothing with *MelaPower Laundry Detergent*.

DESKS

For dusting, nothing works better than *Rustic Touch*. If it's not available, try ½ tsp of *Tough & Tender* and a drop or two of *Sol-U-Mel* in a 16 oz spray bottle filled with water. For ink stains, apply full-strength *Tub & Tile* or *Sol-U-Mel* to the ink spot. Repeat if necessary. (**NOTE:** Do not put full-strength *Tub & Tile* or *Sol-U-Mel* directly onto a wood surface.)

DIAPERS

Most people use disposable diapers now, but for those who still prefer to use cloth ones, odor is sometimes a challenge. Be sure to use a pail with a lid for soiled diapers. Cover the diapers with a combination of water and 1 capful of *Sol-U-Mel*, 1½ tablespoon of *MelaPower 6x* and 1½ tablespoon of *MelaBrite 6x*. Soak them overnight before washing with 1 tablespoon of *MelaPower 6x* (1 pump) and 1 to 2 capfuls of *Sol-U-Mel*. For whiter diapers, add 1–2 tablespoons of *MelaBrite 6x* as well. Treat the diaper pail regularly with *Sol-U-Guard Botanical* to disinfect.

DIRT – CLOTHING

Ground-in dirt stains can be effectively taken care of by applying full-strength *MelaPower Laundry Detergent* before adding the garment to the regular wash load. Wash as usual using *MelaPower* and *MelaBrite*.

An alternate choice would be to spray the dirty area with full-strength *PreSpot*. Let it set for a few minutes and then launder in *MelaPower Laundry Detergent*. **TIP:** *Revive Wrinkle Relaxer* actually works to prevent stains from setting into your fabrics.

HEALTHY HOME

DISINFECTANT

Sol-U-Guard Botanical is the first botanical disinfectant that's 99.99% effective against common germs. Spray wherever germs can be found—kitchen counters, food preparation surfaces, bathrooms, garbage cans, doorknobs, light switches, toys, phones, etc. **Never use *Sol-U-Guard* on natural stone surfaces.**

An alternate solution is to combine one part *Sol-U-Mel* to five parts water in a spray bottle. Spray on and let air dry.

Remember to carry *Clear Defense Hand Gel* or *Wipes* with you everywhere. It can be used in restaurants, public restrooms, and simply after handling doorknobs and shaking hands.

DISHES — DISHWASHER WASHING

When you first begin to use *Diamond Brite* in your dishwasher, run at least one empty cycle with 1 oz of *MelaMagic* and the regular amount of *Diamond Brite*. This will clean out any buildup from the commercial soaps previously used. Then use the *Diamond Brite* as directed. If you have soft water or a high efficiency dishwasher, you may need to use less.

DISHES — HAND WASHING

Use 5 to 7 drops of *Lemon Brite* in a sink full of water. For baked-on food, fill a container with hot water to which 2 or 3 drops of *Lemon Brite* have been added. Let the dishes soak for ½ hour and then wash as usual.

DISHES — STAINS

Soak stained dishes or china in a bucket or sink of hot water containing ⅓ cup of *Diamond Brite*. Let them soak for 1 hour. If stains have not dissolved, soak them overnight.

DRIVEWAYS

Combine 2 oz of *MelaMagic* with water and 1 to 2 capfuls of *Sol-U-Mel* in a 16 oz bottle. Spray on any fresh grease stains. Scrub with a brush and hose the driveway with water. Or use full-strength *MelaMagic* for hard to clean grease stains.

DUST MITES

Sol-U-Mel, when diluted according to directions and sprayed in the air, will kill all airborne germs and viruses and will deodorize at the same time. When sprayed on upholstery, it will suffocate dust mites. Be sure to spray your mattress periodically even if you don't flip it any more.

DUSTING

Always dust before you vacuum so that the dust particles can be picked up by the vacuum cleaner. Keep your air conditioner and heater clean and well serviced so that the amount of dust and bacteria particles floating throughout your home is limited.

Using **Rustic Touch** will condition your wood furniture and woodwork, while it cleans dust and wax buildup and leaves behind a mirror shine. The cleaned surfaces stay non-magnetic and seem to repel dust and dirt for a longer period of time. Use it on natural and artificial wood furniture, laminated surfaces, vinyl, leather and paneling.

On all other surfaces, mix ½ tsp of **Tough & Tender** with water in a 16 oz spray bottle. Spray on a cloth and wipe away the dust. The **Tough & Tender Wipes** are also great for dusting.

ENAMEL

The **Classic Tooth Polish** is a wonderful enamel polish. Save your old tooth polish tubes and slice them open when you are ready to polish your enamel. There is usually enough residue to do the job and it is very economical.

FABRIC DYE STAINS

Spray the affected areas with **PreSpot**. Let it set for about 1 minute and then soak in a container with 1 tablespoon of **MelaPower 6x** (1 pump) in a gallon of water for 30 minutes. If the stain is not completely gone, reapply **PreSpot** and wash in the washing machine as usual.

FINE WASHABLES

To launder wool, nylon or other fine fabrics add 1 tsp of **Tough & Tender** to a basin of cold water. Gently wash and rinse your fine washables.

FINGERNAIL POLISH

Sol-U-Mel is very effective at removing fingernail polish and many other challenging substances. Put a little **Sol-U-Mel** on the area and let it soak for a few minutes and then wipe it with water. Be careful, as full-strength **Sol-U-Mel** may damage painted surfaces.

FIRE ANTS

Spray the ants with **PreSpot**. It is very effective for killing them—and they won't come back! For fire ant pain, splash the area with **Sol-U-Mel**.

For a foolproof way to kill fire ants consider this: After you have mopped the floor with **Tough & Tender** and/or **MelaMagic,** or you have washed the car with **Tough & Tender**, add 5 or 6 drops of **Lemon Brite** and stir. Pour half of the bucket on the fire ant bed. After about 30 minutes pour the other half on the bed.

If you are really mad about the fire ants, like when they have invaded your flower beds, mix the following in a two gallon bucket of water: 1 capful of **Tough & Tender**, 1 capful of **MelaMagic**, 1 capful of **Sol-U-Mel**, 1 capful of **Tub & Tile** and always 10 drops of **Lemon Brite**. Sir and pour half of the bucket on the fire ant bed. Wait 30 minutes and pour on the other half. This kills them "dead" and they won't come back. Plus, that will be the greenest part of your lawn!

HEALTHY HOME

FIREPLACE

For the fireplace glass, use *Clear Power* (diluted to ½ of the strength suggested on the bottle). Wipe with a soft cloth or cheap paper towels.

For the outside of the fireplace, use 2 tbsp of *MelaMagic* with 16 oz of water. Spray on the soiled area and scrub with a brush.

FIRST AID KIT — HOME AND CAR

T36-C5, Clear Defense Hand Gel or *Wipes, Renew Intensive Skin Therapy, Triple Antibiotic Ointment, MelaGel, Sun Shades Sunscreen, CounterAct Extra Strength Pain Reliever, Antibacterial Liquid Soap,* scissors, tweezers, bandages, gauze, a small container of water (for washing wounds), forceps and crush-proof empty containers for tick removal.

FLOORS — LINOLEUM AND CERAMIC

For mopping, use 4 oz of *MelaMagic* in a gallon of water. For a quick clean up, make a spray by mixing 2 oz of *MelaMagic* in a 16 oz bottle filled with water.

To kill bacteria and fungus on nonporous bathroom and kitchen floors use *Sol-U-Guard Botanical* disinfectant as directed.

FLOORS — HARDWOOD

Use 1 oz of *Tough & Tender* in a gallon of water to clean your hardwood floors. Be sure to dry the floors carefully.

FLOORS — SCUFFMARKS

Rub scuffmarks with *Antibacterial Liquid Soap* or full-strength *Sol-U-Mel.* If working on wooden floors check a small area first to be sure that they have been properly sealed.

FLY CONTROL

Spray fly-prone areas daily for one week with a combination of 1 tsp of *Tough & Tender* and 1 capful of *Renew Bath Oil* in a 16 oz spray bottle filled with water. After the first week, spraying only 2 to 3 times each week should control the flies. Spray your porches, decks, and yards after each rainstorm.

FREEZER

To clean spills, use diluted *Tough & Tender.* Spray on and wipe clean with a cloth. Alternatively, try the *Tough & Tender Wipes.* To kill mold or mildew, use 3 oz of *Sol-U-Mel* in a 16 oz spray bottle filled with water. Spray on and let set for 5 minutes. Wipe with a soft cloth.

FRUIT JUICE SPOTS — CLOTHING

Spray the area with full-strength *PreSpot.* Let it set for a few minutes, and then launder with *MelaPower Laundry Detergent* as usual.

Always read and follow product packaging directions and warnings.

FURNITURE

For spot cleaning of fabric, use 1 tbsp of *PreSpot* with 16 oz of water. (You may want to test for color fastness on a hidden area.) For wood, leather or vinyl, use *Rustic Touch* as directed.

FURNITURE — OUTDOOR

Outdoor furniture can easily be cleaned by spraying with 1 tsp of *Tough & Tender* and 1 capful of *Sol-U-Mel* combined in a 16 oz bottle of water. This will loosen the dirt so that the furniture can easily be wiped with a sponge or rag and rinsed with the garden hose.

GARAGE FLOOR

On a sealed garage floor, combine 2 oz of *MelaMagic* with water and 1 to 2 capfuls of *Sol-U-Mel* in a 16 oz bottle. Spray on any fresh grease stains. Scrub with a brush and hose the floor with water.

GARBAGE CANS

Pour ¼ to ½ cup of *MelaMagic* and 1 to 2 capfuls of *Sol-U-Mel* into the garbage can. Fill the can ¼ full with hot water and scrub the sides with a soft brush. Pour the mixture out and rinse with water. To prevent odor, clean them frequently.

An alternate solution would be to use *Sol-U-Guard Botanical* as directed for extra-strength disinfecting power.

GLASS

Use *Clear Power* as directed on the label. Terry towels, old cloths or very cheap paper towels are excellent for wiping windows after spraying. (Try using the *Clear Power* diluted to ½ of the strength suggested on the bottle.) For best results use distilled water with the *Clear Power*. See also *Windows* in this chapter.

GLASS TABLETOPS

Clean with *Clear Power* (diluted to ½ of the strength suggested on the bottle). Mix with distilled water if possible.

To keep the lint off after cleaning, mix ¼ tsp of *MelaSoft* and water in a 16 oz spray bottle. Spray on and dry with a cloth towel.

GRAPE JUICE STAINS — CLOTHING

Grape juice stains need to be sprayed immediately with *PreSpot*. Let soak and then wash as usual with *MelaPower*.

GRASS STAINS — CLOTHING

Spray *PreSpot* or *MelaPower* on the grass stain. Let it set for a few minutes and then soak in a bucket of warm water containing 1 tbsp of *MelaPower 6x Laundry Detergent*, for several hours.

Tough & Tender works well on grass stains too.

GREASE – CLOTHING

For grease stains on clothing, spray before laundering with *PreSpot* and rub gently. Launder as usual with *MelaPower* and *MelaBrite*.

If you are dealing with major grease or extremely stubborn grease, mix a solution of 1 tbsp of *MelaPower 6x Laundry Detergent* and 1 capful of *Sol-U-Mel* with 2 gallons of warm water. Put the clothing in this solution and let it soak for a few hours. If the grease spots are not dissolved, apply a squirt of *Antibacterial Liquid Soap*. Rub it in with your finger or a soft brush. Let this stand for a few minutes before rinsing with warm water.

GREASE SPILLS

Pour full-strength *MelaMagic* on the grease spot and let it set for 15 minutes. Then wipe it up.

GREASE SPOTS – RUGS AND CARPETING

Rub a small amount of *Antibacterial Liquid Soap* into the spots on your rugs or carpeting for a quick clean-up. Rinse and blot the stain with a dry cloth.

GREASY HANDS

Washing with *The Gold Bar* or *Antibacterial Liquid Soap* works well. You might also try a little bit of *MelaMagic*. Rub your hands together and then rinse with water.

GUM

For gum on clothing, pour full-strength *Sol-U-Mel* on the affected area. Let it set for a minute or so. Rub to loosen the gum, and then wash in *MelaPower Laundry Detergent* as usual.

To effectively clean sticky, gummy surfaces, apply full-strength *Sol-U-Mel*. If the sticky area is on wood, carefully check a small area to be sure the wood has been sealed before applying too much *Sol-U-Mel*.

HAIR – STATIC ELECTRICITY

When you are challenged with static hair, spray some diluted *MelaSoft* on your hairbrush or comb. It works wonders to calm a bad hair day.

HARD WATER SPOTS

For heavy duty cleaning of hard water spots, rub the area with concentrated *Tub & Tile*. Rinse and wipe dry. **Never use *Tub & Tile* on marble or granite surfaces.**

HOT TUBS

No Melaleuca products, including *T36-C5*, *Renew Bath Oil*, or *Sol-U-Mel*, should be used in an operating hot tub or permanent Jacuzzi tub. Melaleuca alternifolia oil is not compatible with the filtration system in those sophisticated environments.

To clean an empty hot tub, use full-strength *MelaMagic* and it may require a lot of elbow grease, but it will work.

HOUSE – EXTERIOR CLEANING

Mix 4 oz of *MelaMagic* with a gallon of water. Apply this solution by either spraying or wiping on the surface of the house. Scrub with a brush and rinse with water.

HUMIDIFIER

Adding 1 to 2 capfuls of *Sol-U-Mel* to the water in your humidifier's water chamber will not only keep it clean but will fill your home with fresh smelling air and inhibit the growth of bacteria.

INK STAINS – CLOTHING AND SURFACES

Spray *PreSpot* on ink stains and rub with your finger or a soft brush. Let it set for a few minutes and then rinse with warm water. If it is a stubborn stain, repeat the procedure or soak the spot overnight.

An alternate solution is to use *Tub & Tile* or *Sol-U-Mel* directly on the spot. *Sol-U-Mel* is especially effective if the fabric has been in the dryer before being treated. It may also be used on "dry clean only" fabrics.

Be sure to check all fabrics for colorfastness before applying any product.

For ink on surfaces, try rubbing the area with a combination of 1 oz of *MelaMagic* and 1 capful of *Sol-U-Mel* mixed in 8 oz of water. The ink should be easily removed unless the surface has not been sealed.

INSECT REPELLENT

To rid your home of creatures such as roaches, beetles, crickets, and termites, try treating them with 3 oz of *Sol-U-Mel* in a 16 oz spray bottle filled with water. Spray around baseboards, thresholds, kitchen cabinets, and anywhere you see bugs in the house.

The "ultimate" insect repellent consists of 4 oz of *Sol-U-Mel*, 4 oz of *Renew Bath Oil*, and 5 oz of *Moisturizing Hand Creme*. Spread on exposed skin or over the entire body. Keep in mind, shampooing with *Melaleuca Original Shampoo* also affords insect repellent protection.

Some prefer to simply use 1 tsp of *Moisturizing Hand Creme* or *Renew Intensive Skin Therapy* with 5 drops of *T36-C5* spread over all exposed skin.

For a general outdoor spray, blend ½ oz of *Sol-U-Mel* in a 16 oz spray bottled filled with water.

Also note that *Tub & Tile* will kill wasps and *PreSpot* and *Tough & Tender* will kill ants.

INSECT REPELLENT – PLANTS

Use ½ tsp of *Tough & Tender* in a 16 oz spray bottle filled with water. Spray on any plants that have pests.

KITCHEN – ALL PURPOSE CLEANER

For a general, all-purpose kitchen cleaner, add 1 tsp of *Tough & Tender* and 1 capful of *Sol-U-Mel* to a 16 oz spray bottle and fill with water.

KITCHEN – CEILING AND WALLS

Mix 1 oz of *MelaMagic* in a gallon bucket of hot water. Use a cloth to wash down the ceiling and walls with this solution. Let them air dry.

KITCHEN – COPPER

Pour 2 oz of *Tub & Tile* in a 16 oz spray bottle and fill with water. Spray this solution on any copper pieces. Wipe with a clean cloth.

KITCHEN – COUNTERTOPS

For kitchen countertops add 1 tsp of *Tough & Tender* and 1 capful of *Sol-U-Mel* to a 16 oz spray bottle filled with water. Spray on the counters and use a clean damp sponge to clean. Alternatively, try the *Tough & Tender Wipes* for a quick clean-up.

For removing stubborn stains, use *Sol-U-Mel* full-strength. To disinfect use *Sol-U-Guard Botanical* as directed. **Never use *Sol-U-Guard* on natural stone surfaces.**

PreSpot works great on laminated countertops for tough stains. Spray it on and let it soak for a few minutes before wiping.

Never use *Tub & Tile* on marble or granite surfaces.

KITCHEN – DISHWASHER

To clean the outside of the dishwasher use 1 tsp of *Tough & Tender* and 1 capful of *Sol-U-Mel* to a 16 oz spray bottle filled with water. Spray on the dishwasher and wipe it with a cloth. Fill only ½ of one of the auto-load cups of your dishwasher with *Diamond Brite* to clean your dishes.

NOTE: When you first start using Melaleuca products, the dishwasher should be run empty with Melaleuca products several times to clean out the residue of the more toxic previously-used products.

KITCHEN – FLOORS

Mix 1 oz of *MelaMagic* into a gallon bucket full of hot water. Mop the floor and let it air dry. Also see *Floors – Hardwood* in this chapter.

KITCHEN – ODORS

Add 3 oz of *Sol-U-Mel* to a 16 oz spray bottle and fill with water. Spray this solution to eliminate odors of all kinds.

KITCHEN – OVEN

Mix 2 oz of *MelaMagic* and 1 capful of *Sol-U-Mel* in a 16 oz spray bottle and fill with water. Apply to the oven and let it set for 5 minutes. Wipe it with a damp cloth. If it is a major job, use a soft scrubbing pad and straight *MelaMagic*.

Always read and follow product packaging directions and warnings.

KITCHEN – SINK

For general cleaning, put a few drops of *Tough & Tender* or *Lemon Brite* in the sink and scrub with a soft brush or scrubbing pad.

Use full-strength *Tub & Tile* or *Diamond Brite* to clean the scuffmarks off enamel sinks. Scrub the stains gently, then rinse. Repeat as necessary. You will be amazed! You may also try the *Classic Tooth Polish*. It's a wonderful enamel cleaner. **Never use *Tub & Tile* on marble or granite surfaces.**

KITCHEN – STOVE

For minor stove clean-ups, add 1 tsp of *Tough & Tender* and 1 capful of *Sol-U-Mel* to a 16 oz spray bottle filled with water. Apply and let it set for a few minutes before you wipe and dry the area.

For major clean ups, apply full-strength *MelaMagic* with a spray bottle or soft cloth. Let it set for a few minutes and then use a soft scrubbing pad to lift off the grime. Wipe with a damp cloth.

KITCHEN – VENTILATION HOOD

Clean all the ventilation hood surfaces with full-strength *MelaMagic*. Apply it with a damp sponge or cloth. Allow it to set for a few minutes and then wipe with a clean damp cloth or paper towel.

LABELS

When the countertop gets stained from price stickers or bread bags, spray full-strength *Tub & Tile* on the area and wait 15 minutes or more before rinsing off. **Never** use *Tub & Tile* on marble or granite surfaces.

When you run across a label on a product that does not want to come off or, at least, wants to leave a sticky surface, try wiping with a small amount of *Sol-U-Mel* on a soft rag.

LAUNDRY

Believe it or not, 1 pump (1 tablespoon) of *MelaPower 6x* is sufficient for an average wash load. If you have soft water or a water softener, you may be able to use even less! For high efficiency washing machines, use *MelaPower 6x HE*. To brighten your load considerably, add 1 tablespoon of *MelaBrite 6x*. In all-white loads you may want to use 2 tablespoons for extra whitening. The *MelaSoft* can be added to the wash load or to the dryer, whichever is easier for you. For dryer use, just dampen a soft cloth with *MelaSoft* and throw it in the dryer with the wet clothes, or use the ready-made *MelaSoft* dryer sheets.

If you are washing clothes that have mildew or any other type of odor, add 1 capful of *Sol-U-Mel* to your normal wash load. It is very effective. Some even recommend adding *Sol-U-Mel* to every load for the additional germ protection.

LAUNDRY STAINS

Use *PreSpot*. It will take out almost all stains. Some stains will require full-strength *PreSpot*. However, many lighter stains will

HEALTHY HOME

disappear with a 50% dilution just as well.

For challenging stains, allow the *PreSpot* to soak into the cloth before putting it in the washer. Sometimes it helps to scratch the stain or rub fabric on fabric. If the stain is still visible, repeat the process a time or two. Some find that it is even more effective if you moisten the garment first and then spray *Pre-Spot* on the moistened garment and let it set for a little while before washing.

If you temporarily run out of *PreSpot*, use full-strength *Tough & Tender* on the fabric stain. After applying with a damp cloth, allow it to remain for a few minutes before rinsing.

If you have tried everything else and simply can't get a stain out of a white fabric, use *Melaleuca's Whitening Tooth Polish*. It is amazing on everything from polyester to cotton and even some delicate fabrics.

For removing red stains such as catsup, spaghetti sauce or blood, try rubbing the area with *Antibacterial Liquid Soap*. It works wonders!

If you are away from home, *Hot/Cool Shot Breath Spray* is the best as an instant spot and stain remover. Spray the spot with *Hot/Cool Shot* and then rub with a fingernail before rinsing with cold water. It's magic!

LAWN FURNITURE

Mix 1 tsp of *Tough & Tender* and 1 capful of *Sol-U-Mel* to a 16 oz spray bottle filled with water. Spray this solution on the furniture and wipe it with a cloth.

LAWN MOWERS

To remove dirt and grease marks from your lawn mower, mix a solution of 1 tbsp of *MelaMagic* with ½ gallon of water. Spray or wipe the solution on your mower and allow it to set for a few minutes before rinsing. Repeat if necessary.

LEATHER CLEANER

Rustic Touch cleans vinyl and leather. It is also great for cleaning the dash of your car. **NOTE:** Spray it on a cloth to apply. If you spray it directly on the dash, you will get it on the inside of your windshield.

An alternate choice would be to use a 1:2 solution of *Antibacterial Liquid Soap* and water. It is very effective for removing dirt and scuffmarks from leather.

LEATHER SOFTENER

Try rubbing *Moisturizing Hand Creme* into stiff, old leather. It works like magic.

LIPSTICK — CLOTHING

Spray *PreSpot* on a lipstick stain and let it set for a few minutes. If this does not work, soak the clothing for a few hours in a 2-gallon bucket of cold water containing 1 tbsp of *MelaPower 6x Laundry Detergent*. Rinse with cool water. Add 1 to 2 capfuls of *Sol-U-Mel* to your regular wash and launder as usual.

Try using *Sol-U-Mel* as a pre-spot treatment on "dry clean only" fabrics.

MACHINE PARTS

Add 1 oz of *MelaMagic* to a 16 oz spray bottle and fill with water. Spray on the part and let it soak. Wipe it with a damp cloth. If the part is grimy, soak it in the above solution and then scrape off as much of the build-up as possible. Remove the remainder with a stiff brush (natural, wire, or brass) that is kept wet with the cleaning solution. For small parts, clean with a rag soaked in either full-strength *MelaMagic* or in the above solution.

MAGIC MARKER

Concentrated *Sol-U-Mel* can be used to remove permanent marker stains, but you must be very careful that the surface to be cleaned has been sealed. *Sol-U-Mel* can remove a surface's finish.

MICROWAVE

Mix 1 tsp of *Tough & Tender* and 1 capful of *Sol-U-Mel* in a 16 oz bottle of water. Apply to the microwave and wipe it with a damp cloth. Alternatively, try the *Tough & Tender Wipes.*

MIRRORS

Regularly use *Clear Power* to clean your mirrors. If *Clear Power* is unavailable, try adding 2 to 3 drops of *Tough & Tender* to a 24-oz spray bottle filled with water. Just spray it on and wipe with a soft cloth or cheap paper towels.

MOSQUITO SPRAY

Looking for an excellent mosquito spray that will not harm your family? Try combining 1 tsp of *Tough & Tender* with 1 capful of *Sol-U-Mel* and 1 capful of *Renew Bath Oil* in a 16 oz spray bottle and fill with water. This is safe not only for your clothes and the outdoor area in general, but you can spray it directly on your skin.

MOLD AND MILDEW

In some areas of the country mildew and mold are prevalent due to the humid environment. When the mold count is high, spray your home with diluted *Sol-U-Mel*. It can help prevent those "morning headaches."

An alternate solution is to place *T36-C5* in an open container in your bedroom at night. Even a drop or two on your pillow will help.

See the section on *Bathroom – Mold & Mildew* in this book.

NON-MAGNETIC SURFACES

To repel the dust and keep television and computer screens clean and static free, wipe them with a damp cloth and *Tough & Tender*.

HEALTHY HOME

ODORS

Use diluted *Sol-U-Mel* to eliminate odors of all kinds, including pet odors, smoke, and other strong odors. Spray in the air or on surfaces. In the laundry, add 1 to 2 capfuls of full-strength *Sol-U-Mel* to eliminate odors and boost the cleaning strength of *MelaPower*.

OIL – CLOTHING

Spray *PreSpot* on oily spots on your clothing and let it dry before washing. It will even remove motor oil.

OVENS

See *Kitchen – Oven* and *Toaster Oven*

PAINT

Spray *PreSpot* on paint spots or splatters. Rub with your finger or a soft brush. Let it set for a few minutes and then rinse in warm water. This method works very well for most paint stains, but you must remember that some paints are there to stay. Try soaking an old paint brush in undiluted *Sol-U-Mel*. Often, it will clean up like new.

PAINT – ACRYLIC

Spray acrylic paint spots with *PreSpot*. Give the paint time to dissolve and then rub the area with your fingernail or a brush. Rinse with cold water and repeat if necessary.

PAINT – OIL AND WATER BASED

Apply *PreSpot* to any paint stain. Wait a few minutes to allow it to soak in before rubbing cloth against cloth. If any paint remains after you rinse the garment, repeat before washing with *MelaPower* and *MelaBrite*.

PANELING

Clean old looking paneling by wiping with a cloth dampened with diluted *Tough & Tender*. Wipe on and dry with a clean cloth. Then enhance the look of the wood by wiping with *Rustic Touch*. It has a tremendous renewing ability.

PET ODORS

See *Odors*

PET STAINS

Sol-U-Mel is great for removing pet stains from the carpet.

PIANO KEYS

With a soft cloth dampened with a little diluted *Tough & Tender*, carefully wipe the piano keys and then thoroughly dry. Alternatively, try the pre-moistened *Tough & Tender Wipes*.

Amazingly enough, some people will stick tape on their piano keys, or even worse, write the names of the notes on the keys with marker pens. *Sol-U-Mel* seems to be the best cleaner for removing not only the tape and the pen marks, but also for cleaning the age-old dirt off the fronts of the keys. **Be careful, however, with the black keys.** If they are painted wood instead of natural wood or plastic, *Sol-U-Mel* will remove the black paint. Either isolate the white keys while cleaning them, or do a small test on the black keys before applying the *Sol-U-Mel*.

PLANTS

Add 1 tsp of *Tough & Tender* to a 16 oz spray bottle and fill with water. Spray on the roses to kill aphids and other undesirables. *Tough & Tender* can even be effective against webworms and a great deal safer than the normally recommended webworm spray. See the *Healthy Garden* chapter in this book for additional gardening applications for Melaleuca products.

PLASTIC

Use *Rustic Touch* to clean your plastic sunglasses. It is also an excellent way to clean plastic covers.

POTS AND PANS

Use *Tub & Tile* to clean stainless steel pots and pans, especially when they have been boiled dry or have baked-on grime on them. It seems to eat away at the black mess and make it much easier to restore to their original condition.

Tub & Tile is also very effective when cleaning copper pans.

REFRIGERATOR

Mix 1 tsp of *Tough & Tender* and 1 capful of *Sol-U-Mel* in a 16 oz bottle of water. Spray the inside and outside of the refrigerator with this solution and dry with a soft cloth. For extra-strength disinfecting and deodorizing use *Sol-U-Guard Botanical* as directed.

RUST

To remove rust stains from clothes, soak the area in concentrated *Tub & Tile*. When the rust spots have faded, wash as usual with *MelaPower* and *MelaBrite*.

Rust spots can be removed from a number of other surfaces by using *Tub & Tile* as well. **Just remember not to use it on marble or granite.**

SAW BLADES

To clean resin buildup from saw blades, shaper bits, or router bits, apply *MelaMagic* full-strength. Wipe them with a damp cloth. Soaking or scrubbing with a soft bristled brush may be necessary. Dry thoroughly and coat with a thin film of light oil (3-in-1, WD 40, vegetable oil, etc.) to guard against rusting.

HEALTHY HOME

Always read and follow product packaging directions and warnings.

SCUFFMARKS

See *Floors – Scuffmarks*

SHOES

To remove scuffmarks from shoes, spray them with **Rustic Touch**. What a difference it will make in your "professional" shoe-polishing job.

SINKS

See *Bathroom – Sink* or *Kitchen – Sink*

SILVER CLEANER

Classic Tooth Polish is excellent silver cleaner. Apply with a soft cloth and then rinse and dry. The shine will last much longer and is considerably safer than toxic silver polishes. (Save your empty tubes and when it is time to polish the silver, slice them open and you will find enough of the **Tooth Polish** residue to do quite a cleaning job. It is very economical, too!)

Diamond Brite can be substituted if **Tooth Polish** is not available.

SOFTENER – CLOTHING

Add 1 or 2 capfuls of **MelaSoft** to the final rinse for an average load of laundry, or use **MelaSoft** dryer sheets.

An alternate choice would be to dampen a small cloth with **MelaSoft** and toss it in with the wet clothes in the dryer.

SPILLS

To clean up spills, wet a cloth or paper towel with **Tough & Tender** (1 tsp to a 16 oz spray bottle). Also spray the stain and begin to blot from the outside edge in. After the stain is removed, rinse and soak up all the moisture from the article.

If you use paper towels, use cheap paper towels. Expensive towels have added softeners and the good Melaleuca products will release these ingredients and sometimes leave streaks.

You may try the handy **Tough & Tender Wipes** for quick clean-ups and small spills.

Hot/Cool Shot will take out spaghetti or coffee stains when you are out to dinner and don't have your **PreSpot** with you. Simply spray the spot and let it dry. Then scratch off the stain.

STARCH, SPRAY

Try **Revive** for a spray starch. It works wonders.

Another solution would be to use diluted **Tough & Tender**. It doesn't make your clothes stiff like starch, but certainly helps with the ironing.

STATIC CLING

If you have a garment that tends to have static cling, lightly spray *MelaSoft* to the underside. This will alleviate the static and allow the material to fall naturally.

Revive is also very effective for static cling. Dilute it by 50% and it works just as well.

STOVE

See *Kitchen – Stove*

TAR

Soak a cloth with *Sol-U-Mel* and wipe the affected area. This should dissolve the tar right away.

When you find tar on your clothes, apply concentrated *Sol-U-Mel* with a toothbrush and you will find that the tar will roll right off.

For tar on your car, try *PreSpot*. It is also very effective in taking tar off without hurting the finish on cars.

TOILET

See *Bathroom – Toilet*

TOYS

Frequently treat washable toys to a good soaking in a sink or container of water with 1 capful of *Sol-U-Mel* and 1 tsp of *Tough & Tender* added. After the toys have soaked, rinse them well and dry carefully.

Toys that cannot be soaked can be treated with *Sol-U-Guard Botanical* disinfectant as directed.

Machine washable stuffed animals, dolls, and blankets should be washed as usual with *MelaPower* (1 pump). Add 1 capful of *Sol-U-Mel* to wash to help disinfect.

TUBS

See *Bathtub*

VINYL

See *Leather Cleaner*

WALLS

For a very effective general cleaning disinfectant, mix 1 tsp of *Tough & Tender* in a 16 oz bottle of water, or add 1 oz of *Tough & Tender* to a gallon bucket of water. If you need a stronger mixture, add 1 capful of *Sol-U-Mel* to either the spray or the bucket.

WASHER – CLOTHING

See *Laundry*

WATER STAINS ON WOOD

Rub *Moisturizing Hand Creme* into the water stain. Let it set for a while, then buff it with a soft cloth.

HEALTHY HOME

WINDOWS

Use *Clear Power* on the glass as directed. Clean with cheap paper towels. The Melaleuca products are effective enough to bring out the additives in the more expensive paper towels which can leave streaks. They can also release the ink on the newsprint from the old-time popular newspaper-cleaning trick. Old towels and cloths can leave lint. Cheap paper towels are by far the most effective when cleaning windows.

Also try using *Clear Power* diluted to ½ the strength recommended on the bottle. For most uses this is sufficient and even more economical.

WINDSHIELD WASH

In the summer, use a combination of diluted *Tough & Tender* and *Clear Power* to replace the windshield wash in your vehicles. (Make sure to use nonfreezing washer fluid in the winter.)

WOOD FLOORS

See *Floors – Hardwood*

WOOD FURNITURE

To clean dirt from wood furniture, mix 1 tsp of *Tough & Tender* and 1 gallon of water. Apply this solution with a rag or sponge. Carefully towel dry the furniture. For heavy stains, use 1 tbsp of *Sol-U-Mel* and 1 gallon of water. Finish cleaning with *Rustic Touch* and a soft rag.

WRINKLES — CLOTHING

When schedules have been too busy and you are just too tired to fold those freshly washed clothes, never fear, *Revive* is here! Just spray and shake the clothes and hang them or lay them over a chair until they dry. Not only will the wrinkles come out, but they will smell fresh, too. Some suggest diluting it by half. It seems to work just as well.

HEALTHY HOME

CHAPTER EIGHTEEN

Healthy Dogs & Cats

PRECAUTIONS

If you are like most pet owners, your pets are very special to you. It is important to you to take the best care of them that you can. If you have not already done so, removing all of the grocery store brand cleaning and personal care products from your home is probably the easiest thing you can do to prolong the good health of your pets. Animals are more sensitive to toxic chemical vapors than we are because they are much lower to the ground where the vapors accumulate.

When using Melaleuca, or any other products, be sure to follow the package directions carefully. When using **T36-C5** or **T40-C3** on your pets, apply a diluted solution to a small area and check for sensitivity for 48 hours. If no reaction occurs, it should be safe. See *Dilution Formulas* below.

Always consult your veterinarian before starting any course of supplementation or treatment for your pet. Every effort has been made to ensure that the information contained in this book is complete and accurate. However, neither the publisher nor the author is engaged in rendering professional advice or services to the individual reader. The ideas, procedures and suggestions contained in this book are not intended as a substitute for consulting with your veterinarian. Neither the author nor the publisher shall be liable for any loss, injury, or damage allegedly arising from any information or suggestion in this book.

GENERAL INFORMATION

The hair and skin of most animals should not be overly washed with harsh detergents or shampoos. Cats and dogs can develop sensitivity and produce dry skin as a result of overwashing. Preventive care during seasonal infestation with fleas, ticks, mites and other insects can be accomplished by proper nutritional support to the animal. Dogs appear to have a particularly high requirement for extra calcium and magnesium. Cats appear to require additional B-complex, often in the form of brewers yeast. Dogs appear to fare very well when treated with **Sol-U-Mel, Renew Bath Oil,** and diluted *T36-C5*. Cats are more sensitive, and should not be treated with these products without consulting a veterinarian first. Optimum nutritional support should be provided based on the individual animal. Your natural veterinarian should be consulted if you are uncertain as to what your pet may need.

DOGS

PRECAUTIONS FOR DOGS

Your dog(s) can benefit greatly by using diluted *T36-C5* for minor first aid applications. But remember, there is an increased risk of an adverse reaction the stronger the dilution, the longer it is used, and the larger the area covered (even more so if your dog is light haired or gray). It is better to use a weaker dilution initially over the affected area and only use for the duration of the first aid application as stated. If there is any adverse reaction discontinue use immediately.

RECOMMENDED T36-C5 DILUTIONS FOR DOGS

Please Note: Use the lesser dilution on areas of sensitive skin. Any carrier oil can be used to dilute T36-C5, but it is worth noting that fractionated coconut oil is a light and fragrance-free oil that is very good for most applications. Jojoba oil is excellent for using on the coat and skin, if only a small amount is used it usually soaks in without leaving a greasy film. Olive oil is a much heavier oil, but has good anti-fungal properties.

- *Large Dog:* Mix 3–4 drops of *T36-C5* in 1 teaspoon of carrier oil. Apply 2–3 times each day until healed.
- *Medium to Small Dog:* Mix 2–3 drops of *T36-C5* to every teaspoon of carrier oil and apply 2–3 times per day until healed.
- *Puppies:* Use the minimum dilution required that is known to be a broad spectrum antiseptic—2 drops of *T36-C5* to every tsp of carrier oil and apply 2–3 times per day. Do not use over a large area of skin.

DOGS – ABSCESS

* Dogs often get into fights defending their territory. When the skin is punctured, it can become infected and an abscess is the most likely result. At the first sign of a puncture wound or abscess, dab with a strong antiseptic mix of 5-10 drops *T36-C5* in a teaspoon of carrier oil, and try to keep the pet from licking the area treated for at least 30 minutes after application. When the abscess bursts, allow it to drain and bathe the area with *Antiseptic Wash,* below. Keep applying the diluted *T36-C5* for 7 days.

If the abscess is large, if it is situated in the mouth or near to an eye, shows no sign of improvement or the animal is in obvious distress, consult a vet as soon as possible. If the abscess appears to be hard or becomes hard, consult a vet. It may not be an abscess.

*See precautions on page 239. See also precautions and dilution recommendations for dogs on page 240.

DOGS – ALLERGIES, CHRONIC

* Just as in humans, allergies in dogs can be treated with *ProVex* or *ProVex-Plus* and *Florify*. For larger breeds, give two capsules of *ProVex* and one capsule of *Florify* per day for the first month and then reduce to one capsule each per day. Give smaller breeds one capsule per day each and then reduce to one capsule each every other day after the first month. Open the capsules and mix it with your dog's favorite food or the capsules can also be coated with malleable dog treats and offered to your dog. If the dog refuses to eat them, you can give the capsules whole. Hold the dog securely and open the mouth with your thumb and index finger each side of the dog's jaw, (with your palm underneath the lower jaw, about half way along). Apply gentle pressure and the mouth should naturally open. Move your thumb and finger further down to keep the jaw open. Tilt the head upwards and pop the capsules on the back of the tongue. Immediately hold the mouth shut, so that the dog cannot move the capsules with its tongue. Never apply more than gentle pressure and talk soothingly to your dog the whole time.

DOGS – ANTISEPTIC WASH

* *T36-C5* is a natural antiseptic for your dog. Bathe wounds, bites, scratches, etc. with an antiseptic wash made by adding 2-3 drops of *T36-C5* mixed with 3 drops of carrier oil, added to a bowl of warm water, agitate the water well to mix and apply with cotton ball. Bathe area twice a day to help stop infection. For larger wounds or wounds that are slow to heal, seek advice from a vet.

As an antiseptic oil, use a dilution of *T36-C5* that is appropriate for your dog. See *Recommended T36-C5 Dilutions* at the beginning of this section.

DOGS – ARTHRITIS

* Painful inflammation of the joints usually causes a dog to limp on one or more paws. Some veterinarians are having excellent results using *ProVex-Plus* for arthritis in dogs. For large breeds, give two capsules per day for the first month and then reduce to one capsule per day. Give smaller breeds one capsule per day and then reduce to one capsule every other day after the first month. One veterinarian claims to have successfully treated 15 to 20 dogs with hip dysplasia, and other serious forms of arthritis, using this treatment.

For immediate care, combine 1–2 drops of *T36-C5* with 1 teaspoon of Jojoba oil and very gently massage the arthritic area. If you follow with a heating pad, be sure that the setting is on low to prevent burning. A chopped up capsule of *Phytomega* can be regularly added to your dog's food, it can help to improve the suppleness of the joints.

It has also been suggested that dogs with arthritis be given one *Replenex* each day. *ProVex* helps to strengthen connective tissue and reduce inflammation. *Replenex* helps to rebuild damaged and worn cartilage. Both are good for reducing the severity of arthritis.

*See precautions on page 239. See also precautions and dilution recommendations for dogs on page 240.

DOGS — BATHING

Bathing your dog could not be simpler with **ProCare Professional Pet Shampoo**, all you need is a teaspoon of the product and shampoo away! Rinse well and your dog's coat will remain in very good condition. It discourages pests too. Melaleuca's **Melaleuca Original Shampoo** also has melaleuca oil and discourages pests and is an exellent solution if you don't have the **ProCare** shampoo on hand.

DOGS — BEDDING & BLANKETS

* Hot- or boil-wash bedding every 2–4 weeks in **MelaPower Laundry Detergent** and **MelaBrite** with an extra tablespoon of salt added. In the winter you may find it very helpful to have two beds for your pet so that you can have one available while the other is being washed. Wipe the area where the bed is normally located often with a diluted solution of **Tough & Tender**.

DOGS — BITES, CUTS AND SCRATCHES

See *Antiseptic Wash*

DOGS — BRONCHITIS, CHRONIC

* **ProVex-Plus** is excellent for dealing with chronic problems caused by impaired immune system function. Give two capsules per day for a large animal and 1 capsule per day for a small animal. **Activate** is a very effective way to boost the immune system for an animal with a chronic infection. See *Allergies* for the best way to give the capsules.

DOGS — CAR ACCIDENT

* A vet must see all car accident victims. Either call a vet to the scene or transport your dog very carefully as soon as possible. Small dogs can be wrapped in a blanket and put into a large box to make traveling easier. Do not attempt to diagnose the damage yourself. There is a likelihood of internal injuries and delayed shock. See also *Fractures*.

DOGS — COAT CARE

* Comb your dog's coat daily, especially on longhaired breeds. If matted, try wetting the matted hair with a mixture of 1 drop of **T36-C5** and ½ teaspoon of oil. Rub it in and try to ease the matted fur a little at a time from the top of the matt with a comb. If you do have to cut the patch of fur, try cutting down vertically instead of horizontally and ease with the comb again. Cutting this way makes less of a bald patch. If the skin is nicked, bathe the wound with **Antiseptic Wash** to prevent infection. See also *Coat Conditioner* and *Bathing*.

DOGS — COAT CONDITIONER

* In between bathing your dog, keep its coat healthy and pest free by mixing 3–5 drops of **T36-C5** in 1½ cup of carrier oil. Jojoba may be a little more expensive but it really does make a difference to the coat.

*See precautions on page 239. See also precautions and dilution recommendations for dogs on page 240.

Store this mixture in a dark glass bottle, in a cool place. Sprinkle a few drops all over the coat, especially around the neck area and comb through the fur. An alternate choice would be to sprinkle a few drops onto a sponge and rub over the dog's coat. Always avoid the eye area.

DOGS — DEODORANT

* You may love your dog, but there is no denying he can really stink. It is even more noticeable to people coming to your home, especially if they have never owned a pet. For a quick fix solution, brush some *Coat Conditioner* through your dog's coat. If you have a little more time, bathe him with *Melaleuca Original Shampoo*. Now drop one drop of *T36-C5* by every door and your guests will not know you have a dog until they see him! See also *Bathing*.

DOGS — DERMATITIS

* Skin conditions, such as rashes, flaky skin, redness, or itchiness, should be treated to prevent secondary infections and reduce any discomfort. You may need to keep the dog isolated to prevent a contagious condition from spreading. Make sure that your dog has not come into contact with air fresheners, spray polishes, or other commercial cleaning products which may be a cause of the problem. Switching to Melaleuca cleaning products will probably help your pet. Cut the hair around the affected area and wash with the *Antiseptic Wash*. Pat the area dry. Apply *Renew Intensive Skin Therapy*, *Triple Antibiotic Ointment*, or a *T36-C5 Antiseptic Dilution* 2–3 times each day until the condition improves. See your vet if the problem persists. See also *Mange*.

DOGS — DEWCLAWS

* Damaged dewclaws should be treated as a wound. If your dog is persistently damaging the dewclaws, seek the advice of a vet. See also *Antiseptic Wash*.

DOGS — DIARRHEA

* If your dog has diarrhea for more than 24 hours or it is chronic, the dog should be taken to a vet. Remember to give plenty of fluids, to prevent dehydration, and a good probiotic such as *Florify*, may help. Just open a couple of capsules and mix the contents into food or drink twice per day until diarrhea has stopped. See also *Soiling*.

DOGS — DRY SKIN

* Dry skin is usually a sign of either improper nutrition or the use of harsh chemicals in certain shampoos or household cleaners. See *Bathing*.

For shorthaired dogs, *Renew Intensive Skin Therapy* can be used to relieve itchy, dry skin. If the itchy skin continues, consult your vet to select the proper diet for your dog.

DOGS — EARS

* Dogs often get ear infections. They can be caused by parasites or a scratch or bite from another dog. When treating the ears, use a

dropper and massage the ears after medicating them. Be careful of the animal shaking its head. Do not put the dropper inside the ear. Apply a slightly warmed mixture of the following twice each day if possible until alleviated. Swab excess along the flap of the ear with cotton ball.

Mix 1–2 drops of **T36-C5** with 2 teaspoons of olive oil, apply a couple of drops of this mixture to each ear as directed above.

To discourage ear mites or to simply keep the ears clean, apply 1 or 2 drops of the above mixture on a cotton swab and wipe the inside of the ear every week. Remember to always use a clean swab for each ear.

Alternatively, it has been suggested to flush both ears with about a teaspoon of **Sol-U-Mel** diluted as directed daily if the dog is prone to ear infections.

DOGS — ECZEMA

See *Mange*

DOGS — EPILEPSY

* **ProVex-Plus** has been used to successfully prevent seizures. Give 2 capsules per day, overlapped with the regular seizure medication, for one week. Then ask your vet if you could try weaning the animal off the seizure medication gradually. See *Allergies* on the best way to give the capsules to your dog.

DOGS — FEEDING BOWLS

* Always wash a dog's feeding and water bowl every day. Wipe the area around the bowls with ½ a capful of **Sol-U-Mel** in a cup of hot water blended with a squirt of **Lemon Brite**. Dry with a paper towel.

DOGS — FLEAS

* If your dog is prone to pick up fleas, the best thing you can do is keep the fur well groomed and bathe every week with the following mixture: For every 2 teaspoons of **Melaleuca Original Shampoo** add 1 teaspoon Jojoba oil. Mix well. Shampoo the dog, avoiding the eyes and rinse well. Apply *Coat Conditioner* between washes.

Your dog should love the taste of Brewer's yeast and even garlic, but fleas hate it. Why not give it a try, some pet owners swear by it.

DOGS — FRACTURES

* Your dog will need optimum nutrition to get it quickly back to its old self again. Using 1 capsule per day of **ProVex-Plus** will speed the healing rate of fractures. Give the capsule to your dog whole or opened and the contents mixed with its food. See *Allergies* for the best way to give capsules to your dog. See also *Car Accident*.

DOGS — HEART PROBLEMS

* **ProvexCV** and **Phytomega** are excellent supplements to give your dog as it gets older. Give 2 **ProVexCV** and 1 **Phytomega** per day for a large animal and 1 each per day for a small animal. See *Allergies* for the best way to give the capsules to your dog.

*See precautions on page 239. See also precautions and dilution recommendations for dogs on page 240.

DOGS – HIP DYSPLASIA

* Hip dysplasia is sometimes caused by congenital arthritis in the hip joint. Two **ProVex-Plus** taken daily for one month by a large dog seems to help. At the end of the first month, cut the dose to 1 per day. Continue this dose, as it is a natural anti-inflammatory. The severity of the condition will help determine the amount to use. For a small dog, start with 1 per day for the first month and then 1 every other day after that. See also *Arthritis*. See *Allergies* for the best way to give your dog the capsules.

DOGS – HOT SPOTS

* Hot spots and abrasions on the body respond well to diluted *T36-C5* applied frequently to reduce the pain, prevent infection, and promote healing. *MelaGel* can be applied if drying or scaling results. **Triple Antibiotic Ointment** is very healing and may help prevent the dog from chewing on the hot spots and making them worse. **Renew Intensive Skin Therapy** has also been successfully used to heal hot spots. See *Recommended T36-C5 Dilutions* at the beginning of this section.

DOGS – INSECT BITES AND STINGS

* Carefully remove the stinger by scraping out with thumbnail or flat card. Be careful not to agitate the sac of poison. Apply diluted *T36-C5* (as in *Recommended T36-C5 Dilutions*) with a cotton swab to soothe the pain and neutralize the venom. If your dog is stung in the mouth by a bee or ant, apply bicarbonate of soda and ice and consult a vet as soon as possible. If your dog is stung in the mouth by a wasp, dab with vinegar and ice to avert swelling, and consult your vet as soon as possible.

If your dog shows any signs of abnormal swelling, wheezing, coughing, sneezing, panting, or anything that you are worried about, consult your vet immediately. Your dog may be having an allergic reaction to the sting.

DOGS – ITCHING

See *Bathing*, *Coat Conditioner*, *Dry Skin*, *Fleas*, and *Mange*

DOGS – JOINT AND MUSCULAR DISORDERS

* Combine 3 drops of *T36-C5* with 1 teaspoon of Jojoba oil and massage into the affected area. If you choose to cover with heating pad, use it only on the lowest temperature to prevent burning. Give a large pet 2 **ProVex-Plus** and 1 **Phytomega** per day, and a small pet 1 of each per day to help reduce pain and inflammation and speed healing. Open the **ProVex-Plus** capsules and chop up the **Phytomega** and mix both into the food. See *Arthritis*.

DOGS – KENNEL COUGH

* Giving a large pet 2 **ProVex-Plus** per day and a small pet 1 **ProVex-Plus** per day can help the immune system fight kennel cough. Give the capsules to your pet wrapped in a piece of soft dog treat or in the center of a hotdog. Or open the capsules and mix them with your dog's food.

DOGS — KENNEL HYGIENE

*If you have to keep your dog in a kennel, wash the kennel down every few weeks during late spring and summer. (Be sure it is not damp during the winter.) Use a squirt of *Antibacterial Liquid Soap* or *Lemon Brite* with 32 ounces of hot water and a 2 capfuls of *Sol-U-Mel*.

DOGS — KIDNEY PROBLEMS, CHRONIC

* *ProVex-Plus* is excellent for helping your dog with chronic problems. Give 2 capsules per day for a large animal and 1 per day for a small animal. *Activate* is a very effective way to boost the immune system for an animal with a chronic infection. Give the capsules to your dog wrapped in a piece of soft dog treat or in the center of a piece of hotdog. Or open the capsules and mix them with your dog's food. For dogs with kidney problems do not use a strong dilution of *T36-C5* (higher than 2 drops per teaspoon of carrier) on the skin or in the mouth.

DOGS — LEECHES

*If you live by marshy ground, your dog could pick up a leech. Dab the leech with *T36-C5* and gently pull it off the skin with tweezers. Treat the wound as suggested in the *Recommended T36-C5 Dilutions* section.

DOGS — LICE

See the sections on *Bedding, Coat Conditioner, Dermatitis, Fleas, Kennel Hygiene*, and *Mange* in this section. Lice are species-specific. If a vet has determined your pet has lice, they are not the same head lice that often infest humans. Isolate your pet from other animals to keep the lice from spreading. Mix half to one teaspoon of *Sol-U-Mel* with 1-2 cups of warm water. Place in a spray bottle and shake well to mix before each application. Spray the pet liberally with this mixture. Brush it in well to soften and dislodge the eggs of the lice. Let this stand for at least 10 minutes. Bathe thoroughly with *Melaleuca Original Shampoo or ProCare Professional Shampoo*. Pat the dog dry with paper towels and dispose of the towels. Repeat daily until all signs of the lice are gone. Add 2 ounces of *Sol-U-Mel* to 16 ounces of water, and apply to areas where your dog sleeps or rests during the day and evening.

DOGS — MANGE

Mange is generally caused by mites that bore into the skin and may be difficult to treat. If these suggestions don't work, contact your veterinarian. Isolate your pet to keep the condition from spreading to other animals.

*Diluted *T36-C5* is very good for areas of unidentified rashes, it doesn't matter if it is Mange or any other cause, *T36-C5* is so broad-spectrum that it will help to alleviate itching and inflammation. Apply a mixture of 3-5 drops of *T36-C5* and 1 tsp. of Jojoba oil to the infected area twice a day.

For larger dogs and dogs that have no problem with *Melaleuca oil*, 10 drops per teaspoon of Jojoba oil may be applied. Dab it on with a cotton ball. If no improvement within 4 weeks, or an adverse reaction occurs, discontinue use. See *Dermatitis*.

DOGS — MOUTH ULCER

* A mouth ulcer is caused by a minor viral infection and is usually located on or under the tongue or on the inside of the dog's cheek. Combine 3–6 drops of *T36-C5* (depending on the size of the animal) with half a teaspoon of olive oil, mix with 1 cup of warm water in a spray bottle and shake vigorously. Spray the area as needed for three days. The oil will not only heal but it should help with the pain as well.

DOGS — NAIL (CLAW) CARE

* Cutting a dog's claws/nails usually needs to be done by a professional with a special claw/nail clipper. Just before your appointment, soak the claws in a mixture of 5 drops of *T36-C5* and 2 teaspoons of Jojoba oil. (A little warm water in a basin, add the oil and stand the paw in the mixture is a good way of doing this). Prepare the claws two days before and two days after they have been clipped to help prevent splitting and infection.

DOGS — NAIL OR PAD INFECTION

* Apply 2–5 drops of *T36-C5* blended with 1 teaspoon of carrier oil to any pad/claw/nail that appears to be infected. Treat twice each day for 7–10 days. Try to discourage your pet from licking the area. If the infection persists or gets worse, consult a vet.

DOGS — OIL (DIESEL) SATURATION

See *Tar*

DOGS — PAW ABRASIONS

* Dogs' paws can become cracked and sore. Bathe in antiseptic wash (See the *Recommended T36-C5 Dilutions* and *Antiseptic Wash*.) and apply a few drops of the following mixture: 5 drops of *T36-C5* blended with ½ cup of carrier oil. Store this mixture in a dark glass bottle and apply it to the paws 2–3 times each day. If your pet will wear little socks, it will assist in the healing and help to keep the area clean. An alternate solution is to treat paw abrasions with *MelaGel* or *Triple Antibiotic Ointment*. Apply twice daily as long as needed.

See also the section on *Nail (Claw) Infections* and *Splinters*.

DOGS — RASHES

See *Dermatitis*, *Eczema*, *Itching*, *Lice*, and *Ringworm*

DOGS — RINGWORM

* Ringworm usually appears as a ring-shaped sore on the skin with patchy hair growth. It is caused by a fungus and is very contagious, so keep the dog isolated until the treatment is successful. Cut the remaining hair away from the affected area and wash thoroughly with

the *Antiseptic Wash* detailed at the beginning of the chapter. Apply a dilution of *T36-C5* (5 drops *T36-C5* in a teaspoon of olive oil) directly to the area with a cotton ball 3–4 times a day. Be aware of any signs of sensitivity. **Dermatin**, **MelaGel**, or **Triple Antibiotic Ointment** are also effective. It may take a couple of weeks to clear up this condition. Make sure that your dog is well fed with the proper nutrition to help him fight the infection.

DOGS — SCENT MASKING

See *Soiling*

DOGS — SERIOUS INJURIES

See *Car Accidents*, *Fractures*

DOGS — SKIN INFECTIONS

See *Mange*, *Bathing*, *Coat Conditioner*

DOGS — SKUNK ODORS

* When your dog has had an encounter in with a skunk, run a large outdoor tub full of water, add 3–4 tablespoons of sodium bicarbonate (bicarbonate of soda), and wash him/her with **Melaleuca Original Shampoo** or **Antibacterial Liquid Soap**. Let it stand for a few minutes then rinse. Repeat if necessary. (The next bath will probably need to be yours!).

NOTE: If a skunk has sprayed your pet, act immediately to eliminate the odor. The longer it stays on the pet, the more difficult it is to remove. Immediately rinse the pet with cool water. (Warm water only amplifies the odor.) Then wash and rinse as suggested above.

DOGS — SOILING

* To clean an area, mask the smell and prevent re-soiling, clean any fecal matter from the area, and blot liquid with a paper towel. Wash with a solution of 1½ cups of hot water and a squirt of **Lemon Brite**. For seriously soiled areas, you may need to add 20 drops of *T36-C5* or 1–2 capfuls of **Sol-U-Mel** to increase stain removing power, sanitation, and deodorizing. Always patch test before applying to the area and, if no discoloration, clean and blot dry. Or use a combination of **Sol-U-Mel** and **Tough & Tender** to spray on the fabric stains and then wipe with a damp cloth. If you do not already have a spray mixture ready, just pour diluted **Sol-U-Mel** on the spots and then spray with **Tough & Tender**. The cleaning effect will be the same. Rinse area and blot dry. See also *Diarrhea*.

DOGS — SORE MUSCLES

See *Joint* and *Muscular Disorders*

DOGS — SPLINTERS

* If your pet picks up a splinter or thorn, carefully remove with a pair of tweezers and apply 1 drop of diluted *T36-C5* mix twice per day until the area is healed. See the *Recommended T36-C5 Dilutions* section.

*See precautions on page 239. See also precautions and dilution recommendations for dogs on page 240.

DOGS — SPRAINS

*Add 3 drops of *T36-C5* to 1 teaspoon of carrier oil and mix well. Massage the mixture into the sprained area and apply a heating pad. Be very sure that the heating pad is on the lowest temperature to prevent burning. See *Joint and Muscular Disorders*

DOGS — STAINS

*Mix 2 capfuls of *Sol-U-Mel* in a 16-ounce spray bottle of water. Saturate the stain and then blot it with a white towel until all the residue and odor is gone. Or try this same procedure using undiluted *PreSpot*.

DOGS — SUNBURN

*Cool your pet down and give plenty of drinking water, apply *Renew Intensive Skin Therapy* or *MelaGel* to the area 2 to 3 times each day. Keep the pet out of the sun as much as possible.

An alternate solution is to apply 2 drops of *T36-C5* in a teaspoon of vitamin E and Jojoba oil to the sunburned area. Keep it cool and moist. Keep your pet out of the sun for at least a week.

DOGS — TAR

*If your dog has stepped or rolled on the road where there is wet tar, mix ½ tablespoon of *Melaleuca Original Shampoo* and 2 teaspoons of salt. Rub into the tar. Rinse with warm water and shampoo with *Melaleuca Original Shampoo* and rinse very well. Repeat the process if necessary.

DOGS — TICKS

*Use a pair of curved forceps to grasp the tick as close to the dog's skin as possible and pull straight out. Do not apply anything to the tick (such as a match, vaseline or *T36-C5*) before removal because of the risk of salivation back into the bite site and possible transmission of disease. Do not crush the tick.

Apply *Triple Antibiotic* or *MelaGel* to the bite site after tick removal. Bathe dog with *Melaleuca Original Shampoo* or *ProCare Professional Shampoo* and rinse. Allow it to dry naturally. This will not only beautify the pet's coat but will help to prevent fleas and ticks. Make sure that the animal gets no lather on the immediate eye area. **NOTE: When pulling ticks off your dog, always have a barrier between your hand and the tick itself. Lyme disease and Rocky Mountain Spotted Fever can be transmitted.**

DOGS — TOYS

*Wash your dog's toys often. Soft toys can be washed in a solution of hot water and *Lemon Brite*. A capful of *Sol-U-Mel* could be added to the water if the toys are particularly dirty. Rinse and dry thoroughly. Wipe plastic and rubber toys with the same solution.

*See precautions on page 239. See also precautions and dilution recommendations for dogs on page 240.

DOGS – URINARY PROBLEMS, CHRONIC

* *ProVex-Plus* is an excellent supplement for dogs with chronic problems. See *Allergies* for the best way to give the capsules.

DOGS – VACCINATIONS

* To prevent infection, apply diluted *T36-C5* with a cotton ball to the affected area 2–3 times each day. See *Recommended T36-C5 Dilutions* at the beginning of this section.

DOGS – VOMIT STAINS

PreSpot can be used after the matter is scraped up and discarded. See also *Soiling*.

DOGS – WARTS

* Warts are small, usually hard, tumor growths on the skin. A virus causes them and moisture helps them to live. To soothe the pain of bleeding or itching warts, apply 1–2 drops of *T36-C5*, on a cotton swab directly to the warts. If your dog has sensitive skin mix with 1–2 drops of olive oil before applying on a cotton swab. Keep the area dry. Watch your pet for adverse reactions. If one occurs stop the treatment immediately. Be patient; it can take weeks for the warts to disappear. **NOTE:** Certain types of warts do not respond to Melaleuca oil.

DOGS – WATER BOWLS

* Add one cup of *Melaleuca Herbal Tea* to your dog's water bowl each day for 7 days. They need to detoxify too. Repeat every two months. One opened capsule of *Florify* added to the water bowl for 7 days following treatment is also beneficial.

DOGS – WORMER

* Show dogs tend to have stomach problems as a result of using too much worming medicine. Try saving the used *Melaleuca Herbal Tea* bags, and mix one in with your dog's food. The probiotic *Florify* can also help to balance your dog's system after too much wormer.

CATS

PRECAUTIONS FOR CATS

It has been published that several cats have had an adverse reaction to tea tree oil. It should be noted that the owners of these cats used tea tree oil either undiluted or in a very strong dilution over a large area of coat. Also, there is no information published about the quality of the oil used. A stale, oxidized, low quality oil should never be applied. If a fresh oil from a trusted supplier is used in a low dilution, and the area is spot-tested for 48 hours, it should be safe to use as directed here. If at any time a reaction occurs, discontinue use immediately. Never use undiluted *T36-C5* on your cat. Never use *T36-C5* on a cat with impaired liver or kidney function, or on young kittens, without the guidance of a vet. *The recommendations listed in this section are for information purposes only. They should not replace care by a veterinarian.*

RECOMMENDED T36-C5 DILUTION FOR CATS

Your adult cat(s) can benefit greatly by using diluted *T36-C5* for minor first aid applications. But remember, if your cat is light haired or is a pedigree, there is an increased risk of an adverse reaction the stronger the dilution, the larger the area covered, and the longer it is used. It is better to use a weak dilution and only use for the duration of the first aid application as stated. Any carrier oil can be used to dilute *T36-C5*, but it is worth noting that fractionated coconut oil is a light and fragrance-free oil that is very good for most applications. Jojoba oil is excellent for using on the coat and skin, if only a small amount is used it usually soaks in without leaving a greasy film. Olive oil is a much heavier oil, but has good anti-fungal properties.

- *Adult Cats:* Mix 2 drops of *T36-C5* in 1 teaspoon of carrier oil, mix well, and apply twice a day to the immediate area, until healed. Do not saturate the skin more than is necessary.

CATS – ABSCESS

*Cats often get into fights. It is a natural territorial trait. When the skin is punctured, infection can set in and an abscess is the most likely result. At the first sign of a puncture wound or abscess, dab with a strong antiseptic mix of 5 drops *T36-C5* in a teaspoon of carrier oil, and try to keep the pet from licking the area treated for at least 30 minutes after application. When the abscess bursts, allow it to drain and bathe the area with *Antiseptic Wash*, below. Keep applying the diluted *T36-C5* for 7 days. If the abscess is large, if it is situated in the mouth or near to an eye, shows no sign of improvement or the animal is in obvious distress, consult a vet as soon as possible. If the abscess appears to be hard or becomes hard, consult a vet, it may not be an abscess.

*See precautions on page 239. See also precautions and dilution recommendations for cats on page 251.

CATS – ALLERGIES, CHRONIC

* One *ProVex-Plus* capsule per day will help your cat deal with chronic allergies. Open the capsule and mix it with your cat's favorite food. If the cat refuses to eat it, you can give the capsule whole. Hold the cat securely; it may help to wrap it in a towel. Open the cat's mouth with your thumb and index finger each side of the cat's jaw (and your palm on top of the cat's head). Apply gentle pressure and the mouth should naturally open. Pop the capsule on the very back of the cat's tongue. Immediately hold the cat's mouth shut and up, so that it cannot move the capsule with its tongue. Never apply more than gentle pressure and talk soothingly to your cat the whole time. A *Florify* capsule, opened and mixed into drinks or food may also help allergies.

CATS – ANTISEPTIC WASH

* *T36-C5* is a natural antiseptic for your cat. Bathe wounds, bites, scratches, etc. with an antiseptic wash made by adding 2 drops of *T36-C5* mixed with 4 drops of carrier oil, to a bowl of warm water. Agitate the water well to mix and apply to a localized area with a cotton ball. Bathe twice a day to help stop infection. For larger wounds, or wounds that are slow to heal, seek advice from a vet. After bathing, apply an antiseptic oil—either use a dilution of *T36-C5* that is appropriate for your cat or apply *MelaGel* to the area. See *Recommended T36-C5 Dilutions*.

CATS – ARTHRITIS

* Combine 1–2 drops of *T36-C5* with 1 teaspoon of Jojoba oil and very gently massage the arthritic area. If you follow with a heating pad, be sure that the setting is on low to prevent burning. A chopped up capsule of *Phytomega* can be added to your cat's food, it can help to improve the suppleness of your cat's joints.

CATS – BEDDING

* Hot- or boil-wash bedding every 2–4 weeks in *MelaPower Laundry Detergent* and *MelaBrite* with an extra tablespoon of salt added. In the winter you may find it very helpful to have two beds for your cat so that you can have one available while the other is being washed. While the bed is being washed, wipe the area where the bed is normally located with a diluted solution of *Tough & Tender*.

CATS – BITES AND SCRATCHES

See *Cats Antiseptic Wash*

CATS – CAR ACCIDENT

* A cat that has been in a car accident must be checked over by a vet. Either call a vet to the scene or transport them very carefully as soon as possible. They can be wrapped in a blanket and put into a large box to make traveling easier. Do not attempt diagnosis yourself; there is a likelihood of internal injuries and delayed shock. See *Fractures*.

---

*See precautions on page 239. See also precautions and dilution recommendations for cats on page 251.

CATS – DERMATITIS

*Skin conditions, such as rashes, flaky skin, redness or itchiness, should be treated to prevent secondary infections and reduce any discomfort for your cat. You may need to keep the cat in a clean cage or pet carrier to prevent a contagious condition from spreading to others. Make sure that your cat has not come into contact with air fresheners, spray polishes, or other commercial cleaning products, which may be a cause of the problem.

Switching to Melaleuca cleaning products will probably help your pet. Cut the fur around the affected area and wash with the *Cats Antiseptic Wash*. Pat the area dry. Apply *Renew Intensive Skin Therapy*, *Triple Antibiotic Ointment*, or a *T36-C5* dilution (see *Recommended T36-C5 Dilutions*) 2 times each day until the condition improves. See your veterinarian if the problem persists.

CATS – DIARRHEA

*If your cat has diarrhea for more than 24 hours or it is chronic, it should be taken to a vet. Remember to give plenty of fluids, and a good probiotic such as *Florify* may help. Just open a capsule and mix the contents into food or drink twice per day until diarrhea has stopped. See also *Soiling*.

CATS – EARS

*Cats are often prone to ear infections, sometimes caused by parasites. When treating the ears use a dropper and massage the ears after medicating them. Be careful of the animal shaking its head. Do not put the dropper inside the ear. Apply a slightly warmed mixture of the following, twice each day if possible, until alleviated. Swab excess with cotton ball. Mix 1 drop of *T36-C5* with 2 teaspoons of olive oil. Apply a couple of drops of this mixture to each ear as directed above. To discourage ear mites or to simply keep the ears clean, apply 1 or 2 drops of the above mixture on a cotton swab and wipe the inside of the ear every 7–10 days. Remember to use a clean swab for each ear.

CATS – ECZEMA

*Diluted *T36-C5* is very good for areas of unidentified rashes. It doesn't matter if it is eczema or any other cause. *T36-C5* is so broad-spectrum that it will help to alleviate itching and inflammation. Apply a mixture of 2 drops of *T36-C5* and 1 tsp. of Jojoba oil to the infected area twice a day. Dab it on with cotton ball. If no improvement within 2 weeks, discontinue use. See also *Dermatitis*.

CATS – FEEDING BOWLS

*Always wash a cat's feeding bowl every day. Wipe the area around the bowls with ½ teaspoon of *Sol-U-Mel* in a cup of hot water blended with a squirt of *Lemon Brite*. Dry with a paper towel.

*See precautions on page 239. See also precautions and dilution recommendations for cats on page 251.

Cats – Fleas

* If your cat has a flea problem, the best thing you can do is keep the fur well combed and every 7–10 days bathe the cat with the following mixture: 1 teaspoon *Melaleuca Original Shampoo* and 1 teaspoon Jojoba oil. Mix and shampoo the cat avoiding the eyes. Rinse well.

Your cat should love the taste of Brewer's yeast, but fleas hate it. Why not give it a try, some cat owners swear by it.

Cats – Fractures

* Your cat will need optimum nutrition to get it quickly back to its old self again. Using 1 capsule per day of *ProVex-Plus* will speed the healing rate of fractures. Give the capsule to your cat whole, or opened and the contents mixed with its food. See *Allergies* for the best way to give your cat the capsules. See also *Car Accident.*

Cats – Fur Care

* Comb your cat's fur daily, especially on longhaired breeds. If matted, try wetting the matted hair with a mixture of 1 drop of *T36-C5* in 1 teaspoon Jojoba oil. Rub it in and try to ease the matted fur a little at a time from the top of the matt with a comb. If you do have to cut the patch of fur off, try cutting down vertically instead of horizontally and ease with the comb again. Cutting this way makes less of a bald patch.

Cats – Heart Problems

* *ProVex-Plus* can be used with heart medication, but consult your vet before doing so.

Cats – Infections of the Skin

See *Dermatitis, Eczema, Fleas* and *Itching*

Cats – Insect Bites and Stings

* Carefully remove the stinger by scraping out with thumbnail or flat card. Be careful not to agitate the sac of poison. Apply diluted *T36-C5* (see *Recommended T36-C5 Dilutions*) with a cotton swab to soothe the pain and neutralize the venom. If your cat is stung in the mouth by a bee or ant, apply bicarbonate of soda and ice and consult a vet as soon as possible. If your cat is stung in the mouth by a wasp, dab with vinegar and ice to avert swelling, and consult your vet as soon as possible. If your cat shows any signs of abnormal swelling, wheezing, coughing, sneezing, panting, or anything that you are worried about, consult your vet immediately. Your cat may be having an allergic reaction to the sting.

Cats – Itching

If your cat is constantly itching, bathe with the following mixture: 1 teaspoon *Melaleuca Original Shampoo* and 1 teaspoon Jojoba oil, mix well. Shampoo the cat, avoiding the eyes and rinse very well. See *Lice.*

*See precautions on page 239. See also precautions and dilution recommendations for cats on page 251.

Cats – Joint and Muscular Disorders

See *Arthritis*

Cats – Kidney Problems, Chronic

* *ProVex-Plus* is excellent for helping your cat deal with chronic problems. Give 1 capsule per day. It is a very effective way to boost the immune system for an animal with a chronic infection. See *Allergies* for the best way to give your cat the capsules. For cats with kidney problems do not use *T36-C5* on the skin or in the mouth.

Cats – Leeches

* If you live by marshy ground, your cat could pick up a leech. Dab the leech with *T36-C5* and gently pull it off your cat with tweezers. Treat the wound as suggested in the *Recommended T36-C5 Dilutions* section at the beginning of this section.

Cats – Lice

See the sections on *Bedding*, *Fleas*, and *Itching* in this section. Lice are species-specific. If a vet has determined your pet has lice, they are not the same head lice that often infest humans. Isolate your pet from other animals to keep the lice from spreading. Mix half a teaspoon of *Sol-U-Mel* with 2 cups of warm water. Place in a spray bottle and shake well to mix before each application. Spray the pet liberally with this mixture. Brush it in well to soften and dislodge the eggs of the lice. Let this stand for at least 10 minutes and bathe thoroughly with *Melaleuca Original Shampoo*. Pat the animal dry with paper towels and dispose of the towels. Repeat every couple of days until all signs of the lice are gone. Add 2 ounces of *Sol-U-Mel* to 16 ounces of water, and apply to areas where your cat sleeps or rests during the day and evening.

Cats – Litter Tray Hygiene

* Apply 1–2 drops of *T36-C5* diluted with oil into corners of the cat litter tray to deodorize. Apply only a small amount at first for your cat to get accustomed to it. When changing the litter box, it is often advisable to put an opened supermarket carrier bag, as a liner, onto the base of the tray. Tuck the edges under the tray (or a couple of pages from a newspaper folded to fit) and fill with cat litter, sprinkle on a couple of teaspoons of bicarbonate of soda and mix well. This can then be scooped up and disposed of when the litter is very soiled. Wipe out the litter tray with a piece of dampened paper towel soaked in a solution of ¼ cup of hot water, *Lemon Brite*, and half a capful of *Sol-U-Mel* before putting the liner down.

Cats – Nail or Pad Infection

* Apply 2 drops of *T36-C5* blended with 1 teaspoon of carrier oil to any pad/claw/nail that appears to be infected. Treat twice each day

for 7–10 days. Try to discourage your pet from licking the area. If the infection persists or gets worse, see your vet.

CATS — OIL (DIESEL) SATURATION

See *Tar*

CATS — PAW ABRASIONS

* Cats' paws can become cracked and sore. Bathe in antiseptic wash (See *Cats Antiseptic Wash*) and apply a few drops of the following mixture: 1–2 drops of *T36-C5* blended with ½ cup of carrier oil. Store this mixture in a dark glass bottle and apply it to the paws 2–3 times each day. If your pet will wear little socks, it will assist in the healing and help to keep the area clean.

An alternate solution is to treat paw abrasions with *MelaGel* or *Triple Antibiotic Ointment*. Apply twice daily as long as needed. See also *Splinters*.

CATS — RASHES

See *Dermatitis*, *Eczema*, *Itching*, and *Ringworm*

CATS — RINGWORM

* Ringworm usually appears as a ring-shaped sore on the skin with patchy hair growth. It is caused by a fungus and is very contagious, so keep the pet isolated until the treatment is successful. Cut the remaining hair away from the affected area and wash thoroughly with the *Antiseptic Wash*. Apply a dilution of *T36-C5* (2 drops *T36-C5* in a teaspoon of olive oil) directly to the area with a cotton ball 2 or 3 times a day. Be aware of any signs of sensitivity. *Dermatin*, *MelaGel*, or *Triple Antibiotic Ointment* are also effective. It may take a couple of weeks to clear up this condition. Make sure that your cat is well fed with the proper nutrition to help him fight the infection.

CATS — SCENT MASKING

See *Soiling*

CATS — SERIOUS INJURIES

See *Car Accident*

CATS — SOILING

* To clean an area, mask the smell, and so prevent re-soiling, clean any fecal matter from the area and blot liquid with a paper towel. Wash with a solution of 2 cups of hot water and a squirt of *Lemon Brite*. For seriously soiled areas, you may need to add 1 capful of *Sol-U-Mel* to increase stain removing power, sanitation, and deodorizing. Always patch test before applying to the area and, if no discoloration, clean and blot dry. Or use a combination of *Sol-U-Mel* and *Tough & Tender* to spray on the fabric stains and then wipe with a damp cloth. If you do not already have a spray mixture ready, just pour diluted *Sol-U-Mel* on

*See precautions on page 239. See also precautions and dilution recommendations for cats on page 251.

the spots and then spray with **Tough & Tender**. The cleaning effect will be the same. Rinse area and blot dry. See *Diarrhea*.

Cats – Sore Muscles

See *Arthritis*

Cats – Splinters

* If your pet picks up a splinter or thorn, carefully remove with a pair of tweezers and apply 1 drop of antiseptic oil mix twice per day until the area is healed. See the *Cats Recommended T36-C5 Dilutions* section.

Cats – Spraying Toms

* Spraying is a natural habit for tomcats. They are marking their territory. Neutering the cat usually stops this annoying habit, but when a cat feels insecure by the addition of another pet (even another family member), changing houses, etc., your tomcat could revert to his old ways again. Make your cat as secure as you can with lots of reassurance. Mask the area he sprays with a solution of 1 cup of hot water combined with a squirt of **Lemon Brite** and half a teaspoon of **Sol-U-Mel**. If all else fails and your tomcat is still spraying inside the home, fill a new spray bottle with water. When (and only when) you actually catch him spraying inside the house, give him 2–3 short bursts of water to his tail (always avoid spraying head and eyes). Within a few days he should get the message and stop spraying indoors. To clean those sprayed spots, pour diluted **Sol-U-Mel** onto the area and then spray with **Tough & Tender**. Wipe the area with a damp cloth. (The two products can also be used blended together into a spray.)

Cats – Stains

* Mix 2 capfuls of **Sol-U-Mel** in a 16-ounce spray bottle of water. Saturate the stain, and then blot it with a white towel until all the residue and odor is gone.

Cats – Tar

* If your cat has stepped or rolled on the road where there is wet tar, mix ½ tablespoon of **Melaleuca Original Shampoo** and 2 teaspoons of salt. Rub into the tar. Rinse with warm water and shampoo with **Melaleuca Original Shampoo** mixed 50:50 with Jojoba oil and rinse very well. Repeat the process if necessary.

Cats – Thorns

See *Splinters*

Cats – Ticks

* Use a pair of curved forceps to grasp the tick as close to the cat's skin as possible and pull straight up. Do not apply anything to the tick (such as a match, vaseline or **T36-C5**) before removal because of the

risk of salivation back into the bite site and possible transmission of disease. Do not crush the tick. Apply **Triple Antibiotic** or **MelaGel** to the bite site after tick removal. Bathe cat with **Melaleuca Original Shampoo** mixed 50:50 with Jojoba oil, and rinse. Allow it to dry naturally. This will not only beautify the pet's coat but will help to prevent fleas and ticks. Make sure that the animal gets no lather on the immediate eye areas. **NOTE: When pulling ticks off your cat, always have a barrier between your hand and the tick itself. Lyme disease and Rocky Mountain Spotted Fever can be transmitted.**

CATS – TOYS

* Wash your cat's toys often. Soft toys can be washed in a solution of hot water and **Lemon Brite**. If the toys are particularly dirty, a capful of **Sol-U-Mel** can be added to the water. Rinse and dry thoroughly. Wipe plastic and rubber toys with the same solution.

CATS – URINARY PROBLEMS, CHRONIC

* **ProVex-Plus** is an excellent supplement for helping cats deal with chronic problems. Open the capsule and mix it with your cat's favorite food. If the cat refuses to eat it, you can give the capsule whole. See *Allergies* for the best way to give your cat the capsules. A good probiotic like **Florify** in the cat's drink may also help.

CATS – VACCINATIONS

* To prevent infection, apply diluted **T36-C5** with a cotton ball to the affected area 2–3 times each day. See *Recommended T36-C5 Dilutions* at the beginning of this section.

CATS – VOMIT STAINS

* **PreSpot** can be used after the matter is scraped up and discarded. See also *Soiling*.

CHAPTER NINETEEN

Healthy Horses

PRECAUTIONS

Always consult your veterinarian before starting any course of supplementation or treatment for your animal. Every effort has been made to ensure that the information contained in this book is complete and accurate. However, neither the publisher nor the author is engaged in rendering professional advice or services to the individual reader. The ideas, procedures and suggestions contained in this book are not intended as a substitute for consulting with your veterinarian. Neither the author nor the publisher shall be liable for any loss, injury, or damage allegedly arising from any information or suggestion in this book.

HORSE LOVERS – PLEASE READ!

We sincerely hope you'll find the tips in this section helpful with your horse(s). If you should find an application for Melaleuca products that works well for you that is not already in this book, please tell us about it. If we publish your suggestion, we'll send you a free copy of the book it's published in. Send your suggestion to the address in the front of this book, or by email to uses@rmbarry.com.

We would also be very interested to know how these suggestions work for you. We greatly appreciate your input.

Many thanks to all the horse owners, farmers, ranchers, and veterinarians who contributed to this chapter. You epitomize the spirit of "enhancing lives." We sincerely hope and expect your contributions will help horse lovers all over North America, Australia, and eventually, the world.

HORSES – ABSCESSES

* For a hoof abscess, wash thoroughly with *Antibacterial Liquid Soap* and then soak the area with *T36-C5*. Wrap the hoof after treating it so that it will remain as clean as possible. Repeat this process three times each day even after the abscess has drained, for a full ten days. If the condition does not improve within twenty-four hours, contact your vet.

An alternate solution would be to put a capful of *Sol-U-Mel* in about a quart of warm water and soak the abscessed foot.

HORSES – ALL PURPOSE SPRAY MIXTURE

* Combine 16 ounces of *Sol-U-Mel* and 4 ounces of *Tough & Tender* in a 1-gallon bucket of water. (Use distilled water if possible.) Blend thoroughly and use this as a spray for challenging areas.

HORSES – ARTHRITIS

* *Replenex* is very effective for arthritic conditions in horses as well as other animals. Check with your veterinarian for the proper dosage.

HORSES – BARBED WIRE CUTS

* Combine 2 ounces of *Sol-U-Mel* with 1½ teaspoons of *Tough & Tender* and 10 drops of *T36-C5* in a 16-ounce spray bottle with water. Treat the cut with this mixture twice each day. It is amazing how little scarring there will be.

HORSES – BATHING

See *Horses – Washing*

HORSES – CLEANING

* Treat buckets and water troughs used for your horses with *Sol-U-Guard Botanical*. *Tough & Tender* can also be used for cleaning the containers for your horse's water. After cleaning, a few capfuls of *Sol-U-Mel* can be added to the water trough when you fill it to kill the bacteria.

Clean bits and leather with *Tough & Tender*, and shine the bits with *Tub & Tile*.

Wash the saddle pads with *MelaPower* after each use. Don't use *MelaSoft*, as it is better that the pads remain absorbent. The winter blankets can also be washed in *MelaPower*.

Use *Moisturizing Hand Creme*, with approximately 5 drops of *T36-C5* added to it, to soften any leather and make it pliable again. Use it on leather riding gloves (when you are finished using them, leave them on your hands and put this mixture on just like you would put it on your hands). They will stay soft and last much longer. It is also very effective on dry bridles.

Another suggestion is to condition the leather with *Rustic Touch* after it has been cleaned with *Tough & Tender* or *Antibacterial Liquid Soap*. (It can also be used to condition vinyl—like the interior of your old truck!)

Moisturizing Hand Creme can be used instead of *Rustic Touch* to condition leather after cleaning and your hands will love it, too!

Tough & Tender can be used to clean tack, and it can be used in a power sprayer to clean the barn or house. Some spray it on the walls to repel flies. It is perfect to wash the horse trailer that has sat around all winter and has mildew.

See also *Horses – Washing* in this book.

HORSES – CUTS, SCRAPES AND BURNS

*On any cut, scrape or burn use the *Horses – All Purpose Spray Mixture* on the injured area twice a day until it is healed. Cuts, scrapes, and burns can be serious if left untreated. *T36-C5* is very effective when used on almost any injury as is the *MelaGel* and the *Triple Antibiotic Ointment.*

A quick way to clean an open wound is to sponge on *Sol-U-Mel*. It is a very effective cleanser.

MelaGel is also very effective for cuts on horses. *Body Satin Foot Spray* can also be used to spray on small wounds.

HORSES – CROSS-FIRING WOUNDS

See *Horses – Over Reaching*

HORSES – DERMATITIS

*Dermatitis is usually seen on horses that have not received proper care. Place your horse in a dry, clean, isolated, area or stall and bath thoroughly. (See the section on *Horses – Washing* in this book.) Apply *Renew Intensive Skin Therapy*, or *Triple Antibiotic Ointment* 2–3 times each day until the condition improves. *T36-C5* can also be applied to certain conditions with a cotton ball.

Provide your horse with plenty of fresh, clean water and proper food and contact your vet if the condition does not improve in a reasonable amount of time.

HORSES – DRY CRACKED HOOVES

*A mixture of 1 ounce of *Sol-U-Mel* blended into 32 ounces of water in spray bottle is a very effective spray for dry hooves. Spray the hoof walls and soles.

HORSES – FLY CONTROL IN STALL AREAS

*For fly control in the stall areas, spray the area liberally with a 16-ounce spray bottle of water mixed with 1 teaspoon of *Tough & Tender* and 2 ounces of *Sol-U-Mel*. Carefully protect the horse's eyes and face from any type of spray. Apply liberally early in the day. This solution may be sprayed on the horse's body to repel flies.

It has also been suggested to try blending 2 tablespoons of *Tough & Tender* with 2 capfuls of *Renew Bath Oil*, ½ capful of *Sol-U-Mel*, and 5-10 drops of *T36-C5* in 32 ounces of water in a spray bottle. This is a strong mixture for the worst part of fly season and in the fall as the bug population decreases, the *Sol-U-Mel* and *T36-C5* can be decreased. This works on face flies, both flies and horse flies, as well as black houseflies.

Some mix ¼ cup of *Tough & Tender* with 2 oz. of *Sol-U-Mel*, and 2 oz. of *Renew Bath Oil* in a gallon of water. This spray is more effective the more you use it. It seems that the oil accumulates over time so you need

---

*See the precautions at the beginning of this chapter.

to have some patience in the spring. You have to start off spraying more often. This mixture can also be used to repel bugs on you.

Combining **Moisturizing Hand Creme** with 5 drops of **T36-C5** makes a very effective mixture for preventing small black flies on horses' ears and muzzles. (It is great for your arms, face and neck as well.)

HORSES – FLY BITES

* Apply **T36-C5** directly to the area of the bite. Repeat application every two hours until swelling and itching disappear. Cover the oil with **MelaGel**, **Triple Antibiotic Ointment** or any type of moisturizer to prevent dryness.

Body Satin Foot Spray can be very helpful to stop itching from bites.

HORSES – FOOT ROT

* Spray the hoof(s) twice each day with the *Horses – All Purpose Spray Mixture*. If the feet are severely affected, clean and trim the hoof(s).

HORSES – FUNGUS

* Horses with white feet will get dew poisoning or a fungus on their white feet or on their noses at certain times of the year. Dry the horse's legs when they come in and apply **Dermatin** or **Triple Antibiotic Ointment** or **MelaGel**.

HORSES – GALLS

See *Horses – Saddle Sores*

HORSES – GIRTH ITCH

* Fill a 16-ounce spray bottle with water and 2 teaspoons of **Nature's Cleanse.** Spray this on areas that are affected by girth itch and other fungicidal or pesticidal skin irritations. No rinsing is necessary. Two applications will usually completely clear up serious problems.

Body Satin Foot Spray can be very helpful to stop itching from fungal conditions.

HORSES – GNATS

* **Triple Antibiotic Ointment** used on the horse's ears will keep the gnats away for a day or so. **MelaGel** used the same way will keep them away for 3 or 4 days. Also, it will heal any bites in the ears. Put a dollop on the end of your thumb and run it up the inside of the ear and on the underside in the tender area where the gnats bite.

HORSES – GREASY HEEL

* Clean the affected area with **Antibacterial Liquid Soap** and warm water. Spray twice a day with a mixture of ¼ teaspoon of **T36-C5** and ½ cup of water. If the area cracks, apply *MelaGel* or *Triple Antibiotic Ointment*. If the area oozes, keep it as dry as possible by treating it only with the oil mixture. After it dries, dust the area with pure cornstarch. This is a very sensitive area and if you encounter challenges with the treatment, try spraying the mixture on the horse's leg or soaking it in a bucket. Covering it with a cotton sock can help, too. Be sure to change it twice a day.

HORSES – GROIN INJURY

* Horses can easily get injured on fences, especially if they get spooked. Generally an injury will have to be sutured and the recommended treatment is to inject the area with betadine solution three times a day for perhaps months. Try using *Sol-U-Mel* in water in place of the betadine. You will be amazed how quickly the area will heal.

HORSES – HOOF ROT

* Mix 8 ounces of *Sol-U-Mel*, 1½ teaspoons of *Tough & Tender* and 1½ quarts of water. Clean the foot with the solution and then wrap it with gauze soaked in the solution. Remove the bandage after four days and if the foot still needs treatment, start spraying the solution on the unwrapped foot two times each day until the foot is healed.

HORSES – INSECTS

*Mix ⅓ of the small bottle of *T36-C5* with 32 ounces of water in a spray bottle. It is a very effective insect repellent and costs approximately $2 per bottle as opposed to $7–$10 for insect spray from the discount tack stores. (Shake before applying.)

Triple Antibiotic Ointment, *MelaGel* and *T36-C5* should be used for tick bites and other insect bites.

Horses have been known to be allergic to mosquito saliva. In such cases, giving the horse a saturation dose of *ProVex* and then cutting back until the maintenance dose is determined, has been very effective. Even more economical is to give the horse *ProVexCV* to manage the condition.

HORSES – LEG MANGE

* This condition can be contagious and therefore the horse should be isolated and all space and equipment should be disinfected after the condition is cleared up. This includes destroying or burning any straw or shavings that have been in contact with the infected horse. See the section on *Horses – Cleaning* in this book.

Clean the area thoroughly with *Antibacterial Liquid Soap* and warm water. Then saturate a cotton ball with *T36-C5* and treat the affected area. Repeat twice a day until the condition clears. Gloves should be worn for protection.

*See the precautions at the beginning of this chapter.

An alternate treatment is to soak a leg wrap in *T36-C5* and wrap the leg. Change the bandage 1–2 times each day.

Leg mange can also be treated by spraying the affected area with 1 tablespoon of *T36-C5* mixed with ½ cup of water. Spray the affected area and the surrounding area to prevent spreading of the mange.

HORSES – LICE

* Use *Melaleuca Original Shampoo* to get rid of lice and discourage ticks. It also softens mane and tail hair, encourages growth and prevents tangles. It is anti-static, which means dust does not collect as readily. In addition, it helps prevent any skin fungus.

HORSES – MANGE

* The horse should be isolated in a clean, dry stall and the affected areas should be washed thoroughly with *Antibacterial Liquid Soap* and warm water. Apply *T36-C5* with a cotton ball and allowed to dry. Treat your horse twice a day with 7–10 days or until signs of the mites are gone. To prevent recontamination, disinfect the stall as well as all brushes, tools and other equipment that were used while caring for the horse. (See the section on *Horses – Cleaning* in this book.)

HORSES – MUSCLE SORENESS

* Dr. Wang said that if a horse will eat the *Access Bar* (broken up into small pieces) that it would not hurt them and could help prevent lactic acid build up in their muscles just like it does for us. They would probably need a couple of bars at a time.

HORSES – NAIL PUNCTURE WOUNDS

WARNING: If the nail is still in the horse's foot, do not remove it until a veterinarian has decided whether or not to x-ray.

* The position of the nail near the bone must be determined to predict the outcome of this injury. Horses have very poor circulation in the frog of their feet. Sometimes surgery may be needed. Otherwise, begin soaking the foot in a mixture of 2 capfuls of *Sol-U-Mel* and 1 capful of *Antibacterial Liquid Soap* in 2 quarts of warm water for 30 minutes morning and evening. After soaking, apply *T36-C5*, then *MelaGel* and cover the area with gauze. Repeat for 3 weeks even if the horse walks without a limp before that time.

HORSES – NEWBORN FOAL

* The umbilical cord of newborn animals must be treated shortly after the animal's birth to prevent infection. Treat the umbilical cord with *T36-C5* and it will dry up in a few days with no signs of infection. The ability of the Melaleuca oil to penetrate and kill harmful bacteria without irritating sensitive tissues is ideal for this purpose.

HORSES – ODOR CONTROL

* Blending 1 ounce of **Sol-U-Mel** into a 32-ounce spray bottle of water is a very effective mixture for stall odor control. Spray on any wet urine spots in the stall and it will immediately take the odor away.

HORSES – OVER REACHING

* These wounds can be very painful and tend to be very sensitive. You may want to spray the wound first with a mixture of **T36-C5** and water to take out the initial pain before cleaning. Wait a few moments and then clean the wound thoroughly with **Antibacterial Liquid Soap** and warm water. Treat again with **T36-C5**, **MelaGel** or **Triple Antibiotic Ointment.** Put a cotton sock over the foot and secure. This will allow the area to breathe while protecting it. Repeat the treatment daily until the foot heals.

HORSES – PRESSURE SORES

See *Horses – Saddle Sores*

HORSES – QUITTOR

* Clean the hoof wall thoroughly with **Antibacterial Liquid Soap** and warm water, allow to dry. Apply **MelaGel** or **Triple Antibiotic Ointment.** This is a very sensitive situation and straight **T36-C5** is not recommended, although some prefer to spray the area with a mixture of ¼ teaspoon of **T36-C5** and ½ cup of water. A vet should see serious or neglected conditions.

HORSES – RINGWORM

* Spray the affected area with the *Horses – All Purpose Spray Mixture* as needed to heal.

It has also been suggested that **T36-C5** is good for treating small areas of ringworm or any fungal challenges.

Your horse should be isolated, as ringworm is a very contagious fungus. This condition can be challenging to heal so don't give up. After the horse is clean of any signs of ringworm, disinfect the stall, halter, buckets and any grooming tools that were used during treatment. (See the section on *Horses – Cleaning* in this book)

HORSES – SADDLE SORES

* These types of sores are usually caused by ill-fitted equipment or by abuse. Combine 15–20 drops of **T36-C5** with ¼ cup of water and dab on the area with a cotton ball. **Renew Intensive Skin Therapy**, **MelaGel** or **Triple Antibiotic Ointment** can also be used to help heal these sores. Allow the sores to heal and correct the cause to prevent scarring.

HORSES

*See the precautions at the beginning of this chapter.

HORSES – SARCOID WART

*A type of wart called a sarcoid sometimes appears on young colts. It apparently is pretty common in colts and many times they will outgrow them. The common suggestion is to use iodine on them. Try *T36-C5* instead, and see how quickly they will heal and not return.

HORSES – SHEATH CLEANING

Antibacterial Liquid Soap is great for sheath cleaning. It melts the smegma, as it is a natural solvent and very gentle. It is also good for washing manes and tails to stop itching.

An alternate choice is to combine ¼ teaspoon *T36-C5* with 1 cup of sunflower seed oil and use in a squirt bottle.

HORSES – SORES ON MOUTH CORNERS

*Apply *T36-C5* to the sore areas followed by *Renew Intensive Skin Therapy*.

HORSES – SUMMER SORES

See *Horses – Fly Bites*

HORSES – SUNBURNED NOSES

*If your horse has white markings on their faces, the pink skin at the bottom of their face and on their nose and lips doesn't grow hair in the summer and can be extremely sensitive to sunburn. Rub the *Sun Shades Sunscreen* on their faces each morning to prevent sunburn. It is also good for healing sunburn.

Using *Sun Shades* on darker horses such as black or liver chestnuts, will keep them from fading in the summer.

HORSES – TICKS

*Use a pair of curved forceps to grasp the tick as close to the horse's skin as possible and pull straight up. Do not crush the tick. Apply *Triple Antibiotic* or *MelaGel* to the bite site after tick removal. **NOTE: Wear latex gloves when handling ticks, as Lyme disease and Rocky Mountain spotted fever can be contracted from such handlings.**

HORSES – THRUSH

* Two teaspoons of *Nature's Cleanse* combined with 16 ounces of water is a very effective treatment for minor thrush. In more severe cases, increase the *Nature's Cleanse* to 3 teaspoons with the 16 ounces of water. In 48 hours there should be no sign of thrush. To prevent the return of dry hoof walls and heels, spray with this mixture when the hoof is trimmed or cleaned. This will instantly deodorize the smell of thrush.

Others use 1 tablespoon of *Nature's Cleanse* and 1 tablespoon of *Renew Bath Oil* in one pint of water. Spray on the hoof walls and sole.

*See the precautions at the beginning of this chapter.

Minor thrush and dry hoof walls and heels will usually be cured in a single application.

Try blending 2 tablespoons of **Tough & Tender**, 2 capfuls of **Renew Bath Oil**, ½ capful of **Sol-U-Mel** and 5–10 drops of **T36-C5** in 32 ounces of water in a spray bottle and spraying on the hoof sole and around the frog to kill thrush.

An alternate solution would be to blend 1 ounce of **Sol-U-Mel** in 32 ounces of water in a spray bottle and spray on the entire hoof to treat thrush.

It has also been suggested that 4 ounces of **Sol-U-Mel**, 1½ teaspoons of **Tough & Tender,** 10 drops of **T36-C5** mixed together in a 16-ounce spray bottle with water, works very well for thrush. Spray generously 2–3 times each day and leave the area open to the air.

Some horseshoers say that **Body Satin Foot Spray** is the best product ever to clear up thrush and other foot problems.

To prevent the thrush condition that occurs on the bottom of the horse's feet, have the shoer put **Sol-U-Guard Botanical** on when he takes off the old shoes.

Horses – Timber Wolf Attacks

* Combine 4 ounces of **Sol-U-Mel**, 1½ teaspoons of **Tough & Tender,** 10 drops of **T36-C5** with water in a 16-ounce spray bottle. Spray the injured area generously 2–3 times each day. Leave the wound open to the air. (One rancher saved a horse that had been treated for four months with Combiotic and the vet had recommended that it be put down. The horse not only recovered when treated with this combination, but later had a foal.)

Horses – Trimming

* If the farrier trims your horse too short, it can become lame. Put 8–10 drops of **T36-C5** in a dish and mix with enough **MelaGel** to be able to apply to all four feet. Put this mixture on the sole and hoof wall of each foot with a toothbrush. You should notice a difference within ½ hour. Continue this treatment morning and night for about a week and a half. The mixture takes away a lot of the pain and promotes healing.

Horses – Warts

*Although most warts clear up on their own, some do bleed. Putting **T36-C5** on the wart will not only aid in the healing, but will help with the discomfort as well. This may need to be applied for several weeks. If the wart is bleeding, coating it with **MelaGel** or **Triple Antibiotic Ointment** will help.

See the section on *Horses – Sarcoid Wart* in this book.

HORSES – WASHING

** Use **Melaleuca Herbal Shampoo** to wash your horse's coat. The **Herbal Shampoo** has a conditioner in it so it will make it easy to get tangles out of the mane and tail. It will also decrease flaking and dry skin. This can be followed with a rinse of **Sol-U-Mel** and **Renew Bath Oil** to keep the coat healthy and shiny. This is also good for cleaning gummy spots on the legs.*

An alternate choice would be to bathe the horse in **Tough & Tender**.

Koala Pals Conditioning Hair Wash can be used on the face, as it is gentle and won't burn their eyes.

A mixture of **Tough & Tender** and **Sol-U-Mel** with water in a spray bottle is an excellent spray on the oily dirty dock of a tail that hasn't been washed in a while. Just spray on liberally and rub in. Wait a few minutes and then wash the tail with **Melaleuca Herbal Shampoo**. It cuts right through the dirt and you won't have to work so hard to get it clean and shiny.

Antibacterial Liquid Soap can also be used on the dock of the tail to cut through the greasy buildup and clear up any skin problems in that area. Try it on the mane as well.

Use **Renew Bath Oil** on their faces, legs and groin area for showing (instead of Vaseline). It will also help to repel bugs.

---

*See the precautions at the beginning of this chapter.

CHAPTER TWENTY

Healthy Farm Animals

PRECAUTIONS

Always consult your veterinarian before starting any course of supplementation or treatment for your animal. Every effort has been made to ensure that the information contained in this book is complete and accurate. However, neither the publisher nor the author is engaged in rendering professional advice or services to the individual reader. The ideas, procedures and suggestions contained in this book are not intended as a substitute for consulting with your veterinarian. Neither the author nor the publisher shall be liable for any loss, injury, or damage allegedly arising from any information or suggestion in this book.

FARMERS – PLEASE READ!

We sincerely hope you'll find the tips in this section helpful in your farming operation. If you should find an application for Melaleuca products that works well for you that is not already in this book, please tell us about it. You'll be helping hundreds of farmers and ranchers who use this guide regularly. If we publish your suggestion, we'll send you a free copy of the book it's published in. Send your suggestion to the address in the front of this book, or by email to uses@rmbarry.com.

We would also be very interested to know how these suggestions work for you. Let us know, and tell us if (and how) you were able to save money in your operation by using Melaleuca products. We greatly appreciate your input.

Many thanks to all the farmers, ranchers, and veterinarians who contributed to this chapter. You epitomize the spirit of "enhancing lives." We sincerely hope and expect your contributions will help farmers and ranchers all over North America, Australia, and eventually, the world.

GENERAL INFORMATION

ANT KILLER

* Spray concentrated ***PreSpot*** on all ant prone areas. Or add a little ***T36-C5*** to your regular ***Sol-U-Mel*** and spray the ants. It may take 2–3 days, but by the fourth day they will be gone and won't come back. This formula will also control flies, mosquitoes, and paper wasps.

*See the precautions at the beginning of this chapter.

FARM ANIMALS

ANT PREVENTATIVE

* Combine 2 ounces of *MelaMagic* with 8 ounces of water and spray all areas where ants tend to congregate.

FLY CONTROL

* For very effective fly control, combine 1 teaspoon of *Tough & Tender* with 1 capful of *Renew Bath Oil* in 16 ounces of water. Spray your animals and the animal areas daily for 7 to 10 days. Follow this with a weekly spray until the fly problem is under control. **DO NOT** spray this or any mixture directly into an animal's face or eyes.

Some prefer to combine 1 teaspoon of *Tough & Tender* with 1 teaspoon of *Renew Bath Oil* and 10 drops of *T36-C5* in 16 ounces of water.

An alternate choice might be to use 2 capfuls of *Sol-U-Mel* and 10 drops of *T36-C5* added to a 16-ounce spray bottle filled with water. Spray all barn and stall confinement areas several times each week.

Another choice would be to combine 2 ounces of *Sol-U-Mel* with 16 ounces of water. Spray directly on the animal.

For personal use, any of the above combinations will work or you might try combining 4 ounces of Moisturizing Hand Lotion with 4 ounces of *Renew Bath Oil* and 4 ounces of *Sol-U-Mel*. It works great for camping as well as for farm work.

By the way, these will also work as mosquito repellents.

PRESSURE WASHING

* Use *MelaMagic* in your pressure washer. Dilute as directed and add *Sol-U-Mel* to boost the cleaning power of the mixture.

CLEANING GREASY EQUIPMENT

* Since *MelaMagic* is a grease cutter, it is generally accepted as the product of choice for cleaning farm equipment. However, some have found that concentrated *PreSpot* makes it easier to remove the grease and grime.

WOUND SPRAY

* Mix 2 capfuls of *Renew Bath Oil*, 3 capfuls of *Sol-U-Mel*, 2 capfuls of *Nature's Cleanse*, 5 drops of *Antibacterial Liquid Soap* and 1 quart of water. Use twice daily on superficial cuts and abrasions. This is **NOT** for deep cuts or puncture wounds.

*See the precautions at the beginning of this chapter.

CATTLE

CATTLE – ABSCESSES
*Scrub the hoof well with *Antibacterial Liquid Soap* and water. Rinse and, using a dropper, put several drops of *T36-C5* directly on the affected area. Confine the animal to a clean area during treatment.

CATTLE – BLOATING
*Add 4 tablespoons of *Tough & Tender* to a pint of water and give it orally to an adult cow. It will break down the surface tension and allow the gas to pass.

CATTLE – CASTRATION
* Follow the remedies and recipes listed just below under *Cattle – Cut, Scrapes, and Burns* for healing the cut site following castration.

CATTLE – CUTS, SCRAPES AND BURNS
* Treat an injured area twice daily with a combination of 16 ounces of *Sol-U-Mel* and 4 ounces of *Tough & Tender* in a gallon bucket of water. Continue using until the area has healed. Cuts, scrapes, and burns can be serious if left untreated. If a more severely injured animal will allow you in close enough to treat it, apply *MelaGel* or *Tripe Antibiotic Ointment* to the injury as well. *T36-C5* is also very effective when used on injuries. For cement burns, apply a liberal amount of *T36-C5*, followed by *Pain-A-Trate*, particularly if there is swelling. As with other injuries, continue treating until the injury has healed.

CATTLE – DEHORNING INFECTIONS
* For dehorning infections, flush the infected areas with a syringe filled with a mixture of 2–4 tablespoons of *Tough & Tender* and 2 capfuls of *Sol-U-Mel* blended in a gallon of water. After flushing, allow to dry and apply *T36-C5* to the infected area. Repeat daily as necessary.

CATTLE – HOOF ROT
*Clean the hoof thoroughly with *Antibacterial Liquid Soap* and water. Then simply use ½ cup of *Tough & Tender* in a plastic or rubber booty tied or taped onto the leg. Inspect daily and repeat until the condition is cleared up.

CATTLE – PHOTOSENSITIZATION
See *Cattle – Sunburn*

CATTLE – MANGE
* This condition is contagious and caution should be used when treating the animals. They should be isolated and any articles used during the treatment should be destroyed or carefully disinfected after

FARM ANIMALS

each use. Bedding should be changed daily and disposed of so that no other farm or domestic animal can come into contact with it. Be sure to wear gloves at all times. See the section on *Calf – Pens and Mange* in this book.

Scrub the affected area thoroughly with **Antibacterial Liquid Soap** and water and rinse. Clip away any matted or unwanted hair and dab **T36-C5** on the affected area and the surrounding area with a cotton ball. Repeat this treatment once a day until the condition clears.

Using **Melaleuca Original Shampoo** when bathing your cattle will help maintain good hygiene. **Sol-U-Guard Botanical** is an excellent disinfectant for any tools.

CATTLE – RINGWORM

* Since ringworm is contagious, the affected animal should be isolated and any articles used during treatment must either be disposed of or carefully disinfected. See the section on *Calf – Pens and Mange*.

Scrub the affected area thoroughly with **Antibacterial Liquid Soap** and water and rinse. Once the area is dry, dab **T36-C5** onto the ringworm with a cotton ball. Repeat the treatment several times per week until the condition clears. Be patient as this is a very challenging condition to eliminate.

CATTLE – SUNBURN

* **T36-C5** is very soothing for the cattle that get sunburn and photosensitization. Mix ¼ teaspoon of **T36-C5** and ⅓ cup of water and spray the affected area. Be careful to avoid the eyes. Provide shade, if necessary, for severe cases and avoid excessive direct sunlight until the condition clears.

Photosensitization occurs worldwide and is most common in cattle and sheep. It seems to be triggered by ingestion of certain plants such as St. John's Wort.

CATTLE – THRUSH ON THE FEET

* Apply **Sol-U-Mel** or **T36-C5** directly on the affected area. Then use a clean, large cotton sock that has been soaked in four ounces of the all-purpose mixture combined with 12 ounces of water to form a good solution. (See the section on *Cow – All Purpose Spray Mixture* in this book.) Make sure the sock is thoroughly soaked. Then fit the sock over the affected foot and wrap with rubber or cotton straps to keep in place. Keep the foot wet with this solution and consider isolating the animal, as thrush can be extremely contagious.

CALVES

CALF – BIRTHS

* When a calf has a difficult birth place put 5 to 10 drops of **T36-C5** down each nostril, and 5 to 10 drops on the back of the tongue, as soon as it is born.

*See the precautions at the beginning of this chapter.

CALF – MILK REPLACER TIPS

* Dissolve 3 *Vita-Bears Children's Vitamins* in a cup of milk and add it to the warm milk replacer. This will assure that the calves are receiving their needed vitamins and minerals.

When calves are switching from milk to milk replacer, add 1 oz. of *Nature's Cleanse* to the pail for the first two feedings and the calves should not have a problem with the switch.

CALF – PENS AND MANGE

* You should be able to keep mange under control by washing out the pens using a garden sprayer and then spraying down the bedding using a mixture of 1 ounce of *Sol-U-Mel* and 16 ounces of water. This should be done once a week.

CALF – PNEUMONIA

* When a calf develops pneumonia, put 5–10 drops of *T36-C5* in each nostril and 6 drops on the back of the tongue. Repeat daily for 7 to 10 days.

CALF – NAVAL ILL

* Combine 2 ounces of *Sol-U-Mel*, 1½ teaspoons of *Tough & Tender* and 10 drops of *T36-C5* in a 16-ounce spray bottle of water. Use as a preventative in newborn calves. If the navel is swollen, change the 2 ounces of *Sol-U-Mel* to 4 ounces for the treatment.

(One rancher said that they have not lost a calf to navel ill since switching from iodine to this mixture.)

CALF – SCOURS

* For scours, orally administer, with a syringe, 1 ounce of *Nature's Cleanse* diluted in 4 ounces of water. The calf should be treated twice daily (morning and evening) until the bowel movement firms up. **Do not give *Nature's Cleanse* full strength!** This can also be put in the milk if the calf is drinking. It usually takes about 2 days of treatment.

(In 1991, one rancher spent $1,000 on medicine and lost 25 calves. In 1992 this same rancher spent $70 on four bottles of *Nature's Cleanse* and lost no calves.)

CALF – SCOURS – PREVENTION

* Combine ¼ cup of *Sol-U-Mel* in a 16-ounce spray bottle filled with water. Spray the bedding or wherever they sleep, weekly. This even works outside and in dirt floor barns that you cannot wash. Spray more often if you notice scouring stool in the bedding. Spray the scouring stool when you see the piles. When possible move the calves to clean ground.

CALF – UNTHRIFTY

* Unthrifty can be dealt with effectively by enhancing the calf's nutrition. Add 3 dissolved *Vita-Bears Children's Vitamins* to the calf's milk both morning and night.

*See the precautions at the beginning of this chapter.

FARM ANIMALS

COWS

COW – ALL PURPOSE SPRAY MIXTURE

* Mix 16 ounces of *Sol-U-Mel* and 4 ounces of *Tough & Tender* in a gallon bucket and fill with water. This can be used as an all purpose spray.

COW – CHAFED OR SORE TEATS

* Use the *Cow – All Purpose Spray Mixture*, listed in this book, 2 to 3 times daily until the sore or chafed teats have healed.

COW – COWPOX

* The incubation period for cowpox is from 4–7 days and there are several recognizable stages. *T36-C5* can be applied to the lesions at any stage and will help with the healing process as well as soothe the pain and sensitivity. This condition is contagious, so the animals need to be isolated. Using latex or rubber gloves clean the affected area with *Antibacterial Liquid Soap* and water. Rinse and thoroughly spray the area with a mixture of ¼ teaspoon of *T36-C5* and ½ cup of water. Some prefer to apply the oil directly on the lesions with a cotton ball. Be sure all tools and bedding are carefully disinfected.

See the section on *Calf – Pens and Mange* in this book.

COW – INFECTION POSSIBILITY

* Combine 2 ounces of *Sol-U-Mel*, 1½ teaspoons of *Tough & Tender* and 10 drops of *T36-C5* in a 16-ounce spray bottle filled with water. Use this mixture after dehorning, brisket tagging or anytime you see a threat of a possible infection.

COW – MASTITIS

* An infected quarter should be treated twice each day with a liberal application of liquid *Pain-A-Trate*. Continue this treatment as needed until the cow is free of infection. If mastitis is severe, apply a liberal amount of *T36-C5* before applying the liquid *Pain-A-Trate*.

When you have an outbreak of herd mastitis, mix 1 ounce of *Sol-U-Mel* with 10 ounces of water and use it as a teat dip.

It has even been suggested that for very serious cases 10cc of *Sol-U-Mel* be injected directly up the teat canal, followed by massaging the quarter. **This procedure should be used with caution.** An injection of 3cc of *Nature's Cleanse* and 20cc of water generally works very well.

COW – PREDIP OR SPRAY

* To prepare a predip to clean the cows before milking, combine 4 ounces of *Antibacterial Liquid Soap*, 16 ounces of *Tough & Tender,* and 2 ounces of *Sol-U-Mel* in enough water to make 5 gallons. This is very cost effective compared to the usually recommended brands of dip.

*See the precautions at the beginning of this chapter.

COW – POST DIP

* Post dip should be used after milking to prevent infection (mastitis). Combine 2 gallons of Prop-glycol, 4 ounces of **Antibacterial Liquid Soap**, 16 ounces of **Tough & Tender**, and one tube of **Alloy Body Wash** with enough water to make 5 gallons. This is used to moisturize the teats. Shake before filling the dip containers. This is a high emollient dip for frost and sun protection. The Prop-glycol is the anti-freeze ingredient.

Use red food coloring in one of the dip containers to help identify the different dips.

COW – PROLAPSED UTERUS

* Combine 4 ounces of **Sol-U-Mel**, 1½ teaspoons of **Tough & Tender** and 10 drops of **T36-C5** in a 16-ounce spray bottle with water. Wash the uterus with this solution. Remove as much of the after birth as possible and spray liberally with this solution before putting back in the cow while she is on her feet. Once in, with your arm up her uterus, whip back and forth as hard as you can to straighten the uterus out. This mixture will not only take out the swelling but it will also prevent infection.

COW – RINGWORM

* Wash the area with **Antibacterial Liquid Soap** and then apply **T36-C5**, **MelaGel** or **Renew Intensive Skin Therapy**.
See the section on **Cattle – Ringworm** in this book.

COW – TEAT CUTS

* Teat cuts and sore teats can quickly be treated with **Triple Antibiotic Ointment**.

COW – TEAT SPRAY

* Spray the teat and the teat end with a mixture of 1 ounce of **Sol-U-Mel** combined with 5 ounces of water. Rinse and repeat the treatment.

COW – UDDER EDEMA OR FRESH UDDER

* Use the **Cow – All Purpose Spray Mixture**, listed in this book, on the udder twice daily.

COW – UDDER SORES

* Use the **Cow – All Purpose Spray Mixture** listed in this book to liberally spray any sores that appear between the quarters, or between the udder and the leg area. Repeat at least twice a day until the sores have healed.

An alternate solution is to mix 2 teaspoons of **Sol-U-Mel** and 1½ teaspoons of **Tough & Tender** in 16 ounces of water. First clean and dry the sores. Then, spray the solution twice daily on the weeping lesions. Spraying on dried up sores isn't necessary.

*See the precautions at the beginning of this chapter.

FARM ANIMALS

COW – UDDER WASH

* For a very effective udder wash, combine 1 quart of *Tough &
Tender* with 3 quarts of water. Use 2 ounces of this mixture with
1 capful of *Sol-U-Mel* in 5 to 10 gallons of water. Immediately prior
to putting on the milkers, spray the udders with a mixture of 1 part of
Sol-U-Mel combined with 5 parts of water.

(In a week's time, one farmer reduced his somatic cell count from
52,000 to 15,000. This was the lowest count in the county. Later,
Federal Inspectors investigated for peroxide use and found nothing
wrong in what he was doing.)

CHICKENS

CHICKEN – COCCIDIOSIS

* Spray the chicken bedding with 1-ounce of *Sol-U-Mel* mixed in a
quart of water.

CHICKEN – DISEASE REDUCTION

* Adding 3 to 4 drops of *Sol-U-Mel* in the small drinking water
reservoirs or 2 to 3 tablespoons of *Sol-U-Mel* in a 500-gallon reservoir,
will reduce the incidence of disease.

CHICKEN – EGG ROOM SALMONELLA
AND ASPERGILLUS

* Spray the egg room weekly using 1-ounce of *Sol-U-Mel* mixed in
a quart of water.

CHICKEN HOUSE – FOGGING BARNS

* Use 1oz of *Sol-U-Mel* to every 5 oz of water when fogging the barns.

CHICKEN HOUSE – SALMONELLA

* Use 1-ounce of *Sol-U-Mel* in a quart of water when spraying the
chicken house to kill salmonella. This will also kill other types of
bacteria.

CAUTION: Avoid direct contact with the birds when spraying.

GOATS

GOATS – ABSCESSES

* If an abscess has not erupted in an injured area, dab full-strength
T36-C5 on the site with a cotton ball or cotton swab. If it is draining, clean
the area with *Antibacterial Liquid Soap* and water and after it dries, drop
1-2 drops of *T36-C5* on the site. Repeat the cleaning and treatment
1-2 times each day until the abscess is healed.

*See the precautions at the beginning of this chapter.

GOATS – CUTS, WOUNDS, BITES AND STINGS

* *T36-C5* can be used on most cuts, wounds, bites and stings. Once the area is cleaned with *Antibacterial Liquid Soap* and water, rinse and pat dry. In most cases you can apply the oil directly on the affected area with a cotton ball or cotton swab. *MelaGel* and *Triple Antibiotic Ointment* are very effective treatments as well.

GOATS – ECZEMA

*Any disturbance affecting the skin is generally covered under the broad term, Eczema. The affected area should be thoroughly washed with *Antibacterial Liquid Soap* and water and patted dry. Clip away any excess hair and apply *T36-C5* with a cotton ball. Treat the condition daily until it clears. If it becomes stubborn or worsens, contact your vet.

GOATS – GOAT POX

* Goat pox in goats, unlike other farm animals, can become serious. A specific virus is responsible for this condition and it can become contagious. It is much like treating an abscess. First clean the area thoroughly with *Antibacterial Liquid Soap* and water. Saturate a cotton ball with *T36-C5* and dab in onto the area if it has not erupted. Using a dropper, place *T36-C5* onto the area after it has begun to drain. Be sure to wear gloves when treating this condition.

GOATS – HOOF CONDITIONS

* Remove your goat from a damp environment and wash the hoof thoroughly with *Antibacterial Liquid Soap* and water. Put ½ teaspoon of *T36-C5* and ½ cup of water in a spray bottle and spray the hoof well. Keep the goat in a clean environment and treat daily or every other day, depending on the severity of the condition.

GOATS – MANGE

* There are four types of mange that can affect goats, psoroptic mange, sarcoptic mange, demodectic mange and chorioptic mange. Psoroptic mange is much less severe than other types of mange, but if left untreated it may become infected. Sarcoptic mange is a more severe type, which untreated, can leave the skin leathery and wrinkled. Young kids are susceptible to this condition. Demodectic mange involves hair follicles and looks like small abscesses. Chorioptic mange is known as the "leg mange."

In all cases the goat should be isolated during treatment. Thoroughly clean the affected area with *Antibacterial Liquid Soap* and water. Rinse and clip away any matted or unwanted hair. Dab the affected area and the surrounding area with a cotton ball saturated with *T36-C5*. Repeat the treatment 1–2 times each day until the condition clears.

If you're working around the ears, clean them thoroughly and then wipe with one drop of *T36-C5* on a cotton ball. Do not drop *T36-C5* directly into the ear canal. As with any condition, if it gets worse, contact your vet.

*See the precautions at the beginning of this chapter.

GOATS — PHOTOSENSITIZATION

See *Goats - Sunburn*

GOATS — RINGWORM

* Ringworm is not as common in sheep and goats as it is in other species, but it they do get it, they must be isolated as it is very contagious. Clean the affected area with **Antibacterial Liquid Soap** and water. Pat dry and clip away any unwanted or matted hair. Dab the affected and surrounding areas with **T36-C5** on a cotton ball. Repeat the treatment once a day and be patient, as it is a challenging condition to clear up.

GOATS — SEEDY TOE

* The condition called seedy toe may cause your goat to become lame. Carefully clean the area with **Antibacterial Liquid Soap** and water and rinse well. Pat dry and, using a dropper, put **T36-C5** directly on the site. Protect the area from dirt by putting an old cotton sock over the foot. Repeat the treatment 1–2 times each day depending on the severity.

GOATS — SKIN CONDITIONS

* There are various skin conditions which goats are susceptible to, similar to those in cattle and sheep. They will vary in severity and many will respond to **T36-C5**. Regular shampooing with **Melaleuca Original Shampoo** will help the goat remain in good condition and will help to prevent many skin conditions. See the areas of special skin conditions for goats listed in this book.

GOATS — SUNBURN

* Sunburn is more likely to be seen on goat breeds such as Saanen and Norwegian Dairy, although it can be seen on others as well. St. John's Wort seems to be triggering factor in photosensitization, as it appears to be associated with ingestion of certain plants. Photosensitization is most common in cattle and sheep but is does occur worldwide and can affect many species.

Keep your goat in a shaded area when being treated. Clip away any matted or unwanted hair and clean the area with **Antibacterial Liquid Soap** and water. Coat the affected area with **T36-C5**, **MelaGel** or **Triple Antibiotic Ointment**. If the condition reoccurs, consider keeping your goat in a shaded area during the intense sunlight hours.

GOATS — WARTS

*A virus causes warts on the teats and although not usually serious, they are prone to bleeding. Applying **T36-C5** will aid in healing as well as soothe the pain and sensitivity. It may take several weeks to clear when applying the oil daily or every other day.

FARM ANIMALS

HOGS AND PIGS

HOGS – ABSCESSES
*At the acute or early stage of an abscess, the site is particularly sensitive to the touch. Saturate a cotton ball with **T36-C5** and dab it on the site several times each day. Continue the treatment, keeping the area clean, while it comes to a head and drains.

HOGS – BATHING
* Wash the hogs in **Antibacterial Liquid Soap** and it will not only clean them, it will heal their sores from scratching and keep their skin from drying out.

HOGS – CANDIDA
*Clean the site thoroughly with **Antibacterial Liquid Soap** and water. Pat the area dry with a paper towel and carefully dispose of the sued towels. Saturate a cotton ball with **T36-C5** and dab onto the site several times each day until the condition clears.

HOGS – COCCIDIOSIS
* Spray the bedding and pen with 1 ounce of **Sol-U-Mel** in a quart of water. Isolate the animal from others until the condition subsides.

HOGS – CONFINEMENT CLEANING
* Use a pressure washer to clean the walls and the ceilings of any confinement area with 32 ounces of **MelaMagic** blended into 24 gallons of water. Adding 3 to 4 tablespoons of **Sol-U-Mel** can boost the strength of this mixture. One spraying should eliminate mold re-growth.

(One hog farmer reduced his cost of cleaning his confinement area from $36 to $7 per cleaning by using this method.)

Another suggestion is to spray all the walls and ceilings with a mixture of 1 ounce of **Sol-U-Mel** in a quart bottle filled with water.

HOGS – CUTS, WOUNDS, BITES AND STINGS
*Always clean any cut, wound, bite or sting thoroughly with **Antibacterial Liquid Soap** and water. Rinse and dry carefully. Check to be sure that no foreign matter is imbedded in the injury and then treat with a cotton ball and **T36-C5**. Repeat the treatment daily until a healthy scab is formed or until the bite or sting disappears.

HOGS – DISINFECTING UDDER AT FARROWING TIME
* Use 1 ounce of **Sol-U-Mel** combined with 20 ounces of water.

HOGS – FOGGING BARNS
* Use up to 1 ounce of **Sol-U-Mel** with 5 ounces of water when fogging the barns.

*See the precautions at the beginning of this chapter.

HOGS – LICE

* When the hogs get lice, wash them with *Antibacterial Liquid Soap* and then spray them with *Sol-U-Mel* and *Tough & Tender* mixed together in a spray bottle. If you will also spray the pens, you will usually get rid of the lice in one treatment.

HOGS – MASTITIS

* When the sows have mastitis or are holding their milk, apply *T36-C5* to the bag followed by *Pain-A-Trate*.

HOGS – PENS – MANGE

* Wash out the pen area with water. Then use 1-ounce of *Sol-U-Mel* combined with 30 ounces of water to spray the empty hog pens and their bedding. The bedding may need to be sprayed weekly to keep the mange under control.

HOGS – PHOTOSENSITIZATION

See *Hogs – Sunburn*

HOGS – PITYRIASIS ROSE

* This condition of unknown origin effects young pigs and particularly those of the Landrace breed. Wash the affected area with *Antibacterial Liquid Soap* and water and rinse well. Pat the area dry and with a cotton ball, apply *T36-C5* onto the area 1–2 times each day until the condition clears.

HOGS – RINGWORM

* This condition is contagious, so isolate your animal while treating for ringworms. Wash the area with *Antibacterial Liquid Soap* and water and rinse thoroughly. Pat the area dry and dispose of the used paper towels. Saturate a cotton ball with *T36-C5* and dab it on the site several times each day. Be patient as this is a challenging condition to treat. Be sure to wear gloves when treating ringworms and carefully dispose of or disinfect any items in contact with the animal during treatment.

HOGS – SALMONELLA IN BARNS

* Spray the barn area at least once a month with a solution of 1-ounce of *Sol-U-Mel* and 30 ounces of water to decrease the likelihood of salmonella.

HOGS – SOW WASH

* Spray the sow using a mixture of 1 tsp of *Tough & Tender* and 1 capful of *Sol-U-Mel* combined in a 16-ounce spray bottle filled with water. Spray the bedding using 1 oz of *Sol-U-Mel* and 30 oz of water.

HOGS – SUNBURN

* Animals exposed to intense sunlight may be affected by either sunburn and/or photosensitization. Occurring worldwide, photosensiti-

*See the precautions at the beginning of this chapter.

FARM ANIMALS

zation is more commonly seen in sheep and cattle and seems to occur at the onset of ingesting certain plants or grasses, such as St. John's Wort, rape and alfalfa. White breeds are more frequently affected.

Provide shade for your animal during periods of intense sunlight and during treatment. Bathe with *Antibacterial Liquid Soap* and water and rinse. Use a light coat of *MelaGel* or *Triple Antibiotic Ointment*. *Renew Intensive Skin Therapy* or *Sun Shades Sunscreen* would also provide some healing and protection.

PIGLETS – FOOT ROT

* This condition affects pigs up to six months of age and if neglected can lead to septicemia. Clean the hoof carefully with *Antibacterial Liquid Soap* and water. Rinse and spray the entire hoof and around the coronary band thoroughly once a day with a mixture of ½ teaspoon of *T36-C5* and ½ cup of water. If possible, isolate the pig and keep it in a clean environment until the condition is eliminated.

PIGLETS – GREASY PIG DISEASE

* Rubbing your piglets every day with *Moisturizing Hand Lotion* will help to alleviate greasy pig disease. In more serious cases, you may have to apply it 2 or 3 times each day until the condition is clear.

An alternate solution would be to spray the pigs daily using a solution of one part of *Sol-U-Mel* and five parts of water.

PIGLETS – ITCH PROBLEMS

* Lightly spray or sprinkle the piglets with a water can using a mixture of 1 ounce of *Sol-U-Mel* and 50 ounces of water will help with an itch problem.

WARNING: Flaky skin may develop if the piglets are treated more than once a week.

PIGLETS – RESPIRATORY PROBLEMS

* Misting the farrowing pens daily with 1 ounce of *Sol-U-Mel* combined with 5 ounces of water will help to reduce the number of piglets with respiratory challenges.

SHEEP AND LAMBS

SHEEP – CUTS, WOUNDS, BITES, STINGS

* Clean any injured area with *Antibacterial Liquid Soap* and water. Rinse and pat dry. Be sure that there are no foreign objects in the injured area that need to be removed. Saturate a cotton ball with *T36-C5* and squeeze out the excess. Dab the oil on the affected area and repeat 1–2 times each day until the condition clears.

*See the precautions at the beginning of this chapter.

SHEEP – FOOT ABSCESSES

*Foot abscesses are more likely to develop when the soil and pastures are wet. The animal needs to be removed from the damp environment and placed in a clean, dry area. Wash the foot thoroughly with *Antibacterial Liquid Soap* and water. Rinse and dry carefully and then apply a mixture of ½ teaspoon of *T36-C5* and ½ cup of water with a spray bottle. Spray the area thoroughly. Keep the wound clean and allow it to drain. Repeat the treatment 1–2 times each day until the condition is clear.

SHEEP – FOOT ROT

*This condition is very contagious under warm, moist conditions. Place the animal in a clean, dry environment during treatment. Wash the foot with *Antibacterial Liquid Soap* and water. Rinse and dry carefully. Spray the foot thoroughly with a mixture of ½ teaspoon of *T36-C5* blended with ½ cup of water. Repeat the treatment 1–2 times each day until the condition clears.

SHEEP – MANGE

*If your sheep appears to have any type of mange, shear and wash the animal with *Antibacterial Liquid Soap* and water. Rinse carefully and apply *T36-C5* directly to the site with a squeezed out cotton ball. This should be applied 2–3 times each day until the condition clears. The animal should be isolated during the treatment period.

SHEEP – ORF

*The infectious dermatitis that affects both sheep and goats is called Contagious Ecthyma (Orf). It is important that the animals be isolated until the condition is clear. Treat by putting 1 drop of *T36-C5* on a cotton ball and dabbing it onto the lesion of the lips and/or feet 1–2 times each day until a scab appears and falls off.

SHEEP – PHOTOSENSITIZATION

*Photosensitization is most common in cattle and sheep. The skin of lightly pigmented animals becomes inflamed from long-term exposure to ultraviolet rays. Thus the animal should be placed in the shade during treatment and until the condition is clear. Saturate a cotton ball with *T36-C5* and squeeze out the excess. Apply this directly to the affected area. It will not only promote healing but will help with the discomfort as well.

SHEEP – RINGWORM

*Ringworm is uncommon in sheep and goats, but it does occur. It is very contagious, therefore the animal must be isolated and any tools used during the treatment time must be carefully disinfected. *Sol-U-Guard Botanical* is an excellent disinfectant for this purpose. Be sure to wear gloves when treating your sheep and be very patient, as this will take some time to clear.

Wash the affected area with *Antibacterial Liquid Soap* and water.

*See the precautions at the beginning of this chapter.

Rinse and pat dry with paper towels. Carefully dispose of the used towels. Saturate a cotton ball with *T36-C5* and after squeezing out the excess, dab it directly on the ringworm site. Repeat this treatment 2–3 times each day until the condition clears.

SHEEP – SHEEP KED

* Sheep ked (sheep tick) can spread rapidly through a flock as this insect can spend its entire life on its host. After shearing, put ½ teaspoon of *T36-C5* into ½ cup of water and spray the animal thoroughly.

SHEEP – SHEEP POX

* Characterized by wide spread skin eruptions, Sheep Pox is a virus that is serious, and often fatal for sheep. *T36-C5* can help with the pain and irritation of the lesions, but a vet should be consulted immediately.

SHEEP – SKIN CONDITIONS

* Applying *T36-C5* directly on the site with a cotton ball can treat dermatitis or lumpy wool or strawberry foot rot. The infected animal should be isolated and the wool around the affected area sheared away. Treat the area 1–2 times each day until the condition is clear.

SHEEP – WARTS

* Warts are rare in sheep. However, if they do occur, they can be transmitted to other sheep. Treat them with a cotton ball saturated with *T36-C5*, squeezed out, and dabbed directly onto the affected area. Repeat the treatment 2–3 times each day until the condition clears. This treatment can take weeks.

LAMBS – MAGGOTS

* If your lamb gets blowfly larvae (maggots) in a wound, clean it with diluted *Sol-U-Mel* and pack the wound with *Triple Antibiotic Ointment*. The maggots will not be able to move out fast enough! It will also prevent reinfestation.

TURKEYS

TURKEY – DRINKING WATER

* Use 2 capfuls of *Sol-U-Mel* to 10 gallons of water for drinking. This same combination can be used to spray around the water tanks and feeders.

TURKEY HOUSE

* The empty turkey house should be misted weekly with a combination of 1 ounce of *Sol-U-Mel* and 5 ounces of water.

(One farmer used this in his turkey house and received the cleanest results ever on his pre-shipping blood tests.)

*See the precautions at the beginning of this chapter.

FARM ANIMALS

TURKEY HOUSE – SALMONELLA

*To prevent the growth of Salmonella in the turkeys and the spread of it to their eggs, spray the turkey house with 1 ounce of either *Sol-U-Mel* combined with 30 ounces of water. This spray should kill most bacteria including salmonella. **Do not spray the birds.**

TURKEY LINE FLUSHING

*Flush all of the water lines using a mixture of 2 capfuls of *Sol-U-Mel* combined with 1 tablespoon of *Tough & Tender* and 5 gallons of water and let them soak overnight. Rinse them well with plain water before reusing.

FARM ANIMALS

CHAPTER TWENTY-ONE

Healthy Garden Solutions

This is a beginning chapter in our book. It contains some exciting ideas shared by our readers. As you read it and think of other ways Melaleuca products have worked in your garden, please share them with us. You can send your suggestions to us at the address in the front of this book, or email us at uses@rmbarry.com.

Please use caution when using these suggestions in your garden. Thank you and happy gardening.

ANT KILLER

Spray concentrated ***Pre-Spot*** on the areas where ants congregate. Be aware of the surface of these areas when using ***Pre-Spot*** as it can take the finish off of some wooden floors.

An alternate idea is to combine 1 ounce of ***MelaMagic*** and 1 ounce of ***Sol-U-Mel*** in a 16-ounce bottle filled with water. This works particularly well with large black ants.

Another simple solution is ***Tough & Tender***. It will kill ants.

ANTS, FIRE

Spray fire ants with ***PreSpot***. It is very effective. For fire ant pain, splash the area with ***Sol-U-Mel***.

For a foolproof way to kill fire ants consider this: After you have mopped the floor with ***Tough & Tender*** and/or ***MelaMagic*** or you have washed the car with ***Tough & Tender,*** add a 5 or 6 drops of ***Lemon Brite*** and stir. Pour half of the bucket on the fire ant bed. After about 30 minutes pour the other half on the bed.

If you are really mad about the fire ants, like when they have invaded your flower beds, mix the following in a two gallon bucket of water: 1 capful of ***Tough & Tender***, 1 capful of ***MelaMagic***, 1 capful of ***Sol-U-Mel***, 1 capful of ***Tub & Tile*** and always 10 drops of ***Lemon Brite***. Sir and pour half of the bucket on the fire ant bed. Wait 30 minutes and pour on the other half. This kills them "dead" and they won't come back. Plus, that will be the greenest part of your lawn!

ANT PREVENTION

If you prefer to just prevent ants, simply spray the most likely areas with 2 ounces of *MelaMagic* combined with 16 ounces of water.

APHIDS

Spray for aphids, spider mites and fungus on roses and other plants with a mixture of 2 teaspoons of *Nature's Cleanse* and 16 ounces of water. This can be sprayed on the plants daily if needed.

An alternate solution would be to use *Sol-U-Mel* to get rid of aphids on your roses. Mix it a little stronger than is recommended on the bottle.

It has also been suggested that a 3% solution of *Tough & Tender* is very effective for killing aphids and stopping the onset of mildew on rose bushes without damaging the plants.

See the section on *Rhubarb* in this book.

APPLE SPRAY

Spray apples in the orchard with one bottle of *Renew Bath Oil* mixed into 5 gallons of warm water.

ARMY WORMS

Mix ½ cup of *MelaMagic* in 2 gallons of water to spray for army worms. Spray the cocoon, nest and "whatever that webby thing is called." The web will dissolve and the worms shrivel up instantly. Spray any new evidence of the worms as soon as they appear. By the way, it will also stop ant invasions.

BAGWORMS

Spray the nest of bagworms with diluted *Lemon-Brite*. It may take a couple of heavy sprayings to do more than make them sick.

BUGS — YARD

Mix 1 cup of *Lemon Brite* dish liquid soap and 1 cup of already mixed *Breath-Away Mouthwash* into a 20 gallon hose-end sprayer and soak your lawn, garden beds and trees to the point that the fluid is running off. Bugs hate it! This will also remove dust, dirt and pollution from grass blades, making any lawn fertilizer work twice as well.

Tough & Tender diluted and used in a lawn sprayer unit makes an excellent bug spray.

Diluted *Sol-U-Mel* is very effective for crickets and crawling bugs.

CREPE MYRTLES

Mix *Sol-U-Mel* in a spray bottle, as directed, and use to combat the fungus that grows on crepe myrtles.

DISINFECTANT

Occasionally you will need to disinfect your pruning sheers to keep mold spores from spreading. The **Antibacterial Liquid Soap** will do an excellent job and clean your hands as well.

FERTILIZER

Tough & Tender diluted through a lawn sprayer unit is an excellent fertilizer for your rose bushes.

FLOWERING BUSHES

To rid your flowering bushes of a collection of bugs, spray liberally with diluted **Sol-U-Mel**. Cover the bush with a plastic bag overnight. The bugs will disappear.

FRUIT TREES

See *Trees*

FUNGUS

See *Aphids*, *Crepe Myrtles* and *Zinnias*

GARDEN BEDS

See *Bugs - Yard*

GNATS

See *Lawn Spray*

GRASS

See *Bugs - Yard*

GREEN HOUSE

Spray your green house with **Tough & Tender** as a deterrent to the growth of mold.

An alternate solution would be to dilute 4–5 drops of **T36-C5 Melaleuca Oil** in a spray bottle of water and spray throughout the greenhouse.

HELIOPSIS

See *Red Spider Mites*

HOUSEPLANTS

If you have found little brown spots on your variegated green houseplants, which have caused the leaves to turn brown and sticky, wipe the leaves with a diluted solution of **Tough & Tender**. Then pour the same solution around the base of the plant.

Diluted **Tough & Tender** is also an excellent product to clean the leaves of other houseplants.

GARDEN

INSECT REPELLENT

A mixture of 3–5 drops of *T36-C5* and 1 cup of distilled or cold boiled water in a spray mister is very effective in ridding plants of parasites or insects. Continue to use the spray for at least a week after the infestations appears to be gone. Make sure that the immediate area and other plants surrounding the affected one are also treated for the duration. This prevents a recurrence of the challenge.

LAWNS

See *Bugs – Yard*

LAWN SPRAY

Spray your lawn with a diluted mixture of **Tough & Tender** in a lawn sprayer unit. It will kill the little gnats as well as mushrooms that grow in your yard.

MILDEW

See *Mold – Gardens*

MITES

See *Aphids*

MOLD – GARDENS

With a 1:5 mixture of *Sol-U-Mel*, spray the moldy areas around the foundation of your house. This will also work well for mildew and the musty areas in your garden where mushrooms crop up.

It has also been suggested that a mixture of 3–5 drops of *T36-C5* blended with 1 cup of distilled or cold boiled water in a spray mister is very effective on mold and aphid infestation on rose bushes and other household plants. Shake the mixture vigorously and mist the plants on the tops and bottoms of the foliage and the soil. Make sure to totally mist the affected area.

MOLD SPORES

See *Disinfectant* and *Green House*

MUSHROOMS

See *Lawn Spray* and *Mold*

MUSTY AREAS

See *Mold – Gardens*

PLANTS

See *Trees*

PLANT – INDOOR

Spraying your indoor plants with *Sol-U-Mel* is very effective.

Plant Sprays

See *Insect Repellent – Garden Use*

Red Spider Mites

Mix 1 cup of *Tough & Tender* in a lawn sprayer unit and fill with water. Spray the plants thoroughly and saturate the ground surrounding the plants. This works especially well on Heliopsis or "Summer Sun" plants.

Rhubarb

Spray diluted *Tough & Tender* on your rhubarb and get rid of all of the aphids without harming the plant.

Rose Bushes

See *Fertilizer* and *Aphids*

Scale

See *Trees*

Shrubs

See *Trees*

GARDEN

Slugs

Sol-U-Mel blended into a diluted spray will rid your garden of slugs and other bugs. It does not work as fast as salt, but it does not hurt the plants and is far cheaper and safer than pesticides.

Soil Surfactant

Tough & Tender is an excellent soil surfactant. Putting it in the ground before you plant your garden in the summer will help the water stay in the ground when it gets hot and there is no rainfall.

Spiders

See *Aphids*

Summer Sun

See *Red Spider Mites*

Tomatoes

Add ⅛ cup of *Tough & Tender* to a 5-gallon water can and water the soil around the tomato plants every other day. They will need about three applications. Not only will it get rid of the blight, but also you will have delicious tomatoes from your "mini forest." (Spraying the tomato plants themselves does not seem to work.)

TREES

Mix *Tough & Tender* in your lawn sprayer unit and spray on the aspen trees to prevent scale and other bug challenges.

Use *Sol-U-Mel* in a 1:5 solution to spray your fruit trees, shrubs, plants and grass. It wipes out the aphids, ants, and all the other bugs that you do not want eating your garden.

See the section on *Bugs – Yard* in this book.

WEBWORMS

Tough & Tender is a very effective spray for webworms. Spray them liberally and be sure that the pressure of the spray breaks into the web. Your yard will smell much better and be a great deal safer than those sprayed with pesticides.

ZINNIAS

Spray diluted *Sol-U-Mel* directly on the leaves of your zinnias. They will usually show improvement in one day. This will even work on leaves that have been slightly affected by the fungus and restore them to their green color.

GARDEN

CHAPTER TWENTY-TWO

Alternative Uses

For Melaleuca Products

This is the "fun" chapter. When we asked our creative readers for unique uses of Melaleuca products we received all kinds of ideas. Most of them had already been included or were added to previous chapters where they obviously belonged. Some of them belonged here. All of them are real but you may not believe it! Have fun! Keep reading and enjoy.

AROMATHERAPY

Add a few drops of *T36-C5* to an aroma light, or to a small pan of boiling water to keep annoying insects away from your house. For your own benefit, add a drop or two to your pillow before you go to bed at night.

ATTAIN SHAKES

Here are some new ways to enjoy your *Attain* shakes:

Root Beer Float
½ cup diet root beer
7 oz. skim milk or water
1 scoop *Attain Vanilla Shake Mix*

Mix ingredients in blender and enjoy this "old-fashioned" low-fat snack.

Piña Colada
6 pieces of canned pineapple   7 oz. crushed ice
1 tbsp. coconut flakes   7 oz. water
2 oz. coconut juice   1 scoop *Attain Vanilla Shake Mix*
1 tbsp. 100% pineapple juice

Mix all ingredients in a blender and enjoy this fruity, tropical treat.

Banana Wonder
½ ripe banana
2 tbsp. non-fat vanilla or banana yogurt
7 oz. non-fat milk
1 scoop *Attain Vanilla* or *Milk Chocolate Shake Mix*

Mix ingredients in a blender and top with the other half of the banana.

BANDAGES

T36-C5 is excellent for removing the "goo" from bandages. And, it doesn't mess up your nail polish! It is good for both the skin and the injury as well.

BEDBUGS

Bedbugs (*Cimex lectularius*) are nocturnal parasites that prefer feeding on human blood. They are not known to transmit diseases. They like to hide in or near mattresses, especially at the seams, as well as in tiny cracks in the wall, in the baseboard, and in other furniture. They can live for months with no food. Bedbugs are most common in areas of high occupant turnover like hotels, apartments, shelters, and dormitories. Infestations are spread when the bedbugs hide in luggage and clothing of travelers. The bugs can also crawl from one apartment to another through the walls. As an indicator to an infestation, look for brown blood stains on the sheets, a possible foul odor, as well as red marks on your skin.

Pull the bed and headboard away from the wall. Smear the bed frame legs with petroleum jelly. Buy extra vacuum bags. Do a daily thorough vacuum of the seams in the mattress, the box spring, the headboard, baseboard, and floor. After each vacuuming, seal the used vacuum bag in plastic and discard. Launder bedding and clothing in hot water and dry on hottest setting. Repair all cracks and crevices, glue down any loose wallpaper. Spray the mattress and surroundings with *Sol-U-Guard Botanical* or *Sol-U-Mel*. Be vigilant because bedbug eggs hatch in 6–17 days.

Also, look up "Diatomaceous Earth" on the internet for a solution to your quest for a natural insecticide.

BEEKEEPING

Professional beekeepers have been known to use tea tree oil for the control of the varroa mite that can devastate an entire colony. Late fall or early winter seems to be the best time of year for treatment of strong colonies. Tea tree oil kills the mite on contact. Upon ingestion of bee larvae that contain essential oils, the mite's reproduction cycle is interrupted.

Grease patties are made from 4 cups of granulated sugar, 2 cups of vegetable shortening, and 21cc *T36-C5*. Mix well and form 4-oz patties, then place on top of each brood box. One batch can treat about 6 hives. For more information, see the West Virginia University web site at www.WVU.edu/.

BILGE CLEANERS

Mix *Tub & Tile*, *Sol-U-Mel* and *MelaMagic* together to use as a bilge cleaner in place of the usual caustic substances.

CAR PARTS

Oily car parts can be easily cleaned with a mixture of 4 ounces of *MelaMagic* and 1 capful of *Sol-U-Mel* in a 16 ounce bottle of water. Generously spray the surfaces and wipe away the oil.

CONVERTIBLE TOPS

Rustic Touch is an excellent choice for convertible tops and car interiors. It makes them shine and contains no alcohol.

ALTERNATIVE

CUTICLES

Apply *Melaleuca Oil* (*T36-C5*) to dry and cracked cuticles. Follow this with *Moisturizing Hand Creme*. For prevention of the damaged cuticles, wash your hands thoroughly with the *Gold Bar* and apply a thin layer of *Renew Intensive Skin Therapy* before beginning the activity that is so damaging to your skin.

It has also been suggested to use *Sun Shades Lip Balm* on your damaged cuticles. It will soften them right up.

DOG – ODOR REMOVER

During your daily walk in the woods, or elsewhere, your dog may decide to roll in something that resembles the smell of dead fish. If bath time is not handy, trying wiping off the brown color with paper towels and *Tough & Tender*. Follow this with diluted *Sol-U-Mel* to remove the remainder and especially the smell. It works great.

DOG HAIR REMOVAL

Sol-U-Mel is very effective in removing the dog smell and dust from old sofas and chairs. In five minutes or so you should be able to clean, deodorize and remove all the dog hair. Just spray with diluted *Sol-U-Mel* and wipe with a paper towel. The old sofa will look new again and it is easy to do every day.

Another solution might be to keep the dog off the couch!

EAR INFECTIONS

To relieve the pain and pressure from ear aches, infections and even fluid in the ear:

Take a paper towel and rip it in half. Fold it into a square about 2 inches in diameter. Take a small juice glass (4 oz. size) and stuff the paper towel into the bottom of the glass. Slightly dampen the paper towel with water (do not saturate it), and then put 5–6 drops of *T36-C5* on the towel. Microwave the glass for 10–20 seconds. Take the glass (You'll see the steam coming up from the paper towel) and put the mouth of the glass completely around your child's ear (It shouldn't be hot, but make sure first!). It works best to have your child sitting down, and just have them tilt their head over the mouth of the glass. Your child can hold the bottom of the glass, as it is not hot. Have them hold it for at least 5 minutes. Repeat 1–2 times each day until the problem clears up. (This treatment has been known to prevent the insertion of ear tubes.)

EYEGLASSES

An alternate use for *Rustic Touch* is to clean your eyeglasses. Spray one squirt 8–10 inches from the lenses and buff with a soft cloth. This will keep your eyeglasses dust free and quick and easy to clean the next day.

FEET – SOOTHING

Try using *Clear Defense* to cool and soothe your feet after long hours at work or shopping. The anti-bacterial aspect is also beneficial and it won't dry out your feet.

FINGERNAILS

When working in the garden and other particularly dirty areas, sometimes it is very challenging to clean your nails. Try washing them with *MelaBrite*. They will come clean almost instantly and remain snow white.

If your nails have a tendency to split and break, try rubbing them with *MelaGel* or *Triple Antibiotic Ointment* (which ever is handy), 2–3 times each day. Within a month you should see a significant difference and they should be very healthy by the end of two months. This can even be used on top of *Nicole Miller's Nail Color*. The *MelaGel* and *Triple Antibiotic Ointment* will penetrate right on into your nails.

HAIR GROWTH

It has been suggested that *Antibacterial Liquid Soap* be used on your hair (scalp) to promote hair growth. It couldn't hurt. What have you got to lose?

JEWELRY

Use a mixture of *PreSpot* and water to soak your rings. They will sparkle! If you have difficulty removing your rings and/or tight fitting bracelets, just spray *Clear Power* on the fingers and/or the top of the hand and the items will slip off like magic!

LAUNDRY

If your washer does not have a rinse dispenser, trying putting a capful of *MelaSoft* on an old rag and throwing it in with the clothes in the dryer. Every so often throw it in the washer of clothes and it will not only work in there but you will have a clean cloth to start over with.

LAUNDRY WHITENER

Save your 96 ounce container of *MelaPower* and the pump. It works great for this laundry whitener.

½ cup of *Diamond Brite Gel*	¼ cup of *MelaMagic*
¼ cup of *Tub & Tile*	1½ cup of *PreSpot*

Pour in the 96 ounce container and fill the rest of the way with water. Shake well before using. Use 2 to 3 pumps of the laundry whitener, in place of bleach, per large load of whites.

LEATHER

Use a cotton ball and full strength *Sol-U-Mel* to clean your good leather purses. (Try it on the bottom first just to be safe.) It will usually take off blue jean stains, pen marks, dirt etc. and look like new!

MANURE

Try a diluted mixture of *Tough & Tender* to get manure out of clothes. Just spray it on and wash in *MelaPower Laundry Detergent*, *MelaBrite*, and *MelaSoft* as usual.

MOSQUITO BITES

Try putting the *Sun Shades Lip Balm* on your mosquito bites. It works like magic! It will stop the itching almost instantly and you will rarely have to repeat the process. Besides it is convenient as you should have the *Lip Balm* in your pocket or purse at all times.

MUSICAL INSTRUMENTS

Tub & Tile is great for cleaning the strings on musical instruments. It makes them work better, it shines them and it makes them last longer.

NAIL POLISH REMOVER

Melaleuca nail polish remover has been in most of our homes for years. It is *Sol-U-Mel*. Use the *Sol-U-Mel* full strength on a cotton pad and hold it on the coating for a moment. Gently rub to remove the polish. It takes longer than the toxic forms of fingernail polish remover but it is much safer and even helps to condition and heal the nails, bed and cuticles. Follow the polish removal with *Clear Defense* and your nails won't even know that they had polish on them. It works!

PAINT

When oil based paint has attacked your skin for whatever reason, gently rub a small amount of full strength *Sol-U-Mel* onto the area. It will come out. Try applying the *Sol-U-Mel* to paint stained clothes as well. They will usually come out of the laundry with no paint on them.

PAINT BRUSHES

When your brushes dry with paint in them, soak them in ½ strength *Sol-U-Mel* for a few hours. You should then be able to strip out the dried paint and reuse a soft and pliable brush.

RAZOR BLADES

Use *T36-C5* on your razors occasionally. It will help if you have sensitive skin or get razor rash. Of course, continue to use your shaving cream.

RING AROUND THE COLLAR

If ring around the collar is a challenge for your washday, try pumping some *MelaPower Laundry Detergent* full strength directly on the dirty area. Rub the material together and throw it in the wash.

SHIN SPLINTS

Shin splints can be quite painful. Try massaging *Pain-A-Trate* into the sore area a couple of times during the day and at bedtime. The pain and discomfort will generally be gone by morning.

SHOESHINE

Try **Rustic Touch** when you want a quick and easy shoeshine. It is also very effective when shining leather purses.

SORE THROAT

In addition to following the suggestions for *Sore Throat* in the *Healthy Body* section of this book, try rubbing **Pain-A-Trate** on the front of your neck at the first onset of a sore throat. Apply it several times a day, especially right before bedtime.

STAINLESS STEEL APPLIANCES

Try cleaning stainless steel refrigerator and oven doors with **Rustic Touch**. It will shine them up beautifully. Repels the fingerprints, too!

SUPER GLUE

If you have ever glued your fingers together with super glue, you will really appreciate this suggestion. Apply a couple of drops of Melaleuca's **T36-C5** to the glued area and rub for a couple of minutes. Voila, the glue comes off and the skin stays on. (This works for crazy glue, too.)

SUSTAIN MUFFINS

Make a batch of these delicious muffins and freeze them. A quick turn in the microwave will give you a fresh muffin every morning.

1 scoop **Sustain** (any flavor)	½ cup juice (orange, pineapple, etc.)
2 cups flour	1 egg
½ tsp. salt	1 tbsp. baking powder
¼ cup butter	¼ t. baking soda
1 cup sugar	2 tbsp. milk

Heat oven to 350 degrees. In a small bowl combine flour, baking powder, **Sustain**, salt and baking soda. In a large bowl beat sugar and butter than add milk and egg. Gradually add the dry mix and blend well. Pour into muffin cups and cook 15–18 minutes.

TEA STAINS

Try using **PreSpot** to clean the tea stains out of a pan. Simply spray the inside surface and let it stand for several minutes. Then wipe clean.

WINDOWS

Try **Lemon Brite** to clean your windows, especially if you live near the ocean. The sheeting action seems to help with the salt residue.

An alternate solution is to add a few drops of **Lemon Brite** to your **Clear Power**. Not only does it seem to help with heavy residue, but the windows seem to stay cleaner longer.

ALTERNATIVE

Tea Tree Oil Research

From Chapter 2, *That Amazing Tea Tree Oil!* by Karen MacKenzie

Altman, P.M. "Australian Tea Tree Oil," *Australian Journal of Pharmacy,* 69, 276-78, 1988.

Altman, P.M. "Australian Tea Tree Oil – A Natural Antiseptic," *Australian Journal of Biotechnology,* 3:4, 247-8, 1989.

Altman, P.M. "Australian Tea Tree Oil – An Update," *Cosmetics, Aerosols & Toiletries in Australia,* 5:4, 27-9, 1991.

Anon, "A Retrospect," *Medical Journal of Australia,* 85-89, 1930.

Anon, "Tea Tree Oil," *Australian Journal of Pharmacy,* 274, 1930.

Anon, *Journal of the National Medical Association,* (USA), 1930.

Anon, "Ti-trol Oil," *British Medical Journal,* 927, 1933.

Anon, "An Australian Antiseptic Oil," *British Medical Journal,* I, 966, 1933.

Australian Standard, "Essential Oils, Oil of *Melaleuca* Terpinen-4-ol Type," AS 2782 1985, Australian Standards Association, Sydney, 1985.

Bassett, I.B., Pannowitz, D.L. and Barnetson R.St.C. "A Comparative Study of Tea Tree Oil Versus Benzoyl Peroxide in the Treatment of Acne," *Medical Journal of Australia,* 153:8, 455-458, 1990.

Belaiche, P. "Treatment of Chronic Urinary Tract Infections with the Essential Oil of *Melaleuca alternifolia*-Cheel," *Phytotherapy,* 15, 9-12, 1985.

Belaiche, P. "Treatment of Vaginal Infections of *Candida albicans* with the Essential Oil of *Melaleuca alternifolia*-Cheel," *Phytotherapy,* 15, 13-14, 1985.

Belaiche, P. "Treatment of Skin and Nail Infections with the Essential Oil of *Melaleuca alternifolia*-Cheel," *Phytotherapy,* 15, 15-18, 1985.

Beylier, M.F. "Bacteriostatic Activity of Some Australian Essential Oils," *Perfumer and Flavorist International,* V4, 23-5, 1979.

Bishop, C.D. "Anti-viral Activity of the Essential Oil of *Melaleuca alternifolia* (Maiden & Betche) Cheel (Tea Tree) Against Tobacco Mosaic Virus," (Research Report) *Journal of Essential Oil Research,* 7, 641-644, 1995.

Blackwell, A.L. Tea Tree Oil and Anaerobic (Bacterial) Vaginosis. *The Lancet* 337-300 (1991).

Blamann, A. and Melrose, G.J.H. 4-Terpinenol. *Perfumery Essential Oil Record.* 50, 769 (1959).

Brophy, J.J., et al. "Gas Chromatographic Quality Control for Oil of *Melaleuca* Terpinen-4-ol Type Australian Tea Tree," *Journal of Agriculture and Food Chemistry,* 37, 1330-1335, 1989.

Buck, D.S., Nidorf, D.M. and Addino, J.G. "Comparison of Two Topical Preparations for the Treatment of Onychomycosis: *Melaleuca alternifolia* (Tea Tree Oil) and Clotrimazole," *Journal of Family Practice,* 38, 601-5, 1994.

Carson, C.F. and Riley, T.V. "Antimicrobial Activity of the Essential Oil of *Melaleuca alternifolia* (A Review)," *Letters in Applied Microbiology,* 16, 49-55, 1993.

Carson, C.F. and Riley, T.V. "The Antimicrobial Activity of Tea Tree Oil," *Medical Journal of Australia,*160, 236, 1994.

Carson, C.F. and Riley, T.V. "Susceptibility of *Propionibacterium acnes* to the Essential Oil of *Melaleuca alternifolia*," *Letters in Applied Microbiology.* 19, 24-25, 1994.

Carson, C.F., Cookson, B.D., Farrelly, H.D. and Riley, T.V. "Susceptibility of Methicillin-resistant *Staphylococcus aureus* to the Essential Oil *Melaleuca alternifolia*," *Journal of Antimicrobial Chemotherapy,* 35:3, 421-4, 1995.

Carson, C.F., Hammer, K.A. and Riley, T.V. "Broth Micro-dilution Method for Determining the Susceptibility of *Escherichia coli* (*E coli*) and *Staphylococcus aureus* to the Essential Oil of *Melaleuca alternifolia*," Microbios 82:332, 181-185, 1995.

Carson, C.F. and Riley, T.V. "Antimicrobial Activity of the Major Components of the Essential Oil of *Melaleuca alternifolia*," *Journal of Applied Bacteriology,* 78:3, 264-9, 1995.

Carson, C.F. and Riley, T.V. "Toxicity of the Essential Oil of *Melaleuca alternifolia* (or Tea Tree Oil)," (Letter) *Journal of Toxicology-Clinical Toxicology,* 33:2, 193-4, 1995.

Carson, C.F., Hammer, K.A. and Riley, T.V. "In-vitro Activity of the Essential Oil of *Melaleuca alternifolia* against *Streptococcus Spp.*" *Journal of Antimicrobial Chemotherapy,* 37:6, 1177-8, 1996.

Carson, C.F., Riley, T.V. and Cookson, B.D. "Efficacy and Safety of Tea Tree Oil as a Topical Anti-microbial Agent," (editorial) *Journal of Hospital Infection,* 40:3, 175-8, 1998.

Coutts, M. "The Bronchoscopic Treatment of Bronchiectasis," *Medical Journal Australia,* 1937.

Dabbous, K.H., Pippin, M.A., Pabst, K.M., Pabst, M.J. and Haney, L. "Superoxide Release by Neutrophils is Inhibited by Tea Tree Oil," College of Dentistry, UT Memphis, Unpublished 1993.

Davies, P. "Ti-Tree Oil for an Adult with Chicken Pox," *Aromatherapy Quarterly,* 12, 1986.

Elsom, G. "Susceptibility of Methicillin-resistant *Staphylococcus aureus* to Tea Tree Oil and Mupirocin," *Journal of Antimicrobial Chemotherapy,* V43, 427-428, 1999.

"Essential Oils – Oil of Melaleuca, Terpinen-4-ol Type." Standards Association of Australia. Standards House, 80 Arthur St. North Sydney, N.S.W. 1985.

Feinblatt, H.M. "Cajeput Type Oil (Tea Tree oil) for the Treatment of Furunculosis (boils)," *Journal of the National Medical Association* (USA), 52: 32-4, 1960.

Goldsborough, R.E. "Ti-Tree Oil," *The Manufacturing Chemist,* 57-60, Feb 1939.

Guenther, E. "The Essential Oils," *Van Nostrand NY,* V4, p526, 1950.

Guenther, E. "Tea Tree Oils," *Soap and Sanitary Chemicals,* Aug/Sept. 1942.

Guenther, E. "Australian Tea Tree Oils," *Perfumery and Essential Oil Record,* Sept. 1968.

Halford, A.C.F. "Diabetic Gangrene," *Medical Journal of Australia,* 2, 121, 1936.

Hammer, K.A., Carson, C.F. and Riley, T.V. "Susceptibility of Transient and Commensal Skin Flora to the Essential Oil of *Melaleuca alternifolia* (Tea Tree Oil)," *American Journal of Infection Control,* 24:3, 186-9, 1996.

Hammer, K.A., Carson, C.F. and Riley, T.V., "In-vitro Susceptibility of *Malassezia furfur* to the Essential Oil of *Melaleuca alternifolia*," *Journal of Medical and Veterinary Mycology,* 35:5, 375-7, 1997.

Hammer, K.A., Carson, C.F. and Riley, T.V. "In-vitro Activity of Essential Oils, in Particular *Melaleuca alternifolia* (Tea Tree Oil and Tea Tree Oil Products) against *Candida spp.*," *Journal of Antimicrobial Chemotherapy,* 42:5, 591-5, 1998.

Hammer, K.A., Carson, C.F. and Riley, T.V. "In-vitro Susceptibilities of *Lactobacilli* and Organisms Associated with Bacterial Vaginosis to *Melaleuca alternifolia* (Tea Tree oil)," (Letter) *Antimicrobial Agents and Chemotherapy,* Jan 1999.

Humphrey, E.M. "A New Australian Germicide," *Medical Journal of Australia,* I, 417-418, 1930.

International Standard, "Essential oils – Oil of *Melaleuca* Terpinen-4-ol Type Tea Tree Oil," ISO 4730:1994 & 1996, International Standards Organization, Geneva, 1996.

Laakso, P.V. "Scientae Pharmaceuticae," *Czechoslovak Medical Press-Prague,* 485-492, 1966.

Laakso, P.V. "Fractionation of Tea Tree Oil." *25th Congress of Pharmaceutical Science,* Prague. 1,485-492, 1965.

Lassak, E.V. and McCarthy, T.M. "Australian Medicinal Plants," Sydney, NSW. Methuen Australian Pty Ltd. (Publishers).

Low, D., Rowal, B.D. and Griffin, W.J. "Antibacterial Action of the Essential Oils of Some of Australian Myrtaceae," *Planta Medica,* 26, 184-189, 1974.

MacDonald, V. "The Rationale of Treatment," *Australian Journal of Dentistry,* 34, 281-285, 1930.

Maruzzella, J. and Ligouri, L. "The in vitro antifungal activity of essential oils." *Journal of the American Pharmaceutical Association.* 47,250-4 (1958).

McCulloch, R.N. and Waterhouse, D.F. "Laboratory and field tests of mosquito repellents." *Australia Council of Science and Industry Research Bulletin.* 213,9-26 (1947).

McDonald, L.G. and Tovey, E. "The Effectiveness of Benzyl Benzoate and Some Essential Oils as Laundry Additives for Killing House Dustmites," *Journal Allergy and Clinical Immunology,* 1993.

Merry, K.A., Williams, L.R. and Home, V.N. "Composition of Oils from *Melaleuca alternifolia, M. Linariifolia* and *M. dissitiflora.* Implications for the Australian Standard, Oil of *Melaleuca* Terpinen-4-ol type. In Modern Phytotherapy – The Clinical Significance of Tea tree Oil and Other Essential Oils." *Proceedings of a Conference 2/12/1990 Sydney and a Symposium 8/12/1990 Surfers Paradise,* II, 107-104, 1990.

Murray, K.E. "The essential oils of five western Australian plants." *Royal Australian Chemical Institute Journal and Proceedings.* 17,398-402 (1950).

Nenoff, P., et al. "Antifungal Activity of the Essential Oil of *Melaleuca alternifolia* (Tea Tree oil) Against Pathogenic Fungi In-vitro," *Skin Pharmacology,* 9:6, 388-394, 1996.

Oleum Melaleuca; *British Pharmaceutical Codex,* 597-98, 1949.

Olsen, M.W. "Control of *Sphaerotheca fuliginea* on Cucurbits with a 1.5% Dilution of an Oil Extracted from the Australian Tea Tree," *Phytopathology,* 78:12, 1595, 1988.

Peña, E.F. "Melaleuca alternifolia: Its Use for *Trichomonal vaginitis* and Other Vaginal Infections," *Obstetrics and Gynecology,* 19:6, 793-795, 1962.

Penfold, A.R. "The Essential Oils of *Melaleuca linariifolia* and *Melaleuca alternifolia*," *Journal Proceedings of the Royal Society of NSW,* 59, 318-325, 1925.

Penfold, A.R. "Essential oil of Melaleuca alternifolia," *Perfumery Essential Oil Record,* 25,121 (1934).

Penfold, A.R. and Grant, R. "The Germicidal Values of Some Australian Essential Oils and Their Pure Constituents," *Journal Proceedings of the Royal Society of NSW,* 59:3, 346-50, 1925.

Penfold, A.R. and Morrison, F.R. "Some Notes on the Essential Oil of *Melaleuca alternifolia*," *Australian Journal of Pharmacy,* 18, 274-5, 1937.

Penfold, A.R. and Morrison, F.R. "Australian Tea Trees of Economic Value," *Technological Museum Sydney,* 1:3, Bulletin 14, 1946.

Penfold, A.R. and Morrison, F.R. "Australian essential oils in insecticide and repellents." *Soap, Perfumery and Cosmetics.* 25,933-4 (1952).

Penfold, A.R., Morrison, F.R. and McKern, H.G. "Studies in the Physiological Forms of the Myrtaceae' Part 2, The Occurrence of Physiological Forms in *Melaleuca alternifolia* (Cheel), (Research on Essential oils of the Australian Flora)," *Museum of Technology and Applied Science,* 18-19, 1948.

Pickering, G.B. "Cedarwood Oil Compounds, Silica Gel Separation and Tea Tree Oil as Nutmeg Substitute," *Manufacturing Chemist,* 27, 105-6, 1956.

Priest, D. "Tea Tree Oil in Cosmetics-The Promise and the Proof," (Technical paper) *Cosmetics, Aerosols & Toiletries in Australia,* Main Camp Tea Tree Oil, 9:4, 1995.

Shapiro, S., Meier, A. and Guggenheim, B. "The Anti-microbial Activity of Essential Oils and Essential Oil Components Towards Oral Bacteria," *Oral Microbiolog. Immunology* (Denmark), 9:4, 202-8, 1994.

Shemesh, A. and Mayo, W.L. "A Natural Antiseptic and Fungicide," *International Journal of Alternative and Complementary Medicine,* Dec. 1991.

Small, B.E.J. "Tea Tree Oil," *Australian Journal of Experimental Agriculture and Animal Husbandry,* V21, 1981.

Southwell, I., Markham, J. and Mann, C. "Why Cineole is Not Detrimental to Tea Tree Oil," *Rural Industries Research and Development Corporation, Research Paper Series* 97/54, 1997.

Swords, G. and Hunter, G. "Composition of Australian Tea Tree Oil (Melaleuca alternifolia)," *Journal of Agriculture and Food Chemistry,* 26:3, 734-5, 1978.

Tong, M.M., Altman, P.M. and Barnetson R.St.C. "Tea Tree Oil in the Treatment of Tinea pedis," *Australian Journal of Dermatology,* 33:3, 145-9, 1992.

Van Hulssen, C.J. and Meyer, T.M., "Ethereal oils from Melaleuca alternifolia and Melaleuca bracteata," *Inorganic Nederland-Indie,* 8, VII, 84-7 (1941).

Veal, L. "The Potential Effectiveness of Essential Oils as a Treatment for Head Lice, Pediculus Humanus Capitis," *Complementary Ther. Nurs. Midwifery,* 2:4, 97-101, 1996.

Walker, M. "Clinical Investigation of Australian *Melaleuca alternifolia* Oil for a Variety of Common Foot Problems," *Current Podiatry,* April 7th to 15th, 1972.

Walsh, L.J. and Longstaff, J. "The Antimicrobial Effects of an Essential Oil on Selected Oral Pathogens," *Periodontology,* V8, 11-15, 1987.

Williams, LR, Home, V.N., Zhang, X. and Stevenson, I. "The Composition and Bacteriocidal Activity of Oil of *Melaleuca alternifolia* (Tea Tree oil)," *International Journal of Aromatherapy,* 1:3, 15-17, 1988.

Williams, L.R., Home, V.N. and Asre, S. "Antimicrobial Activity of Oil of Melaleuca alternifolia. Its Potential Use in Cosmetics and Toiletries," *Cosmetics, Aerosols & Toiletries in Australia,* 4:4, 1990.

Willix, Dr. Robert D. "A Must for Your Medicine Chest," *Health for Life,* 3:5, 4-5, May 1996.

Disinfectant Properties

of T36-C5® Compared to Other Agents

The following table is a summary of clinical research and is based upon direct contact of the agent with the organism. Standard concentrations were used. This demonstrates the disinfectant ability of Melaleuca alternifolia oil which contains at least 37% terpenols and less than 7% cineol. Please note that although many organisms show sensitivity to certain agents, mutant strains are developing which resist control. Many disinfectants are toxic or cause damage to skin when used over a prolonged time period. For these reasons, a number of these agents are no longer used clinically.

Disinfectant Agent	S	E	B	F	V	C	TOXIC?
Isopropyl Alcohol	K	K	O	P	P	O	
Phenolics	K	K	O	P	O	P	
Chlorine Solution	K	K	O	P	P	P	Yes
Iodine Tincture	K	K	O	P	O	P	
Acetaldehyde	K	K	P	K	K	K	Yes
Mercury Salts	K	P	K	K	K	K	Yes
Hexachlorophene	K	P	O	K	O	O	
Quaternary Ammonium	K	P	O	P	O	O	
Boric Acid	P	P	O	O	O	O	
Cidex	K	K	P	K	K	K	
T36-C5	K	K	K	K	K	K	

K = Kills organism
P = Partially effective
O = Does not kill organism

S = Staph Aureus
E = E. Coli
B = Bacteria Spores
F = Fungi
V = Viruses
C = Candida Albicans

Melaleuca Oil

and Healthy Skin

Healthy skin produces many different essential oils to maintain equilibrium with the environment. Each cell of the body has a double fatty envelope that makes up its membrane. This is what separates the cell from its environment. It is the character of this envelope to allow highly selected gases, nutrients, vitamins, minerals, hormones, and water into the cell while excreting wastes with a precision unique to life itself.

When *Melaleuca alternifolia* oil is put in contact with healthy cells, only the Creator of both could describe the complex interactions which take place. Several things are known about plant oils and human skin. Incompatible ones such as oils of Poison Ivy activate a response to flush the substance away from the system. Essential oils are absorbed and mix delicately with the equilibrium and further the harmony of health.

Bacteria have an electrical charge on their surface, much like the electric polarity of a battery. Friendly bacteria have a similar electrical charge to the skin cells they protect. Essential oils, such as found in *Melaleuca alternifolia* oil, encourage the growth of these friendly bacteria. Potentially dangerous bacteria have a lower electrical charge and are destroyed by these oils. Viruses do not carry any appreciable electrical charge and their protective lipid coats are dissolved by essential oils, allowing them to be chemically destroyed by the body's natural defenses.

What do we understand about *Melaleuca alternifolia* oil and this symphony of life at the molecular level? Actually, not much more than what the native Australian people shared with Captain Cook—try it and see what its properties can do for you.

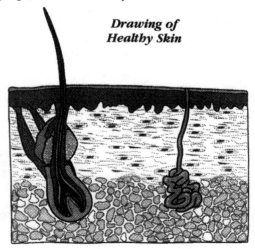

Drawing of Healthy Skin

Technical Information

Although there are over 300 known species of tea trees (*Melaleuca*) in Australia, only one, the *Melaleuca alternifolia*, is known to have substantial therapeutic properties. The most closely related species to Melaleuca alternifolia is the *M. linarifilia* that yields an oil that is somewhat bacteriostatic, but is too high in Cineole, a natural skin irritant.

The pure oil of *Melaleuca alternifolia* is known to contain at least 100 compounds. A few of these compounds are not yet identified. A unique compound, viridiflorene, is found only to exist in oil of Melaleuca. Two other compounds, Terpinen-4-ol and Cineole, are regulated by the Australian Standards Association to designate therapeutic quality.

In Australia, the minimum amount of Terpinen-4-ol allowed is 30%, and the maximum amount of Cineole is 15%. Terpinen-4-ol is one of the more important therapeutic ingredients in the oil. Therefore, one would want oil high in Terpinen-4-ol. And since Cineole is caustic to the skin, the higher quality oil is low in Cineole. High quality oil should have at least 35% Terpinen-4-ol and less than 10% Cineole.

Since pure oil of *Melaleuca* is entirely natural and the genetics of one tree varies slightly from the other, the quality of oil from one grove of trees may vary substantially from another. In fact, much of the oil that has been distilled from *Melaleuca alternifolia* trees does not meet the minimum standards of quality oil.

Much research still needs to be done to determine exactly why *Melaleuca oil* works as it does and what extract proportion of each of the compounds produces the most effective blend of oil.

In order for any product to give repeatable, expected results, it must be consistent from batch to batch. For this reason, we strongly recommend that anyone purchasing products labeled as or containing oil of *Melaleuca* do so from a reputable firm that has its source of oil and quality of oil well documented.

The following lists 48 of the 100 known compounds in pure *Melaleuca alternifolia* oil.

48 Known Compounds of Pure *Melaleuca alternifolia* Oil

1. α-Pinene
2. Camphene
3. β-Pinene
4. Sabinene
5. Myrcene
6. α-Phellandrene
7. 1,4-Cineole
8. α-Terpinene
9. Limonene
10. 1,8-Cineole
11. γ-Terpinene
12. p-Cymene
13. Terpinolene
14. Hexanol
15. Allyl hexanoate
16. α-p-Dimethyl-styrene
17. β-Phellandrene
18. α-Cubebene
19. (a Sesquiterpene)
20. α-Copaene
21. Camphor
22. α-Gurjunene
23. Linalool
24. (a Sesquiterpene)
25. α-Thujene
26. 1-Terpineol
27. 1-Terpinen-4-ol
28. β-Elemene
29. β-Caryophyllene
30. (a Sesquiterpene)
31. Aromadendrene
32. β-Terpineol
33. Allo-aromadendrene
34. Globulol
35. α-Humulene
36. *tr*-p-menthen-2-ol
37. γ-Muurolene
38. α-Terpineol
39. Viridiflorene
40. Piperitone
41. α-Muurolene
42. Piperitol
43. Viridiflorol
44. δ-Cadinene
45. 4,10-Dimethyl-7-isopropyl bicyclo [4.4.0]-1,4-decadiene
46. Nerol
47. 8-p-Cymenol
48. Clamenene

Product Price Comparison
WalMart vs. Melaleuca

Survey Date: May 27, 2009 (WalMart in Centennial, Colorado)

WALMART	Size/Use	No. of Uses Per Purchase	Ratio* to Melaleuca	Cost of Each Pkg.	TOTAL COST
Tide 2x Ultra Liquid	100 oz.	64 loads	3.00	$ 10.84	$ 32.52
Bounce Dryer Sheets	80 sheets	80 uses	1.25	4.12	5.15
Windex	32 oz.		3.00	2.50	7.50
Tilex	32 oz.		3.00	3.74	11.22
Pledge Multipurpose Wipes	25 wipes	25 uses	1.20	3.88	4.65
409 Degreaser	32 oz		3.00	2.16	6.48
Listerine Tartar Control	33.8 oz.		.95	5.32	5.00
Glide Dental Tape	54.7 yds.		1.01	3.50	3.50
Scalpicin Medicated Shampoo	1.5 oz.		5.33	6.47	34.51
Lamisil Antifungal Ointment	.42 oz.		1.19	8.13	9.67
Tylenol PM	50 caplets	50 uses	1.00	6.87	6.87
	SUB TOTAL				$ 127.07
	Tax (6.85%)				$ 8.70
	WALMART TOTAL				**$135.77**

MELALEUCA	Size/Use		No. of Uses Per Purchase	Ratio* to Melaleuca	PC Cost of Each Pkg.	Total COST
MelaPower 6x Laundry	96 oz.	=	192 loads	1	$29.99	$ 29.99
MelaSoft Dryer Sheets	100 sts	=	100 uses	1	5.69	5.69
Clear Power Glass Cleaner	16 oz.	=	96 oz.	1	5.69	5.69
Tub & Tile Bathroom Cleaner	16 oz.	=	96 oz.	1	5.69	5.69
Tough & Tender Wipes	30 wipes	=	30 uses	1	3.49	3.49
Tough & Tender Cleaner	16 oz.	=	96 oz.	1	5.69	5.69
Breath-Away Mouth Rinse	8 oz.	=	32 oz.	1	5.69	5.69
Classic Dental Floss	55 yds.			1	3.99	3.99
Melaleuca Original Shampoo	8 oz.			1	7.69	7.69
Dermatin Antifungal Creme	.5 oz.			1	7.89	7.89
CounterAct P.M.	50 caplets		50 uses	1	4.09	4.09
	SUB TOTAL					$ 85.59
	Shipping ($3.90 + 5.4% of order total)					8.52
	Tax (6.85%)					5.86
	Less Advantage Rewards (Preferred Customers)					–4.40
	MELALEUCA TOTAL					**$ 95.57**

WALMART TOTAL = $135.77
MELALEUCA TOTAL = $95.57
MELALEUCA SAVINGS = $40.20

*For example: it takes three 100 oz. bottles of Tide 2x Ultra Liquid to equal the 192 loads in Melaleuca's *MelaPower 6x*; it takes three 32 oz. bottles of Tilex to equal one bottle of *Tub & Tile*.

Problems Index

Use this index when you have a problem or condition and you want to discover which products will help. Use the "Products Index" on page 311 when you have a Melaleuca product and you want to discover its various uses.

Products Index

Use this index when you have a Melaleuca product and you want to discover its various uses. Use the "Problems Index" on page 304 when you have a problem or condition and you want to discover which products will help. **Note:** This index covers the "Healthy Body" and "Healthy Home" chapters only.

BOOK ORDERING INFORMATION

The
Melaleuca
Wellness Guide

BOOK PRICES

(Prices are in US dollars.)

Quantity	Price Each
1–4	$12.50
5–9	$10.75
10–19	$9.50
20–49	$8.25
50–99	$6.95
100+	$5.75

IF ORDERING BY PHONE (US and Canada)

We accept all major credit cards, and checks by phone (US customers only). Most orders ship the same day we receive them. Smaller orders are shipped by First-Class Mail or Priority Mail. Larger orders are shipped by United Parcel Service. Call:

Toll-Free 1 (888) 209-0510
Local (303) 224-0277
Fax (303) 568-0224

IF ORDERING BY MAIL (US and Canada)

We accept money orders (payable in US funds) or US checks. We usually dispatch mail orders the day after we receive them. Smaller orders are shipped by Mail. Larger orders are shipped by United Parcel Service. Send order to:

RM Barry Publications
PO Box 3528
Littleton, CO 80161-3528

OTHER COUNTRIES
(Australia, New Zealand, UK, Ireland, Puerto Rico, and Singapore)
Place orders online at: **www.rmbarry.com**
Questions? Email us at: **info@rmbarry.com**

0110 15M